# ARCHETYPAL PSYCHOLOGIES

James Hillman at Eranos
(Photograph courtesy of the photographer, Jan Marlan.)

# ARCHETYPAL PSYCHOLOGIES

*Reflections in Honor of James Hillman*

Edited by
Stanton Marlan

Spring Journal Books
New Orleans, Louisiana

Published by
Spring Journal, Inc.
627 Ursulines Street #7
New Orleans, Louisiana 70116
Tel.: (504) 524-5117
Website: www.springjournalandbooks.com

Cover design:
Michael Mendis
24 Blackfriars Street
London, Ont. N6H 1K6
Canada

Cover art:
*The King's Vessel* by J. Karl Bogartte

Printed in Canada
Text printed on acid-free paper

Library of Congress Cataloging-in-Publication Data Pending

*For*

JAMES HILLMAN

*Analyst, Mentor, Colleague, and Friend*

# Contents

## Philosophy



## Poetry, Myth, Art, and Religion

# Acknowledgments

I first want to thank James Hillman for his friendship over many years of association. His originality, passion, and commitment to psyche and soul have continued to inspire my work as an analyst and writer.

I would also like to express appreciation to all of the authors who have made contributions to this book and whose work I deeply value. As a community, they have contributed to an ongoing re-visioning of psychology and of our cultural imagination. Their continued personal and intellectual companionship and exchanges have helped me to sharpen and refine my ideas. I would especially like to thank David Miller for his sage advice and continuing intellectual companionship throughout the process of this work.

Much appreciation to Paul Kugler for his contribution of photographs from his personal collection, as well as for providing historical photographs of James Hillman, colleagues, and friends, many of which are from the Eranos Foundation collection and the Hillman family photo archive. I want to thank the Eranos Foundation, and James Hillman, Margot McLean, and the Hillman family for permission to publish these historical images. Thanks also to Patricia Berry for sharing some additional photographs from the early days, and to Peter Kupersmith and the Joseph Krauskopf Memorial Library for providing information and pictures relating to the Krauskopf Library. A number of photographs are from my wife Jan's and my personal collection, and some others were given to us over the years by friends, and I am appreciative of these as well.

I want to express my deep gratitude to Claudette Kulkarni, without whose assistance this book would never have reached completion. Claudette has been an exemplary partner to my work, with her superb technical skills, typing, editing, and formatting. Even more importantly, she has been an invaluable emotional support and intellectual companion through the thicket of preparing this work.

I would also like to thank Nancy Cater for her continuing counsel, her courage as a publisher, and the remarkably fine work she, Greg Mogenson, and superb copyeditor Michael Mendis continue to produce at Spring Journal Books.

I would also like to acknowledge and thank surrealist artist J. Karl Bogartte for contributing his artwork for the cover of this book, as well as for his interesting ideas and our many enjoyable exchanges.

Finally, I would like to thank my wife and colleague Jan Marlan, not only for her support and enthusiasm for my work, but also for her astute critique and challenging dialogue. Her insights and subtle sensibilities always carry my thoughts forward and enrich my life and work.

Stanton Marlan
2008

# Introduction

The title and content of this book take their lead from a comment made by James Hillman in response to being asked if he considered himself to be the founder of the school of Archetypal Psychology. He answered, "I am not the only founder of this school. There is not one single Archetypal Psychology, but many Archetypal Psychologies."[1] At another time in an interview, when Hillman was asked about the representation of Archetypal Psychology, he stated: "If there were a clearly formulated thing called 'archetypal psychology' then someone could 'represent it.' But I see it as represented (this 'it') by individual people in all sorts of professions and callings, working from the insights that my work releases ..."[2]

This book testifies to the fecundity of Hillman's work and to the energy it has released and continues to release worldwide. The dissemination of his ideas has influenced writers in philosophy, religion, history, myth, language, urban studies, politics, the men's movement, feminist criticism, ethics, art, film studies, poetry, analytic practice, and more. His psychology points beyond any single vision and has contributed generally to the enrichment of our cultural imagination.

No single book can adequately represent the scope of Archetypal Psychology, if it can be "represented" at all, and it is not the purpose of this book to do so. Rather, its intention is simply to honor the contributions of James Hillman and other authors who have responded to, challenged, amplified, carried forward the body of ideas signified by the name Archetypal Psychology. While this collection contains the work of several well-known authors, there are many whose work is absent from these pages but who have, nonetheless, made equally important contributions. In essence, this book lays no claim to being comprehensive or objective. It does, however, present some unique offerings: an historical reflection by Hillman's official biographer, a photographic retrospective of seldom-seen photographs, a provocative current interview, thoughts on Hillman's self-revisioning process, polemics, reflections on our intellectual family, and much more—on myth, art, legend, poetry, practice, dreams, imagination, culture, and community.

The ferment created by these ideas supports Hillman's notion that "[t]he psyche has to keep working its logos, i.e., making psychology."[3] *Archetypal Psychologies: Reflections in Honor of James Hillman* sets out to do just that, to continue the process of making psychology not simply in the sense of a separate discipline among others, but as a continuing expression of what "being psychological" has come to mean in Hillman's vision. It is a vision that continues to challenge and delight his readers.

Ed Casey in his paper for the current volume, "Quelle Surprise! Going to the Edge of Things," notes:

> One of the most remarkable gifts of James Hillman to his readers is his capacity to *surprise* them. Time and again, his articles and books move into new territories not anticipated by his readers. … [T]ransportation problems are discussed after earlier brilliant analyses of fantasy and imagination, the literal furniture of the analyst's office is described following an emphasis on the role of myth in the patient's discourse, money after many adversions to angels, the open city in contrast to the sealed consulting room, beauty in the wake of death and the underworld, war straight after beauty! The effect is not only exhilarating and inspiring—and provocative—but it invokes a special state of mind that is ever more open to surprise.[4]

The papers in this book are equally diverse. Their publication here in no way suggests that they represent all of archetypal psychology or that Hillman would necessarily agree with the ideas in them. It is my hope, however, that he will be honored by them. It is my wish and expectation that this collection of essays *will* exhilarate, inspire, and provoke its readers—and if it does invoke this special state of mind that Casey alludes to, it will have accomplished its mission.

## *NOTES*

[1] James Hillman, as quoted in Marcus Quintaes, "Hillman Re-Visioning Hillman: Polemics and Paranoia," p. 88 below.

[2] James Hillman, in Jan Marlan, "Interview with James Hillman: Past, Present, Future," p. 48 below.

[3] *Ibid.*, p. 49.

[4] See p. 97-98 below.

# Reverie, Ancestry, Photography, Interview

We are born into a family and, at the last, we rejoin its full extension when gathered to the ancestors. Family grave, family altar, family trust, family secrets, family pride. Our names are family names, our physiognomies bear family traits and our dreams never let us depart from home—father and mother, brother and sister—from those faces and those rooms. Even alone and only ourselves, we are also always part of them, partly them ....

—James Hillman, *Blue Fire*, p. 196

... [W]e start in myth and live myth in biography. That's why you have to read my myths—my books—to get my biography.

—James Hillman, *Inter Views*, p. 146-147

James Hillman and Stanton Marlan. (From the archives of Jan and Stan Marlan.)

---

Stanton Marlan, Ph.D., ABPP, LP, is a Jungian psychoanalyst and archetypal psychologist in private practice in Pittsburgh, PA, and an adjunct Clinical Professor of Psychology at Duquesne University. He is a training and supervising analyst with the Inter-Regional Society of Jungian Analysts, a member of the C. G. Jung Institute of New York, and a licensed psychoanalyst in that state. He is also President of the Pittsburgh Society of Jungian Analysts. He holds diplomates in both clinical psychology and psychoanalysis from the American Board of Professional Psychology. Dr. Marlan has a long-time interest and involvement in Archetypal Psychology and the work of James Hillman, particularly in the area of dreams and alchemy.

# 1

# Transference, Friendship, and Other Mysteries: A Reverie

Stanton Marlan

When I was beginning this book, I found myself wondering about place, about being placed, and placing myself in the company of James Hillman. I have known James for nearly thirty years, first as an analyst and later as a mentor, colleague, and friend. After reading *Re-Visioning Psychology*, I fell in love with this book and with its ideas. I felt that I wanted to know this man. Prophetically, I first met him in a swimming pool outside of a meeting of the Inter-Regional Society of Jungian Analysts. I thought he was considering joining the Society and I remember that he asked me what was going on in the meetings. I responded rather glibly, "Just a lot of politics," expecting an introverted nod of recognition. Instead he said, "Everything is political." This response was a surprise, one of many to come, but it was also a delight, and I recall my pleasure in discovering later that he was indeed going to join the Society. So, the swimming pool became the first of many meeting places that were to follow, including: the consulting room, our society gatherings, Eranos lectures, dinner tables, birthday parties, playing fields, and later—and most enigmatically—the library, about which I will speak below.

In the early days, reading Hillman's work was challenging. I found it strikingly original, profoundly insightful, spirited, provocative, and truly psychological. It was also freeing. His discussion of "pathologizing" liberates the imagination and allows one to see through to the depths of soul. As I felt the effects of my engagement with Hillman's ideas, I wanted to learn more. Though I had already been in analysis for many years, I began to think about working analytically with him. Although I had some ambivalence about this, I did think it would be a great way to extend and deepen my understanding of his ideas and of archetypal psychology.

Before talking to Hillman about entering analysis, I had an uncomfortable dream. It was an image of "lying down with Hillman." When I did speak with him, I reported the dream and all the ambivalence that came with it. After some consideration he said: "Why not lie down with me for a while." Somehow this relieved my tension and I did lie on his metaphoric couch for about four or five years, and I never regretted it. I not only learned more about Hillman's ideas, but, more importantly, about my own, and about myself. The work sharpened my mind, deepened my soul, and opened me further than I expected to life beyond my consulting room.

Hillman's naturalness and humility were part of my experience of working with him. I remember his telling me once that he enjoyed, when he made an interpretation, that I never asked how to apply it. Another time, when we were stuck in relation to an image, he said he wished he knew more that might be helpful. What I did not tell him was how satisfied I was with what he did offer. His insights into dreams and images were often astounding. I felt his respect for psyche and his interest in what could be learned from it. At the same time, while he would challenge and confront me, his judgments always seemed to come from an objective engagement with psyche and not simply from his own values or from some form of countertransference. He had a keen eye and an uncanny wit and never turned away from what was impenetrable or dark. I had the feeling of working with the minutest details and yet, at the same time, towards an expansive horizon.

After some years of personal analysis, I began to participate in a small group of analysts and scholars who met with Hillman periodically to exchange ideas and talk about theory and cases. Present at these meetings were: James Hillman, Hayao Kawai and Kazuhiko Higuchi from Japan, Wolfgang Giegerich from Germany, Patricia Berry, Paul Kugler, Tom Kapacinskas, Robert Bosnak, Mary

Watkins, Nor Hall, and Angelyn Spignesi (see Fig. 1 and Fig. 2). The excitement of those early meetings continued to catalyze my interest

**Fig. 1:** Group photo taken in the 1980s. **Front row, left to right**: James Hillman, Kazuhiko Higuchi, Paul Kugler, and Mary Watkins. **Middle row, left to right:** Hayao Kawai, Nor Hall, and Stanton Marlan. **Back row, left to right:** Robert Bosnak, Thomas Kapacinskas, and Pat Berry. (From the archives of Jan and Stan Marlan.)

**Fig. 2:** Group photo taken in the 1980s. **Front row, left to right:** Thomas Kapacinskas and Paul Kugler. **Middle row, left to right:** Angelyn Spignesi, Robert Bosnak, Nor Hall, and James Hillman. **Back row, left to right:** Stanton Marlan, Wolfgang Giegerich, Mary Watkins, and Pat Berry. (From the archives of Jan and Stan Marlan.)

in archetypal psychology, and I made a number of good friends, who now constitute the diverse core of a growing intellectual family. Our group, including some of the authors in this book, was of course only one small enclave of the many colleagues and friends of James Hillman worldwide who were engaged in exploring and developing archetypal psychology.

Over the years, James Hillman has remained an important presence in both my inner and my outer life. He has helped to shape the way I imagine my own work and he remains an interlocutor to whom I am grateful for his intellectual generosity, for his taking the time to read and comment on my work, for our exchange of letters, ideas, and personal reactions, and for his mentoring and collaborative spirit. I remember once sending James a paper that included some of my thoughts about Lacan, Derrida, and postmodernism. I knew he was not particularly favorable to the French and asked if he felt my point of view was moving away from his perspective. He responded: "I do not believe you have distanced yourself from what I have been doing; I find your mind on the same track (not derivative, but parallel)!"[1] While James was very articulate, engaging, and challenging, I never felt anything but intellectual friendship and collaboration from him. Nor did I ever feel that he wanted or cultivated disciples. On the contrary, I always sensed that what was important for him in colleagues was precisely that they have their own ideas and opinions and not simply be followers or, worse, adoring imitators. In fact, he once wrote in another letter: "You do quote Hillman too much! You need to assume some of your thoughts as *yours*."[2] This sort of respectful challenge and continued normalizing of my "idealizing transference" were of great value in my own development.

As my relationship with James Hillman developed over the years, I particularly enjoyed our exchanges about alchemy. His vision of the alchemical processes and non-linear transformations of color was unique. His emphasis on blackness, the *nigredo,* and his views about the stone of the philosophers and the goal of alchemy particularly inspired my own work.

James Hillman has a dark eye, but he is anything but an introverted, melancholic man. His love of life and beauty is infectious. He has always loved to combine stimulating intellectual exchange with good food, frolic, and foolishness. James loves to eat, to talk, and to play. He loves poetry and baseball, tap dancing and shopping for hats.

I remember our archetypal weekends and celebrations as nourishing to the psyche and senses, the body and soul. I recall one evening when colleagues from many countries were sitting around the dinner table and the conversation turned to how animal sounds are heard. It was both hilarious and instructive to discover how cows moo, dogs bark, or snakes hiss in other languages and through our varying sociolinguistic contexts.

Laughter was always a part of these meetings, as was a deep sense of the world's beauty. On one occasion, I remember driving somewhere with James, and in the middle of our discussion, he paused. He was looking out the car window. The sun was shining through the trees and he called my attention to the quality of the light and the landscape, commenting on how truly beautiful this world is. As I think of James Hillman now, through the many archetypal moments described above, what strikes me most profoundly is his love of nature and of Aphrodite, and his vital engagement with the life around him.

It would not honor James Hillman to speak only of the light and to not say something about his dark side. At times my relationship with James has been difficult. He can be irascible and impatient; he has terrible phone manners; and he is often in a hurry and even rude. But my experience is that if one doesn't wilt in the face of his passions, one discovers an uncommon gentleness of spirit and a large soul. It is a gift to know him.

I would like to end this reflection with an enigmatic story that remains a hallmark of what feels like a more-than-personal connection to James Hillman. Over the years, as I became increasingly involved with Hillman and his work, a friendship developed between us as well, and at one point, I visited him when he was living in Dallas. In his house he had a small, two-story library with a balcony, and this room enchanted me. I asked him about it. He told me that as a boy he had spent time in his grandfather's library and had loved it, and that was why he had modeled his library after it.

Some years later, when my wife Jan and I were preparing to buy a new house, we had asked the realtor to look for one with a large room that I could use for a library. When the realtor called to say, "I have just the house for you," we went to see it, fell in love with it, and bought it. It had a large, domed room that the previous owners had called "the ballroom," which would be ideal for the library. In fact, we discovered that when the house was first built, this room had been a library, and the original owner, Rabbi J. Leonard Levy, had used a small inglenook room off to one side as his study. We restored the library back to one with two levels and a balcony, connected by a spiral staircase (see Fig. 4).

I had not thought too much about any of this until one day when Hillman came for a visit to Pittsburgh. I had invited him to speak at a local conference, and he was staying with us. When he first saw my library, he paused at its threshold with an odd look on his face. He asked me whether there was a small room over on the left of the library. I said, "Yes," but how did he know that? He told me that it was a lot like his memory of his grandfather's library, the one he had told me about. I recounted to James the story we had been told of the Rabbi who built the house and library when he moved to Pittsburgh from Philadelphia to assume a new position here, and who had loved his mentor's home in Philadelphia so much that he modeled this new house after it. These happenings seemed to be oddly synchronistic, and the mysterious feeling was palpable.

When James went back home, he did some research on Rabbi Levy. He discovered that while in Philadelphia, Rabbi Levy had been an associate of Joseph Krauskopf, James's very own grandfather. It turned out that Rabbi Krauskopf had been Levy's mentor and that Levy had been inspired to design his own home and library to replicate Krauskopf's. I was stunned to realize that, in essence, I was living in a house with a library that replicated the one that James had loved so much as a child. The whole experience felt very numinous to me and I wondered about a deeper connection to James Hillman than I had imagined possible.

A year or two later, I went to Philadelphia to find James's grandfather's house to see the original library. The house was very similar to mine but, unfortunately, the library had been torn out. I asked whether there were any shelves left from it and was told that there were some stored in the basement of the house. The new owners graciously gave me two shelves. I kept one and gave one to James with a little plaque on it commemorating his grandfather's library and this odd synchronistic event.

In the following paper published in this volume, "Legacy of the Ancestors," Dick Russell, Hillman's biographer, writes about Hillman's grandfather. Russell describes the library in Krauskopf's home as containing "busts of Shakespeare, Dante, and other literary giants,"

**Fig. 3:** Interior of the Joseph Krauskopf Memorial Library. (Used by permission of the Joseph Krauskopf Memorial Library, Delaware Valley College, Doylestown, Pennsylvania.)

**Fig. 4:** The restored library at the Marlan home. (Photograph by Jan Marlan.)

and notes that "as a boy, his grandson James would sometimes stand there, gazing upon the bookshelves."[3] Hillman's grandfather was directly involved with the founding of Delaware Valley College in Doylestown, Pennsylvania, and it too contains a library modeled after the one Krauskopf had in his home. When I visited this library, I was able to find some photographs of the interior (see Fig. 3, previous page, and Fig. 5) and a relief carving of Dr. Krauskopf (see Fig. 6) that is currently being installed above the entrance to the library.

As I conclude this reflection—sitting here in my own library, staring at my own bookshelves—I am left with Russell's image of James as a young boy gazing at his grandfather's library. I find myself likewise in a reverie—about this strange confluence of souls … about the mysterious series of events … about my relationship with James Hillman. I find myself full of wonder listening to the echo of the ancestors.

**Fig. 5:** Interior of the Joseph Krauskopf Memorial Library. (Used by permission of the Joseph Krauskopf Memorial Library.)

**Fig. 6:** Stone relief of Rabbi Krauskopf commissioned for the 150th anniversary of his birth in 2008 by the Friends of the Joseph Krauskopf Memorial Library. The relief is by noted Bucks County sculptor Charles Wells and will be placed above the redesigned entryway to the library. It captures the rabbi in a pensive moment with his hand on a book, a visual reminder of how important his personal library, now housed in the Krauskopf Library, was to him. (Description by Peter Kupersmith, College Librarian. Image used by permission of the Joseph Krauskopf Memorial Library.)

## *NOTES*

[1] Personal communication from James Hillman to the author, December 18, 1997.

[2] Personal communication from James Hillman to the author, January 26, 1996.

[3] p. 21 below.

James Hillman and Dick Russell, Hillman's official biographer. (Used by permission of Dick Russell.)

---

DICK RUSSELL is the author of five books, including *Eye of the Whale*, named among the best books of the year (2001) by three major newspapers. A recipient of the citizen's Chevron Conservation Award, he is a longtime environmental activist who worked closely on projects with Robert F. Kennedy, Jr. He first met James Hillman through a mutual friend who sells both of them organic vegetables. He divides his time between Boston, Los Angeles, and Baja Mexico.

# 2

# *Legacy of the Ancestors*[1]

DICK RUSSELL

Blow on a dead man's embers
And a live flame will start.

Let his forgotten griefs be now,
And now, his withered hopes;
. . .

—Robert Graves,
"To Bring the Dead to Life"

Nearly all biographies begin with the antecedents of their subject, to one degree or another. Most do not linger long on the forbears, perhaps because not enough is known about them, generally because the life of the "main man" or woman is what the reader is most interested to know about. In the case of James Hillman, however, we must digress, meditate, reflect upon the ancestors, from whom much seems to have been passed down to him.

From the earliest societies to contemporary civilizations, genealogical methods have been utilized to trace ancestries back to gods, animal totems, and legendary heroes. Originally, it was the oral history narratives of clan or tribe that bequeathed the lineage. In ancient Sumeria, Babylon, Egypt, India, and China, kings and heads of state traced their rights to the throne through genealogy. Adam, Abraham, and Noah all have their "begats" sketched in the Old Testament, where the House of David traces a royal bloodline. Muslims track their descent to Mohammed, while of course the Greeks and Romans sought to link their heritage to the gods.

In the last book of his *Republic*, Plato sets down the Myth of Er, in which he uses the word *daimon* to describe a "soul-companion" that guides us during our time on earth. The idea is that we each have a unique image or pattern that our soul selects before we are born, forgotten by us in the process of arrival, but remembered by the *daimon*—which becomes, in effect, the carrier of our destiny. "Other cultures have many words for those 'spirits' that seem to guide us," Hillman has said, "terms like 'the invisibles'"—or what we often describe as fate or destiny.[2]

Confucius described two souls of humankind, the living and the spiritual, the latter containing the departed ancestors. The dead are given a greater reality by the memory of them that the living keep alive, and they are thus invoked on important occasions such as births and marriages. In today's Africa, the Ibo and Kalabari peoples of Nigeria continue to believe in the presence of two souls, much like the ones that Confucius advanced. A person is always being watched by the ancestral spirits, and "to be cut off from relationships with one's ancestors is to cease to be a whole person."[3]

Many Australian aborigines believe that a newly-born infant is a reincarnation of a deceased ancestor. Certain Indonesian peoples say that ancestral souls reside in sacred animals, sometimes in preparation for a new human incarnation. In the western Amazon, tribes eschew eating particular animals, such as deer, because the ancestral souls have entered the animal's bodies. Native peoples of central Mexico traditionally believed that the migrating monarch butterflies were their returning ancestors.

The importance of ancestry to soul appears in Anglo-Saxon and Scandinavian genealogies. In Germanic folklore the soul was considered, in certain respects, something inherited. And it was out of this German Romantic tradition—the one that gave us poets such as Goethe, philosophers such as Kant and Nietzche, composers such as Beethoven—that C.G. Jung came to prominence in the early years of the 20$^{th}$ century.

Himself a pastor's son, Jung had a maternal grandmother who often fell into trances and awoke uttering prophecies, while his maternal grandfather was an Old Testament scholar who "spoke" frequently to spirits. It was by the legend of his grandfather—not the living example of his father—that Jung measured himself as a young man. By the time he was nineteen, Jung was convinced that his existence was somehow deeply entwined with his ancestors and the spiritual mysteries.[4]

As a pioneer in the nascent field of psychiatry, Jung's chief disagreement with Sigmund Freud was his belief that the unconscious was a far vaster realm than Freud hypothesized. Across time and divergent cultures, behaviors, fears, and thoughts proved remarkably similar. Jung termed this the "collective unconscious," composed of archetypes, or primordial images inherited from our ancestors. From the infant's attachment to the mother and fear of the dark, to the images of sun, moon, angels, evil, and the wise old man, there was a consistency of influence upon the human personality, no matter its origins.

In the course of giving a seminar in Zürich in 1925, Jung went so far as to espouse a belief in "ancestor possession." Under certain circumstances in your life, he said, particular hereditary units could activate themselves and, in effect, "take over" your own actions. "I know no answer to the question of whether the karma which I live is the outcome of my past lives, or whether it is not rather the achievement of my ancestors, whose heritage comes together in me," Jung would write in his autobiography, *Memories, Dreams, Reflections*. "Am I a combination of the lives of these ancestors and do I embody these lives again?"[5]

In 1975, James Hillman published his landmark book, *Re-Visioning Psychology*, in which he refines some of Jung's ideas into what has come to be known as archetypal psychology. Here Hillman harkened to the Neoplatonists of the Renaissance, to whom "the great men of the past were living realities ... because they personified the soul's needs for spiritual ancestors, ideal types, internal guides and mentors who can share our lives with us and inspire them beyond our personal narrowness."[6] In reaching back to "Greek and Roman mythical figures—not as allegories, but as modes of reflection," these Renaissance thinkers had rediscovered soul and its paradoxical nature: Soul is in us, but we are also in *it*.

Later, in his essay "Extending the Family" (1985), Hillman wrote: "The ancient home gave plenty of place to the invisibles that live in a family, propitiating and domesticating its daimones, which it acknowledged as rightfully belonging." He went on to add: "With the passing of time a sense of its power grows within one's psyche, like the movements of its skeleton inside one's flesh, which keeps one in servitude to patterns entombed in our closest attitudes and habits. From this interior family we are never free. This service keeps us bonded to the ancestors."[7]

Yet, as he would elaborate in *The Soul's Code* (1995): "Only if a member of the natural family (itself not always determinable), say a grandparent or an uncle or an aunt, is worthy enough, powerful enough, knowledgeable enough, may he or she become an ancestor in the sense of a guardian spirit."[8]

Even as a young man, Hillman had found himself compelled to know all he could about his ancestors. "I am grateful to you for thinking of me in connection with a box or boxes of personal papers of Grandfather's," he once wrote his parents. "These things mean much to me ...." Another time, he wrote of being "delighted to be getting all this family information." Today, their portraits all hang in an upstairs bedroom, and in the attic there are literally thousands of pages about Hillman's forbears—letters and postcards, faded newspapers and photographs, genealogical charts—reaching back two centuries. Indeed, so much was recorded and kept, by so many branches of the family, that it is almost as if we are scrutinizing some Egyptian or Chinese "cult of the ancestors."

There is, perhaps, one distinction. This particular one saved the menus from all the great occasions.

---

The dedication page of Hillman's first book, *Emotion* (1960), reads: "To the spirits of my grandfathers—JOEL HILLMAN and JOSEPH KRAUSKOPF."

James Hillman never knew Krauskopf, his maternal grandfather, who died in 1923, three years before his birth. Yet Krauskopf remained a dominant, even legendary, figure in the household, an oil portrait peering down intensely from the living-room hearth in Atlantic City. An immigrant youth who spoke no English upon arriving at Ellis Island, Krauskopf had risen to become the most prominent Reform rabbi in the United States.

He had spent his youth in the forests of eastern Prussia (today's Poland), helping his wood contractor father haul small bundles to the local villagers. At fourteen, Krauskopf sailed in steerage to join his older brothers in America, the "land of opportunity." But after the brother supposed to take him in was robbed and murdered on the road, Krauskopf ended up alone in the textile town of Fall River, Massachusetts. He took part in amateur theatricals to facilitate learning the language, and sold trinkets door to door. One of his customers, a Christian schoolteacher named Mary Slade, took a keen interest in the uncommonly bright teenager—and eventually requested a scholarship for him to the new Hebrew Union College in Cincinnati.[9]

Years later, Krauskopf reflected: "Neither environment nor family tradition could have exercized [*sic*] an unconscious impelling influence on me, for I knew of no minister in my family; and when I felt myself drawn toward the Jewish pulpit I lived in a gentile community, and far removed from a Jewish congregation .... I felt within me what I believed to be a divine call, and I obeyed."[10]

His mentor at the college was Rabbi Isaac Mayer Wise, then the leading advocate for Reform Judaism, who conducted services in English instead of Hebrew, and on Sundays rather than the customary Saturday Sabbath. A fellow student would describe Krauskopf as a born leader, one who "struck out into original paths" with a "veritable passion for work" and an "apparently inexhaustible fund of energy."[11] Krauskopf would be among the first four young men to become American-trained ordained rabbis.

His initial posting was to Kansas City, then a booming cattle town. There, Krauskopf was taken under the wing of a prosperous local merchant named Benjamin Arnold Feineman, whom everyone called B. A. He was married to a Binswanger, one of four daughters of an immigrant shopkeeper, who had been shot to death in frontier Missouri after refusing to open his store and sell liquor to a customer on the Sabbath. Although Feineman's diaries record his enchantment with the Binswanger widow, he had ended up wedded to daughter Bettie when she turned sixteen. The reception supper provided, according to the local newspaper, "everything that the daintiest epicure could desire."

Feineman had been among the founders of Kansas City's Reform temple, and Krauskopf wasted no time in pushing the envelope. The new theory of evolution was not in conflict with religion, he preached, and Jesus possessed traits that Jews should emulate. He fought against child labor, became active in prison reform, and arranged low-cost housing for impoverished families. Embodied in Krauskopf, a contemporary wrote, "we can hear the longing of the new American rabbi for the emancipation of Judaism from its outlandish, outmoded Oriental cloak."[12]

After four years in Kansas City, in 1887, Krauskopf was summoned by the Reform Congregation Keneseth Israel in Philadelphia to be its spiritual leader. He was only twenty-nine when he and his wife, Rose, boarded the railway coach eastbound with three children. During his first year, Krauskopf initiated what conservative members viewed as "unwarranted innovations" —calling for more art, music, and dancing in the temple's religious school and beginning a young people's society of "Knowledge Seekers." The fallible Bible, he told his congregation, "is the work of man and shares all the faults that characterize the religious writings of bygone ages .... No religion, if it is to serve its purpose, is to be permitted to become congealed or fossilized."[13] Religion had to confront the social issues of the day and address the needs of the poor, the ill, and the imprisoned. "He discards ... the idea of a coming Messiah, believing that the Messianic age will have dawned when all mankind shall be one brotherhood," it was written of Krauskopf.

His "Sunday Lectures," delivered from memory with "literary charm," proved so popular that they were published weekly in pamphlet form. A new synagogue had to be built to hold the burgeoning crowds, which included many non-Jews. The rabbi himself designed the edifice, in the style of the Italian Renaissance: "A square and graceful tower, capped by a minaret, rises above the front façade; and the inner structure is crowned by a dome of grand proportions."

Krauskopf launched the Jewish Publication Society of America, a non-profit cooperative venture whose objective was to bring books on Jewish subjects to a wider American audience. (Now based in New York, it remains a leader in religious publishing). His call for a public library helped push Philadelphia to establish it first in 1892. The prestigious *National Encyclopedia of American Biography* was by then describing Krauskopf as "giving the Jewish reform movement a direction and a force hitherto unthought of."

His ongoing interest in slum conditions led to the Model Dwelling Association, an attempt to bring private enterprise into low-income housing. He was among the first to call for a federal Secretary of Labor. He was also an early environmental champion who, in speaking out for pure food and smog-control laws, proclaimed: "It is not an unwarranted assumption of power for the state to interfere with the food we eat and the air we breathe." According to a later chronicler, "Many of his suggestions were far ahead of his time, especially the notion that poverty and crime were largely functions of the environment and child development."[14]

In 1894, following the expulsion of all Jews from Moscow and concerns that pogroms there were intensifying, Krauskopf arranged a trip to Russia after meeting with several wealthy Americans. His intent was to discuss, with the Czar, the purchase of a large tract of available land where Jews might be resettled as farmers. While this effort did not bear fruit, Krauskopf did make a pilgrimage to the rural home of Count Leo Tolstoy, already world renowned as the author of *War and Peace*. Tolstoy had condemned persecution of the Jews, and had been denounced as an anarchist by the Russian hierarchy for advocating collective ownership of land.

From Moscow, it took six hours by rail and horse-drawn wagon to reach the ancestral estate where Tolstoy continued to work the land like an ordinary peasant. Krauskopf was mightily impressed, later recalling "the fire of humanity beaming" from the man's eyes as they shared a frugal evening meal. Expressing doubt that the Czarists would ever accept Krauskopf's plan, Tolstoy suggested that he instead open an agricultural school in America "where young Jews could learn the skills of their ancestors."

Krauskopf, who would later describe Tolstoy as "one of those rare geniuses of whom Emerson speaks, who prove their greatness by being greatly misunderstood,"[15] followed Tolstoy's advice. Raising funds to purchase 122 acres in Doylestown, Pennsylvania, he would open the National Farm School two years later, its first students being a dozen boys taken off the streets of Philadelphia. "Gradually, Krauskopf recognized that his interest in agriculture as the means for helping Jews in the American slums and European ghettos began to coincide with Zionist efforts to establish agricultural colonies in Palestine," according to an article in *American Jewish History*.[16] Those would become the first kibbutzes. Yet Krauskopf himself continued to believe that "there will never be a return to Palestinian Zion unless there will first be a return to Eden nearer home" in America. Today, his original school is called Delaware Valley College, stretching across 940 acres; with more than a thousand students, it is the only private college in America that offers a Bachelor of Science degree in agriculture.

Following the unexpected death of his wife, Krauskopf was left a widower with three children to raise. Then, in 1896, the same year that he established the National Farm School, he returned to Kansas City to marry Sybil Feineman. She was a primary schoolteacher, the eldest daughter of B. A. and Bettie and, thirteen years younger than Krauskopf, had in fact been part of his first confirmation class. Sybil's sole attendant at the wedding was her grandmother, Elise Binswanger.[17]

Elise's murdered husband, Solomon Binswanger—great-great-grandfather of James Hillman—had been the last of nine brothers. One of those, Ludwig, had remained in southern Germany, and become a well-known medical "psychiatrist" before the term was ever used. In 1857, Ludwig had founded the Bellevue Sanitorium in Kreuzlingen, Switzerland. This private asylum would eventually become famous, caring for such luminaries as F. Scott Fitzgerald's wife, Zelda. This Binswanger's grandson, also named Ludwig, ended up a student of Jung's, and through Jung was introduced to Freud. All through the Freud-Jung letters, he is described as a go-between in their relationship.

Another Binswanger descendant would later be elected to the governing Curatorium of the Jung Institute. Hilda Binswanger, a Jungian analyst in Zürich, would translate James Hillman's book, *Suicide and the Soul*, into German. Yet another Binswanger would be Hillman's family physician during his years in Zürich. Hillman himself knew nothing of these ancestral connections before he moved to Zürich in 1953, where he would remain for almost a quarter of a century.[18]

During the Spanish-American War, Joseph Krauskopf had been one of several field commissioners enlisted to visit hospitals at the front in Cuba and military camps in the U.S. There he became acquainted with Theodore Roosevelt and his Rough Riders. In 1906, Roosevelt would write Krauskopf from the White House, praising the National Farm School: "[N]o nation can afford to forget that in the last resort its well-being rests upon the well-being and high character of the man who tills the soil."[19] When Roosevelt died in 1917, Krauskopf dedicated to his memory a stained-glass window in his Broad Street Temple.

In the early years of the 20th century, while that temple boasted the largest Jewish congregation in America, Krauskopf went on to work for civic improvements and became a fervent supporter of women's suffrage and civil rights, while adamantly opposed to capital punishment and later Prohibition.[20]

Accompanied by his wife Sybil and daughter Madeleine in the summer of 1912, Krauskopf returned to visit their ancestral German homeland. Sybil wrote to her father, B. A., of visiting a woman, who "took us to the house where you were born Papa .... Madeleine and I delighted ourselves by plucking some of the beautiful poppies and cornflowers." Later that year, B. A. Feineman died, lauded by the *Kansas City Star* for having "contributed in a very substantial manner to [the city's] development, especially along humanitarian and philanthropic lines."

Krauskopf's congregation paid for his family to take a year-long trip around the world in the summer of 1913. Their journey took them across Asia, through the Middle East and Europe, up the Nile, to Jerusalem and Bethlehem, Delphi and Olympia, the trip ultimately being cut short by the beginning of World War I. While America's entry into the war would turn the tide against the Axis powers, the rabbi's sermons grew increasingly pessimistic. He was disappointed with Woodrow Wilson's failure to bring the country into the new League of Nations; he was disillusioned with the vengeful Treaty of Versailles, which ended the War; above all, he was embittered by the ongoing persecution of Jews in both Eastern and Western Europe.

The large library in the rabbi's home contained busts of Shakespeare, Dante, and other literary giants. As a boy, his grandson James would sometimes stand there, gazing upon the bookshelves. Krauskopf's last sermon, delivered on Christmas Eve 1922, concerned the value of art in the worship of God. "Take the best sermon and see how dull it is alongside a good play," he had once written in a lecture entitled "The Stage as a Pulpit."[21]

After collapsing in his home, Krauskopf, who loved the ocean, was taken by his family to the seaside resort of Atlantic City. There, his oldest daughter, Madeleine, lived with her husband, Julian Hillman, who, with his father, managed a Boardwalk hotel, the Breakers. The *Philadelphia American* reported that Krauskopf "spent his last days sitting on the porch of the hotel, wrapped in blankets." He died of arteriosclerosis in a room at the Breakers, on June 12, 1923. Less than three years later, his grandson James Hillman would be born—also in a room at the Breakers, overlooking the water.

A crowd of thousands came to pay respects to "a man who was an institution," as the Philadelphia newspaper editorialized. Joseph Krauskopf "stood in the forefront of those who believe that ancient religion should not stand still, but keep pace with the changing needs of mankind. This attitude made him for many years a storm center, with the forces of orthodox Judaism openly arrayed against him."

As Krauskopf had said in one of his Sunday Lectures (1912), "Progress has ever been the gift to the many by the few who have had the courage to differ, who have dared to stand alone."[22]

---

The paternal grandfather, Joel Hillman, had, like Krauskopf, been on his own since his early years. Born in Memphis a year after the Civil War ended, he had been raised by a shopkeeper family in Okolona, Mississippi after his father died in a cholera or yellow fever epidemic and his mother disappeared. At fourteen, Hillman left whatever home he knew and found work selling sandwiches, cigars, and magazines from a pushcart for the Illinois Central railroad, which ran between New Orleans and Chicago. In the latter city he remained, later sweeping out a slaughterhouse in the Union Stockyards, described in Upton Sinclair's *The Jungle* as a "square mile of abominations."

Standing more than six-foot-two, Hillman caught the eye of one of the meatpacking companies. After a few years apprenticing as a butcher, he was dispatched to open a branch office in Washington, D.C. There, he sold butter, eggs, and chickens to local restaurants. His occupation, at the time of his marriage to Sarah Lulley in 1891, was listed as "porkpacker."[23]

Sarah was a petite young lady who enjoyed wearing fantastic hats, jewelry, and costumes. Well-educated at a private girls' school in Washington, she was the grand-daughter of a Hungarian revolutionary. During the initially successful rebellion against Hapsburg Austrian rule led by Louis Kossuth in 1848, Emanuel (Mano) Lulley had been the "spymaster," or chief of intelligence. After Russia sent a huge army to maintain the *status quo*, Kossuth and his men were forced to capitulate. "Lulley was one of the five men who buried the crown of Hungary and refused to reveal its hiding-place."

Lulley, along with his wife and five children, were among fifty of Kossuth's band to be rescued from a refugee camp in Turkey by the American steam frigate *Mississippi*. Upon landing at the Brooklyn Navy

Yard, Lulley is said to have dressed his children in Hungarian national costumes and sent them marching ashore to wild applause. Invited to Washington to meet President Fillmore, he was given "a splendid silver medal" and decided to remain.

During the Civil War, Lulley sought to raise a volunteer regiment called the Kossuth Corps for the Union Army. (Hungarian participation in the Civil War exceeded that of any other ethnic group). He and one of his sons were sutlers in the nation's capital, merchants who followed the army selling various provisions—possibly a "cover" for Lulley's real work as a secret agent for Lincoln's Department of Justice.[24]

In more recent years, his great-great-grandson, James Hillman, would tramp through at least fifteen of the Civil War battlefields, from Pennsylvania to Mississippi.

> Writing books for me is anyway much like a military campaign. I confess to fighting my way through with military metaphors. There is a strategy, an overall concept, and there are tactics along the way. ... Tradition would say I was a "child of Mars."[25]

After the war, Lulley set himself up in the auctioneering and commission business on the same block as Harvey's Restaurant and Oyster Saloon, whose steamed oysters were considered the beginning of real American cuisine. Since Harvey's was one of Joel Hillman's customers, this may have been where he first encountered Lulley's grand-daughter Sarah, "a proud little Hungarian princess," as her grandson James Hillman would recall.

Julian, the young couple's second child, came along in 1894. And Joel's business enterprise continued to gather momentum. Although lacking any formal education, he read prodigiously and could quote Keats and Shelley. He had "style and taste, a gentleman's fantasy," James remembers. "He was extremely distinguished, spoke with a slight Southern accent, and had the kind of presence where he was often mistaken for a senator."[26]

In 1906, a Washington newspaper headline announced: "Harvey's Changes Hands: Hillman, the Purchaser." Joel had bought the restaurant business for $140,000. Under his management, the *New York Times* reported, Harvey's "became well known as a rendezvous for members of Congress, the diplomatic corps and the press." The restaurant was famed for its Imperial crab and steaks broiled to perfection. Joel selected the meat personally; the market kept a skewer with his name on it. He made an "epicurean trip" to Europe, about which the *Washington Herald* interviewed him: "On the other side eating is a recreation and a pleasure. … [O]ver there we can learn the lesson that in our rush and hurry we sacrifice some of the real pleasures of life."[27]

Sarah's father, Anthony Lulley, also a merchant, had retired to Atlantic City, New Jersey, at the time the leading resort community in the U.S. And in 1907, Joel Hillman acquired the lease on a Boardwalk hotel then called the Rudolf. It was a five-story wood-frame building, with a ballroom that could accommodate 500 dancers. While maintaining his interest in Harvey's, Joel moved his family to Atlantic City and was soon elected the first president of the New Jersey Hotel Association.

After building an addition and changing the hotel's name during World War I, Hillman's Breakers now stood ten stories high, "with a magnificent green copper roof, like a French chateau," and baths in each of the 450 rooms.[28] His son, Julian, intent upon marriage to Madeleine Krauskopf, the attractive rabbi's daughter, decided to join his father as assistant manager.

The families came together for the first time when the Krauskopfs invited the Hillmans to a meal in Philadelphia, at which Sybil Krauskopf prepared what she considered a very special dinner. Yet, as they all sat down in front of the platters, Joel Hillman said, loud enough for all to hear: "Why do they think they always have to have squab?" The fare, it seemed, was too bourgeois for his "refined European" tastes. Or perhaps the Southern-born "aristocrat" felt the need to upstage the prominent Reform rabbi.[29]

The marriage ceremony in the Krauskopf garden was a lavish affair hailed as "one of the most artistic weddings ever witnessed" by the *Atlantic City Press*. The magnificent tiered wedding cake, a creation of the Breakers' head baker, stood more than three feet high and required five men to deliver it from Atlantic City to the bride's home in the Germantown section of north Philadelphia.[30]

During the Roaring Twenties, the couple traveled across the Atlantic on luxury steamers, while Joel sat in the smoker's lounge regaling people with his stories. In 1927, Joel and Julian became the American partners in the building of a new luxury hotel in Paris. It would be called the George V, rising a luminous whiteness of high marble and stone walls, in a "modern French style" that drew admirers from the international design world. Guests would come to include Franklin D. Roosevelt and the Prince of Wales. The glory was fleeting, as the Hillman family was bankrupted by the advent of the Great Depression and lost its ownership interest in the George V. (Today, the hotel is owned by His Royal Highness Prince Al Waleed of Saudi Arabia).

Years later, Madeleine Hillman would remember her father-in-law once stopping their chauffeured car on a Paris street to point out something in a butcher's shop and remark at how beautiful it was. Espying a *foie gras* that had opened up, he marveled, "Look at that, it's like a sunset. It should be painted." Not surprisingly, Joel became the first American member of the Escoffier Society, a Parisian group of epicurean chefs and hoteliers that gathered for long dinners to compare notes on gourmet cuisine.

When he died at 85 in 1951, the *Atlantic City Press* wrote: "Mr. Hillman represented a glittering era in which hotel reputations were made when a host was almost as great as the famous guests who visited his establishment." He was a man with "a genius for hotel keeping and a magic touch ... known to literally thousands of visitors in his heyday."

---

So let us reconsider Jung's question: "Am I a combination of the lives of these ancestors and do I embody these lives again?" What do we see reflected in the life of James Hillman?

In Joseph Krauskopf, we encounter the reformer, both of his own discipline and in aspiration of the larger world beyond it. In the Binswanger line is the therapeutic-psychiatric element. In B. A. Feineman, the sense of civic duty and involvement. In Emanuel Lulley, the revolutionary warrior. In Joel Hillman, the quality of worldliness and international style. Also in these ancestors, we find the ongoing link between the undaunted self-made American and the European tradition. We observe a combination of luck, privilege, ability, and chutzpah.

Of course, all these expansive aspects of the ancestors leave their shadow traces. With the light comes darkness. Ancestral blessings are not unaccompanied by ancestral curses.

---

In the summer of 2007, Robert Bly, the poet and a longtime friend of James Hillman's—born the same year, 1926—is sitting over breakfast in his Minneapolis kitchen for an interview. "My first impression of Jim was of someone who came from a line of very good innkeepers," Bly is saying. "I saw him as host at a hotel that served wonderful food, had great rooms—and the feeling that you were always welcome. He's standing behind the desk, checking you out. And he's going to do things for *you*—I mean, the room service is superb!"

Later that morning, Bly adds: "Jim expands outward into the universe from an object or an idea. He is honoring what used to be called 'angels'—all the invisible beings, both in the psyche and in the world."

## *NOTES*

[1] The following are excerpts from a work-in-progress, the first biography of James Hillman, by Dick Russell.

[2] Bert H. Hoff, "Authenticity, Character and Destiny: An Interview with James Hillman," 1998, <www.menweb.org/hillmaiv.htm>, accessed October 13, 2007.

[3] Jack Partain, "Christians and Their Ancestors: A Dilemma of African Theology," <www.religion-online.org/showarticle.asp?title=1078>, accessed October 13, 2007.

[4] "The Enigmatic Origins of the Jung Cult," talk presented to the Unitarian-Universalist Fellowship in April 1999. <www.wku.edu/~jan.garrett/jung.htm>, accessed October 13, 2007.

[5] Jung also wrote: "I feel very strongly that I am under the influence of things or questions which were left incomplete and unanswered by my parents and grandparents and more distant ancestors. It often seems as if there were an impersonal karma within a family, which is passed on from parents to children. It has always seemed to me that I had to answer questions which fate had posed to my forefathers, and which had not yet been answered ...."—C. G. Jung, *Memories, Dreams Reflections* (New York: Pantheon Books, 1963), p. 233.

[6] James Hillman, *Re-Visioning Psychology* (New York: Harper Colophon, 1992), p. 198.

[7] James Hillman, *A Blue Fire* (New York: Harper & Row, 1989), p. 204.

[8] James Hillman, *The Soul's Code* (New York: Random House, 1996), p. 89.

[9] Krauskopf's background was compiled from various sources including family archives and William W. Blood, *Apostle of Reason: A Biography of Joseph Krauskopf* (Philadelphia: Dorrance & Co., 1973). See also Glenn D. Kittler, *Profiles in Faith* (New York: Coward-McCann, 1962), pp. 131-151.

[10] Blood, p. 12.

[11] David Philipson, quoted in Blood, p. 17.

[12] Rabbi Stuart E. Rosenberg, quoted in Blood, p. 28.

[13] *Ibid.*, pp. 41-42.

[14] "The Early Years of Joseph Krauskopf at Reform Congregation Keneseth Israel," paper by Martin P. Beifeld, Jr., January 1973, unpublished paper, p. 11.

[15] Joseph Krauskopf, *Gleanings from our Vineyard: Seven Lectures by Rabbi Jos. Krauskopf* (Philadelphia: Oscar Klonower, 1895), p. 3.

[16] Martin P. Beifeld, Jr., "Joseph Krauskopf and Zionism: Partners in Change," *American Jewish History* (September 1985), pp. 49-50.

[17] Ethel R. Feineman, "A History of the Jews of Kansas City," *The Reform Advocate,* March 28, 1908; Howard F. Sachs, "Development of the Jewish Community of Kansas City, 1864-1908," *Missouri Historical Review* 60, no. 3 (1966): 30-360; newspaper clippings, James Hillman's personal archives.

[18] Conversations with James Hillman and C. George Boeree, "Ludwig Binswanger 1881-1966," <http://webspace.ship.edu/cgboer/binswanger.html>, October 26, 2007.

[19] Theodore Roosevelt, personal letter to Joseph Krauskopf, March 19, 1906, from the personal archives of James Hillman.

[20] Beifeld.

[21] Krauskopf, p. 4.

[22] Blood, p. 183.

[23] Joel Hillman's background was compiled from interviews with James Hillman and Joel Hillman, Jr.

[24] The Lulley family background was compiled from various sources including materials sent by Steve Beszedits, University of Toronto; also Lois Hechinger England, "The Lulley Family: From the Danube to the Potomac and Beyond," *The Record, The Jewish Historical Society of Greater Washington Annual* 18 (1991): 24-30.

[25] James Hillman, *A Terrible Love of War* (New York: The Penguin Press, 2004), p. 15.

[26] Author's interviews with James Hillman.

[27] Obituary and editorial, *Atlantic City Press*, August 17, 1951; obituary, *New York Times*, August 18, 1951.

[28] Bryant Simon, *Boardwalk of Dreams: Atlantic City and the Fate of Urban America* (Oxford: Oxford University Press, 2004), pp. 78, 84.

[29] Author's interview with James Hillman.

[30] "Wedding," *Atlantic City Evening Union*, September 20, 1919.

PAUL KUGLER received his Ph.D. from the State University of New York and completed a Diploma in Analytical Psychology from the Jung Institute, Zürich (1979). While in Zürich, he worked at the Clinic and Research Center for Jungian Psychology (Klinik am Zürichberg) before returning the United States to teach at SUNY / Buffalo and work in private practice in East Aurora, New York. He is the author of numerous works ranging from contemporary psychoanalysis and experimental theater to postmodernism and clinical supervision. Dr. Kugler is the author of *The Alchemy of Discourse: Image, Sound and Psyche* (rev. ed., 2002) and editor of *Jungian Perspectives on Clinical Supervision* (1995). His most recent book is *Raids on the Unthinkable: Jungian and Freudian Psychoanalyses* (2005). He is a past president of the Inter-Regional Society of Jungian Analysts and currently serves as an officer of the International Association of Analytical Psychologists.

# 3

# James Hillman and Friends: A Photographic Retrospective

PAUL KUGLER

We are all familiar with photographs, especially the family album. But what actually is a photograph and how is it related to our history? A photograph is an encounter between the photographer, the photographed, and the viewer, and somewhere in this encounter a certain psychically ambiguous experience begins to emerge. The photograph stops the flow of time and is retrospective in experience. Photographic images are always about the past. How different this is from film and its anticipatory nature, which draws the viewer into the future, waiting to see "what comes next." Photographs, on the other hand, are of an earlier time, a moment that has been "shot," "captured," "arrested"—and yet, unlike a lived past experience, the photograph cannot "develop" into the present. Through the act of taking a photograph an unbridgeable gap is opened up between the moment of capture in the photograph and the present moment of its viewing. In this existential abyss and its temporal discontinuity, we find the mystery of the photograph. While viewing it, the psyche makes use of this "space," this temporal gap, to imagine the nature of the image. The viewer wonders about the photograph: What was the occasion? Where did the event occur? Who were the people? What was happening? Why did the photographer take this picture? And as the viewer struggles with these questions, the precise details of the picture become clearer, and at the same moment, our imagination begins to work on the image, lending it a past and a future, and the precise instant that has been "captured" in the photograph begins to acquire meaning and duration. As the viewer is drawn into the picture and begins to fantasize about its story and what motivated the photographer to preserve this unique moment, the photograph begins to take on psychological significance.[1]

The photographs in this retrospective of James Hillman and a few of his friends come from several sources. Several of the earlier photographs are from Hillman's personal collection, others are from the Eranos archive, and the remainder are from my own photographs taken between 1976 and 2004. It is my hope that these photographs might be viewed, not so much biographically, but with an imaginative eye towards that mysterious gap between the captured moment of the photograph and the moment of your viewing. [2]

## *NOTES*

[1] For a more extensive discussion of the psychic significance of "lived time" see E. Minkowski, *Lived Time: Phenomenological and Pathological Studies* (Evanston, IL: Northwesters University Press, 1970). Also see John Szarkowski, *Looking at Photographs* (New York: Hill and Wang, 1989) and John Berger (with Jean Mohr), *Another Way of Telling* (London: Writers and Readers, 1982) for a discussion of the experience of viewing photographs.

[2] I would like to thank The Eranos Foundation for their permission to reproduce the Eranos photographs. I would also like to thank James and Margot Hillman for granting permission to reproduce photographs from the Hillman family collection.

James Hillman at the Barcelona IAAP Congress in 2004. (Photograph by Paul Kugler and used with his permission.)

Adolf Guggenbühl and James Hillman in Houston, Texas during a visit to America in 1963. (Used with the permission of James Hillman).

James Hillman in his study in Thompson, Connecticut, August 1983. (Photograph by Paul Kugler and used with his permission.)

Gilbert Duran, Alfred Zeigler, and James Hillman standing on the veranda of Casa Eranos at the 1980 Eranos Conference (Used with the permission of The Eranos Foundation.)

Left: James Hillman's High School Yearbook photograph (1942/43). (Used with the permission of James Hillman.)

Right: James Hillman in 1993 in Pomfret, Connecticut. (Photograph by Paul Kugler and used with his permission.)

Michael Adams and James Hillman at the East Aurora Seminar on Archetypal Psychology, August 1999, Roy Croft Inn. (Photograph by Paul Kugler and used with his permission.)

Back row, from left to right : Jan Marlan, Stanton Marlan, Michael Adams, Nor Hall, Greg Mogenson, Ginette Paris, James Hillman, Kazuhiko Higuchi. Front row, from left to right: Karen Wolff, David Miller, Margot McLean, Tom Kapacinskas, Kevin Wolff. Photograph taken in August 1999 in East Aurora, New York. (Photograph by Paul Kugler and used with his permission.)

James Hillman is on the far right with his classmates from The Friends School in Atlantic City, 1933/34. (Used with the permission of James Hillman.)

James Hillman at the East Aurora Seminar on Archetypal Psychology, August 1999, Roy Croft Inn. (Photograph by Paul Kugler and used with his permission.)

Left to right: Paul Kugler, James Hillman, and Wolfgang Geigerich, 1987 Eranos Conference. (Photograph by Luciano Soave and used with the permission of The Eranos Foundation.)

From left to right: Michael Adams, James Hillman, Stanton Marlan, Margot McLean, Kazuhiko Higuchi, Ginette Paris, and Greg Mogenson at the East Aurora Seminar on Archetypal Psychology, August 1999, Roy Croft Inn. (Photograph by Paul Kugler and used with his permission.)

James Hillman 1940's. (Used with the permission of James Hillman.)

James Hillman and Enrique Pardo sitting on the veranda of Casa Eranos at the 1985 Eranos Conference. (Photograph by Luciano Soave and used with the permission of The Eranos Foundation.)

David Miller at the East Aurora Seminar on Archetypal Psychology, August 1999, Roy Croft Inn. (Photograph by Paul Kugler and used with his permission.)

Wolfgang Giegerich in the shadows of Casa Gabriella, 1987 Eranos Conference. (Photograph by Paul Kugler and used with his permission.)

James Hillman sitting at a typewriter while in a Swiss sanitarium for tuberculosis in the 1949. (Used with the permission of James Hillman.)

James Hillman at the Alchemy Weekend Seminar at Spring House, Zürich, Summer 1976. (Photographed by Paul Kugler and used with his permission.)

David Miller presenting his 1986 Eranos lecture. (Photograph by Luciano Soave and used with the permission of The Eranos Foundation.)

James Hillman presenting his 1985 Eranos Lecture. (Photograph by Luciano Soave and used with the permission of The Eranos Foundation.)

Nor Hall at the East Aurora Seminar on Archetypal Psychology, August 1999, Roy Croft Inn. (Photograph by Paul Kugler and used with his permission.)

Charles Boer at the 1983 Eranos Conference. (Photograph by Luciano Soave and used with the permission of The Eranos Foundation.)

Margot McLean, 2004. (Photograph by Paul Kugler and used with his permission.)

---

JAN MARLAN is a Jungian analyst and forensic psychologist who lives and practices in Pittsburgh, PA, USA. She is vice-president of the Pittsburgh Society of Jungian Analysts and a member of the Inter-Regional Society; and was the former editor of the *IAAP Newsletter* (1999-2004).

4

# Interview with James Hillman: Past, Present, Future

JAN MARLAN

[*Editor's Note:* *This interview was conducted in October 2005 and was originally published by the International Association for Analytical Psychology in its IAAP Newsletter, Issue 26, March 2006, and is reprinted in this volume by permission of the publishers.*]

**Jan Marlan:** Very nice to have this opportunity to reflect with you about your evolution in the Jungian world. First of all, I'm curious about the things that mattered to you in your early days in Zürich—*who* mattered, *what ideas* mattered, who most influenced you at first? What was it all about in those early days?

**James Hillman:** Looking back, what mattered to me was asylum. I was in shaky shape; and, equally important, in an inspiring climate of ideas. I was thoroughly *in* analysis, amplifying my dreams, and listening to the lectures, and "all shook up." This was February 1953 through the first exam and first supervised patients two years later. I loved the Institute and was a complete convert to anything

Jungian—and hated the University (where I'd signed up for a Ph.D. in November '53, against great resistance in a great sweat.) I'd had a pretty broad education before this, knew languages, had read pretty much. But now I was confronted with mysteries beyond my ken: myths, fairy tales, symbolism, rituals. And then all this psychopathology and Freudian theory! I was dreaming like a whirling dervish and studying books by the lecturers—Kerényi, Eliade—and the required books—like Lévi-Strauss and Bleuler. And all the folks around Jung had ... "power." I thought I had come home to the intellectual and emotional place where I belonged. That lasted quite a while, and it was shared with my close friends of that time: Evangelos Christou, Molly Tuby, Francesco Caracciolo, Robert Stein, Marvin Spiegelman, David Hart, Pit Pope, and Richard Pope.

**JM:** Interesting—sort of possession and initiation at the same time. That energy must have been electrifying. Do you relate it specifically to Jung? ... That he was still alive and present at that time? Or, what exactly made it so gripping? You use the word "power." Power, like magical and compelling?

**JH:** Of course it had to do with Jung, and the way he was shielded by the group around him. Mostly we got gossip and rumors, and once in a rare while, we got an actual session with him, or a dream of ours was taken by our analyst to him. When I was president of the students' organization in '56 or '57, I asked Frau Jaffé (his secretary then) whether we might come and have a session with him. No problem! It was like the Wizard of Oz—all the shielding and mystique—and then, there we were, about 15 of us students, asking him our questions directly. Civilized, friendly; but the "mana" was clear (power was indeed there!).

The first meeting of the IAAP, when it was formed in Zürich (1955) in honor of Jung's 80th birthday, is another illustration. I remember the meetings of the "powers" there, and a sort of anima-animated argument between Fordham and Neumann about "the Mother." It was British empiricism vs. German-Jewish philosophizing, and it got nowhere until Esther Harding in her clear, sharp voice intervened and straightened everyone out. Animus over anima! I collected the ballots at the organizational session on Gemeindestrasse 27. C. A. Meier was pro-tem president, I believe, and Robert Moody was then elected president. I was 29 years old, already a father, but I felt like a boy among presences!

**JM:** Great story! I can imagine the energy of these early years; it must have been incredible to be in the midst of that. I wonder, though: at what point did it dawn upon you that you were an innovator and one who would ultimately change the course of Jungian thought?

**JH:** My self-understanding does not paint a comforting picture. I did not decide at a certain point to "innovate." I don't foresee; I have no classical prudence. I work from anger, when something feels insulted. When I heard von Franz attack the *puer aeternus* in her lectures in the 1950s, and Esther Harding talk against inertia and in favor of the hero killing the dragon (so moralistic!), and Erich Neumann go on and on about "Die Grosse Mutter" until you felt swallowed up, and other lecturers assault Freud, and the whole atmosphere of the teachers promoting the earth and tradition and introversion, I would feel insulted. I was the *puer*, I was from Atlantic City, New Jersey, where there is no earth at all (it's a sandbar, actually) and show business counts! And this moralism offended the life I knew before, in India, Paris, Dublin, among all sorts of remarkable people.

Another instance: My friend Robert Stein went off to London in 1957 or so, to try English analysis for a spell and came back all but crushed by the transference frame and the oppression of his spontaneity, of his "madness." I was insulted—angry! The first paper I wrote and presented "officially" was in London, to the London Jungian Club in the very early 1960s; it was called "Friends and Enemies," in which I emphasized the classical idea that you don't have friends unless you also have enemies and that friendship is one of the oldest cultured emotions/loves we know of, predates transference, is more "archetypal;" and transference may be friendship emotion arising with no place to go. That's innovation—but only because I was angry and wanted to destroy something. From one perspective, everything I have been building arises (if it rises at all) from an urge to destroy.

**JM:** What comes to mind for me here is Sabina Spielrein, and her "Destruction as the Cause of Coming into Being" piece. I am struck by the parallel, that innovation and one's own "power" can arise from aspects of destruction. I guess it's de-struction! (Very alchemical.)

**JH:** Even if the emotion is anger, the act is not sheer destruction because it produces a work.

**JM:** Turning more to the present, Pacifica [Graduate Institute] now seems to be the keeper/steward of your work, both literally (the manuscripts, papers, etc.) and figuratively (in the way their graduate programs appear to be grounded, etc.). Would you agree with this impression? And are you satisfied with the way they are representing archetypal psychology in general?

**JH:** If there were a clearly formulated thing called "archetypal psychology," then someone could "represent it." But I see it as represented (this "it") by individual people in all sorts of professions and callings, working from the insights that my work releases—both the higher elements that are inspiring and the lower elements that are caustic and critical and hardnosed. Pacifica offers ideals and dedication and a pioneering psychological climate that is immensely important today when academic and therapeutic psychology are so institutionalized.

**JM:** That reminds me of something. When I was first accepted into training, I recall excitedly sharing this with you, and you saying: "Oh, I'm *so* sorry ...!" This was around the time you had published *We've Had a Hundred Years of Psychotherapy—and the World's Getting Worse*, so I took your reaction to mean you were fairly pessimistic about the whole course of the analytic discipline. Yes?

**JH:** Yes, I am critical of the "whole analytic discipline." I see it as a remarkable genius reflection of a period of Western history, and I think it has become years later a kind of New Age substitute for life, on the one hand, and a substitute for rigorous education in culture, philosophy and religion, on the other; and third, a "helping profession." It's perfectly legitimate to perform any of these tasks, or all three of them. I just think [Wolfgang] Giegerich is right—and [Alfred] Ziegler was, too—that the whole thing has lost its way. Something is deeply missing: the soul-in-the-world ... the political and the aesthetic, and the adventure that was there at the beginning. It's become too humanized, feminized, personalized, and its language feels dead. I guess where it is still exciting is in the new "countries" of psychotherapy—Eastern Europe, Latin America—part of their becoming globalized. But doesn't that say something about what our task is in the Western "advanced" cities: to realize if *they* find it new and exciting, then *we* are fifty years out of tune? The psyche has to keep working its logos, i.e., making psychology.

**JM:** At this point, your cumulative writings comprise what could be gathered into a "collected works" in their own right, and I've heard that this might happen.

**JH:** Yes, there is a project under way to gather my papers, essays, lectures, and dialogues (interviews), even perhaps scripts for TV, into a Uniform Edition which Spring [Publications] is currently publishing. The Dallas Institute has helped sponsor this series. Volume 1, *Archetypal Psychology*, includes a huge reference list of works by many, many hands in the fields, plus a complete checklist of my writings in all languages. Volume 2, *City and Soul*, is in preparation (right now I'm finishing up on it). It will be released next spring, and includes papers on politics and beauty and the environment and urban architecture, etc. Volume 3 *Senex and Puer,* is at the printer. All the alchemy writings (which Stan [Marlan] did so much work for) will be in Volume 5, which should appear in 2007, and so on. It's all described on the web. It doesn't include my books, but the 10 volumes—hardcover and rather beautifully designed—will probably have about 2,500 to 3,000 pages.

**JM:** Do you have a particular favorite of your own works (or maybe several)? Or put another way: for which of your works would you most want to be remembered?

**JH:** Different "me's" have different favorites. As for being remembered for this one or that one, I'd like to think that different kinds of people with different interests in different times in history will turn to this or that book. They reflect different moods and different "gods."

**JM:** I thought you might say *Re-Visioning Psychology*, which would probably be my own answer to this question. But I see your point here: it's hard to privilege one work over another, when each marks a particular hallmark of your thinking. The later books, of course, are more accessible to a wider audience. What's that like for you? Have you been pleased with the response?

**JH:** I confess that I'm always into the next thing and don't give a lot [of attention] to the response to my books. I am a production addict, and rarely enter into controversy with critics about books published. I was delighted that *The Soul's Code* struck a popular spark, of course, and unhappy that the most personal and intense writing I've ever done and my final book, *A Terrible Love of War*, fell altogether flat publicly (though not with the individuals who've written me [about it]). In Italy, there is a huge response—all my books are in print and reprinted, and some have been steady bestsellers; and I'm read there by both students and intellectuals. There's even a book called *Caro James* [*Dear James*], which is made up of letters by 25 Italian writers, analysts, thinkers, etc., with questions and critiques, to each of which I respond. Italian culture rests on the same style, the same base of thought, the same aesthetic and rhetoric that I tend to use. It's a pleasure and an honor to be met on this intelligent level in Italy.

**JM:** I hadn't heard about this book—would be great to have it translated into English. You must be moving into your turn towards aesthetics and the importance of "beauty" throughout these responses, I am thinking—is this right?

**JH:** Yes, it is what first and most moves the soul and what seems neglected to the detriment of our theory and our patients. The whole business has to find a new basis in aesthetics, and Jung's separation of ethics from aesthetics has to be by-passed. Remember, Plotinus said the soul is always an Aphrodite, and the figure of Psyche in Apuleius's tale was the most beautiful of all beings. Doesn't this suggest the line to pursue, the area to explore, and the feelings to invite, to invoke in practice, if Jungian analysis is to keep faith with the psyche's essential nature?

# 5

# A Celebration of Images

James Hillman with his nephew on his 70th birthday. (From the archives of Jan and Stan Marlan.)

**Top left**: James Hillman. (Photograph by Paul Kugler; used with his permission.) **Top right**: Rafael López-Pedraza. (Photograph courtesy of Rafael López-Pedraza.) **Bottom left**: Nor Hall at the East Aurora Seminar on Archetypal Psychology, August 1999, Roy Croft Inn. (Photograph by Paul Kugler; used with his permission.) **Bottom right**: David Miller and Jan Marlan. (Photograph by Paul Kugler; used with his permission.)

**Top left**: Thomas Kapacinskas. (From the archives of Jan and Stan Marlan.) **Top right**: Stanton Marlan. (Photography by Gateway Associated Photographers.) **Bottom left**: Lyn Cowan. (From the archives of Jan and Stan Marlan.) **Bottom right**: Wolfgang Giegerich. (From the archives of Jan and Stan Marlan.)

# early days . . .

Jeffrey Satinover, Pat Berry, and Robert Bosnak. (Used by permission of Pat Berry.)

Mary Watkins, Robert Bosnak, Wolfgang Giegerich, and Nor Hall. (From the archives of Jan and Stan Marlan.)

Wolfgang Giegerich lecturing at the 1983 Eranos Conference. (Photographed by Luciano Soave and used with the permission of The Eranos Foundation.)

*... collegiality*

Lyn Cowan (standing), Jan Marlan, and Pat Berry. (From the archives of Jan and Stan Marlan.)

# revelries . . .

Greg Mogenson. (From the archives of Jan and Stan Marlan.)

Ronald Schenk. (From the archives of Jan and Stan Marlan.)

Stanton Marlan, Edward Casey, and Robert Bosnak. (From the archives of Jan and Stan Marlan.)

Stanton Marlan and Kazuhiko Higuchi. (Photograph by Jan Marlan and used with her permissions.)

# conviviality ...

James Hillman and Kazuhiko Higuchi. (Photograph by Paul Kugler and used with his permission.)

Michael Vannoy Adams and James Hillman. (Photograph by Stanton Marlan; used with permission.)

*... scholarship*

Pacifica Graduate Institute, Lambert Road Campus. (Photograph courtesy of Erik Davis, Pacifica Graduate Institute.)

Interior of the Joseph Campbel & Marija Gimbutas Library at Pacifica Graduate Institute, where the James Hillman Collection is housed. (Photograph courtesy of Erik Davis, Pacifica Graduate Institute.)

The Dallas Institute of Humanities and Culture in Dallas, Texas, established in 1980 by Donald Cowan, Louise Cowan, Gail Thomas, James Hillman, Robert Sardello, and Joanne Stroud. (Photograph courtesy of Larry Allums, Director, The Dallas Institute of Humanities and Culture.)

**Left:** Robert Bly, with whom James Hillman collaborated in spearheading the Men's Movement. (Photograph © Janice Applegate, courtesy of Blue Flower Arts.) **Right:** Klaus Ottmann, Editor-in-Chief, Spring Publications, Inc. (Photograph by Herb Lotz, Santa Fe, courtesy of Klaus Ottman.)

**Top left**: Greg Mogenson, 2002. (Photograph by Paul Kugler; used with permission.) **Top right**: Nancy Cater, Publisher, Spring Journal Books. (Photograph courtesy of Nancy Cater.) **Bottom left**: Ginette Paris. (Photograph courtesy of Ginette Paris.) **Bottom right**: Marcus Quintaes. (Photograph courtesy of Marcus Quintaes.)

**Top left**: Edward Casey at the East Aurora Seminar on Archetypal Psychology, August 1999, Roy Croft Inn. (Photograph by Paul Kugler; used with permission.) **Top right**: David Miller, East Aurora Seminar, 1999. (Photograph by Paul Kugler; used with permission.) **Bottom left**: Pat Berry. (Photograph courtesy of Pat Berry.) **Bottom right**: Mary Watkins. (Photograph courtesy of Mary Watkins.)

**Top**: Paul Kugler, August 2007. (Photograph by Tessa Gerling and used with her permission.) **Bottom left**: Robert Romanyshyn. (Photograph by Paul Kugler and used with his permission.) **Bottom right**: Thomas Kapacinskas, 1993 (Photograph by Paul Kugler and used with his permission.)

# *Intellectual History*

The great men of the past were living realities ... because they personified the soul's needs for spiritual ancestors, ideal types, internal guides and mentors who can share our lives with us and inspire them beyond our personal narrowness.

—James Hillman, *Re-Visioning Psychology,* 1992, p. 198

By calling upon Jung to begin with, I am partly acknowledging the fundamental debt that archetypal psychology owes him. He is the immediate ancestor in a long line that stretches back through Freud,, Dilthey, Coleridge, Schelling, Vico, Ficino, Plotinus, and Plato to Heraclitus—and with even more branches which have yet to be traced.

—James Hillman, *Blue Fire*, p. 22

GINETTE PARIS is Core Faculty, Mythological Studies Program at Pacifica Graduate Institute, Santa Barbara, California. She is the author of *Pagan Meditations* (Spring Publications) and *Pagan Grace* (Spring Publications). This article is an adaptation of the last chapter of her most recent book, *The Wisdom of the Psyche: Depth Psychology after Neuroscience,* Routledge, London, 2007.

6

# Our Intellectual Family: We Fight and We Love

GINETTE PARIS

The work of James Hillman provided me with many of the ideas I think with; but even better than an expansion of my thinking, his work has given me a *definition of reality*, one that has amplified for me the joy of being alive. We all have a choice as to which kind of reality we pay attention to, every day, every minute. There are many kinds of realities, and some require an initiation, as is the case for imaginal reality. The field of archetypal psychology can be appreciated *as an intellectual initiation into the richness of inner life.* All initiations provide for the neophyte a group, a clan, a subculture, a family of some sort. I wish to explore, in this article, the kind of clan "we" constitute, and in this "we" I am including all of us who feel that imagination is an essential form of reality.

Each author writing in the field of depth psychology presents a different definition of the reality of inner life, sometimes concordant, sometimes discordant. The clan of depth psychologists has a family tree starting with Freud and a few other revered ancestors. The many dissensions, divorces, and rebellions are part of our family saga, like structural tension in the frame of an old ancestral house, which requires our attention and repair. In most families, discord leads to tension, not murder; to divorce, not deadly shunning. At Christmas or Thanksgiving, a "good enough" family is still able to share a meal together, in spite of internal battles and tensions. Intellectual families have the same range of possibilities and allow the younger members to build their identities through two distinct processes.

The first is a polemical approach—the confrontation of ideas—which strengthens one's capacity to fight, eventually, with any idea. An oral defense, as the word "defense" suggests, is a testing of a newcomer's capacity to defend ideas and serve them as a good soldier defends his or her country. This mode exists because hatred and wars do arise in the world of ideas, as much as in the world of families and nations. Intellectual wars exist because of a basic philosophical dilemma that no finessing will dissolve: how tolerant can one be of intolerance? Theories in psychology are not immune to those tensions and territorial wars.

Tolerance is easy when the values of the other do not threaten my sense of survival; it is not quite so easy for a girl discovering that her homosexuality is interpreted as being caused by sickness or sin. To survive psychically, the girl will have to *fight* the theory, engage in a war against "family values." Many of the students studying at the Institute where I teach need to deconstruct oppressive myths as much as they need air to breathe. The history of ideas is full of fascinating wars of ideas, where those who refused to go to war for their ideas ended up victimized. My guns are always ready against the sexism and racism of the three great monotheisms and I try to be a brave little soldier when it is time to attack. Ideas are intellectual territories; left undefended, they will be colonized.

The second approach that is necessary to build an intellectual community is a Dionysian one. It involves regularly falling in love with ideas offered by other members of the clan. One then wants to incorporate these ideas, digest them, become a living symbol of them. It begins with an attraction, a desire to melt into that particular cultural pot, a hunger for the delicious new recipes for thinking. *I like the way the people in this group think, I want to join them, study with them, become one of them.* I felt that kind of appetite when I first read Hillman's *Re-Visioning Psychology* (1975) when it came out. His massive oeuvre kept me busy for quite a while. I felt like a cat let loose in a creamery—here at last was the Dionysian orgy of ideas that I craved.

The Dionysian mode, however, also has its own way of becoming destructive: when the strongly held enthusiasms are short-lived, when they follow one charismatic star after another, then any real training of the mind is rendered impossible. Instead of a group, there is a master and his groupies. The group may have fun and a great sense of belonging, but the thinking becomes shallower and shallower. *Everybody gets an A; let's hold hands in a circle, honor the ideas of the master, and not discuss anything that may spoil the fun!*

As for the polemical, war-like mode, it becomes self-destructive when a school of thought rigidifies in its position, like a scorpion turning its poison against itself. The symptoms of that form of decadence are the same everywhere: a tendency to consolidate group identity through exclusion, condemnation, contempt, issuing one intellectual *fatwa* after another, shunning anyone who strays away from the orthodoxy or who dares contradict the Theory. An intellectual *fatwa* is issued each time a clique gains control of teaching positions and tenure, research grants, scholarships, media.

An example of intellectual *fatwa* can be found in Professor Alan Dundes' public contempt for Joseph Campbell's work, especially around Campbell's broad definition of the word "myth." None of Dundes' students, if they wanted to survive academically, could admit to having been interested in or delighted by Campbell. Discovering at a conference that the bookstore had put the folklore and mythology books under a sign that read "Joseph Campbell," Professor Dundes wrote: "I remember being almost relieved that at least none of my books were to be found in that section."[1] Professor Dundes' critique of Campbell is informed, intelligent, and articulate, yet it is so contaminated with contempt and even rage, that one feels there is some complex at work. That kind of intellectual milieu self-destructs because academics sooner or later will migrate elsewhere to avoid the intellectual dictatorship. Academic freedom is supposed to stage confrontation, not give a show of hysterical contempt and shunning.

In order to have a balance, one should feel the freedom to diverge, but with enough group libido that there is a certain pleasure in confronting ideas. Some milieus won't allow real conversation; over the years, I had my share of having to learn empty technical terms, the meaning of which is, too often, to keep others at a distance and erect theoretical boundaries. I have to answer, every semester in my classes, the same question: what is archetypal psychology and how is it different from the other depth-psychological perspectives? How can one interested in the unconscious dimensions of the psyche answer that questions *simply*? Most of my kind (professors/practitioners) have professional identities that are like a minestrone, a soup made of whatever vegetables happen to be in season (or in the refrigerator). My vocation being to teach and not to preach, I have mostly refused to belong to "a" school, but this does not mean that I refuse to follow a disciplinary track or a master as far as I can go, because that is precisely how one learns. There is also such a thing as intellectual manners: one has to listen to one's teacher or master long enough for the full logic of the argument to be expressed, all the while keeping under control the tendency to interrupt with too many instances of "yes, but I myself think ...."

If schools of thought are families, bibliographies are their family tree. Looking at the list of the authors that have shaped my vision of inner life, beginning with Freud and the post-Freudians, Jung and the post-Jungians, the work of James Hillman stands out because of his radical reinterpretation of the theories of Jung. His work is a window with a view on the history of psychology, its philosophy, its roots in ancient Greece, and its future as a renaissance of psychological imagination. The Hillmanian approach has for me the supplementary advantage of being acceptable in academic milieus that are still very critical of Jung. Jung via Hillman is a strategy that has worked with the most critical minds. Hillman's take on Jung (which takes some and leaves some) travels through the Jungian country and then continues the voyage beyond. His approach is that of someone who has consistently called for a renaissance of psychology, a call that his own work is answering. He represents the part of depth psychology that is opening up to an ecological thinking as well as a spiritual renaissance, reaching for the future and establishing itself back in the humanities and into the flow of the rising eco-revolution.

Although Hillman's oeuvre is now mostly behind him, it belongs to the next incarnation of depth psychology.

## NOTES

[1] Alan Dundes, "Folkloristics in the Twenty-First Century," Presidential Plenary Address to the American Folklore Society, 2005, subsequently published in *Journal of American Folklore* 118, no. 470 (2005): 385-408.

Marcus Quintaes is an Archetypal Psychologist currently living in Rio de Janeiro, Brazil. He did his postgraduate work in Mental Health at the Federal University of Rio de Janeiro. One of the founders of the group Rubedo (www.rubedo.psc.br), he is also a coordinator for Himma—Studies in Imaginal Psychology (www.himma.psc.br). He is a member of the International Association for Jungian Studies (IAJS). Having dedicated himself to the study of the works of James Hillman and other major exponents of Archetypal Psychology for the past 17 years, he has worked tirelessly to disseminate Hillman's ideas among the Jungian community in Brazil, and has organized several seminars on Archetypal Psychology and Post-Jungian thought in Rio de Janeiro and São Paulo. (e-mail: mvquintaes@gmail.com)

# 7

# Hillman Re-Visioning Hillman: Polemics and Paranoia

MARCUS QUINTAES

> I trust my anger. It's my favorite demon.
> Writing and anger go together.
>
> —James Hillman

I would like to begin with three images.

In a recent interview, given to the International Association for Analytical Psychology (in a special issue dedicated to the celebration of its 50 years of existence), when asked about the precise moment that, in his opinion, he had made a real contribution with ideas and books to the course of Jungian thought, James Hillman answered:

> My self-understanding does not paint a comforting picture. I did not decide at a certain point to "innovate." I don't foresee; I have no classical prudence. I work from anger, when something feels insulted. When I heard von Franz attack the *puer aeternus* in her lectures in the 1950s, and Esther Harding talk against inertia and in favor of the hero killing the dragon (so moralistic!), and Erich Neumann go on and on about "Die Grosse Mutter" until you felt swallowed up, and other lecturers assault Freud,

> and the whole atmosphere of the teachers promoting the earth and tradition and introversion, I would feel insulted. I was *puer*, I was from Atlantic City, New Jersey, where there is no earth at all (it's a sandbar, actually) and show business counts! And this moralism offended the life I knew before, in India, Paris, Dublin, among all sorts of remarkable people.[1]

Another instance:

> My friend Robert Stein went off to London in 1957 or so, to try English analysis for a spell and came back all but crushed by the transference frame and the oppression of his spontaneity, of his "madness." I was insulted—angry! The first paper I wrote and presented "officially" was in London, to the London Jungian Club in the very early 1960s; it was called "Friends and Enemies," in which I emphasized the classical idea that you don't have friends unless you also have enemies and that friendship is one of the oldest cultured emotions/loves we know of, predates transference, is more "archetypal;" and transference may be friendship emotion arising with no place to go. That's innovation—but only because I was angry and wanted to destroy something. From one perspective, everything I have been building arises (if it rises at all) from an urge to destroy.[2]

In another text entitled "Back to Beyond: On Cosmology," Hillman reveals:

> Mars guides me more than Saturn, Hermes more than Athene. I feel claustrophobic when submitting to generalizations and laws, and call out "paranoid" when required to enter any unifying system.[3]

In his book *A Terrible Love of War*, undoubtedly the most confessional of all his books to date, Hillman writes:

> I confessed in an earlier excursion to being a "child of Mars," as the Renaissance humanists describe basic kinds of characters with names from the planetary gods. An affinity with martial rhetoric is natural to my method. My path in life and way of being calls up enemies. I like to sharpen oppositions and set fire to the passions of thought: I take pleasure in cracking numbskulls. (Mars finds dumbness everywhere because he is so dumb himself). It is as if there is a native need to be at war, as if I must enact Heraclitus and not merely consider his words as

> "ancient Greek cosmology." War thus becomes my constant season of spring, of April, Mars's month.[4]

He continues:

> Writing books for me is anyway much like a military campaign. I confess to fighting my way through with military metaphors. There is a strategy, an overall concept, and there are tactics all along the way. When stuck, don't dig in; keep moving forward. Don't obsess trying to reduce a strong point by sheer force or laying siege. Isolate it and in time it will fall by itself. No pitched battles with the interior voices of saboteurs, critics, adversaries. A light skirmish, a shower of arrows, and disappear into the next paragraph. Camouflage your own vulnerability, your lack of reserves with showy parades and bugles—remember everyone else is equally vulnerable. Pillage the storehouses of thought, refurbish old material and use it to reinforce your lines. Abandon ground you can't exploit, but when you've got an issue on the run, take all the territory you can.[5]

And more:

> Now its challenge is standing in my history, for my history with pride and pleasure, an old veteran on parade whose wars were "only" psychological.[6]

According to the single rule of Archetypal Psychology, let us stick to the images: anger, insult, fury, enemies, destruction, war, Ares. That is James Hillman, a man who defines himself as a thinker, who prefers the violent passions of war as a source of ideas rather than a naïve and inert pacifism which ends up sterilizing and blunting the ability to think. Through a careful and attentive reading of Hillman's writings, we are able to say that because Archetypal Psychology affirms the existence of one or more gods, because it is a polytheistic psychology, it allows for the idea that peace is necessary to maintain a condition of stability and safety, but this peace is always in jeopardy. To assume the possibility of many gods—in other words, to be polytheistic—means to defend a tolerance of differences and an acceptance of diversity represented by the gods themselves. Polytheism is a condition for polemics. The rhetoric of polemics rules polytheistic discourse, which is characterized by an avoidance of any totalitarian thought or unification around a single center, a single way, a single discourse, or a single truth.

Wherever a single God reigns, there is no room for polemics. Monotheism, the exclusive worshipping of one single God, easily lends itself to a narcissistic attitude. The Brazilian composer Caetano Veloso sings it very well: "Narcissus thinks that anything is ugly that is not in the mirror." To abandon the mirror's perfect narcissist mirage—a place in which there is no difference since the differences have been subtracted or erased—and to step into the rich, fertile field of the other's diversity: this could be considered one of the intentions of James Hillman's Archetypal Psychology.

Polytheism means to consider otherness in its radical difference. It is a dialog with alterity, and polemics is one form that this dialog may assume. In this way, to polemicize is to affirm one's identity; it is a refusal to submit to the will of another, it is a condition of individuation. To polemicize is to declare war on sameness, to arouse friction, and to generate resistance. I believe that Hillman and his Archetypal Psychology are heirs to Heraclitus, the pre-Socratic thinker, when the latter asserts that "Polemos is the father of all things."

Let us be guided by these ideas: polemics as a severance, polemics as a transgression, polemics as a foundation, and polemics as a first gesture. If we examine the history of Archetypal Psychology, we will realize that James Hillman is the one person who has undoubtedly mastered the art of rhetoric and polemics. Hillman's style is similar to the furious power of an acid that burns and eats its way through whatever it encounters, corroding surfaces that are flat and shining, and opening furrows through which something different arises, destroying to create.

Hillman and his writings gather a whole pantheon of mythic possibilities, from Ares' argumentative violence to Aphrodite's aesthetic sense; from Hermes' intellectual traps to Dionysus's nomad and errant aspect; from an erotic love of ideas to the Apollonian character of his erudition. Hillman's writings are sceneries and landscapes for the gods' parade, the gods that make up his particular polytheism. Since his untimely exit from Zürich's Jung Institute, where he worked as Director of Studies for ten years, Hillman has been involved in many ardent and polemic struggles with various figures in the Jungian world and with the Jungian community itself. The relationship between Hillman and many Jungians is one of extreme, yet delicate, tension. Some segments of the Jungian community regard the work of Hillman with suspicion and reserve, and have made every effort to separate him from the Jungian collective in an attempt to diminish and weaken the impact of his thinking. One possible factor that may justify this attitude towards Hillman and his writings is that he violently challenges some certainties that these Jungians strenuously seek to preserve.

One of the main objectives of Hillman's Archetypal Psychology is to carry Jung's work and thoughts beyond inner circles and clinical institutes, in order to approach and dialogue with the main intellectual streams of our culture. Archetypal Psychology finds in the postmodern intellectual tradition a major interlocutor for its purposes. In his books, Hillman engages the thoughts of Heidegger, Nietzsche, Bachelard, Freud, Deleuze, and Levinás. In many interviews, he mentions the works of Foucault, Derrida, and Lacan. Despite his (dis)agreement with these authors' points of view, the important thing to know is that Hillman reads and challenges these thinkers. In recent years, Hillman has redefined himself as a "therapist of ideas," someone who works with theories and ideas rather than with clients and clinical cases. Moreover, Hillman may undoubtedly become quite a disturbing character for any clinical analyst who gives his or her full attention and interest to the clinical field and has no inclination towards philosophical thought.

## Polemics I: Giegerich vs. Hillman

Hillman has struggled polemically with a number of important thinkers in the Jungian world. One of these encounters was with Rafael López-Pedraza, one of the fathers—as much as Hillman himself—of Archetypal Psychology. He has also argued with C. A. Meier, a famous traditional classical Jungian analyst (his "favorite enemy," as Hillman calls him), with Richard Noll, and with Wolfgang Giegerich. Here, I would like to dwell on the famous controversy with Giegerich. Throughout this discussion, we must understand clearly that polemics is an essential condition of polytheism. This does not mean in any way that we cancel out the other's existence, but rather that we live together in diversity.

The first international festival for Archetypal Psychology, in honor of James Hillman, was held in July 1992. The event took place at The University of Notre Dame, and brought together 500 people—Jungian analysts, artists, philosophers, students, and writers—for the purpose of assessing Hillman's work as well as his influence in the fields of culture, art, politics, urbanism, and psychotherapy. My comments here are based on the beautiful and important review written in *The Round Table Press: Review of Contemporary Contributions to Jungian Psychology* by Pamela Donleavy, member of the C. G. Jung Center of Philadelphia.[7]

At the opening of the festival, Hillman said that he was looking forward anxiously to the opportunity of being together for a whole week with a community focused on soul, since the practice of psychology has an insidious tendency to create isolation and make us stay inside the "white ghettos of observing mind."[8] Hillman challenged the participants to transgress, to summon Dionysus. He challenged the participants to overcome what is usually considered proper; he did this by making pornography the main theme of his opening lecture.

Undoubtedly, one of the crucial moments of the Festival, as well as one of the most polemical, was the participation of the Jungian analyst Wolfgang Giegerich. Hillman invited him to go beyond the "usually correct," and Giegerich did just that. He began his lecture, entitled "Killings: Psychology's Platonism and the Missing Link to Reality," by asking if Archetypal Psychology is really a psychology in the company of gods or if "the small talk of gods is just a glamorizing slang, fundamentally distant from the reality formerly referred to by the word 'gods'?"[9] Giegerich argues that it is not possible to give up the sacrifice of the bull and assume the belief in Zeus, both at the same time. When one promotes a festival in honor of the gods, the killing sacrifice is most necessary. The sacrifice is the summoning of the divine presence that changes the day into a festive, sacred one. This is the controversial question raised by Giegerich: Is it possible to sacrifice without slaughter? His question alludes to the fact that Archetypal Psychology has reduced the experience of sacrifice to a simple metaphor, a mere symbol. He emphasizes that without sacrifice, i.e., without a real killing, Archetypal Psychology will remain in an "unreality bubble," as he calls it.

Giegerich's lecture caused a huge uproar at the festival. Many participants wanted to discuss the questions raised by the challenge he proposed, while the festival's organizers chose to maintain the official schedule. In many lectures that followed the audience cried: "We want to discuss the questions that Giegerich presented!" Something had been constellated and the organizers, rather than follow the first rule of Archetypal Psychology—stick to the image—chose to stick to the official schedule, and did not give space for discussion on the questions raised by Giegerich's lecture.

Many of the festival's participants believed that the sacrificed victim was Hillman himself. In this event, Hillman, a polemicist at heart, got a taste of his own medicine and became the target of the polemics. One month after the event, Hillman sent a letter to all the participants, presenting his own opinion about the division that erupted at the festival. Hillman wrote:

> I think this divisiveness—that what happens must meet our personal expectations—derives in part from the many-sidedness of the polytheistic background to an archetypal psychology. It does invite pandemonium.[10]

I would like to emphasize the expressions used by Hillman: divisiveness, many-sidedness, polytheistic. Nevertheless, Hillman's conclusive answer to the tension triggered by W. Giegerich would come up only two years later. In 1994, Hillman published an article entitled "Once More into the Fray,"[11] in which he used all his irony, all his erudition and fine literary sensibilities to deconstruct and answer each one of Giegerich's accusations against Archetypal Psychology. Hillman's main point was that Giegerich based his criticism on three essential misconceptions: the fallacy of historic models, the ontological fallacy, and the fallacy of concretism.

The debate proceeded with a reply from Giegerich to Hillman's article, and with the publication of Giegerich's book, *The Soul's Logical Life*, a severe and consistent criticism of the methods of Archetypal Psychology.[12] However, it is crucial to emphasize that Hillman and Giegerich, despite the controversy between them, are best friends and prolific colleagues in Archetypal Psychology. This debate occurred only in the field of ideas, and there was no necessity to be faithful to the thought of the founder. After all, what does it mean to be loyal to someone in the field of ideas? To think through polytheism is to slide through many different places, to occupy new stands, and to create unprecedented positions to fulfill.

## The Four Moments of Hillman's Work

Let us follow our own path by asking about the itinerary of this challenging thinker. Although after one hundred years of psychotherapy the world is getting worse, we do have many years of Hillman to guide us. We may divide his enormous work into four specific moments. I am going to use the division proposed by David Tacey, in an article entitled "Twisting and Turning with James Hillman: From Anima to Word Soul, from Academia to Pop."[13] David Tacey is a professor of literature at La Trobe University in Melbourne, Australia, and Hillman was his analyst for many years while he studied and worked in Dallas, Texas, in the United States. These four moments are:

**The First Moment:**

Hillman worked as a Jungian analyst and Director of Studies for the C. G. Jung Institute in Zürich for 10 years (1959-1969). He was already the author of countless works, in which he had presented his immensely vigorous and well-articulated thought. Hillman at this time already revealed the originality that distinguished him in the midst of classical Jungian psychologists. The following publications of his date from this period: *Emotion* (Northwestern University Press, 1960), *Suicide and the Soul* (Spring Publications, 1964), and *Insearch: Psychology and Religion* (Spring Publications, 1967).

**The Second Moment:**

Hillman and the creation of Archetypal Psychology. This initiated a profound critique of Jungian thought and was the first consistent post-Jungian movement; it brought with it important theoretical innovations rather than sterile repetition. It seems to me that James Hillman and Michael Fordham were undoubtedly the two great innovators and original thinkers of post-Jungian thought. The major works by Hillman during this period were *Re-Visioning Psychology* (Harper and Row, 1975), *The Dream and the Underworld* (New York: Harper and Row, 1979), *Healing Fictions* (Spring Publications, 1983), and *The Myth of Analysis* (Northwestern University Press, 1972).

During this period, Hillman's thought approaches the postmodern movement that privileges plurality and multiplicity and renounces meta-discourses and totalizing narratives. Hillman stands back from the metaphysics of the archetypes and of their essentialism; he upholds phenomenology as a method for dealing with the images. If the golden rule of psychoanalysis is free association, Hillman follows the orientation of Rafael López-Pedraza by saying that the golden rule of Archetypal Psychology is to stick with the image.

In this period, he published three important articles in *Spring Journal* about the issue of the image: "An Inquiry into Image,"[14] "Further Notes on Images,"[15] "Image-Sense."[16] In these articles, now classics of Archetypal Psychology, Hillman proposed a modification of the term "archetypal," giving priority to its adjectival aspect rather than to the use of "archetype" as a noun. We should now consider the archetype as a value, an attribute, a quality of the image. To consider the notion of "archetypal" from this perspective means to renounce any attempt at possessing a previously established list of archetypal or non-archetypal images, as well as any attempt at having an *a priori* and universalized meaning that already exists, such as those in a dictionary of symbols.

These are fundamental texts in which Hillman seeks, more and more radically and consistently, to deconstruct the usual notion of image as it is defined by the classical Jungian school. He proposes a theoretical critique of the notion of image, changing the work with image from a visual perspective to a literary ethics and appreciation. Working with images is not literal but literary. The search for the origins and the construction of patterns and structures called archetypes is abandoned in favor of praising and privileging the phenomenon, that is, the image. We must not confuse a therapy using images with a therapy using archetypes. The goal of Archetypal Psychology is an imaginative and ethical relationship with images, one that invests them with adjectival value as archetypal. Beyond the essentialist, normative, ahistorical, and pasteurizing tendency of the classical theory of archetypes, Archetypal Psychology has chosen to emphasize the primacy of differences, of particularity, of context, of the plot that images present us.

During this same period, Hillman showed a keen interest in academia. Attempting to bring the discourse of Archetypal Psychology into academic circles, he took up positions at universities such as Yale, Chicago, Syracuse, and Dallas. Meanwhile, his ideas sparked an interest among Jungian thinkers steeped in contemporary thought and drawn to postmodernism and the issue of language. Here I will mention only a few of them.

Michael Vannoy Adams is a Jungian analyst who explored comparisons and parallels between Hillman's ideas and those of the French philosopher Jacques Derrida. Adams argued that the ideas of

Archetypal Psychology were similar in many ways to the deconstructing philosophical exercise proposed by Derrida. Paul Kugler is another Jungian analyst who developed Hillman's ideas by exploring his own interest in the question of language from an archetypal perspective. In his book *The Alchemy of Discourse*, originally his graduation thesis at Zürich's C. G. Jung Institute, Paul Kugler worked with the thoughts of Jung and Hillman, finding parallels to the ideas of Jacques Lacan and thus broadening the question of the relation between the unconscious and language. Other important figures at this time were David Miller, with his extended and rigorous interest in postmodernism, and Edward Casey, with his study on the phenomenology of place inspired by the phenomenology of Heidegger. These were some of the thinkers who found in Hillman points of similarity and points of convergence between Archetypal Psychology and the contemporary thought of the times. The contributions they made were indispensable to Hillman's goal of extending the horizons of Archetypal Psychology beyond the tight circles of Analytical Psychology.

**The Third Moment:**

This was the moment of a complete overturning in Hillman's thought, characterized by a vigorous revival of the Neo-Platonic notion of *Anima Mundi*. Hillman was responsible for the creation of an eco-political discourse. He launched an unprecedented and furious attack on the subjective and intrapsychic preoccupation of all psychotherapies, criticizing their tendency to over-value individual subjectivity at the expense of the real problems of the world.

Psychotherapy personalizes and subjectivizes everything in the world, and thus turns the subject into an apolitical entity, robbing him of his status as a citizen. To counter this, Hillman proposed a new concept of the Self. He re-conceived the Self as the interiorization of community. He also proposed a new view of Archetypal Psychology by affirming the thing he longed for, namely, to create a profound psychology of extroversion. In this endeavor, he was sustained by ideas inherent in the rhetoric of *Anima Mundi*: beauty, aesthetics, depth, inner life, political activity.

Important works of this period include: *The Thought of the Heart and The Soul of the World*; *Anima: An Anatomy of a Personified Notion*; a very beautiful article published in *Spring Journal* in 1989 entitled

"From Mirror to Window: Curing Psychoanalysis of its Narcissism"; and his polemical book *We've Had a Hundred Years of Psychotherapy—and the World's Getting Worse.*

It was towards the end of this period that Hillman presented his swan song, "The Yellowing of the Work," at the IAAP Congress in Paris, in 1989. In it he announced to the Jungian community the end of his activities as an analyst. Hillman gave up his clinical practice and began to pursue more vigorously his activities as a writer and lecturer, and his interest in psychological practice with larger groups.

**The Fourth Moment:**

Finally, according to the classification of David Tacey, Hillman entered into in his "pop" phase, into an apparently Platonic essentialism and the use of metaphysical categories, with his book *The Soul's Code.*[17] According to Tacey, Hillman was fulfilling his dream to be widely recognized and to increase the size of his readership.[18] (Tacey's interpretation is not necessarily to be accepted, but it should be mentioned nevertheless.) It is not by chance that *The Soul's Code* remained on the bestseller list for a whole year, according to *The New York Times,* and it was certainly the best-selling book of Hillman's career.

At this point, Hillman also entered the international circuit of conferences and interviews. He began using a more accessible, less erudite language. *The Soul's Code* and *Kinds of Power* both belong to this phase. It was a delicate moment for Hillman: many classical Jungians had long since lost respect for him, and the postmodern Jungians now felt confused and betrayed. However, nothing could be more in keeping with the spirit of the man, a man moved by Hermes: he ardently defends an idea in one book and reverses it in the next, always altering his positions and refusing coagulation into fixed meanings. This hermetic move fits his innovative, creative spirit—the spirit of the *puer.*

Here, Hillman reveals another side of his daemon: the one that resists his followers wish for leadership, always changing direction and confusing those who follow him, who find themselves surprised by where he ends up. Ideas that he once dismissed may suddenly become the object of his interest and the cornerstone of his new work. An idea comprehensively and intensely defended in one book may become a vague memory after a while. This is the consequence of an obedience to a mercurial spirit.

## Polemics II: Hillman vs. Hillman

Faithful to the plural and multiple rhetoric that characterizes Archetypal Psychology, Hillman refuses (cunningly, in my opinion) to occupy a place of absolute truth, of last reference, of the Founding Father or First Master. Hillman rejects all claim to being the one in possession of the final word. He refuses to occupy a central position at meetings and conferences. Hillman does not maintain a fixed, stable, or static image of the Self, but puts himself entirely at the disposal of the archetypal forces of Hermes. Hillman is a true apprentice of Hermes: oscillating in his thoughts, enigmatic in his language, inconsistent with his ideas, and resistant to any fixed definitions or propositions.

It is against this backdrop that I would like to discuss three precise moments in which Hillman takes issue with his own work, becoming the target of his own methods—in other words, Hillman re-visioning Hillman. In 1992, Hillman published *We've Had a Hundred Years of Psychotherapy—and the World's Getting Worse*, a dialogue and exchange of letters between him and Los Angeles writer Michael Ventura. In this book, he turns against the motto that had oriented him for fifteen years and sustained the main ideas of Archetypal Psychology. The motto is a statement from a letter by John Keats: "Call the world if you Please, 'The vale of Soul-making.' Then you will find out the use of the world ...." Comenting on the phrase "the vale of soul-making," Hillman writes:

> So, I want to clear this up here, because Keats's phrase which has sustained my therapy for so long, contains a major mistake! It actually neglects the world, even while finding a soul use for it. You go through the world for your own sake, making your own soul. But what about the world's soul, Michael? What about the *anima mundi* and making that?[19]

In *Hundred Years*, Hillman acknowledges the errors in meaning that for a long time misled him in his practice in Archetypal Psychology, and he seeks rectification. Analysis, by becoming the core of all the emotions of life, turns the object libido into a narcissistic reflection towards itself. Hillman's alternative is to break the containment of analysis so as to release the object libido into the world: for Hillman, "object libido is but a psychoanalytic name for the drive which loves the world, the erotic desire for *anima mundi*, for soul in the world."[20]

To propose a psychology of *Anima Mundi* is to invite oneself to a relationship of intimacy with the soul of the world and its objects. These objects are not the only ones to have a soul, whether natural or human, but situations and occurrences also have a soul. From this point of view, the psychic reality of the world's soul becomes available from the images. There is no way to separate our soul from the souls of others—and by "others" I mean people as well as everything that we can consider as environment. It is, thus, no longer possible to work with the classical notion of individuation and its rhetoric of "my travel," "my process," "my journey," the blind, frenetic pursuit of an inner Self, and to ignore the individuation of the soul of the world and its objects. The care of the soul does not necessarily mean introversion or denying the reality of the world, its substance and objects. There is no way to engage in soul-making if we keep ourselves attached exclusively to the Self, and exclude the world. In 1989, in an article entitled "Back to Beyond: On Cosmology," Hillman wrote about the place of metaphysics, which had been missing within his own construction of Archetypal Psychology to date:

> In my work so far I have shunned metaphysics. I have kept mainly within the critical tradition. The action of psychology I have called "seeing through," "psychologizing." And I have often enough spoken against norms for psychological actions because they become normative and normalizing, against ideals because they become idols to be smashed, against positive goals for psychology and therapy because they become positions and positivism, against affirmative actions and supportive grounds because they become delusional densities that prevent the primary critical activity of seeing through. .... If anything, the depth psychology of soul-making as I have been formulating it is a *via-negativa*. No ontology. No metaphysics. No cosmology. A Knight errant, always off at a tilt, iconoclastic. .... I have tried to follow Jung the psychologist of the soul but not Jung the metaphysician of the spirit. And, for all its puer impetus and anima aroma, my work has been stringently dedicated to lowland tactics, to the discipline of image, of phenomena, of pathologizings, in the mode of critical skepticism. Something further is needed, and I have known this for some time.[21]

In this same article, he comments on a meeting, "Science and Consciousness," which took place in Cordoba, Andalusia, and which was attended by many thinkers such as David Miller, Gilbert Duran, and David Bohm. Hillman says:

> It struck me in Córdoba that what I had been doing was merely another strand of Western skepticism and nihilism. Worse: by declining to engage in metaphysics I was abetting the decline of the civilization into the catastrophe of concretized nihilism. My *via-negativa*, though different in content because of its call of soul-making, the vivification of imagination, and the restoration of the gods, still retained as method the critical, skeptical, analysis such as we find in bare existentialism, linguistic philosophy, operationalism, and deconstruction theory. Was I really so different from those I opposed? One thing we held in common: the failure to grapple constructively, positively, with metaphysics. .... What soul does—make fantasy images—has, moreover, been condemned by metaphysics as untrue, unreal, and amoral. Could one stay in soul and yet take seriously the soul's need to go beyond itself? I had been literalizing the need to stick with the soul by staying stuck in soul. In other words, how to fulfill Jung's suggestive phrase *esse in anima* with a psychological metaphysics?[22]

By revising his position on the issue of metaphysics, considering it from that moment on as a legitimate need of the soul in its attempt to go further, Hillman is able to work towards the construction of a "Psychological Cosmology," sustained by the notion that the planets possess existence and action. Thus, one could calculate astronomically and astrologically what lies beyond human subjects. In other words, one could find out the mathematics of literal movements from real planets. This way, one could psychologically imagine what goes on beyond mythical fictions: the beyond itself is an almost literal mythical place, even a mythical region of poiesis, producing images. According to Hillman, one can reach this region through the imagination, unlike other types of primary principles, which are accessible only through self-evident intuition or through deductive or inductive reasoning.[23] But beyond merely reaching it, the imagination is stimulated by mythical fiction. Mythical fiction generates the mythological imagination and, afterwards, the speculative freedom of the soul.

Later, in 1996, in an article entitled "'Psychology: Monotheistic or Polytheistic?' Twenty-Five Years Later,"[24] Hillman reviewed one founding classic text of Archetypal Psychology, namely, his earlier 1971 article, "Psychology: Monotheistic or Polytheistic?"[25] In the article, he points out that what he had written twenty-five years earlier had been intended to expand psychology beyond the consulting room, towards philosophy and mythology. He had also wanted to call attention back then to the serious schism at the core of Western culture: the opposition between pagan and Christian, between polytheism and monotheism. In the later article, Hillman recapitulates his earlier points, retracing the course that his thoughts took at the time. He argues that the historical conflict between polytheism and monotheism persisted for centuries and was never resolved; it remained alive in poets, painters, and composers who tried to restore ancient myths and gods. It could also be found at folk festivals with evident marks of Mediterranean paganism, as well as in the councils of the Christian Church, which promoted theological controversies concerning images and heretical teachings. The conflict between monotheism and polytheism has also been constellated within psychological practice, in which pagan forces came back with full power, as noted by Freud and Jung, who saw myths in pathologies and gods in sickness. Again, as I have been trying to demonstrate, Hillman writes self-critically:

> And, as you also know in that essay of twenty-five years ago, I tried to rejuvenate the faded awareness of that war between monotheism and polytheism by throwing myself full tilt into the battle on the side of pagan polytheism. Though an old warrior, and living in a rural retreat, unlike Cincinnatus I have not retired from warfare. What I did not then recognize and now begin to see is that a monotheistic vision informed my own eyes when reading and interpreting the monotheistic position. In other words, I was fighting in my martial manner—intemperate, unrelenting, and blind—not as an old Roman Pagan, but with the very, almost fanatical, attitudes of what I was attacking! I was acting as a monotheist even while defending polytheism. I took the Bible—Hebrewism, Christianism—with the very literalism that I accused it of.[26]

At the three moments discussed above, we witness Hillman in the process of coming to a realization about himself and his own theoretical positions. James Hillman, the great archetypal deliteralizer of Jungian thought, is in some of his texts a victim of his own literalism. He realizes that he is in many ways no different from those who suffered the blast of his implacable martial fury—no different to a much greater extent than he would like to be.

Here I would like to focus on one aspect of the process that interests me in particular. By revisioning his own work, Hillman inaugurates an open space for re-thinking Archetypal Psychology, not as a closed system of ideas or a static group of dogmatic thoughts, but as a forum in which to imagine, re-imagine, and create metaphors from different places, points of view, and narratives, giving ourselves unreservedly to the field of infinite meanings.

By practicing the brave act of re-visioning his own work, Hillman injects his own poison, his *pharmakon*, into Archetypal Psychology and transforms it by freeing "Archetypal Psychology" from a fixed meaning. I propose calling this task the creation of the individuation of the text. Hillman thus produces in those who are interested in his ideas a unique, personal, non-dogmatic relationship with this nexus of ideas called "Archetypal Psychology." There is here an opening to the possibility of having multiple transferences with an author and his works, i.e., from each reading there emerges a new text, a new understanding, a new image. Each reading unceasingly creates new and polysemic networks that generate unprecedented interpretations, deeply enlarging and increasing the frontiers of Archetypal Psychology in an infinite metamorphosis. Different interpretations of Hillman's texts produce and revitalize Hillman's own texts. Here we might imagine the value of *Mercurius Duplex* as a reading practice and an ethic.

At a symposium coordinated by Hillman in California in 2000, entitled "Archetypal Psychology: Retrospective and Recent Acquisitions," someone asked Hillman if he considered himself the founder of a new school of thought. He answered: "I am not the only founder of this school. There is not one single Archetypal Psychology, but many Archetypal Psychologies,"[27] and he went on to mention several other exponents, including Paul Kugler, David Miller, Ginette Paris, Wolfgang Giegerich, Stanton Marlan, Noel Cobb, and others.

Would that not indicate the plurality that characterizes the practice and teaching of Archetypal Psychology and Hillman's ideas in Brazil? After all, how many points of view about Hillman are there in Brazil? There can only be a plural answer: many. There are many who have had a long relationship with James Hillman's thought. We have Gustavo Barcellos, a Jungian analyst, and his pioneering work of translating and teaching Hillman's ideas, as well as the original project proposed by John Burns in Vila Serena, São Paulo, of treating chemical dependence using Archetypal Psychology. There is the interest of Farley Valentin, of the Jungian group "Sizígia" in Fortaleza, as well as the work of Joel Brinco Nascimento, in Vitória, Espírito Santo, using Hillman's and Giegerich's thought. In addition, there are those who work with the group Kairós—Ajax Salvador, Rosa Blanco, Wladia—and others from Himma—Studies in Imaginal Psychology group. There are works from Santina Rodrigues, André Mendes, Aline Fiamenghi, Sérgio Anaute, Gulherme Scandiucci and others. And there is the very important group Rubedo, which includes Carlos Bernardi, Henrique Pereira, Marta Chagas, Luiz Granato and myself.

Thus, there are many groups, many readings, many interpretations, many "Hillmans."It is in this positive acceptance of plurality and multiplicity—the distinctive mark of Hillman's thought—that I believe we may find a way to protect Archetypal Psychology from what might be the opposite of its discourse: paranoia.

## Paranoia's Discourse and Reason: The Death of Archetypal Psychology

It is no accident that Hillman turned paranoia into a theme for one of his most important works: it was the topic of his lecture at the Eranos Conference in 1986.[28] In this lecture, Hillman points to two fundamental ways of understanding paranoia. The first relates to paranoia as a disorder of meaning. If the archetype of meaning is the Self, then paranoia is the disorder of the Self. The second, Hillman proposes, is to see paranoia as the imposition of literalism upon the metaphoric reality presented in any psychic event. In other words, paranoia is the insanity of literalism and the failure of the art of metaphor. I would like to further this analysis by proposing a third understanding: paranoia as the tyranny of unification, or the curse of the One. But what exactly does this mean?

What clinical practice teaches us is that unlike the schizophrenic's experience, which is characterized by a high degree of splitting and fragmentation, the experience of the paranoiac is characterized by a pervasiveness of meaning. In fact, paranoia is the empire of meaning, a meaning that always moves against the subject. Our concern here, however, is with a different dimension of meaning: in paranoia meaning is always unique, unchangeable, fixed, and unequivocal. From this we can conclude that every paranoiac is a narcissist *par excellence*, for everything in his or her experience is self-addressed. The paranoiac is continually self-absorbed, a fact that explains the megalomaniac character of his or her delusion.

In paranoia, megalomania appears in the form of many images, because the subject believes himself or herself to be the center of the world. Everybody seems to be looking at you, talking about you, hating and wanting to destroy you, even wanting to love you. Consequently, to the paranoiac, betrayal is inevitable and imminent, and there are always spies everywhere. You cannot be careless; you can trust no one. It is necessary to be alert at all times to avoid betrayal. As a paranoiac, you do not trust; you watch. One important detail: the paranoiac always has the feeling of being unique. The belief in one's uniqueness is inherently paranoid. It is what allows the paranoiac to believe he or she is the model for everybody else. The paranoiac is always the one who knows what is good for everyone, who knows the best paths, who knows how to act properly in issues of ordinary life. This belief in one's uniqueness leads to all kinds of fantasies of betrayal, plots, distrust, and suspicion, since anyone who does not admire you wants to destroy you and displace you from the favored place you believe you occupy.

Then there is what we may call an extremely common phenomenon in the dynamics of paranoiacs: the betrayal delusion. The paranoiac appoints himself or herself as the leader of a group, whatever this group may be, and, in a jealous delusion, inevitably chooses from among his or her followers the one who will be the betrayer. This is how we may understand mass paranoia and the horrible atmosphere that prevails within groups that have a paranoiac for a leader. Such a leader always acts through self-reference, believing that all his or her followers' actions are directed towards him or her in a hostile way, and this implies a plot, a conspiracy, a *coup d'état* to bring the paranoiac down from his or her position of power.

Perhaps we have here one of the reasons for the endless history of schisms and divisions that have marked the path of many great thinkers in depth psychology. Could this apply to the Freud-Jung relationship, as well as to the relationship between Lacan and the International Psychoanalytic Association, and to so many other conflicts? Could the dynamics of paranoia, in some cases, be the unconscious shadow condition of mass institutions or any other human gathering? Does Hillman escape this paranoia trap by realizing that he never wished to found an institution or any sort of official body in Archetypal Psychology? Do his wandering and nomadism, represented by his constant displacements, work as an antidote against the paranoid script of being a model for everybody? Perhaps that is why we find him at the University of Dallas, together with Robert Sardello, Patricia Berry, and Gail Thomas, during the 1970s; in London, during the 1980s, with Noel Cobb and Eva Loewe at the London Convivium for Archetypal Studies; and at the Pacific Graduate Institute with Mary Watkins, Ginette Paris, and David Miller during the 1990s?

By revising his work constantly and refusing to become fixed at a certain point, Hillman escapes the paranoid literalism of a correct reading, i.e., from the paranoid belief in the existence of a correct reading, a final, definitive, and univocal one. A belief in the uniqueness of meaning would be the death of the plurality of differences. By proposing different perspectives on his text, opening it up to the multiple fields of meaning, Hillman escapes from falling into the temptation of the paranoia of the One, the tyranny of unification; he escapes from the belief of being unique. We have here polemics as an antidote against paranoia, Archetypal Psychology as an anti-paranoia method.

If paranoid reason is the place of homogeneity, centralized discourse, a discourse that kills all difference and establishes a place of unique truth and knowledge of reality, Hillman resists falling captive to this web. He remains faithful to his mercurial way, to the spirit of the *puer* and to his astrological descent: Pluto in ascension, Sun and Moon in Ares, a true "son of Mars." To struggle against paranoia is to defend multiplicity and difference as founding conditions for the exercise of the cultivation of the Soul, the love for images. It is an ethical imperative in the name of the image's freedom of speech and the free exercise of thought and ideas. This is the battle. This is the combat.

I want to conclude by saying that in order to struggle against the paranoid tyranny of unification, of single-minded thought, it is necessary that one have a true love of war. Here, war is not the annihilation of the other; it is a condition of respect toward otherness, the rescue of heterogeneity, the struggle on behalf of the ethical imperative to find ways to live together in our differences and even to love them. Eros, Aphrodite, and Ares. Together.

This is the invitation: Welcome to war!

## *NOTES*

[1] James Hillman in "Jan Marlan Interviews James Hillman." *IAAP Newsletter* 26, 2006, p. 192.

[2] James Hillman, *We've Had a Hundred Years of Psychotherapy—and the World's Getting Worse* (San Francisco, CA: HarperCollins, 1995), p. 75.

[3] In *Archetypal Process: Self and Divine in Jung, Hillman and Whitehead*, ed. D. R. Griffin (Evanston, IL: Northwestern University Press, 1989), p. 218.

[4] James Hillman, *A Terrible Love of War* (New York: Penguin Books, 2004), p.111.

[5] *Ibid.*, p. 15.

[6] *Ibid.*, p.123.

[7] Pamela Donleavy, Lila Stonehewer, and Murray Shugar, "Hillman: A Festival of Archetypal Psychology—Three Views," in *The Round Table Review of Contemporary Contributions to Jungian Psychology* 1, no. 1 (1993): 8-11.

[8] *Ibid.*, p. 10.

[9] Wolfgang Giegerich, "Killings: Psychology's Platonism and the Missing Link to Reality," *Spring 54* (1993): 6-7.

[10] James Hillman in a personal note entitled "A Thank You," which was sent to all those who had attended the "Festival of Archetypal Psychology" at Notre Dame in July 1992.

[11] James Hillman, "Once More into the Fray: A Response to Wolfgang Giegerich's Killings," *Spring* 56 (1994): 7-19.

[12] Wolfgang Giegerich, *The Soul's Logical Life: Towards a Rigorous Notion of Psychology* (Frankfurt am Main: Peter Lang, 1998).

[13] David Tacey, "Twisting and Turning with James Hillman: From Anima to World Soul, from Academia to Pop," in *Post-Jungians Today: Key Papers in Contemporary Analytical Psychology* (London: Routledge, 1988), pp. 215-234.

[14] James Hillman, "An Inquiry into Image," *Spring* (1977): 62-88. The following is a representative passage from the article: "'Archetypal' now is the result of an operation, given not with the image but with what happens with the image—a function of making rather than a function of being. The image grows in worth, becomes more profound and involving, that is, it becomes more archetypal as its patterning is elaborated" (p. 75).

[15] James Hillman, "Further Notes on Images," *Spring* (1978): 152-182. The following passage from the article is worthy of note: "Don't get literal about muteness, as dumb, non-verbal simplistics. The muteness of the image, I said, is a necessary realization for altering our habitual way of experiencing in language, our habitual way of telling our dreams. Our usual ways of speech may keep us from hearing what the image is saying. And a main determinant of the volume of an image resides in the multiple implications of its words. To get at this volume, this amplification, we have to break through the roles assigned by grammar and syntax .... In grammar and syntax is lodged the fundament of our collective unconsciousness and its non-imaginal singleness of mind: We are unconscious in the very instrument of our consciousness: our speech" (p. 162).

[16] James Hillman, "Image-Sense," *Spring* (1979): 130-143. The thrust of Hillman's thought in this article can be seen in the following statement: "Perhaps the key to the training of dream-workers is this retraining of the senses by the image. Perhaps, the reason for collecting our dreams so faithfully, amplifying them with symbols and studying cultural imageries, is not mainly to learn archetypal patterns of content, but to train our eye and ear out of their habitual modes of sense-perceiving, so that we can 'read an image' as Lopez-Pedraza says, and 'hear psyche speaking' as Robert Sardello says" (p. 130).

[17] David Tacey, "Twisting and Turning with James Hillman: From Anima to World Soul, from Academia to Pop," in *Post-Jungians Today: Key Papers in Contemporary Analytical Psychology* (London: Routledge, 1988), p. 216.

[18] *Ibid.*

[19] Hillman, *Hundred Years,* p. 54.

[20] James Hillman, "From Mirror to Window: Curing Psychoanalysis of its Narcissism," *Spring* (1989): 69.

[21] James Hillman, "Back to Beyond: On Cosmology," in *Archetypal Process: Self and Divine in Whitehead, Jung, and Hillman,* ed. David Ray Griffin (Evanston, IL: Northwestern University Press, 1989), p. 214.

[22] *Ibid.*, pp. 216-217.

[23] *Ibid.*, p. 220.

[24] James Hillman, "'Psychology: Monotheistic or Polytheistic?' Twenty-Five Years Later," *Spring 60—Marriages* (1996): 111-125.

[25] James Hillman, "Psychology: Monotheistic or Polytheistic?" *Spring* (1971): 193-208.

[26] Hillman, "Twenty-Five Years Later," p. 112.

[27] James Hillman, from the author's notes of Hillman's lecture "Archetypal Psychology: Retrospective and Recent Acquisitions," delivered at the Pacifica Graduate Institute, Santa Barbara, California, 2000.

[28] *On Paranoia*, Eranos Lectures, Series 8 (Dallas, TX: Spring Publications, 1988).

# Philosophy

Depth psychology was, and remains, a *logos* for the *pathos* of the psyche.

—James Hillman, *Facing the Gods*, p. 1

If … philosophy takes rise in *philo*, it also refers to Aphrodite in another way. For *sophia* originally means the skill of the craftsman, the carpenter, the seafarer, the sculptor. … Aphrodite gives an archetypal background to the philosophy of "eachness" and the capacity of the heart to find "intimacy" with each particular event in a pluralistic cosmos.

—James Hillman, *Blue Fire*, p. 302

---

EDWARD S. CASEY is Distinguished Professor at the State University of New York at Stony Brook. He also teaches at Pacifica Graduate Institute. He served as Chairman of the Philosophy Department at Stony Brook from 1991 to 2001. His books include *Spirit and Soul: Essays in Philosophical Psychology; Imagining; Remembering; Getting Back into Place; Representing Place in Landscape Painting and Maps*; and (more recently) *Earth-Mapping: Artists Reshaping Landscape*. His latest book, *The World at a Glance*, has just been published. He served as co-editor with David Miller for *Spring Journal's* special issue "Philosophy and Psychology" (*Spring 77*, 2007). His recent research bears on the role of edges in human experience.

8

# Quelle Surprise! Going to the Edge of Things (with and for James Hillman)

EDWARD S. CASEY

> The palm at the end of the mind,
> Beyond the last thought,
> Rises in the bronze décor …
> The palm stands on the edge of space …
>
> —Wallace Stevens, "Of Mere Being"

One of the most remarkable gifts of James Hillman to his readers is his capacity continually to *surprise* them. Time and again, his articles and books move into new territories not anticipated by his reader. Even the most dedicated aficionado of Hillmanian thought is subject to surprise: transportation problems are discussed after earlier brilliant analyses of fantasy and imagination, the literal furniture of the analyst's office is described following an emphasis on the role of myth in the patient's discourse, money after adversions to angels, the open city in contrast with the sealed consulting room, beauty in the wake of death and the underworld, war straight after beauty! The effect is not only exhilarating and inspiring—and provocative—but it invokes a special state of mind that is ever more open to surprise. The reader cannot help but ask: Out of what depths come these unexpected new directions? What is their source?

These last questions are perfectly natural ones to ask. I am more interested, however, in another range of consideration: that concerning the edge of thought. Instead of speculating about new depths in the author's fertile mind, I am more struck by how the creative mind seeks out new edges—is always going beyond the most recent accomplishment by tracing out an emerging edge of consideration. *Thinking at the edge*: this is more pertinent than pondering in the depths. And such thinking is in turn a matter of following out emerging *surfaces* of cognition and feeling. And producing such surfaces! The written and printed page is, after all, a surface with edges, and if we are surprised by what we read there, it is not only because of the semantic content of what is articulated on any given page, but also because of what happens *on the next page*: the momentary abyss *between* pages is as important as what arises on an individual page. This is indeed an "edge of space" in Stevens' phrase. And when suspended in this *écart*, this space of not-knowing, we are primed for surprise.

Surprise, then, occurs in two edgy situations: first, at the edge of the writer's habitual mind, where the *scintillae* of new thoughts (and often demi-thoughts) glisten like sparks: Plato, in speaking of philosophical creativity, had spoken of the divine spark that leaps between Forms (*Eidé*) and Mind (*Nous*); second, at the edges of any given text, where the reader's mind is extended in a direction opened up by writing that cannot be anticipated in its results. Clearly, the two kinds of edge are continuous: only to the extent that the author's creative powers have reached out to new edges can they find expression in a text that draws the reader's attention to new vistas. And by "find expression" I point to yet another dimension of the edge/surprise syndrome: the verbal (or, in other contexts, imagistic) means must themselves continually seek new expressive forms. As we see in James Hillman's experimental turns in this domain: from treatise (e.g., *The Emotions*) to polemic (e.g., in his ferocious critiques of an ego-based psychology), from academic lectures (i.e., those at the origin of *Re-Visioning Psychology*, whose final version, however, was far from academic) to keen satire (e.g., *Freud's Own Cookbook*). These ever-changing formats are also integral to the experience of continual surprise familiar to Hillman's close readers.

In this contribution to a collective volume that celebrates James Hillman's achievements in archetypal psychology, I would like to take up in some detail the factor of surprise as such, along with its intimate alliance with edge and surface, in an effort to illuminate more fully the basis for what admirers of Hillman's work know to be the case: his inimitable capacity to delight his readers by surprising them at every turn—or rather, at each edge and on every surface. How does this happen, not only in his own exemplary case, but in the course of human experience more generally? Perhaps we, too, shall find out something surprising if we have not ourselves reflected on these very matters ....

## I

Our first question should not be: What is surprise? Rather, we ought to ask: How does surprise happen at all? Rather than its content as such, we ought to attend to its engenderment, its bearing on a larger world, the history of its effects, its *retentissement* in our lives overall. To emphasize content or subject matter is to be led in the wrong direction: fascination with the fabulous, horror before the devastating, or any kind of preoccupation with what is literally before us: *just there*, "*einfach da*" as Husserl liked to say in his characterization of the "natural attitude" that holds us in thrall but ultimately teaches us nothing of any real significance.[1] This attitude signifies what we are naturally drawn to do—it is perfectly human to focus on perceptual or mental presentations—yet what is not, in the end, a learning experience. The allure of pleasure and horror alike is such as to reinforce what we already know, or have already experienced: in being drawn to such things (or their representational images, as in horror films) we are drawn back and down into the self-replicating. In other words, we are closed to genuine surprise. We must not confuse the entertaining or titillating with the surprising; the former may employ elements of surprise—what will the monster's face really look like once his mask is taken off—but this is to miss the true significance of surprise, which is to unsettle us in our being, not just to distract us in our immediate reactions.

We have to distinguish between the surprising and the shocking. The latter is overwhelming; it so far surpasses the natural attitude as to deliver to us the un-natural, e.g., as the preternatural, the surreal, or the like. It is merely the obverse of the natural and hence dependent on the regularities and predictabilities of the latter. It is akin to trauma, which takes what is otherwise an ordinary physical act, e.g., sexual intercourse, and render it unnatural by the infusion of a degree or kind of violence that makes a mockery of the forceful aspect of such intercourse—a forcefulness perfectly compatible with gentleness.

Trauma de-naturalizes what in other contexts might well be perfectly natural, thereby rendering it shocking. If the surprising is less natural than the shocking, this is only because it is less bound to the paradigmatic presence of the natural in our experience: it ventures beyond the ordinary limits of what is accepted as natural, it takes us to the extraordinary edge of this experience by virtue of its suspension of the natural attitude. It is quietly revolutionary.

This is not to say that the surprising is merely tepid. What surprises us can unsettle us without literally upsetting us. The surprising is uneasily situated between the innocuous and the shocking—between the merely mild and the crashingly overbearing, between the too little and the too much in the realm of affect and perception, between the attitude of just tolerating something and finding it altogether intolerable. This does not imply, however, that the surprising is a golden mean, securely located midway between two extremes. Rather, the surprising moves unsteadily and unpredictably between such extremes, occupying any and all positions in the interim space, yet not in any regular or repetitive sequence. Any such sequence, were it to be established on a consistent basis, would become precisely the *un*surprising!

This indicates that surprise is at once non-extreme but not patterned. It cannot possess the gravitas of traceable shape or known trajectory—or else it would lose its own essence or soul. In short, it would no longer be surprising. It would be part of a natural attitude of accustomed happening: or more exactly, of routine response to the known.

My strategy of negative phenomenology—surprise is not this, but also not that—may seem to imply that the surprising is something arcane or rarefied, something difficult to achieve. But precisely not! The surprising is very much part of ordinary experience; it is the always-arising face of that experience. We need not make any special effort to experience it, since it belongs to ongoing experience itself. Indeed, experience would no longer *be* experience without it, as we can gather from the *peri* root of this latter word, which taken *à la lettre* means "from [*ex*-: 'out of'] making a trial."[2] Just to have an experience, to be in the midst of it, indeed to be capable of it, is to entail the factor of surprise: of not knowing how something is going to turn out—as the German word for experience, *Erfahrung*, implies. Hence, we should not talk of "surprising events," as if there were non-surprising ones as well, but of "the surprise of the event" in Nancy's phrase—where "event" is construed as the occurrence of experience itself.[3] Every event, every experience, is surprising: that is part of its essential being, even if this claim cannot be justified in terms of the natural attitude, which always aims at the elimination of what is surprising from human experience and the events wherein that experience takes place.

## II

And the edge? It has already arisen unbidden and of its own accord, as it were, in my opening discussion of the intrinsic surprisingness of experience. It has come up on the periphery of this experience, indeed *as* its periphery. Far from being external or secondary, however, edge is primary to experience—the same experience (which is to say, *all* of experience) that has shown itself to be so indispensably and surpassingly surprising. How is this so?

To start with (and always), *by means of surface*. If edges are the ends or limits or surfaces, it is by surface that the surprising is at once withheld and revealed: withheld, insofar as the current surface acts to conceal what is to be seen (or what has been seen in the case of a surface that has supervened upon something we have just seen); revealed, to the extent that whatever we see suddenly is itself a surface, or composed of surfaces. Elsewhere, I have argued that the world—which is, in my view, ineluctably a place-world—is constituted by a set of surfaces, their configuration or "layout." This last term is that of J. J. Gibson, who says incisively that "the surface is where most of the action is."[4] What kind of action? Mainly perceptual action and especially the visual action of glancing.

Glances alight on surfaces as if reverting to their natural element. Human beings, who are never not glancing, seek out familiar surfaces, which keep surprise at bay; these are surfaces of easy recognition, surfaces we *know*: the welcome surface of the top of the desk at which we write, the road on which we drive daily, the bathroom floor, our favorite couch in the living room—or our lover's body. But we also hunger for unfamiliar surfaces: why else do we travel to strange places at considerable expense and effort? These are surfaces of new landscapes, or exotic architecture, or groups of people we do not know. On such surfaces the surprising is set forth as such; it is sponsored by them. All we need to do is to take a gander—an easygoing, unobstructed glance—for the surprising to appear in its very nudity and on its own terms. I go to Yosemite for the first time, and El Capitan towers before me: a sheer phenomenon, that which "shows itself ... from itself in the very way in which it shows itself from itself," as Heidegger has put it.[5] Even if I have seen a photograph of this massive and precipitous rock, I am not prepared for the sheer height of this promontory, whose craggy outsize surfaces take me by surprise. It is as if nothing can prepare me for the sheer surprise of the scene, the character and co-ordination of its surfaces. I am not shocked, but I am visibly moved—"taken over" by what I see, as is signified by the literal sense of "sur-prise."

No surprise except in a surface, and no surface that is not seen (or seeable) by a glance—or felt by a touch, the haptic equivalent of the glance. Thanks to their being the point of attachment for glances, surfaces constitute the essential mediatory ground of surprise. They do so in three basic ways:

1. As we have just seen, they may present surprise in an uninhibited and altogether direct way—"surprise as such," without fetters or further complications. This is surprise as we *come upon it*, bold and naked, not hiding; here surprise is set out on a single surface (or coherent group of surfaces) on which the glance can espy the surprising itself;
2. At the opposite extreme are surfaces that allow surprise only begrudgingly, as it were, covering it up in a thicket of occlusions, such that surprise can here arise only by an effort of looking in a series of concerted glances that act to uncover what has been concealed up to that point; in the simplest case, as cited at the beginning of this section, one surface serves to withhold the surprise that a second makes available—once the first surface has been removed, or our look has gone around or under it effectively;
3. Most intriguing is the situation in which 1 and 2 are in effect combined rather than kept separate, and in such a way that the surprising emerges from the unsurprising, the unfamiliar from the familiar; striking cases in point include writing, making love, making music, and certain extraordinary perceptual experiences in which

something singular arises from the tried and true, surprising us in the midst of the known: instead of the surprising being *on* the surface, or *behind* it, it is found *within* it; it is only by delving *into* the surface that the surprising is found, or arises; temporally, this is experienced as two phases in sequence: a first moment of familiarity in which a given surface seems not surprising at all, followed by a second, in which something surprising nevertheless emerges from the same surface or is seen in it; spatially, this translates as a transformation from a known surface (or group of surfaces) into a surface (or set of them) characterized by the sudden appearance of the unknown: typically, an undetected item or pattern is now noticed (e.g., a subtle feature, such as a recessive or shadow color not seen at first); but sometimes the character of the surface as a whole changes under my look, in the perceptual equivalent of what the ancients called *metabolé eis allo genos*: say, the whole body surface of my lover now erotically engaged and experienced as a different body surface, even though I know it is the same throughout. Or, in another avatar, it is like tracing out the finer veinage in a person's hand—"getting down to the capillaries," as Hillman once remarked of the endeavor of phenomenology to discern the subtler structures in a given item of investigation.[6] Not noticed at first, these structures rise into awareness and become focal, changing the sense of what is seen as a whole.

These three vicissitudes outline an entire surprisology of surfaces; between them, they share out the primary ways by which surfaces show surprise, whether by presenting it outright, concealing/revealing it, or letting it emerge from within the unsurprising itself. Further variations occur; but they serve only to specify or spell out what is here set out as eidetically possible.

## III

Not only is the surprising affiliated with surfaces—and thereby implicated in the life of the glance—but it emerges from these surfaces *suddenly*. If surfaces signify the major spatial unit of the surprising, the sudden signifies its most characteristic temporality. It is tempting to think that suddenness is restricted to dramatic instances, as when we come upon El Capitan, or when an entirely concealed surface shows itself, or my lover's body alters quickly under my eye and touch. But a significant factor of the sudden is always at stake in the perception of the surprising. Even when the surprising emerges from within the very familiar, the moment of emergence itself occurs suddenly. This is so even if getting to that point has taken time, as also happens when a certain surface (or an aspect of it) "surfaces" from a period of long concealment. The sudden accrues to the moment of discovery itself, to the realization that things are not the way they look at first—or even over a considerable stretch of time. The process of detection or disambiguation, of erotic arousal or closely descriptive investigation, may take a lot of time—just how long will depend on many circumstantial factors—but this does not matter when it comes to the experience of surprise itself. For that experience occurs suddenly. A lifetime of habitual perception that has become highly routinized, does not preclude such suddenness. Not if it is an issue of surprise. If surprise catches us unawares—as it must to some significant degree, if it is to count as genuinely *surprising*—it must do so with the force of the sudden.

Kierkegaard was struck by this very force as it attaches itself to the moment (*Augenblick*). He posited it as situated between the frozen duration of the Eternal and the ever-changing succession of the Temporal.[7] The sudden is neither time standing still (the *nunc stans* of Aquinas), nor time moving on from one instant to the next. The true Moment, that of the Sudden, deconstructs the double yoke of the supposedly exclusive choice between the synchronic and the diachronic by demonstrating that there is another way to be in time. So, too, there is an extraordinary way of being in space that is the equivalent of the Moment: *being at a place*, where place is situated between infinite Space and the delimited Point. Place, too, is a third term that undoes a putatively exhaustive choice between two extremities—not unlike the way in which the surprising itself exists, by excess, between the anodyne and the overwhelming.

The surprising comes into our ken suddenly—whatever the density of its surrounding circumstance or preceding history. It comes as a disruptive and discontinuous presence: or rather, as no presence at all but a special form of absence—that of the immediately vanishing. No sooner has the surprising arisen, suddenly, than it vanishes again, just as suddenly. These are not two separate moments, but two phases of one Moment—phases that do not exist in succession but in that temporal modality that Husserl designated as the "all-at-once." What surprises us comes to us all at once, and the element of surprise disappears at once in this very first once; and this is so even if *what* has surprised us, the thing or event or aspect that has occasioned surprise, itself persists. I may be surprised at your appearing at my door; you may well linger after I welcome you into my apartment; but my surprise comes and goes even as you stay. (Your staying, moreover, may occasion further surprising moments.) It is as if the surprising were an epiphenomenon that flits on the back of more stable phenomena.[8]

The *all* of all-at-once is also aptly descriptive of the special temporality of the sudden. Despite its brevity and its piggybacking proclivity, the surprising comes to us in whole cloth, as all that it is. Even if a great deal can remain over in the phenomenon to which it attaches—other sides, its imminent fate, etc.—nothing is left over in the surprising as such. We are simply surprised, taken over by it, all of us by all of it: all of us that is prone to surprise (our surprisable self), and all of it that can be surprising (its surprising power), the two locked into each other's full embrace, with nothing of either left over.

A closely related point is this: just as the suddenly surprising (to employ a deliberately pleonastic expression) gives us something all at once, so it gives it to us *just as it is*. Unlike the most ordinary phenomenon, which never gives all of itself nor presents itself just as it is, the surprising as suddenly appearing is *nothing but surprising*. This is more curious than it may appear at first glance. We might have thought that the surprising consists in the excess of the not-appearing over the appearing—that it depends on there being something non-apparent if not altogether concealed. But concealment, as we have seen, is restricted to one of the three basic ways by which surfaces give rise to surprise; and even then, it is not concealment as such that is the essential action of surprise: it is the way by which the moment of un-concealment suddenly shows something surprising to us, thanks to the unexpected appearance of another surface, one that had been withheld from our vision. In this case, there is indeed a circumstance in which we do not at first grasp all that is there, just as it is. Even if it is this same circumstance that gives rise to surprise, the surprise it occasions presents itself as precisely what it appears to be; all is there, nothing is left over; and this all is as it gives itself out to be.

Here at least, *is* is as it *appears to be*: a variation on Wallace Stevens' line "let be be finale of seem."[9] And this is just what it means to be an epiphenomenon: not being phenomenal (substantial, thing-like, three-dimensional), the surprising in its suddenness does not have aspects (sides, surfaces, qualities) that fail to meet our glance—that elude us. Everything comes forward into our immediate perception. All appears just as it is: as something sheerly surprising. Nothing more, nothing less. That is to say: neither a thing, nor nothing, but a non-thing that nevertheless counts as something enough to arrest our attention. A pure appearance in short: the surprising as such, the sudden as such, a surface as such.

## IV

Let us take a moment to review how we have come to where we are.

I began by noting the virtue of surprise when it comes to writing—how surprise is a most effective way by which an author like James Hillman not only holds the attention of his reading public but inculcates a special state of mind in that public: looking forward to being surprised by that author's next work. Knowing that it will be surprising, even if not *what* will constitute the surprise as such, this public experiences a specifically lectorial capacity for surprise. I speculated that corresponding to such a capacity is the ability (and willingness) of the author to follow his own thought to its very edge—to let it exfoliate in ever-new directions, trusting these to be of particular interest to himself and his readers.[10]

From here I observed the close imbrication of surprise and surface—how the surprising always appears on a surface of some kind at which we glance. I classified three basic such situations—the surprising right on a surface, emerging from beneath a concealed surface, and arising from within a given surface. Then I took up the factor of the sudden as the specific temporal format in which the surprising comes to us, reflecting on how such suddenness allows the surprising to be a genuine epiphenomenon and thus something that appears all at once and just as it is, with no hidden remainder and no internal successiveness.

Where now is *edge* in all this? I have hinted at the close relationship between edge and surface. Let us pursue this clue so as to determine the special role of edge in the matrix of ideas I have so far considered. Think of it: every surface, save an infinite and unending one (of which we have no example in ordinary perceptual experience), ends in an edge—or more exactly, a set of edges. What are these? They are the places where the surface ends: where it no longer continues going in a certain direction but abruptly drops off. A first paradox in this familiar situation is this: an edge is at once emblematic of the extension of a surface and of the termination of that same surface. Were a surface not extended at all, it could not have edges; yet the very extension it needs to be a surface at all is eliminated once an edge is reached. Edges are essential to the existence of a surface, yet they also delimit this existence, cutting it off abruptly.[11] For this to be so, edges need not be rigorous or sharp: any edge, even the most mellow and soft-nosed, will act to terminate its own surface. It defines where that surface is going even as it decides where it will not go. Just as an edge may seem to spring up from nowhere—revealing that extra step we had not seen—so it can seem to drop off into nowhere, as when we suddenly see at our feet an abyss on the other side of a ridge we had taken to be an innocuous crease in a landscape.

A corollary of this is that edges direct and guide our glances—the very glances that discover and light on surfaces. A glance can be drawn initially to three kinds of thing: a surface as such, what lies on that surface, and where the surface ends. Edges are involved in all three circumstances. For we cannot apprehend any surface without having some sense of its edge: it need not be in our present perception for its presence to be felt; it may lie only in our belief about where the edge is likely to be. (Think of the way we sense, long in advance of arriving there, the southern edge of the Grand Canyon.) By the same token, when our glance is drawn to something in particular on a surface, we are aware both of the presented edges of this thing and of the (perhaps only adumbrated) edges of the surface on which it rests. Given sufficient mobility on our part, we can become fully aware of either kind of edge, whether it belongs to the thing or to the surface.

It is this latter circumstance that is most salient in everyday life. For we encounter both sorts of edge, that of the thing and of the surface, either by chance—just coming upon it suddenly—or by maneuvering ourselves towards it. Surprise is at stake in both instances. The first form of surprise is the classical case of unexpected discovery, a tychic occurrence, something arising outside of explicit anticipation:

something suddenly underfoot or in the corner of the visual field. But we are equally subject to surprise in the second instance: for we may intentionally move ourselves towards a certain place in the landscape, no matter how familiar it may be, and still be surprised.

As Kierkegaard shows in his *Repetition: An Essay in Experimental Psychology*, returning even to the most accustomed scene, e.g., one's student digs in Berlin as he did, brings with it no guarantee that it will be the same.[12] To the contrary: it will be ever different—so different that we are bound to be surprised. No wonder we so often hesitate to make such a return in person, preferring to maintain the place in memory as persisting just as we once knew it to be. Philosophers and psychologists collude with this powerful temptation by proposing models of "object permanence" (Piaget), "permanence in time" (Kant), or "adumbrational identity" (Gurwitsch, building on Husserl). But the course of daily experience tells us otherwise: the edges of things and surfaces—and their concatenation in places—often refuse to fit into these reassuring paradigms. They shrink, melt, recede, withdraw, and in many ways elude our anticipatory efforts: too many to catalogue. And this is just the point: were such cataloguing possible, uncertainty would be removed for good: there can be no *catalogue raisonnée* of everyday existence—which, as Freud first argued persuasively in *The Psychopathology of Everyday Life*, is forever subject to the literal parapraxis of the unexpected.

## V

I have been unremittingly visuocentrist in this essay, tying surprise to the glance and positing exclusively visual edges and surfaces. But edges and surfaces, as I have briefly conceded, are also tactile. They are more than this: they characterize every domain of human experience. Let us restrict ourselves to edges at this late point. As I have remarked of Hillman's work, edges of a decidedly non-perceptual sort can be an integral part of a lifetime of accomplishment: writing at the edge, thinking at the edge. Eugene Gendlin has proposed an entire new psychotherapeutic technique of "thinking at the edge,"[13] a technique that has no fewer than fourteen steps! Such thinking is not a matter of escaping boredom or of mere restlessness. Thought that is alive and not merely defensive seeks ever new edges, and if it does not find them it makes them! Examples include art works, scientific experiments, dance steps, indeed any creative achievement—each of which brings forth its own surfaces and edges. Hillman once remarked that "every writer must find his own length."[14] To do so, one must create the right edges: those of each page and finally that of the last page of a given piece of writing.

By the same token, there is imagining at the edge, feeling at the edge, and finally living at the edge. These are only so many modalities of edge-work, each representing a special modality of existing in the life-world. Feelings and emotions are not simply endless, or bottomless; even the most encompassing depression has its limit. So, too, any act of imagination, no matter how innovative or idiosyncratic, takes us to some limit of human experience. Indeed, every human accomplishment, including athletic ones, consists in finding one's right length: one's outer limit, even if this is very different from where one began. *To come up to the edge*: this is a very basic action. Here we move beyond issues of expectation and knowledge to arrive at the much more capacious arena of the Event.

I take event to be the ultimate unit of experience, its *non plus ultra*. As such, it is where edge finally belongs, once we take edge beyond the finite receptacles of thing, surface, place, and region.[15] This may seem strange, since we tend to think of event reductively as mere happening or occurrence. But matters are more complicated—and more interesting—than this. Minimally, let us say that if the sudden is primarily temporal, and if surprise is mainly spatial (i.e., in the sense that it arises most strikingly, even if not exclusively, on visual surfaces: the *sur-* shared by "surface" and "surprise" alike is at base a spatial prefix), then event is, at the least, spatiotemporal. *At the least*: for an event cannot be reduced to its spatiotemporal parameters. These latter establish only the field of appearance, the matrix of presentation, the scene of action and perception. They set up the grid for a given thing to appear, or an occurrence to arise.

The Event itself—which I capitalize to mark the difference—is something else again. It is a unique and unrepeatable happening that exceeds the formal conditions of possibility set down by space and time. Being formal, these latter can be located in the human subject, as Kant attempted to do. But the Event they make possible cannot be thus circumscribed; it cannot be subjectified. For it comes *from the world to the subject*—not the other way around. And this makes all the difference. It is from the world that the ultimate edge, the edge that matters, derives. What kind of edge is this?

It is a material, but not necessarily a physical, edge. By this I mean that it has sufficient content—as the German *Sache*, "topic," as well as *Sachverhalt*, "state of affairs," both imply—to have purchase on our experience. The edge of an Event has the bite required to take hold of us; it can effect a *prise* on us—not only on our expectations, but our actions as well. It can *take us over*, literally "surprise" us at a level of surprise that is no longer limited to what is unanticipated and yet that is not shocking or overwhelming. This is surprise at being in the world at all and in the first place: Surprise of the first order. Such primal surprise is a material condition of possibility for the secondary surprises that fill out the course of everyday living—surprises that have formed the focus of this essay (and rightly so, as the quotidian surprises are what matter most from day to day and do so much to configure these days in detail).

Philosophers, from Aristotle to Fink, have a habit of calling such Surprise "wonder." But I persist in my nomenclature. Wonder seems to me closer to awe—which takes us in a very different direction, namely, toward astonishment. This is appropriate for *das Dass*: Heidegger's formula for the wonderment that we exist at all, that there is something rather than nothing.[16] Surprise, albeit a rather material-transcendental form of it, is right for designating the situation to which I am referring in this penultimate section of my essay. I am surprised not that there is a world at all but at *how* this world appears and arises. It does so in the guise of Events, which occasion a very special sort of surprise—surprise at how the world comes forth at every moment as a place-world composed of things and surfaces and their respective edges. But that is just the bite, the edge, of it: the entire coming-forth of the place-world constitutes an Edge for our experience, its outer limit, its final form, its ultimate matter.

## VI

Phenomenology and archetypal psychology converge in a shared concern with *appearing*. For the archetypal psychologist, such appearing takes the form of *image*, whether image is considered as "primordial image" (Jung) or "image sense" (Hillman) or as myth (Kérenyi, Eliade, Campbell, and others). For phenomenologists, it is characteristic to consider it as "phenomenon" (Husserl) or as "what shows itself from itself in the very way in which it shows itself from itself" (Heidegger). Despite the marked difference in preferred terminology, the two groups of thinkers share the conviction that an appearance is not detached from that of which it is an appearance. Every appearing is an appearing *of the thing whose appearance it is.* Kant had already insisted on this in his idea that appearances are appearings of things in themselves. In the wake of Kant, there has been an augmenting appreciation of the sheer variety of ways in which things appear: they appear as images and surfaces, phenomena and epiphenomena, as dreams and myths—and as the finite things of everyday life.

Every single kind of such appearances comes edged. *No appearing without an edge*: that is axiomatic for post-Kantian thought, whether expressly philosophical or resolutely psychological. This means in turn: *no event without edge*. And this in another turn signifies that world itself, the place-world of appearances, is Edge. Being in the world is going out on the edge of it. And if this is so, no world can appear to us except as surprising—in the end, as Surprise itself.

The surprise ending—no surprise!—is Surprise itself.

The intertanglement of edge and event, appearing and world, is thick. But occurring as it does in primary and secondary forms of surprise, this continual co-immersion is experienced as light. As light as the illumination in which the palm at the end of mind appears—there at the edge of space and time alike, there in excess, there ever further out, going out on the edge, out and out ....

## *NOTES*

[1] See Edmund Husserl, *Ideas Pertaining to a Pure Phenomenology and to a Phenomenological Philosophy*, trans. F. Kersten (The Hague: Nijhoff,, 1982), Book One, Sections 30-32.

[2] See the insightful discussion of *peri* in Ann Bergren's monograph *The Etymology and Uses of PEIRAR in Early Greek Poetry*, American Classical Studies, No. 2 (New York: American Philological Association, 1975), especially pp. 22-23. We should reflect on the revealing fact that *peras*, Greek for boundary, is a closely related word, showing up in English words such as "perimeter" or "periphery"—thus in figures that consist almost wholly in having or being an edge. This suggests that the link between experience and edge is as close as that between experience and the surprising: not surprisingly!

[3] See Jean-Luc Nancy, "The Surprise of the Event," in *Being Singular Plural*, trans. Richard D. Richardson & Ann E. O'Byrne (Stanford, CA: Stanford University Press, 2000), pp. 159–176.

[4] See J. J. Gibson, *The Ecological Approach to Visual Perception* (Hillsdale, N.J.: Erlbaum, 1986), p. 23. On layout, see *Ibid.*, pp. 7-8, 12-13, 33-43, 157-158, 161-166.

[5] Martin Heidegger, *Being and Time*, trans. J. Macquarrie & E. Robinson (New York: Harper & Row, 1962), p. 58.

[6] Hillman's remark came in a conversation of circa 1995. He was commenting, not without irony, on the my own tendency to dwell on a certain phenomenon—if not to the edge of doom or to the exhaustion of his readers, then to a certain felt limit of patience!

[7] See "Interlude" in Søren Kierkegaard, *Philosophical Fragments*, trans. Howard & Edna Hong (Princeton, NJ: Princeton University Press, 1985).

[8] "Epi," is the Greek equivalant of French *sur*: both mean "upon."

[9] From Wallace Stevens, "The Emperor of Ice Cream," 1954.

[10] Hillman once remarked that he was always "amazed at how new thoughts keep coming as I write; I have no idea where they are coming from, but they just announce themselves to me" (Conversation of the late 1990s). Here he points to a specifically authorial form of surprise.

[11] This is true not only of physical surfaces but of surfaces of any kind: e.g., surfaces of thought, of memory, of imagination. As my focus in this paper is on perceptual paradigms, however, I continue to invoke visible surfaces. But see my reflections in section V below.

[12] Søren Kierkegaard, *Repetition: An Essay in Experimental Psychology*, trans. W. Lowrie (Princeton, NJ: Princeton University Press, 1941).

[13] See Eugene Gendlin, "Introduction to Thinking at the Edge," *The Folio* 19, no. 1 (2004): 11.

[14] Conversation, late 1980s, with reference to whether one finally prefers essays, or books, or poems, to express one's thought in the most apposite way.

[15] In this essay, I have not discussed the edges of places or regions; in the case of places, they arise in the form of such specific limits as walls, hedgerows, and property lines; in the case of regions, they appear as perceptual horizons or as such "natural" delimitations as rivers, mountain ranges, etc.

[16] "The pure 'that it is' shows itself ... the Being of the 'there' (*Da*) is disclosed moodwise in its 'that-it-is' (*in seinem Dass*)" (Heidegger, *Being and Time*, p. 173).

ROBERT D. ROMANYSHYN is an Affiliate Member of The Inter-Regional Society of Jungian Analysts and a Senior Core Faculty Member in the Clinical Psychology and Depth Psychotherapy programs at Pacifica Graduate Institute. His most recent book is *The Wounded Researcher: Research with Soul in Mind*. He lives in Summerland, CA, with his wife Veronica Goodchild.

# 9

# Thinking in the Space Between: Phenomenology and Archetypal Psychology

ROBERT D. ROMANYSHYN

## Going South

In 1972, Robert Sardello and I began a graduate program in phenomenological psychology at the University of Dallas in Irving, Texas. We had met at Duquesne University in Pittsburgh where Sardello had taught for a while, and where I had completed my clinical doctorate in phenomenological psychology two years prior to making the trek from the hills of Pittsburgh to the flatlands of Irving, Texas. The shock of that southern journey was immediate, but in time I learned to appreciate the big sky and the endless horizons of Texas. I even grew accustomed to grits soaked in honey as a breakfast treat, and, perhaps most surprising of all, I began to like country western music with its themes of love, loss, betrayal, booze, and the occasional lost dog, drawing the line only at line dancing in cowboy hat and boots and beer swilling in cowboy bars on hot and humid Saturday nights. There was, however, a deeper shock in store, one that took time to make its presence felt. The southern journey was in fact more than a change in my geographical location in the world. It was also a change in the landscape of the soul. In 1979, James Hillman blew into Dallas like one of those southwest tornadoes that brought Dorothy and Toto to the wizard in the land of Oz, and "Kansas" was never the same. The move south was, in Hillman's terms, the start of the move to "Florence," which was destined to make my southern journey a matter of heart.

> Awakening the imagining, sensing heart would move psychology itself from mental reflection toward cordial reflex. Psychology may then become again Florentine; for the move "southward" that I have been urging these last twenty years—from the clinics of Zurich and Vienna, from the white laboratories and black forests of Germany, from the positivist and empiricist dissections of Britain and America, to say nothing of the gymnastics of the tongue of France—cannot be accomplished without moving as well the seat of the soul from brain to heart and the method of psychology from cognitive understanding to aesthetic sensitivity.[1]

So said Hillman in his 1982 article, "*Anima Mundi*: The Return of the Soul to the World." Looking back on these events now, a quarter century later, I cannot help but recall how Hillman's call for this "southern journey" from head to heart, from cognitive understanding to aesthetic sensitivity, turned out to be one moment in the long drama of thinking in the space between phenomenology and depth psychology in general and Jung's and Hillman's psychologies in particular.

## The Heart of the Matter

In 1982, I published my first book, *Psychological Life: From Science to Metaphor*, and in that book I wrote a long chapter on William Harvey's 17th-century book, *Exercitatio anatomica de motu cordis et sanguinis in animalibus,* in which the human heart is transformed into a pump. I was guided in this work by my teacher and mentor, J. H. van den Berg, about whom I will have more to say later, through whose vision I saw how Harvey's work was a radical shift in humanity's psychological existence. In his special version of phenomenology called metabletics, van den Berg had, over the course of many volumes, charted these shifts, which, if one were thinking archetypally, would be traced to cultural-historical transformations in archetypal dominants. But van den Berg eschewed explanations in terms of categories, archetypal or otherwise, in favor of extended, copious, and finely detailed descriptions of how changes in one area of human life are reflected in changes in multiple other areas of life. His metabletics spoke in terms of shifts in our collective epistemological structures, in our ways of knowing the world. For van den Berg, the psychology of an age was mirrored or made visible in the ways it built its buildings, worshipped its gods, created its systems of education, medicine, and science, and practiced the arts of living and dying. Quite simply put, his metabletics was a record of not only how people of a different age lived a different existence, but also of how reality was a different matter, of how matter itself was a different reality.

One cannot fully appreciate the depth and scope of van den Berg's work without some exposure to his writings on the changing nature of man, of matter and the human body. So, for example, when William Harvey did his studies of the human heart that becomes a pump, one of the key issues was the question of the nature of the *septum cordis*, that piece of tough, fibrous tissue between the right and left sides of the heart. For Harvey, there were no holes in that structure. When he opened the body, he did not see those holes, which others before him had seen, and which even his contemporary and French rival, Jean Riolan, still saw. Riolan lived in a different world, where the blood of the heart did percolate back and forth through the holes in the *septum cordis*, where the blood moved with the lazy rhythm of the tides. In his disagreement with Harvey, Riolan saved the reality of that tidal heart by saying that the holes existed until one opened the heart and then they disappeared. Two worlds were colliding here, one destined to be eclipsed and the other to triumph. In these two worlds, men and women lived with different hearts. In Riolan's world, the heart did not force the blood into that long journey of circulation throughout the body, whereas in Harvey's world the blood was forced into that journey. The heart had to pump the blood in this fashion in order to keep pace with a changing world in which, for example, the earth had already begun to circulate in the heavens, logarithms, the mathematics of faster motion, came into play, and church buildings in their baroque extravagances began to undulate.

Would Harvey have been able to see the heart as a pump if the heart itself was not ready to lend itself to that vision? Would he have been able to see the heart as a pump if the world had not also changed to support that reality? These are the kinds of questions that van den Berg's work raises, and in response he would say Harvey could not.

The reality of the heart is the heart that we live, and the objection that the real heart is the heart that is a pump, has always been a pump, and will forever more be a pump, misses how for van den Berg our bodies of knowledge are socially constructed realities that mirror shifts in humanity's mutable psychological existence.

This claim does not in any way deny the factualness of the heart as a pump. Van den Berg is a medical doctor and he knows the reality of the pumping heart. But he also knows that this fact is also a way of imagining the heart, and in this structure of participation lies the heart of the matter. It is where we live our lives. Van den Berg calls this structure of participation the first structure of human existence to distinguish it from the second structure of explanation. In the second structure of explanation, water, for example, is, in all its epiphanies, $H_2O$. But no one lives in the second structures of explanation, be they of the heart or of water. A cold-hearted person does not have a defective pump and one who has a broken heart does not need to consult a cardiologist. In the same fashion, no one drinks a glass of $H_2O$ or swims in it on a hot summer day. The first structure of participation is what matters, and, for van den Berg, retreats to the second structure of explanations take us away from the changing nature of the psychological world, the world as we live it and experience it in the first structure.

## Metabletics Is Not Metaphysics

What I want to emphasize here is that for van den Berg the question of what might account for these shifts is not at all the issue. His work was and is averse to explanations in terms of first principles in whatever form or shape. For the phenomenologist what matters is the intentional arc between the noetic act of consciousness and its noematic correlate, with no concern about the ontological status of the noematic referent. I recall, for example, one occasion when van den Berg was lecturing at Duquesne University and a student asked him what accounted for the cultural and historical changes in human life, and he replied simply, directly, and to the point by saying "we don't go there." His point was and is that to go there is to leave the domain of psychology. To go there was to substitute metaphysical speculation for phenomenological description.

At Dallas, I favored the elegant simplicity of van den Berg's metabletic phenomenology, and I found all that talk about soul and archetypes and the gods to be unnecessary distractions that took one away from the world and its historically discontinuous epiphanies. I was especially caught by the notion of the mutability of humanity's psychological life, which was so different from the idea of some archetypal continuity in the psyche. And I was drawn to what I saw as the cultural-historical therapeutic implications of van den Berg's work. Here was a true psychology of liberation, a psychology that invited us to re-collect the origins of our contemporary circumstances for the sake of transforming them into a new beginning. If the heart as a pump had become part of our taken-for-granted ways of living, encrusted in our medical and pharmaceutical industries as well as in our dietary habits and jogging mania, then the recovery of this heart as a moment in the psychological history of the body could only have a therapeutic effect. It would liberate the imagination from the accumulated layers of forgotten origins, those sedimented deposits of history where the unfinished business of humanity lingers as so many possibilities. Here was a psychology that understood the unconscious as the weight of history that we bear, as moments of transition that had become frozen in outworn, unexamined, and enslaving ideologies. Was not Jung's psychology, despite his insistence to the contrary, another ideology, another system of enslavement, and was not archetypal psychology also a wily seduction toward that same kind of entrapment? Was there not some wizardry going on behind the curtain, like there was in Oz?

In his metabletic reflections on history, the specter of such a hidden wizard was not haunting van den Berg's work. Descartes was not behind the drapes. No interior and arcane domain of the mind or the psyche was needed to explore and excavate the ways in which the unconscious betrays its presence through the exercises of power and oppression in our politics and economics, in our architecture and our styles of education. No intrapsychic residue of Descartes's split between a mind divorced from body and world and a world without our mindful presence was in van den Berg's metabletics. In his metabletic studies, he had ripped away the curtain, exorcised that ghost, just as he did in his phenomenological studies as expressed so eloquently, for example, in *A Different Existence*, his simple, small book on the principles of psychopathology, in which he criticized the remnants of a Cartesian dualistic metaphysics in depth psychology. It was clear that such a dualism was at work in Freud. Was it not also there in Jung and perhaps even in archetypal psychology? If one wished to understand the other, one had to understand the world in which he or she dwelt, the landscapes of his or her existence. And since that landscape was composed of so many sediments of history, the weight of humanity's history waiting for us to re-member it, then it was clear that one could find the unconscious only in the world between us, as a phenomenological therapist finds it in the place between himself/herself and the patient. We make the unconscious together van den Berg said. It is an historical creation, made in partnership and in the conspiracies of silence in that partnership, as well as in the subtle tides of time, which remove us from origins into forgetfulness. Metabletics was, then, a work against forgetting, a work of cultural-historical anamnesis.

And so, in this first book I followed this path, with van den Berg the historical person present as a psychological companion, always there at my writing table, like some friend of the heart. What astonishment to discover that the movement and circulation of the blood was of a piece with the movement and circulation of the Copernican earth around the sun, and of a piece as well with changes in the fields of mathematics, church architecture and religion, with devotion to the Sacred Heart making its appearance as a counterweight to the mechanical heart! Chronicling these changes, my intention in that book was to show how this transformation of the heart was, among other developments of that period, one of the foundations for the emergence of psychology in its modern guise as a natural science, and within this context I was calling for a shift away from that development and towards the metaphoric character of psychological life.

## The Metaphoric Character of Psychological Life

For the purposes of this article, it is not necessary to present the steps by which in that first book I arrived at the metaphoric character of psychological life. Let it suffice to say that in addition to van den Berg's work, it was Merleau-Ponty's phenomenology of perception, and especially that wonderful essay "Eye and Mind"[2] and the book, *The Visible and the Invisible*, which he was working on at his death, that guided my way. Our embodied perceptual life draws us into the world, and before we know that we know it we are engaged in the world. We see, for example, because the world wants to be seen, and between the animate flesh and the flesh of the world and the other there is a chiasm, a crossing, a transgression, a mutual and erotic seduction in which we are mirrors for each other. "Man is a mirror for man," Merleau-Ponty had said, and in this mirror-play, the other, the world, is the depth of one's self, and through the other each of us is re-figured as a character in a tale. Through the mirror of the world and the other, one's psychological life is enacted, as if on a stage, and, indeed, for the phenomenologist it is true that all the world's a stage and all of us players upon it. Psychological life has an "as if" quality. It arises between the thickness of things and the thinness of thoughts, a subtle reality between the empirically sensible world of matter and the intellectually reasonable world of mind. Story, I said, is the form of psychological existence, not fact or idea, or fact or idea only as they are storied. As such, the comprehension of psychological life requires those poetic virtues of Keats' negative capability and Coleridge's willing suspension of disbelief. Its comprehension requires a metaphoric sensibility. A story told by van den Berg illustrates these points.

As van den Berg notes, in Carry van Bruggen's book *The Cabin at the Ditch*, there is a description of a simple occasion in relation to the Jewish Sabbath. The little girl who is the central character in this episode notices a recurring ritual that takes place every Sabbath morning: the girl's mother removes the usual red-and-black cloth from the table and puts in its place a gleaming white one. In this simple exchange of cloths the girl notices a profound change in her world. A certain "It" happens, but it is always just beyond her grasp. Van den Berg writes:

> As long as the black and red cloth remains on the table, there is nothing; mother comes, and there is nothing extraordinary about her, either. She takes away the black and red cloth; the bare table is old and full of scratches. Now the white cloth flutters in mother's hand, by the lamp, almost touching it; now it is lowered, it is on the table and—another miss. "It"' has come and no one has seen "it" arrive. Mother suddenly has another face; and every chair and the cabinet and the stove—they all look different.[3]

This "It" that happens and which the child notices is no-thing. But this no-thing is not a void. It is not an emptiness. Rather, it is a subtle no-thing, a pregnant no-thing, a moment when the ordinary world is cracked open and its subtle reality breaks through. The change that the girl sees is there in the world, but no camera could capture it because it is not a fact to be measured any more than it is just an idea in the girl's mind that is projected onto the unchanging things. One has to have a different eye to be able to witness this epiphany. One has to be present to the world in a different way. One has to have that capacity for metaphor that opens up a domain of reality between things and thoughts.

Through van den Berg I had come to appreciate this kind of display by the world, this insistent presence of its subtle epiphanies, and I had come to value his exquisite attention to the details of things and to the ways in which the world of things, the human world as well as the world of nature, hold and reflect the depths of our psychological existence. From how a simple wine bottle carefully placed near the fire in anticipation of a friend's visit can register the disappointment of the evening when the friend calls to cancel because of the cold, snowy weather, to how the shoes that lie unused as one lies in one's sickbed reflect the changed status of one's presence in the world, phenomenology, especially in the hands of one like van den Berg, shows that we belong to ourselves because we belong to the world. The world is an epiphany that demands our presence before any attempt to ascribe meaning. For the phenomenologist the world is an appeal, and between the sensing flesh of the body and the sensible flesh of the world there is a mutual erotic seduction at play. Back to the things themselves Husserl had said, and Erwin Straus had defined phenomenology as the task of un-raveling the unwritten constitution of everyday life. One had only to read, for example, that fine little book by van den Berg, *The Psychology of the Sickbed*, to experience how phenomenology was indeed a work of anamnesis, a work of un-forgetting that returns one to what is already lived in experience before it is known, categorized, conceptualized, or made into some sort of system. In van den Berg's hands, not unlike the hands of Bachelard, phenomenology became for me a work of recovering the animating presence of the things of the world as well as the work of deepening the events of life into experiences.

## Hillman as Symptom

Independently of Hillman's "Anima Mundi" essay, the phenomenology I was practicing was moving "south" along a path parallel to Hillman's "southern journey" to recover what he called the soul of the world. I was recovering the genesis of scientific psychology's "northern exposure" for the sake of returning psychological life to the world. During this time, Hillman was lingering on the threshold of my writing studio. He was present as an absence, like a symptom is when it asks us to remember something too vital to forget but which we forget because it is too inconvenient or disturbing to remember. Hillman as an inconvenient symptom! I like that now as I write this passage. It fits my experience of him so long ago. He was haunting the margins of my thoughts about the mirroring relation of subject and world, the therapeutic value of historical reflection, the metaphoric character of psychological life, the place of story in understanding self and other, and the aesthetic domain of the heart as the organ of psychological gnosis.

While I was working on this book throughout the 1970s, the encounter with "Hillman"—whose name I put in quotes to distinguish the historical person from the symptomatic presence he was as he lingered and would not leave the threshold of my writing studio—was mediated by Sardello, who, in the late 1970s, introduced Hillman's *Re-Visioning Psychology* into our program in phenomenological psychology. This encounter was, to say the least, not pleasant. In *Re-Visioning Psychology*, Hillman had returned soul to psychology and he was quite clear what he meant by the term "soul." It was, he said, a perspective and not a substance. While it could not be identified with anything else, it could not be grasped by itself apart from other things. It was like a reflection in a mirror that deepened events into experiences for a way of knowing that was essentially metaphoric. This news was not pleasant for two reasons.

First, as indicated above, I had arrived at the same conclusions about psychological life, but from a different perspective—and who is not disturbed to discover that someone else has already pitched his or her tent on the same ground? I was, in retrospect, suffering from what Harold Bloom has described as the "anxiety of influence," and, to be quite frank, I was not willing, nor had I the temperament, to become a disciple. Or maybe it is closer to the truth to say that I was already in service to someone else and felt no reason to make a switch. If anything, Hillman was someone to think against and that for the moment was enough.

Second, and really more to the point, I was going south without all that talk about soul. In the mirror of the world and the other the event and the encounter are transformed into an experience, and in the context of description all that talk about soul in the processes of personifying, pathologizing, psychologizing, and dehumanizing seemed loaded with too much metaphysics. In his review of my book, Sardello addressed this point. "Without ever uttering words such as 'archetype,' 'myth,' or 'gods', Romanyshyn works out a 'lateral depth' of the world—seeing through things, others, and the body as the reflections of psychological experience."[4]

In its style, then, phenomenology seemed to offer the same things that archetypal psychology did. "Between us and events, between the doer and the deed, there is a reflective moment," Hillman had written in *Re-Visioning Psychology*, and he added, "soul making means differentiating this middle ground."[5] But if phenomenology was precisely the opening of this middle, metaphoric ground, where the "It" could appear in all its subtle manifestations, what need was there for Hillman's psychology? Between the first moment of being reflected or mirrored back to oneself through the world, and the second moment of reflecting back upon and re-collecting oneself from that dispossession of oneself through the world, phenomenology was a con-spiracy between oneself and the world. It was the practice of learning how to breathe in relation to the world, where thinking or reflection follows the rhythm of breathing with its pause between the moment of inspiration, when we are brought home to ourselves for a moment enriched and deepened by having taken in the world, and the moment of expiration, when we give ourselves back to the world, surrender to it, and even, as the term suggests, expire for a moment, die to who we are as we are seduced by the world.

Moreover, I knew that for phenomenology this middle ground was a place of radical transformation. Merleau-Ponty was addressing this point when he wrote, "There really is inspiration and expiration of Being, action and passion so slightly discernible that it becomes impossible to distinguish between what sees and what is seen, what paints and what is painted." To illustrate his point, he quoted the artist Paul Klee: "'In a forest, I have felt many times over that it was not I who looked at the forest. Some days I felt that the trees were looking at me, were speaking to me ....'"[6] In the circuit of reflection action and passion are so slightly discernible that it is impossible to distinguish between who sees and what is seen, between who knows and what is known, between who is the doer and what is the deed. Indeed, in this circuit of reflection, in this con-spiracy with the world, the dichotomy between self and world is dissolved in that middle ground where subject and object are no-thing. Phenomenology was the art of dissolution, a natural alchemy, an *opus contra naturam*, a work against the natural attitude. As such, it was the practice of learning how to see again, of looking again to see, even if only for a moment, that self "is" world.

In its continuous work of return to re-gard the world, I understood that phenomenology situates itself and is situated within this pause between inspiration and expiration, within that middle ground, which John Sallis called the strife of the difference between the origins that fund one's return and the origins that are made again in the work of return. Reflecting on this strife, he had noted, "one of the names that the tradition has given to the power of persisting in that strife is imagination."[7] In the end, then, phenomenology was for me the exercise of the imaginative capacities of the human heart. In that pause where self and world breathe together in a con-spiracy of Eros and its laws of attraction, imagination was the way of nourishing the reasons of the heart that Reason does not know. In the hot, arid flatlands of Texas, phenomenology was that way of being in the world between thinking and perceiving, where in their mutual mirroring self and world transform each other into no-thing. In a landscape that often struck me as somewhat barren, phenomenology was for me—or did it become?—the practice of recovering no-thing out of the somethings of the world. It was the art of witnessing the moment, the art of doing no-thing.

And so I was reading Hillman while practicing this art of dreaming into the world while awake, and questioning if archetypal psychology was really adding anything to phenomenology. "Hillman" was an irritant, like a pebble in a shoe when one is on a walkabout. "He" would not go away, and when I would be tempted to go further south with him, "van den Berg," whose name also requires these quotation marks to distinguish the historical person from the companion he had become in the landscapes of my psychological world, would caution against it. I had learned from van den Berg the exquisite aesthetics of phenomenology and indeed he had taught me that phenomenology was not mental reflection at all, but the cordial reflex, which Hillman had called for, a way of knowing the world and being in it with heart before mind. If one was to travel south and take the journey to "Florence," one needed only to learn how to breathe in the world. Phenomenology taught me how to breathe better, like poetry, according to Bachelard, helps one breathe better. Was it not enough, then, while on the road to "Florence," to be simply one who breathes well, and in doing so become one who dwells in the world poetically, and who offers for the sake of the things of the world a poetics of their epiphanies? Did we have to load ourselves down with the baggage of a metaphysics of soul? Was it not better to travel light? Was it not enough to be a good phenomenologist? I thought so until I took a detour on the way to "Florence" and headed west after that wonderful experiment in Dallas ended.

## West towards the Setting Sun: Confrontations with the Unconscious

It turns out that the road to "Florence" is marked by many sinkholes where the ground can suddenly and without warning give way beneath one's feet. In such moments one is abducted into the underworld, and in those moments the phenomenologist encounters the depth psychologist. This was one of the other points that Hillman had made about soul in *Re-Visioning Psychology*. He said that soul derives its significance from its special "*relation with death*."[8] I had read those words, of course, but they had not registered. The phenomenology I was practicing had little, if any, shadow in its aesthetics.

Grief is one of those sinkholes, or it can be. It abducts one into the underworld and the dismemberment that occurs is an e-ducation into the reality of soul beyond any mere metaphysical pretensions that mind might have of it. Indeed, grief is, or can be, a kind of forced individuation process where one loses one's mind for the sake of soul. In grief the light that phenomenology brings to the world is tempered by the darkness of the unconscious. If phenomenology is a poetics of the world's epiphanies, then the e-ducation in depth that grief enforces becomes a way of learning how to see the world through the eyes of death, and learning how to see in dark-light. Going west in 1991 to California was also, therefore, more than a change in the geographical coordinates of my life. It became a shift in my psychological landscape. Going west was more than a lateral move on the horizontal plane. It was a vertical move into the personal and collective realms of the unconscious, which eight years later I was able to describe.[9]

The personal story of my descent is not the issue here. Rather, the issue is that without a direct experience of the unconscious that tears one apart, depth psychology is only an idea and often a bad one. Without some experience of dismemberment, depth psychology is often the exercise of power rather than the deepening of humility. I am not suggesting that a direct experience of the autonomous unconscious itself is enough to inoculate one against the temptations of power, nor am I suggesting that it automatically confers a mantle of humility. No, my point is that the unconscious becomes a living presence and a force of transformation through a direct encounter with it. It is no accident that the two founders of depth psychology had "creative illnesses." In 1896, the death of Freud's father started him on the road to his own descent, and in 1912, after his break with Freud, Jung began his own long confrontation with the unconscious. I would suspect the same is true of Hillman too. However a direct experience of the unconscious happens, one cannot later un-have it, or continue to cleverly think it away. It is a mark, a baptism, a wounding and a blessing whose ontological shockwave produces an epistemological revolution.

For me that epistemological revolution has meant a change not only in what I have been writing since the early 1990s, but also in how I have been writing. In this context, Hillman has increasingly become less an irritant and more an ambience, which is much better than a pebble in my shoe, as I have taken up themes from the point of view of soul and its ways of knowing and being in the world. So, in essays such as "The Orphan and the Angel: In Defense of Melancholy," "Alchemy and the Subtle Body of Metaphor," "On Angels and Other Anomalies of the Imaginal Life," "Psychology is Useless; Or, It Should Be," "On Being a Fool: In Defense of the Pathetic Heart," along with several others collected in *Ways of the Heart: Essays Toward and Imaginal Psychology*,[10] my focus has been on thinking in the space between phenomenology and depth psychology more from the side of the latter than the former, a tilt toward the presence of "Hillman" and "Jung" after the descent. Imaginal psychology—a term I am not really very fond of, but which serves for now—has become for me a holding place for a depth phenomenology of the world's subtle body, for a poetics of the depths in those fleeting moments of "It," an attempt to capture for a moment in words what finally always eludes our grasp, making every effort a kind of failed success. In addition, I have come to appreciate in a very direct way Hillman's description of the archetypal point of view, which he gives in *Re-Visioning Psychology*.

In that now-classic book, Hillman situates his archetypal approach within a principle and a method articulated by the neo-Platonic philosopher Plotinus. The principle states that "All knowing comes by likeness," and the method is one of "reversion," which is "the idea that all things desire to return to the archetypal originals of which they are copies and from which they proceed." In all things, this desire is "... imagined as having the intentionality of returning to an archetypal background." The moments, then, when things do fall apart, when things and ourselves become unglued, when those sinkholes on the road to "Florence" open up, have an intelligence about them, or we should perhaps say an-other wisdom than that of our ego-conscious minds. This other wisdom is an archetypal pattern within every act of behavior and every experience of fantasy within which who I am resembles who I am like when I act and feel in a certain way. "These archetypal resemblances," Hillman notes, "are best presented in myths in which the archetypal persons I am like and the patterns I am enacting have their authentic home ground."[11]

So, I think now more in terms of how this or that moment is like something other than itself, which is really thinking metaphorically, and this keeps me in touch with my phenomenological beginnings. But I also think now more in terms of that likeness in relation to some archetypal myth or theme, and that is somewhat anathema to the phenomenologist. However, one of the fruits of being e-ducated and drawn out of oneself into the ways of soul has been that I trust very much more now that I am led into my thinking by what wants to think itself through me, and so I have spent the last few years in the company of Orpheus and Eurydice, being led by them to consider such issues as the role of love and loss in psychological transformation, the place of the orphan as an archetypal presence and companion in the journey of homecoming, and the archetypal presence of Orpheus in Jung's psychology. And, perhaps more significantly, I have recently completed a project that began 15 years ago, when I first arrived at Pacifica Graduate Institute and was asked to develop an approach to research in accordance with its motto of serving the soul of the world. That work, *The Wounded Researcher*, puts me on the road again to "Florence." In calling for a poetics of the research process, it presents an approach to research that, in keeping soul in mind, is under the spell of Orpheus.

## Letting Go of Psychology

As I near the end of this essay, having taken it as an invitation to think back and re-collect origins, I know that "Florence" is nowhere. It is not a place; it is way of being. "Florence" is an imaginal domain, a no-where that is always now-here. To be on the road to "Florence" is, therefore, an ongoing task, and this task consists in always giving psychology away, or letting go of what we make of it in our theories and ideas, of dissolving the metaphysical shrouds in which we entomb it. At its best and at its worst psychology is always a complex about soul, and the one who travels the road to "Florence" must finally be the alchemist who knows that the basic work of alchemy is to coagulate and dissolve. In this regard, a psychology that does keep soul in mind is, as Hillman has always claimed, in touch with the poetic basis of mind. Every poem begins again the work of poetry. To be in touch with the poetic basis of mind is to be a perpetual beginner, the one who is always starting out again on the road to "Florence." And this, as it turns out, is no different for the phenomenologist.

Phenomenology is always a return to beginnings, to origins, a work of homecoming in which the home to which one returns is made over and over again in the very acts of returning. The phenomenologist, says Merleau-Ponty, is a "perpetual beginner."[12] So call it "Florence" or "Dallas" or "California" or even "Kansas"—it does not matter. What counts is what one brings to the journey, the attitude, the style, the way of being in service to soul.

What I have brought to this journey is and has been a devotion to thinking in the place between phenomenology and archetypal psychology. In this between place I have listened to van den Berg and Hillman, to Jung and Merleau-Ponty, as well as to a host of others, poets mostly, but also historians and some philosophers. At times I have even been an eavesdropper on their conversations. By temperament I have been and remain inclined toward phenomenology and toward the work of "van den Berg." But, as I have said, "Hillman" has been an irritant, a pebble in my shoe on that road to "Florence," a symptom, and now an ambience, inviting me to consider some inconvenient truths. He has been someone to think against, and that has been of great value.

True thinking, I think, needs an adversary, someone or something to engage, to struggle with, and to push against. Hillman works in this way. In relation to Jung, Hillman has been the heretic, and as such he has been one of those who has most faithfully carried forward the work of Jung and deepened the work of soul. As there have been and are Jungians, there are also "Hillmaniacs," and in each camp, neither Jung nor Hillman are well served. One serves best when one thinks his/her own thoughts and one thinks those thoughts best when there are companions such as "Hillman" (and "van den Berg") who model the heretic, who model the one who chooses, and as such challenges one to take a second look at his/her thinking, always, and to resist becoming a true believer.

## Closing Time: The Wisdom of the Dream

Two years ago I had a dream and it seems to me that this dream is the best way to conclude this essay about thinking in the place between phenomenology and archetypal psychology. Perhaps it says more than I have been able to say here and perhaps it is better to let the dream and its wisdom have the final say.

In this dream I am in an old Victorian house at an academic conference of archetypal psychologists. The participants are in a large open room for cocktails and are gathered around in a circle engaged in conversation. I recognize many of them as friends and colleagues, but I am on the outside of this circle and feel unseen and unnoticed. I wander through the house, and in a dining room that has dark wood panels, which give the room a feeling of age, I encounter a street poet who is dressed in simple clothes, which contrast sharply with my colleagues, who are all well suited and tied. This poet is instructing a woman whom I know very well in the work of Rilke, and I feel somewhat jealous of the attention he is giving to her. I continue to wander and I find myself in the back of the house in the pantry, where the kitchen help prepare the food. This pantry is airy and has screens on the window that open to the outside. The poet enters and he escorts me to a screen door. He opens it onto a landscape that is filled with people who are enjoying the world. There are couples walking hand in hand, people lying on the grass, and some playing different kinds of games. It is summer there and I am enthralled by the clarity of the light. The scene is filled with life and it reminds me of my boyhood summer days. I can smell the freshness of the air and feel the cool breeze on my skin. The poet gestures with his arm towards this landscape as if to point out the contrast with the interior of the house of academe.

But it is clear that he is not instructing me to cross the threshold and leave the house of academe. The dream ends with us standing on the threshold between these two worlds, just as I stand and have stood on the threshold between the two worlds of phenomenology and archetypal psychology.

On that threshold one is neither this nor that, neither the phenomenologist nor the archetypal psychologist. On that threshold one is aware that "Phenomenology needs the sense of mythic structures in the background and their deep values; archetypal psychology needs the de-literalizing, sometimes humorous, sense of metaphor in the foreground."[13] There on the threshold between the world and "going inside" the work of soul-making is done.

## *NOTES*

[1] James Hillman, "*Anima Mundi*: The Return of the Soul to the World," in *The Thought of the Heart and the Soul of the World* (Dallas, TX: Spring Publications, 1992), pp. 108-109.

[2] Maurice Merleau-Ponty, "Eye and Mind," trans. Carleton Dallery, in *The Primacy of Perception* (Evanston, IL: Northwestern University Press, 1964).

[3] J. H. van den Berg, *A Different Existence* (Pittsburgh, PA: Duquesne University Press, 1972/2001), pp. 60-61.

[4] Robert Sardello "On Seeing Through the World," *Spring* (1983): 207-211.

[5] James Hillman, *Re-Visioning Psychology* (New York: Harper & Row, 1975), p. x.

[6] Merleau-Ponty, "Eye and Mind," p. 167.

[7] John Sallis, *Phenomenology and the Return to Beginnings* (Pittsburgh, PA: Duquesne University Press, 1973), p. 116.

[8] Hillman, *Re-visioning Psychology*, p. x (italics in original).

[9] Robert Romanyshyn, *The Soul in Grief: Love, Death and Transformation* (Berkeley, CA.: North Atlantic Books, 1999).

[10] Robert Romanyshyn, *Ways of the Heart: Essays Toward an Imaginal Psychology* (Pittsburgh, PA: Trivium Publications, 2002).

[11] Hillman, *Re-Visioning Psychology,* p. 99.

[12] Maurice Merleau-Ponty, *Phenomenology of Perception*, trans. Colin Smith (London: Routledge, 1962), p. xiv.

[13] James Hillman, "An Inquiry into Image," *Spring* (1977): 85.

Michael P. Sipiora is Associate Professor of Psychology at Duquesne University where he has received awards for teaching excellence. In addition to archetypal psychology and narrative, areas of Sipiora's teaching and publication include phenomenological philosophy and psychology, and classical rhetoric. He earned Bachelor's and Master's degrees in philosophy at San Jose State University. His Master's and doctoral studies in psychology with a concentration in literature were carried out at the University of Dallas, where he took courses from Hillman on alchemy, myth, and the Neoplatonic tradition, and attended Ricoeur's McDermott Lectures on narrative. He spent four years as Marketing and Distribution Manager for Hillman's Spring Publications, Inc. He is a licensed psychologist who has practiced in both private and community mental health settings and has been active in organizational development consulting and executive coaching.

# 10

# Myth and Plot: Hillman and Ricoeur on Narrative

MICHAEL P. SIPIORA

## Introduction: *Muthos* as Myth or Plot

Aristotle maintains that *Muthos,*[1] "Fable or Plot,"[2] is the "life and soul"[3] of the poetic arts. Both James Hillman and Paul Ricoeur anchor their reflections[4] on narrative in Aristotle's *muthos*. However, they do so from different sides of the "or." The philosopher Ricoeur describes his narrative theory as "prefigured in Aristotle's *Poetics*":

> I have retained from Aristotle's poetics the central concept of emplotment, which in Greek is *muthos* and which signifies both fable (in the sense of an imaginary story) and plot (in the sense of a well constructed story). It is [from] this second aspect of Aristotle's *muthos* that .... I hope to draw all the elements capable of helping me later to reformulate the relationship between life and narrative.[5]

For the psychologist Hillman, it is the imaginary story, myth, which takes precedence. In "The Fiction of Case Histories," he writes:

> Freud's *discovery* of the Oedipal tragedy located psychology at the very beginning of poetics, with Aristotle's use of *mythos* [*muthos*] in his *Poetics*. When we open that book to read in English about plot, we find that wherever "plot" appears the original Greek word is *mythos* [*muthos*]. Plots are myths. The basic answers to *why* in a story are to be discovered in myths.[6]

Hillman and Ricoeur[7] each proceed to develop quite different interpretations of "mimesis"—the activity of "making" in terms of which Aristotle defines *muthos.* Hillman's taking of *muthos* as myth leads to a Platonic conception of mimesis as mythologizing. Continuing with the passage cited above:

> But a *mythos* [*muthos*] is more than a theory and more than a plot. It is the tale of the interaction of humans and divine. To be in a *mythos* [*muthos*] is to be inescapably linked to divine powers, and moreover, to be in mimesis with them.[8]

Mythologizing, as Hillman describes it in *Re-Visioning Psychology*, is an essential component of psychologizing, which is how soul is made in the deepening of events into experience. The activity of soul-making leads to what Hillman later elaborates in *The Soul's Code* as "character." On the other side of *muthos*, Ricoeur's taking the second sense of plot leads to a hermeneutic understanding of mimesis as emplotment. Emplotment, Ricoeur's enriched notion of a threefold mimetic activity, specifies how "fiction contributes to making life, in the biological sense of the word, a human life."[9] The activity of emplotment, in turn, leads to the making of what Ricoeur calls "narrative identity."

Rather than taking a side in reading Aristotle, we will pursue both sides of *muthos*, myth and plot. We will proceed by swiftly laying out the line in Hillman's work that runs from *muthos* to soul-making and the force of character. A digression recounting the story of archetypal psychology as an insurrection against conventional psychology will bring to the fore the critical character of Hillman's work. A quick but attentive treatment of Ricoeur's development of *muthos* into emplotment leads to the correlative notion of narrative identity.[10] We will then be in a position to consider the "practical moves" of making life into story that Hillman lays out in *The Soul's Code*. Within this context we will interweave the dramas of mythologizing and emplotment, crisscross the lines along which Hillman and Ricoeur each take up *muthos,* and arrive at a hybrid of character and identity that can inspire and inform the insurgent practice of crafting a personal narrative.

## *Muthos* as Myth: Mythologizing and Character

Aristotle's claim that *muthos* is the first principle of the poetic arts holds particular importance for Hillman, whose "psychology of soul" asserts the "poetic basis of mind"[11]—indeed, the "poetic basis of therapy, of biography, of our very lives."[12] The key to this importance is to be found among the "fence-posts" with which Hillman stakes out the "idea of soul" in *Re-Visioning Psychology*. Soul "makes meaning possible" and "refers to the deepening of events into experience." Additionally, "by 'soul' I mean the imaginative possibility in our natures, the experiencing through reflective speculation, dream, image, and *fantasy*—that mode which recognizes all realities as primarily symbolic or metaphorical."[13] Soul-making transpires in seeing literal events as "metaphorical enactments"[14] of archetypal dramas. This seeing-through or psychologizing, "*goes on whenever reflection takes place in terms other than those presented*,"[15] and specifies "how" events are deepened into experiences.[16]

In Hillman, psychologizing is a process or operation involving four interconnected, often simultaneous, steps. First is a moment of reflection that disrupts the natural grasp and flow of events. Second comes the "justification" of the operation by an appeal to a latent or hidden reality that is more than the event at surface value. Then an explanation follows, the narrating of the event in terms of this latent reality, which Hillman identifies with mythologizing. And fourth, ideas are used as tools with which to see through, and thereby complicate, enrich, and animate what was literal and merely superficial.

While in psychologizing "all explanations whatsoever may be regarded as narrative fantasies and examined as myth,"[17] "a simple narrative, just a story, is not enough to make soul."[18] Mythologizing is a kind of narrating that offers the symbolic and metaphorical reflection necessary to deepen events into experiences. Mythologizing makes up an account of whatever happens in terms of what has "never happened but always is."[19] This making-up is carried out by taking-up myth as a perspective. In mythologizing, the answer to the question of "why" something happens—the usual role assigned to the plot in configuring events into a story[20]—is given in terms of myth and so cannot be taken literally. Indeed, "myth moves into meaning merely by taking one out of literal objectivities."[21] Mythologizing deepens chronology into story by letting us see symbolic connections and metaphorical references in and through the litany of the literal. Hillman is emphatic that the meaning that mythologizing brings into play is not the certainty of clear and distinct ideas. Instead, in reflecting literal events through a mythic perspective, mythologizing connects us with the multiplicity and ambiguity of "meaning inherent in our lives."[22]

The work of mythologizing in soul-making, its role as the narrative component in psychologizing, is directly related to the Platonist sense in which Hillman takes *mythos* [*muthos*] as myth. Myths recount the encounters of the human and the divine. In their way (which is never literal), myths explain the relationship between above and below, universal and particular, form and matter. For Hillman, "we meet archetypal reality through the perspective of myths."[23] Mythologizing is a mimesis, a poetic making, in which the archetypal is brought into participation with the mundane. In the narrating activity of mythologizing, the mundane imitates the archetypal. As already quoted, "To be in a *mythos* [*muthos*] is to be inescapably linked to divine powers, and moreover, to be in mimesis with them."[24] Through mimesis, the mythologized narrating that makes soul, the particularity of our experience is linked to the claim of divine powers and an archetypal reality informs the meaningfulness of our experience. This narrative component of psychologizing is in play as well in Hillman's notion of pathologizing as the making of soul through suffering: "Gods are in the styles of our suffering, in the *casus*, the way things fall, shaping our case history into their myths."[25] Mythologizing is precisely the shaping, the mimesis that makes soul in both psychologizing and pathologizing.

What is made of us in the making of soul? Who do we become in mythologizing? "Character" is Hillman's answer in *The Soul's Code*. The qualitative notion of character, with its long history going all the way back to Heraclitus's identification of character with fate, is where Hillman's taking of *muthos* as myth ends up. Character is what emerges out of the narrative deepening of life events into meaningful experience. Our character is what is called forth by the mythic claims that make soul. In *The Force of Character*, the companion to *The Soul's Code*, Hillman connects soul, *muthos*, and character.

> It helps to regard soul as an active intelligence, forming and plotting each person's fate. Translators use "plot" to render the ancient Greek word *mythos* [*muthos*] in English. The plots that entangle our souls and draw forth our characters are the great myths. This is why we need a sense of myth and knowledge of different myths ....[26]

Seeing our lives through the great myths, we recognize the archetypal claims that configure the meanings of our experience. We are drawn into our lives as figures enacting dramas that both transcend and subtend the literal events of our chronological histories. Living through the myths brings out qualities in us that mark our character. Hillman follows Aristotle's assertion that "character is revealed through action."[27] How we act in theses stories, what we do as the characters in these stories, reveals our character.

For Hillman, working within a polytheistic mythology, the multidimensionality of character is crucial. Indeed, the Platonist theme of a "one that is many" is implicit in Hillman's notion of character. "Character is characters; our nature is a plural complexity, a multiphasic polysemous weave."[28] In the mythologizing that makes soul, we are figured as characters in many dramas, claimed by many gods. The integrity of character is the configuration of an ensemble of characters assembled in a life story. "Character is a cluster of characteristics."[29] The inherent plurality and complexity, the profound ambiguities of our character accord with the symbolic and metaphorical character of psychological reality itself. The multiple dimensions of character are present in the multiple characters woven into the various and varied strands of a storied life.

In summary, Hillman takes Aristotle's *muthos* as myth because soul is made (in both the seeing-through of psychologizing and the suffering of pathologizing) by narrating events in terms of myth. In the making of such narratives (mimesis as mythologizing), we are claimed by the metaphorical and symbolic dimensions of our experience. Responding to these claims, we are figured as characters in mythologized stories. As such characters, we in turn engage the events in our lives, deepening them into psychological experiences. Qualities, revealed through our actions in these stories, are brought out in us as soul is made in our lives. Our particular and unique character is marked out in the configuration of qualities drawn together by our life story.

## Archetypal Psychology: Plotting an Insurrection

Given the narrative character of soul-making, it is no surprise that Hillman is forever narrating what he does, telling and retelling where archetypal psychology came from, plotting its moves and imagining its future. In these stories, Hillman himself is figured as many characters: the Platonist, the Son of Soul, the Polytheist, the Democrat, the Puer, the Ares, the Old Soldier, and more. His own character is revealed in the actions of these characters. It is revealed in his enacting these characters as author, speaker, analyst, teacher, and publisher in the making of archetypal psychology.

In *A Brief Account* (1983) Hillman writes: "Archetypal psychology can be seen as a cultural movement part of whose task is the re-visioning of psychology, psychopathology, and psychotherapy in terms of the Western cultural imagination."[30] In a later version (1999), the movement is a "war."

> My war—and I have yet to win a decisive battle—is with the modes of thought and conditioned feeling that prevail in psychology and therefore in the way we think and feel about our being. Of these conditions none are more tyrannical than the convictions that clamp the mind and heart into positivistic science (geneticism and computerism), economics (bottom-line capitalism), and single-minded faith (fundamentalism).[31]

He goes on in this passage to "champion" the "idea of character" precisely because it has been obliterated by the dominant "isms" of our day and therefore absent from our daily lives.

Hillman devotes two books to character, *The Soul's Code* and *The Force of Character,* popular books he wrote at the end of the century that began with Freud, locating psychology in *muthos*. At the heart of both works are "the repetitions and returns to basic obsessions" that have plotted the story of archetypal psychology from the start. Hillman's career-long devotion has been to the redemption of psychology and the recovery of soul, "re-visioning psychology from the point of view of soul."[32] Contemporary psychology's poverty of ideas, decried in *Re-Visioning Psychology,* leads directly to the condition observed in *The Soul's Code*: "We dull our lives by the way we conceive of them."[33] Hillman advocates character as a "fresh way of looking at the importance of our lives."[34] He persuades us to entertain "large ideas such as beauty, mystery, and myth,"[35] as well as "big words, such as 'vision' and 'calling'"[36] that come along with the idea of character as its native poetic soil, intellectual tradition, and repressed cultural context.

The critical dimension of archetypal psychology is vital to its story. Michael White's Narrative Therapy[37] can help articulate a plot for telling the story in a way that illuminates the social importance of archetypal psychology itself as a narrative. In this version, archetypal psychology is a "narrative therapy" for psychology and for the culture at large that both performs a soulful critique of the "problem-saturated" discourse of conventional psychology and offers the big words and large ideas that in turn provide the type of "thick" and "rich" descriptions necessary to generate "alternative" stories of individual lives. Re-visioning psychology, according to this plot, is a "re-storying" of the culture's "dominant narratives."

White adopts his overall framework from Michel Foucault's theories of power and knowledge. In this view, the dominant social narratives and their institutionalized, global totalitarian knowledges (like the "geneticism and computerism," "bottom-line capitalism," and "fundamentalism" identified by Hillman) cannot be overturned by a frontal assault waged by some other unitary knowledge. The very configuration of power/knowledge precludes the possibility of re-storying one dominant narrative by replacing it with another. "Instead, he [Foucault] argues for the 'insurrection' of ... subjugated knowledge against the 'institutions and against the effects of the knowledge and power that invests scientific discourse.'"[38] Subjugated knowledges fall into two classes: "erudite" and "indigenous." The first class consists of "previously established or 'erudite' knowledges," that have been obliterated by the dominant narratives, "written out of the record by the revision of history achieved through the ascendance of a more global and unitary knowledge." "These knowledges can be resurrected only by careful and meticulous scholarship."[39] The second class of subjugated knowledge, which Foucault refers to as indigenous or "local popular," "are 'regional' knowledges that are currently in circulation but are denied or deprived of the space in which they could be adequately performed."[40]

Seen within White's framework, the intended cultural movement that became Hillman's war can be narrated according to an insurrection plot. The story of archetypal psychology can be told as an insurrection against the dominant narratives that obliterate indigenous story-telling practices, and a recovery of erudite knowledges that promote mythical understanding. Many chapters in this story have been spent in the intentional and concerted effort to revive traditions subjugated by the dominant narrative of mechanistic, positivistic science and Cartesian literalism. From the publications he has authored (and other volumes for which he has served as editor), to the authors he has published through his Spring Publications, Inc., Hillman has retrieved and contributed to the "tradition of Jung and Corbin" and "their predecessors, particularly the Neo-Platonist tradition via Vico and the Renaissance (Ficino), through Proclus and Plotinus, to Plato ... and most anciently to Heraclitus."[41] Hillman's erudition and scholarship, his passion and literary skill have brought "this Neoplatonic and 'arcane' psychology"[42] to professional and popular notice in a time when the "isms" he decries have dominated not only public but also private discourse.

Archetypal psychology's insurrectionist plot also configures Hillman's conflicted relationship to psychotherapy and analysis. Himself an analyst, as well as teacher of therapists and trainer of analysts, Hillman devoted considerable attention to re-visioning the myth of analysis and re-narrating the fiction of case history. But Hillman also co-authored *We've Had a Hundred Years of Psychotherapy—and the World's Getting Worse,* and the story was that he stopped practicing therapy. His criticisms of psychology's practice have been as intense and as devastating as his derision of the field's impoverished ideas. He has decried the standard psychotherapeutic prescription of pills and coping as fostering compliance with an oppressive *status quo* of crude materialism, vacuous consumerism, and ideological manipulation. He has been outraged at therapy's obsession with our wounded inner child, broken families, and dysfunctional relationships when it all but turns a blind eye to the lack of "satisfactory work" and "satisfactory political community"[43] that threaten our democracy. When narrated in an insurrectionist plot, archetypal psychology is necessarily strident in its critique of psychotherapy's undermining of the natural competencies and indigenous knowledges that empower people to deal with the vicissitudes of life. As Hillman observes, "We're disempowering ourselves through therapy."[44]

## *Muthos* as Plot: Emplotment and Narrative Identity

Returning to the *Poetics*, Ricoeur takes up the sense of *muthos* as plot and broadens it beyond the genres of tragedy and comedy to include the whole range of narrative compositions. Ricoeur uses the term "emplotment"[45] to emphasize *muthos* as a poetic process or operation rather than a structure. And he follows Aristotle in a "quasi-identification" of *muthos* with mimesis, "the imitation or representation of action."[46] Plot is "what" is constructed in mimetic activity at the same time that the poetic imitation of action, mimesis, is governed by the plot's organizing of events. For Ricoeur, "the configuring operation constitutive of emplotment" becomes a process with three moments, which he "seriously and playfully" names: "$mimesis_1$, $mimesis_2$, and $mimesis_3$."[47] These three moments form an arc that connects our pre- and post-narrative experience in a manner that "contributes to making life, in the biological sense of the word, a human life."[48] The connection, as we will see, is made by way of the "synthesis of the heterogeneous" and "discordant concordance" of poetic configuration. Understanding how poetic configuration contributes to life will lead us to Ricoeur's conception of narrative identity.

In $mimesis_1$, it is due to the "*pre-narrative quality of human experience*" that "we are justified in speaking of life as a story in its nascent state, and so of life an *activity and passion in search of a narrative*."[49] Ricoeur grounds $mimesis_1$ in three features.[50] First, our lived understanding of the structure of human action, as implicitly referring to the "who," "what," "when," and "why" of "doing something," is presupposed in our understanding of narratives. Second, human experience can be narrated because action is always already mediated by cultural symbols and available to interpretation. And third, the "within-time-ness" or temporal dimension of human action, as distinct from a series of "nows," belongs as well to the grammar and linguistic expressions out of which narratives are constructed. In identifying $mimesis_1$, Ricoeur references the pre-thematic, pre-linguistic quality of our lived experience that itself calls for reflection and expression in order to reach its fullness as distinctively human.

In $mimesis_2$, languaged reflection configures the possibilities of pre-verbal experience into the action of a story. This articulation of lived experience in a narrative structure occurs by way of the story's plot. Ricoeur depicts plot as "a synthesis of heterogeneous elements"[51] which connects multiple incidents into an intelligible whole, accounts for both continuity and change, and "draw[s] a configuration out of succession."[52] As an actual telling of a "nascent" story waiting to be told out of pre-narrative experience, mimesis$_2$ is the making of a specific story that recounts a particular action. Ricoeur emphasizes the mediating function of mimesis$_2$, in configuring "discordant concordance."[53] Diverse and divergent elements fit together and relate to each other in terms of the narrative's plot. The plot includes an organizing theme, what Aristotle refers to as the "thought" of a poetic composition, in which characters, along with their actions and motives, and the incidents that befall them are rendered intelligible. The action of the story brings together all the things that happen, even the unexpected reversals, in a configuration in which they lead to, follow from, and connect with one another as if by design.

"A life," according to Ricoeur "is no more than a biological phenomenon as long as it has not been interpreted. And in interpretation, fiction plays a mediating role."[54] The third moment of emplotment, mimesis$_3$, is the reconfiguration of lived experience that occurs when that experience is informed by the articulated narrative of mimesis$_2$. If mimesis$_1$ is taken as a nascent story waiting to be told, and mimesis$_2$ is the telling of that story, then mimesis$_3$ is the interpreting of life in terms of the story. The meanings explicated in the storied articulation of lived experience are incorporated into post-narrative sense making and action. "Mimesis$_3$ marks the intersection of the world of the text and the world of the hearer or reader; the intersection, therefore, of the world configured by the poem and the world wherein real action occurs."[55] The arc of emplotment, having traversed the distance between experience and narrative, now reaches back to experience. The emploted narrative mediates post-narrative experience in a manner reverse but analogous to how the explicit narrative had mediated pre-thematic, lived experience. Mimesis$_3$ thus involves the reception of the specific, articulated narrative and the difference it makes in the experience of living. The narrative is now lived insofar as living is now informed by the narrative.

What is made of us in narrative's contribution to making life human? Who do we become in emplotment? Narrative identity is precisely "the sort of identity to which a human being has access thanks to the mediation of the narrative function."[56] Narrative identity is prefigured in the pre-narrative quality of our experience that anchors mimesis$_1$. For Ricoeur, "the very fabric of life" is a "the mixture of acting and suffering" that "narrative attempts to imitate in a creative way."[57] The configuration of action in mimesis$_2$ provides the condition for the explicit generation of identity in relation to the story's characters, the subjects of the narrative's action either as agents of actions performed or those subjected to the outcomes of other actions. Narrative identity arises in the reconfiguration of experience performed in mimesis$_3$ when we interpret our identities through the characters in the story. We make sense of who we are in terms of the possibilities of acting and suffering enacted by the story's specific characters. "What the narrative interpretation properly provides," writes Ricoeur, "is precisely 'the figure-able' character of the individual which has for its result, that the self, narratively interpreted, is itself a figured self—a self which figures itself as this or that."[58]

Such a self has the power to become the "narrator" of its own story. As borne dramatic witness by the beginning and, most often, the end of our life, we are never the sole authors of our story. However,

> Our life, when embraced in a single glance, appears to us as the field of a constructive activity, borrowed from narrative understanding, by which we attempt to discover and not simply to impose from the outside the *narrative identity which constitutes us*.[59]

Culture and the literary tradition provide a store of plots encompassing a host of characters we can try on and through whom we figure ourselves out. By way of "imaginative variations" of our self in terms of these characters, we come to recognize ourselves as the character appearing in our life story.

In summary, Ricoeur's conception of emplotment, his taking of Aristotle's *muthos* as plot, leads to an understanding of the relationship between live and narrative in terms of a threefold mimesis. In mimesis$_1$, the activities of our living call for narrative articulation. The narrating of life's possibilities in mimesis$_2$ in turn invites mimesis$_3$ as the interpretation of our selves in terms of articulated stories. Ricoeur's notion of narrative identity, the kind of identity that emerges from the mediation of emplotment, figures humans as acting and suffering. This narrative identity offers a sense of our selves that is an alternative, Ricoeur suggests, to the "narcissistic, egoistic and stingy ego."[60] "In place of an *ego* enamored of itself arises a *self* instructed by cultural symbols, the first among which are the narratives handed down in our literary tradition. And these narratives give us a unity which is not substantial but narrative."[61]

## Myth and Plot in Personal Narrative

Having sketched the development of narrative approaches from the two sides of Aristotle's *muthos*, first following Hillman's path from myth to character and then portraying Ricoeur's progression from plot to identity, what remains is to converge these approaches on the practical task of making a personal narrative. In "The Fiction of Case History," Hillman concludes that perhaps in the first 100 years of psychotherapy what has really been sought is "not to be loved or to get cured" but "to be told into a soul story and given a plot to live by."[62] In *The Soul's Code* the question becomes: "How do I find the basic plot of my story?"[63]

Hillman begins *The Soul's Code* by telling the Myth of Er from Plato's *Republic*. In telling this myth, Hillman enlists the erudition of the Platonist tradition in staging an uprising against the tyranny of global totalitarian knowledges that have "robbed" us "of our true biography."[64] By retrieving the Platonic discourse on myth and soul that he finds in Plotinus and others in this line, Hillman generates alternatives to the casting of character in the "interplay of genetics and environment."[65] In telling a myth Hillman is also serving the resurgence of indigenous knowledges found in cultures throughout history and now all but lost to our own. "Only our contemporary psychology and psychiatry omit it from their textbooks."[66]

The knowledge omitted from our institutionalized psychological theories is included in the sense of life that inheres in storytelling. This is the knowledge, indigenous to making life human, that is operative in Ricoeur's notion of emplotment, specifically in $mimesis_1$ as living in a nascent story, and then the living through the appropriation of stories in $mimesis_3$. $Mimesis_2$ configures what we know of ourselves, as those who act and suffer in the culturally mediated yet still nascent stories of $mimesis_1$, in terms of the explicit plots provided by our literary traditions. Similarly, Hillman observes in "A Note on Story" that story is part of human life; coming with life, "it is already a perspective to life."[67] The subjugation of indigenous knowledge of our humanity occurs in that the kinds of plots that "prevail in psychology" are those of a global totalitarian variety that so "clamp" our minds and hearts[68] that we lose, rather than appropriate, a narrative perspective on ourselves as acting and suffering. In place of plots in which we can imaginatively figure ourselves and deepen the events of life into experiences, such as those Ricoeur identifies with literature, conventional psychology's literal, causal explanations reduce us to a "narcissistic, egoistic and stingy ego"[69] and all but annihilate our native narrative understanding of life.

While all literature has the power to redeem us from literal reductions, Hillman claims that Plato's myth "has a redemptive psychological function, and a psychology derived from it can inspire a life founded on it."[70] Because cosmological myths, such as the Myth of Er, narrate "reality as primarily symbolic and metaphorical,"[71] they have the power to re-engage us with the depth of our experience repressed in our culture's dominant narratives.[72] Hillman writes:

> … [C]osmological myths place us in the world and involve us with it. The cosmologies of today—big bangs and black holes, antimatter and curved, ever-expanding space, curved and going nowhere—leave us in dread and senseless incomprehensibility. Random events, nothing truly necessary.[73]

Cosmological myths perform the psychological function of configuring our lives within their plots, that is, within an archetypal ordering of events. "It is the identity of the story," as Ricoeur observes, "that makes the identity of the character."[74] A psychology of soul derives from cosmological myths because our character is found in the archetypal claims in which our experience is figured. By envisioning our lives through theses myths, psychology offers a way of narrating our acting and suffering that renders events necessary and our lives meaningful.

"The myth," Hillman tells us "leads also to practical moves"[75] in which, to use Ricoeur's words, "we attempt to discover … the narrative identity which constitutes us."[76] The first move in making a personal narrative is now readily apparent: in viewing the events of our life history, we are to be instructed by mythic cosmologies. By interpreting our experience as mythically figured, we can then recognize and respond to the claims that configure our own character. The fitting response is to "align life" with these claims by narrating our own story. We synthesize the heterogeneous material of our biographies, the many different events and diverse affairs that affect us, into the discordant concordance of a life story that identifies our character.

Next comes the living of our lives in terms of our story, which Ricoeur calls mimesis$_3$. Hillman offers the following instructions: "[F]ind the common sense to realize that accidents, including the heartache and natural shocks the flesh is heir to, belong to [one's character], are necessary to it, and help fulfill it."[77] "[C]oncordance," as Ricoeur observes, "is never found without discordance."[78] Accidents do not accord with the rest of the story but they happen; and when they do, they threaten the coherence of the story. They, along with all the other discordant occurrences in a life of acting and suffering—the things we could never have foreseen and the consequences we never intended, chance encounters and coincidental events, tragic errors and comic reversals—invariably appear in our stories. Living our stories requires making sense of such discordances by realizing that they are necessary to our life story. "The whole problem of narrative *Verstehen* [understanding]," according to Ricoeur, "is contained here in principle. To make up a plot is already to make the intelligible spring from the accidental, the universal from the singular, the necessary or the probable from the episodic."[79] In living life in terms of story, narrative understanding is a kind of common sense that operates at the level of practical knowledge or "prudence."[80] It is the common sense indigenous to life and story that is obliterated by the global, totalitarian knowledges that determine the ways "we think and feel about our being."[81]

Ideas of necessity and fate, foreign to modern science's literal explanations and forgotten in conventional psychology's causal theories, are integral to Aristotle's *Poetics* and are "at the heart" of *The Soul's Code.*[82] They are essential to the making of a personal narrative. We begin to understand how discordant occurrences play a role in our life story when we see events from the perspective of cosmological myth. By narrating our story according to this sense of the connectedness of the things, we can make sense of "accidents, including the heartache and natural shocks the flesh is heir to" as linked to everything else that happens in our lives. The discordant elements in our lives, when configured within the discordant concordance of our personal narratives, become necessary to the appearance of our character. Our narrative identity, as the character in our life story, requires that what has happened—the expected and unexpected, the concordant and discordant—needed to have happened for us to be who we are. "Because of the concordant-discordant synthesis," as Ricoeur explains, "the contingency of the event contributes to the necessity, retroactive so to speak, of the history of a life, to which is equated the identity of character. Thus chance is transmuted into fate."[83]

The convergence of Hillman's and Ricoeur's approaches generates a dynamic understanding of Aristotle's *muthos* as the "life and soul" of our personal narratives. By taking each side of *muthos* in and through the other we see how plot and myth interplay in the making of a personal narrative, how soul-making's deepening of events into experience makes life into a meaningful story, how mythologizing is woven into the emplotment of our life story, and how we find our narrative identity as the character portrayed in our life story. Hillman notes that story is "something lived in and lived through, a way in which the soul finds itself in life."[84] "Psychological living," he writes "implies living in a fantasy, a story, being told by a myth."[85]

## *NOTES*

[1] Aristotle's Greek term will be transliterated as *muthos*. Hillman's use of *mythos* will be retained when appearing in direct quotations with *muthos* inserted in brackets.

[2] Aristotle, *The Poetics*, trans. I. Bywater, in *The Basic Works of Aristotle*, ed. R. McKeon (New York: Random House, 1968), 1450b, 22.

[3] *Ibid.*, 1450a, 39.

[4] The terms "story" and "narrative" will be used interchangeably in what follows. I take story and narrative to contain a plot as distinct from a "chronicle."

[5] Paul Ricoeur, "Life in Quest of Narrative," in *On Paul Ricoeur: Narrative and Inter*

Sanford L. Drob is on the faculty of Fielding Graduate University and New York University Medical School. He is the author of *Symbols of the Kabbalah: Philosophical and Psychological Perspective*, and *Kabbalistic Metaphors: Jewish Mystical Themes in Ancient and Modern Thought* (both Jason Aronson, 2000). He has published numerous papers on the interface between philosophy, psychology, and religion, including several on Jung's relationship to Jewish mysticism. He is currently completing books on Jung and the Kabbalah and Kabbalah and Postmodern Thought. *pretation,* ed. D. Wood (New York:

Routledge, 1991), p. 21.

[6] James Hillman, "The Fiction of Case History," in *Healing Fictions* (Barrytown, NY: Station Hill Press, 1983), p. 11.

[7] Ricoeur certainly belongs with "Owen Barfield and Norman Brown" in Hillman's vaunted "mafia of the metaphor to protect plain men from literalism" (*Re-Visioning Psychology*, p. 149). Indeed both men come to narrative by way of metaphor. Narrative is implicit in Hillman's appropriation of Vico's notion of metaphor as "fable in brief" (*ibid.*, p. 156). For Ricoeur, whose three volumes of *Time and Narrative* are a continuation of *The Rule of Metaphor*, both metaphor and plot are the work of the productive imagination with the former operating at the level of the sentence while the later functions at the level of text. For an insightful and provocative discussion of metaphor in Hillman's work, see: R. Olson, *Deconstructing Hillman: A Derridean Reading of Re-Visioning Psychology*, unpublished dissertation, Duquesne University, 2002.

[8] Hillman, "Fiction of Case History," p. 11.

[9] Ricoeur, "Life in Quest of Narrative," p. 20.

[10] In addition to Ricoeur's multivolume *Time and Narrative* and related essays, I also make use of his development of the notion of narrative identity in *Oneself as Another* (trans. K. Blamey [Chicago, IL: The University of Chicago Press, 1992]). I do not, however, extend consideration to where Ricoeur is led in this later work: "The *autonomy* of the self will appear then to be tightly bound up with *solicitude* for one's neighbor and with *justice* for each individual" (p. 18). Nor does space allow discussion of the ethical dimension of narrative in Aristotle, a dimension that is of great importance in Ricoeur's work. My treatment of Ricoeur is for the same reason limited in other respects as well.

[11] James Hillman, *Re-Visioning Psychology* (New York: Harper and Row, 1973), p. xi.

[12] Hillman, "Fiction of Case History," p. 21.

[13] Hillman, *Re-Visioning Psychology*, p. x.

[14] *Ibid.*, p. 127.

[15] *Ibid.*, p. 135 (italics in original).

[16] *Ibid.*, p. 122.

[17] *Ibid.*, p. 141.

[18] Hillman, "The Fiction of Case History," p. 26.

[19] James Hillman, *The Soul's Code: In Search of Character and Calling* (New York: Warner Books, 1996), p. 46.

[20] Hillman, "The Fiction of Case History," p. 9.

[21] Hillman, *Re-Visioning Psychology*, p. 142.

[22] *Ibid.*, p. 158.

[23] *Ibid.*, p. 157.

[24] Hillman, "The Fiction of Case History," p. 11.

[25] Hillman, *Re-Visioning Psychology*, p. 129.

[26] James Hillman, *The Force of Character and the Lasting Life* (New York: Ballantine Books, 1999), p. 11.

[27] *Ibid.*, p. 36.

[28] *Ibid.*, p. 32.

[29] *Ibid.*, p. 197.

[30] James Hillman, *Archetypal Psychology: A Brief Account* (Dallas, TX: Spring Publications, Inc., 1983), p. 2.

[31] Hillman, *Force of Character*, p. xxiv.

[32] Hillman, *Re-Visioning Psychology*, p. ix.

[33] Hillman, *Soul's Code*, p. 5.

[34] *Ibid.*, p. 33.

[35] *Ibid.*, p. 5.

[36] *Ibid.*, p. 6.

[37] Michael White and D. Epston, *Narrative Means to Therapeutic Ends* (New York: W. W. Norton, 1990).

[38] *Ibid.*, p. 27.

[39] *Ibid.*, p. 25.

[40] *Ibid.*, p. 26.

[41] Hillman, *Brief Account*, p. 4.

[42] *Ibid.*, p. 26.

[43] James Hillman & Michael Ventura, *We've Had a Hundred Years of Psychotherapy—and the World's Getting Worse* (San Francisco, CA: HarperCollins Publishers, 1992), p. 13.

[44] *Ibid.*, p. 6.

[45] I have greatly profited from Polkinghorne's discussion of personal narratives in relation to Ricoeur's notion of emplotment. See: Donald Polkinghorne, "Narrative and Personal Identity," in *Phenomenology and Narrative Psychology: The Fourteenth Annual Symposium of the Simon Silverman Phenomenology Center* (Pittsburgh, PA: Simon Silverman Phenomenology Center, Duquesne University, 1997).

[46] Paul Ricoeur, *Time and Narrative*, vol. 1, trans. K. McLaughlin and D. Pellauer (Chicago, IL: The University of Chicago Press, 1984), p. 34.

[47] *Ibid.*, p. 53.

[48] Ricoeur, "Life in Quest of Narrative," p. 20.

[49] *Ibid.*, p. 28 (italics in original).

[50] Ricoeur, *Time and Narrative*, vol. 1, pp. 54-64.

[51] Ricoeur, "Life in Quest of Narrative," p. 21.

[52] *Ibid.*, p. 22.

[53] Ricoeur, *Time and Narrative*, vol. 1, p. 66.

[54] Ricoeur, "Life in Quest of Narrative," pp. 28-29.

[55] Ricoeur, *Time and Narrative*, vol. 1, p. 71.

[56] Paul Ricoeur, "Narrative Identity," trans. M. Muldoon, *Philosophy Today* 35, no. 1 (1991): 73.

[57] Ricoeur, "Life in Quest of Narrative," p. 28.

[58] Ricoeur, "Narrative Identity," p. 80.

[59] Ricoeur, "Life in Quest of Narrative," p. 32 (italics in original).

[60] *Ibid.*, p. 33.

[61] *Ibid.*

[62] Hillman, "Fiction of Case History," p. 49.

[63] Hillman, *Soul's Code*, p. 5.

[64] *Ibid.*

[65] *Ibid.*, p. 6.

[66] *Ibid.*, p. 10.

[67] James Hillman, "A Note on Story," in *Loose Ends: Primary Papers in Archetypal Psychology* (Dallas, TX: Spring Publications, 1975), p. 1.

[68] Hillman, *Force of Character*, p. xxiv.

[69] Ricoeur, "Life in Quest of Narrative," p. 33. I think it is clear that both Hillman and Ricoeur are critical of this kind of ego, the "heroic ego" as Hillman calls it. What might seem problematic, in light of Hillman's emphatic rejection of any talk of "self" in *The Soul's Code*, is Ricoeur's notion of a narrative self. However, the limitless inflation and endless self-absorption that comes with the term and so disturbs Hillman, are absent from Ricoeur's acting and suffering narrative self.

[70] Hillman, *Soul's Code*, p. 8.

[71] Hillman, *Re-Visioning Psychology*, p. x.

[72] For a related discussion of cosmology and *mythos* in Hillman, see: M. Sipiora, "The Anima Mundi and The Fourfold: Hillman and Heidegger on the 'Idea' of the World," in *Pathways into the Jungian World: Phenomenology and Analytical Psychology,* ed. R. Brooke (New York: Routledge, 2000), pp. 67-83.

[73] Hillman, *Soul's Code*, p. 47.

[74] Paul Ricoeur, *Oneself as Another*, p. 148.
[75] Hillman, *Soul's Code*, p. 8.
[76] Ricoeur, "Life in Quest of Narrative," p. 32.
[77] *Ibid.*, p. 8.
[78] Ricoeur, "Life in Quest of Narrative," p. 32.
[79] Ricoeur, *Time and Narrative*, vol. 1, p. 41.
[80] Ricoeur, "Life in Quest of Narrative," p. 23.
[81] Hillman, *Force of Character*, p. xxiv.
[82] See p. 192.
[83] Ricoeur, *Oneself as Another*, p. 147.
[84] Hillman, "Note on Story," p. 4.
[85] Hillman, *Re-Visioning Psychology*, p. 143.

Sanford L. Drob is on the faculty of Fielding Graduate University and New York University Medical School. He is the author of *Symbols of the Kabbalah: Philosophical and Psychological Perspectives*, and *Kabbalistic Metaphors: Jewish Mystical Themes in Ancient and Modern Thought* (both Jason Aronson, 2000). He has published numerous papers on the interface between philosophy, psychology, and religion, including several on Jung's relationship to Jewish mysticism. He is currently completing books on Jung and the Kabbalah and Kabbalah and Postmodern Thought.

# 11

# James Hillman on Language: Escape from the Linguistic Prison

SANFORD L. DROB

For over four decades James Hillman has offered us a vision of psychology that stands apart from and challenges the conventions in our field. While the majority of us have focused on the psychology of the individual, Hillman has taught us to look at "psyche" as it is manifested in the environment and the world; while the field has focused upon cognition and behavior, Hillman has called for a return to meaning and the soul; while psychology has adopted models from biology, cybernetics and economics, Hillman has turned to mythology and alchemy; while clinicians have preoccupied themselves with the unity, health, and normality of the self, Hillman has applauded the experiences of chaos, multiplicity, and pathology; while the field has (more recently) turned its attention to "positive" psychological traits and character virtues, Hillman has asked us to pay careful and loving attention to such things as suicide, bad parenting, money, and incest. While other psychologists have elevated analysis, reflection, and interpretation, Hillman has taken the view that images and fantasy are the carriers of meaning and should not be interpreted and immediately transformed into reified concepts; while psychology has sought to operationalize its constructs, Hillman has urged us to play with ideas. Finally, while psychology has labored to establish itself as a positivistic science, Hillman sees the psyche as immersed in imagination, poetry, and myth, and science itself as one discourse (or myth) among many others.

While each of Hillman's challenges to conventional psychology are of great interest, it is perhaps the general manner in which he deconstructs the ruling discourse in our field that is most valuable and interesting. "My war," Hillman writes, "is with the modes of thought and conditioned feelings that prevail in psychology and therefore also in the way we think and feel about our being."[1] In this essay, I will focus on some of these "deconstructive" aspects of Hillman's thought, and especially upon how his thought provides a challenge to the view, implicit in much psychology and philosophy, that we are unavoidably immersed, and even imprisoned, by the language of our time and culture. I will consider the possibility that Hillman's philosophy of language provides us with one avenue of escape from the "linguistic prison."

It is important, however, to state from the outset that for Hillman, language is of supreme importance. For example, he writes. "Language can express every shade of emotion, that is precisely its beauty—and its power. Deprived of the sense of words our emotional expressions become primitive, physical, and senseless."[2] As we will see, the issue for Hillman is the *kind* of language that we write and speak.

## The Linguistic Prison

The notion that we are somehow "imprisoned" by language, first espoused by Nietzsche,[3] has been a *leitmotif* both in philosophy and psychology since the middle of the last century. For example, Derrida writes in *Of Grammatology*: "The so-called 'thing itself' is always already a *representamen.*"[4] In his *Ecrits*, Lacan writes: "… [I]t is the world of words that creates the world of things,"[5] and Wittgenstein, in the *Philosophical Investigations*, suggests that any "thing" that we speak of is only what it is insofar as it has a role in a culturally determined "language game."[6]

In psychology, the notion of a "linguistic prison" is perhaps less easy to discern than it is in philosophy, but it is equally influential, in the views, for example, that thought and meaning are largely, if not entirely, linguistic; that cognitions, which are spoken about in propositional and sentential terms, control our moods and behavior; that a "thinking disorder" is present when a "patient" deviates radically from conventional discourse; that the "unconscious is structured like a language"; that the "self" is a function of a *narrative* that is adopted by the ego; that we are born into and psychologically situated by a language that structures and thereby constrains our thought, experience, and behavior, etc. While few, if any, psychologists (or psychoanalysts) would subscribe to each of these propositions, as ideas they are each familiar enough to be part of the conventional discourse in our field.[7]

There is, I believe, a powerful prejudice in favor of regarding language as a system complete unto itself, especially amongst philosophers and psychologists, for whom words (rather than, to take just a few examples, images, musical sounds, or for that matter, lumber) constitute their "stock and trade." Philosophical and psychological theories are spoken, and moreover, written; and once speech and language have taken hold, it becomes difficult to escape from the conclusion that there is no absolute distinction between words and the things they presumably represent, and to hold, with Derrida, that "There is nothing outside the text," i.e., that "reality" is itself constructed by and only accessible through language. One speaks and writes on the basis of all the other words, phrases, and texts one has been exposed to and not through any presumed direct connection between one's words and a transcendental signified or "thing-in-itself." This is true whether one is speaking about the objects of everyday life or science, or the images one has experienced in a dream. Words, it is said, obtain their meanings by virtue of their place within a differential matrix in which each word is defined through its contrast with other words (Saussure) or by the role it plays in a "language game" (Wittgenstein). Words, it is argued, do not have direct empirical referents, and must be disambiguated, and only have sense within a "linguistic context." Even in those cases where one can point to an object in the world that presumably corresponds to a given word, one's pointing is inevitably equivocal until it is clarified *via other words*. In considering the relationship between words and things, it is argued that "thing," "experience," "image," "truth," and "reality" are themselves words that *derive their meaning from the place they have in our linguistic discourse*: it is in this sense that the signified (thing) is another signifier (word).[8] On this view, one would have to, in effect, stop speaking, stop using language altogether if one hoped to somehow grasp a "thing" that was "pre- or non-linguisticized" (i.e., that lay completely outside our linguistic conventions), and even then it could no longer be *said* to be a "thing." Certainly, it is argued, one does not grasp a non-linguisticized thing *with words*. Indeed, if signs and signifiers were truly distinct, and words attached themselves directly to objects, unmediated by other words, we would not be able to say or write anything at all because such objects or "transcendental signifieds" would lie completely outside the matrix of language, the very matrix that is the origin of signification. In such a case, one could make a noise or a mark and point to a presumed object, but one would not be able to say what aspect of the thing one was pointing to, what kind of thing it was, and how it differed from other things, etc. In our actual practice, when we point to an object and make meaningful reference to it we do so only because such reference carries with it implications drawn from an entire language.

One of Wittgenstein's disciples, Norman Malcolm, went so far as to argue that a "dream" attains its significance by virtue of the role that "dream reports" play in a language-game and form of life.[9] For Malcolm, it makes no sense to hold that there is a "dream-in-itself" apart from the role that the word "dream" plays in our dream report language games. While "dreams" have certainly taken on new significance with the advent of psychoanalysis and analytical and archetypal psychology, this is only because the "dream report" has been inserted into a new linguistic practice.

## Reality as Presented by Philosophy

According to Derrida, "From the moment that there is meaning there are nothing but signs."[10] We can't *speak* of an object beyond language (the "transcendental object") because once we attempt to do so we have already entered the linguistic order. For these and other reasons, Derrida, Wittgenstein, and other postmodern thinkers are skeptical regarding the claim that philosophical language can provide us with a view of reality "that is more than reality-as-presented-by-philosophical-language." Philosophers and theologians have long been held in thrall by the notion that they can signify that which lies beyond language, but on the postmodern view this is an illusion. It is not that there is no thing-in-itself or experience beyond language,[11] only that we cannot signify it; for the very act of signifying anything already involves us in theory, language, interpretation, etc. Once I say something about a "pure intuition" or even think something about it, this intuition, image, or sensation becomes a part of a language. Consciousness is thus, for both Wittgenstein and Derrida, unable to penetrate to the pure ideality which Husserl and other earlier philosophers had thought they could describe.

In the *Philosophical Investigations* Wittgenstein says: "So in the end when one is doing philosophy one gets to the point where one would like just to emit an inarticulate sound."[12] Wittgenstein, however, holds that even "such a sound is an expression only as it occurs in a language-game." Any gesture toward a transcendental signified is, like a move in the game of chess, only comprehensible as such within a context, a form-of-life/language game that provides it with sense. When we speak of "reality" or the "extra-linguistic" we are inevitably speaking of "reality" and the "extra-linguistic" as it is defined by a certain discourse, theory, politics, and praxis. We can make no claims to contact with the "things themselves" that are not made within the context of some linguistic-cultural-political system. Derrida and Wittgenstein warn us against taking our own system for the "language of being itself" as opposed to just one more human tongue.[13]

## Problems with Linguistic Reality, Narrative Truth

Hillman places himself in opposition to the modern view that the meanings of our words are simply a function of the role they play in our linguistic conventions. He writes:

> In the modern language games of Wittgenstein, words are the very fundamentals of conscious existence, yet they are also severed from things and from truth. They exist in a world of their own. In modern structural linguistics, words have no inherent sense, for they can be reduced, every single one of them, to quasi-mathematical units.[14]

For Hillman, "the word transcends their nominalistic definitions and contexts and evokes in our souls a universal resonance."[15] Indeed, he says that "*words are persons*"[16] and he speaks of the structuralist position as "a suicide of the word."[17]

Hillman has an enormous respect, and even reverence, for language. He does not seek to escape language altogether (and in fact criticizes therapies that seek to replace "talk" as cure) but rather seeks to rescue language from the prison we have made for it, through our "obsession with language and communication,"[18] and the operationalization and technicalization of our (particularly psychological) vocabulary: "After subtly poisoning our own imaginal potency with this language, we complain of a cultural wasteland and loss of soul."[19]

Hillman does not provide a systematic critique of the structuralist and operationalist views of language. Indeed, to enter into formal argument, would, for Hillman, be to speak the very language he regards as "dead" and devoid of meaning and soul. Instead, Hillman draws our attention to a distinction between "logical" and "mythical" language, the former associated with a certain kind of conventional and scientific truth and reality, the latter associated with the truth and reality of the soul.[20] He distinguishes between the language of "expectations, measuring progressions, ego strengthening and weakening, coping and failing," and the imaginal language of the "underworld."[21] Regarding the language of the underworld, Hillman asserts that it is neither certain nor substantial. He writes: "The dead speak differently: they whisper. Their talk has lost its positive substance, its natural certainty. We must lean in close to hear this kind of speech."[22] The language of death is one that "put[s] our dayworld notions to sleep," and involves a radical shift of consciousness that reveals "soul."[23]

Hillman suggests that there is a listening and thus a discourse that exists quite apart from the language games of ordinary, practical life. For Hillman, "because dreaming is imaging, our instrument for undistorted listening can only be the imagination. Dreams call from the imagination to the imagination and can be answered only by the imagination."[24] Hillman suggests that the world we encounter in dreams is our daylight world "in metaphor."[25] He suggests that once we enter "metaphorical modes" of imagining, perceiving, and speaking "we are finally across the bridge and can look back on the all-too-solid brick structure where we live our lives as manmade defenses against the soul, as (quoting Jung) an 'anthropomorphism called reality.'"[26]

## The Language of Psychology and the Speech of the Soul

Hillman is highly critical of the language of contemporary psychology. He distinguishes "the language of psychology from the speech of the soul,"[27] and he is particularly distrustful of the former, its theories, models, diagnoses, psychodynamics, IQ and projective tests, case histories—indeed, all of the "common conventions of the profession."[28] Hillman argues that even psychoanalysis has lost its contact with the soul: "Once depth psychology spoke with a living tongue. ... The Viennese psychoanalysts let the soul freely associate and make its radical, uncouth statements .... The establishment was shocked by its method and its language .... Psychology was in touch with the soul. ... But today, psychology—even depth psychology—is a tool of the establishment."[29] The language of psychoanalysis has become "common currency," and, as such, Hillman tells us, "[t]his language is dead."[30] In a sense, this development was inevitable, for while Freud recognized the distinction between "logical" and "mythical" language, he held that "rational, reifying, or thing-oriented language, even if a derivative and secondary process, was still the preferable 'way of truth' ... [and] reality."[31] Hillman is kinder to Jung, for while Freud turned myth into conceptual language, "Jung dreamt the myth along."[32]

Hillman warns against a purely pragmatic understanding of language and ideas. While today we believe that a "'good idea' is good because it saves time or money or makes things more convenient," such a pragmatization of ideas robs them of their power to generate further ideas, and thus of their "life-generating force."[33] For Hillman, mythical ways of thinking and speaking are valuable precisely because they leave us free to "wonder, question, and imagine"[34] instead of closing things off via theory and definition. Psychopathology is of interest to Hillman, in part "because it names those phenomena which are most threatening to the language and system of mind we call psychology."[35] For Hillman, the psyche can be described with words such as "distortion," "tortured," and "torment," and it is precisely these characteristics that lend it value.

Playing on the Wittgensteinian metaphor, Hillman asks, in *The Myth of Analysis*, why it is that psychology's "language game departed from the soul's play?"[36] Hillman's answer, a few pages later is that "when psychology becomes a specialism and the psyche is set forth in an academic textbook, the soul disappears."[37]

## Questioning the Ruling Discourse

We might say that for Hillman, the notion that reality as "reality" is defined in the "language game," that is, in *conventional discourse*, keeps us unquestioningly within the confines of the "linguistic prison" and threatens to establish a conservatism in thought and experience that stifles cultural change and personal creativity. The idea that the "ruling discourse" should be so privileged or that it provides a window into the "house of being" gave rise to ego-psychology and ordinary language philosophy, the former equating psychological *well-being* with an adaptation to society and its conventions, the latter holding that all that is or can be meant by "truth," "reality," the good," is precisely what we mean and do with these terms in everyday discourse. By relentlessly writing outside the ruling discourse, by imploring us to stick with our uninterpreted experience and images, and by creating new metaphors that deconstruct and expand our conception of the psyche, Hillman has battled against the view that "truth" or "reality" is defined simply by how these terms function in our conventions and prevailing theories. Hillman again contrasts a conventionalist view of language with what he calls a "mythic, metaphoric language," one that is "evocative and detailed, yet not definitive, not productive of dictionaries, textbooks, or even abstract descriptions … [it is] a speech of stories and insights which evoke, in the other who listens, new stories and new insights, the way one poem and one verse ignite another verse and another song."[38]

Hillman writes of an attitude that welcomes ideas and experiences that shatter our conventional ways of thinking and speaking. "At first," he writes, "better the wacky and the weird than ideas whittled down to fit preconceived slots. Here we need courage to face their destructive force, for ideas can also lay waste cherished habits of mind. We now call this destruction of old ideas, politely, 'a paradigm shift.' 'Catastrophe theory' would be more appropriate."[39]

Indeed, it is the possibility of saying something new that is perhaps most significant in Hillman's conception of language. We have seen the very act of writing about "truth" and "reality," either philosophically or psychologically conceived, begins with language and so prejudices the outcome in favor of language that the very possibility of experiencing a non-linguistic "truth" or "reality" is from the outset lost. Indeed, by talking about philosophical or psychological "truth," "reality," etc., and by making philosophical and psychological interpretations one's preferred mode of entry into these "kingdoms," the possibility of actually experiencing or doing something new and unexpected may well be eliminated. Hillman is particularly opposed to what he refers to as routine and allegorical interpretation:

> When images no longer surprise us, when we can expect what they mean and know what they intend, it is because we have our "symbologies" of established meanings.[40]

For Hillman, the problem with all interpretation is that it endeavors to bring an image or fantasy under conceptual, rational control, and in so doing robs it of its potential to surprise frighten, enthrall, puzzle, or otherwise transform our psyche. Hillman famously discusses a patient's dream of a crawling, huge black snake. He tells us:

> ... [T]he moment you've defined the snake, interpreted it, you've lost the snake, you've stopped it and the person leaves the hour with a concept about my repressed sexuality or my cold black passions ....[41]

For Hillman, in order to make soul and meaning one must "keep the snake there." The psyche, by way of the limitless depths of its images, must "threaten the hell out of you" and keep you in the realm of the unknown for as long as possible, for it is in this way that real psychological work can begin. For Hillman, "the true iconoclast is the image itself which explodes its allegorical meanings, releasing startling new insights."[42]

Hillman wants to foster "an attitude toward dreams in which any positive knowledge would be a daylight move, wronging the dream and wronging the soul."[43] He adds: "Essential for working with what is unknown is an attitude of unknowing. This leaves room for the phenomenon itself to speak. It alone may keep us from delusions."[44] For Hillman, "rationalizing interpretations, by attempting to replace the id with the ego, actually work to drain the unconscious, to reduce its size, to empty it out—all of which are hostile acts."[45] Such metapsychological efforts to tame the dream and bring it into the clearing of knowledge and explanation stop the dream from "working in the soul."[46]

Hillman's writings suggest that "reality" is precisely the opposite of that which we conventionally define to be "real." We often speak of "reality testing," as if it were a measure of one's capacity to see and say what everyone else does. Hillman's thoughts on chaos, the image, the dream, and psychopathology, draw attention to the notion that there is a sense in which our linguistic conventions limit our perspective and prevent us from experiencing ourselves and the world. Hillman might say that conventional discourse about "reality" is a social construct that actually screens us from a *pre-linguistic imaginal real*, one that breaks through only when our ordinary discourse is shattered by something traumatic and unexpected, which we can neither assimilate nor accommodate to our ready-made modes of thinking, feeling, and being.

## Metaphor, the "Monstrous," the "Underworld," and the "Real"

Hillman offers us a notion of "linguistic disruption" that suggests a conception of "meaning" and "reality" that is diametrically opposed to how these terms are *conventionally* understood. I would like here to consider briefly several other conceptions of the relationship between meaning and linguistic disruption that may help shed light on our proposed escape from the "linguistic prison" and which help draw out the philosophical implications of Hillman's thought.

For Hillman, images, myths, dreams, archetypes, and metaphors, as opposed to reason and interpretation, are the seat of "meaning" and thus the bearers of soul. Indeed, one could infer from Hillman that conventional discourse, science, and philosophy are devoid of meaning to the extent that they are divorced from the archetypes that find their home in the imagination. The question of how to draw the line around "meaning" is one that has been considered in recent philosophical debates regarding the semantic status of metaphor. For example, the philosopher Mary Hesse held that metaphor, of which myth is one important example, should be included within the categories of meaning, knowledge, and truth.[47] The failure to do so, according to Hesse, leads to the distorted elevation of science over all other avenues of human inquiry. However, in a critique of Hesse's position, Richard Rorty[48] (following Donald Davidson) countered that metaphors have no meaning other than their literal one and that their power lies not in their capacity to open up new vistas of truth or meaning but rather in the fact that they cause us to change our actions, beliefs, and desires. For Rorty, a metaphor "dies" when its meaning is articulated, i.e., when it becomes a vehicle of knowledge. While Rorty here seems to be opposed to Hillman's view that images and metaphors are the true bearers of meaning, his general point, that metaphors prompt us to change our actions, beliefs, and desires, *as long as their meaning is not articulated*, accords well with Hillman's view that the image or the dream is most therapeutic when it stirs our psyche prior to any interpretation.[49]

Derrida uses the term "monstrous" to refer to that which is totally unanticipated, which cannot be assimilated by our categories of discourse, and which thereby disrupts our linguistic and conceptual schema. In particular, he identifies the monstrous with the unpredictable future, writing that the

> ... future is necessarily monstrous: the figure of the future, that is, that which can only be surprising, that for which we are not prepared, you see, is heralded by species of monsters. A future that would not be monstrous would not be a future.[50]

Derrida suggests that the monstrous, impossible future is necessary in order to maintain an open economy of thought; a future that was clearly determined and known would lead to a dogmatism in thought and presumably a closing off of the creative spirit.

Similarly, Lacan uses the term "real" to denote an "unspeakable," "impossible" (to signify) brute reality that lies completely outside of the symbolic order, and which traumatically breaks apart our psychic and linguistic structures. Lacan speaks of

> ... the essential object which isn't an object any longer, but this something faced with which all words cease and all categories fail, the object of anxiety par excellence.[51]

Lacan contrasts the "real" with what he refers to as the "symbolic order," the order in which things are named, assimilated, and known. The symbolic order is actually what is normally referred to as the "real world," and it is no accident that Lacan reverses the usual mode of description. For Lacan, the "real" is associated not only with trauma and anxiety, but also with *desire*.

Derrida's "monstrous" and Lacan's "real" are by definition unsymbolized; they cannot be understood, assimilated, or processed by our current conceptual and linguistic schemes. The "real" may be something primally sexual, painful, or transgressive. It may be a ghastly confrontation with death or the experience of psychosis, or perhaps a profound intuition that one is certain cannot be described. Later in his career, Lacan increasingly identified the "real" with "*petit a*," the "object of desire," but, however understood, for Derrida, and Lacan especially, that which intrudes and disrupts language can never be linguisticized, never be made part of the symbolic order, for to do so would *ipso facto* mean to tame and conventionalize it. By way of contrast, for Hillman, language has the potential to carry within itself the "real" and the "monstrous," and it is only a perverse technicalization of language that has robbed it of this potential. For Hillman, there can be no doubt that what he calls "the underworld" is something of supreme value:

> Something lives in me that is not my own doing. This demon that speaks in dreams and passions and pains will not let go, and I am forced to give recognition to its value for deepening me beyond my usual notion of myself as ego and for bringing my mind a sense of soul and of death.[52]

Hillman asks, "How can anything of worth and soul be conveyed from one psyche to another … if archetypal significances are not carried in the depths of our words?"[53]

Hillman speaks of dreams as having this kind of extra-linguistic (and certainly extra-conventional) thrust and power, and he tells us that one eliminates this power by interpreting the dream and assimilating it to one's "framework." The only way to experience the radical reality/newness of the dream is to allow oneself to be bitten by it as if by a snake, to "seethe in its juices," to be surrounded by its affect, tone, and flavor, to allow its images to "threaten the hell out of you," to keep you in the realm of the unknown for as long as possible. It is paradoxical that one of the best examples of the extra-linguistic *real* is a dream, which normal discourse considers the prime example of an *unreal* illusion. Indeed, one of the best means that the "ruling discourse" (the discourse of the ego) has for protecting itself from an intrusion by an "extra-linguistic object" is to discount all such objects and label them illusions. In doing this, we come to believe that both psychological and philosophical truth and reality are afforded to us within the "clearing" of conventional meaning, when what we desire (and fear) is actually in the unknown "forest" of the yet-to-be-symbolized and the impossible-to-be-rationalized.

## Revisiting the Linguistic Prison

On the basis of Hillman's writings on language, one can conclude that there is indeed an escape from the linguistic prison, from the infinite regress of words that keep us mired in the matrix of conventional language. But unlike Derrida and Lacan, whose writings suggest that any such escape, if there is indeed one at all, lies beyond the realm of language, or Rorty, who suggests that the escape can be symbolized in metaphors that are not, strictly speaking, meaningful, Hillman suggests that at least one avenue of escape from our linguistic prison lies within meaningful language itself, the polyvalent language of myth, metaphor, dreams, pathology, death, and the "underworld."[54] It is the attitude we take toward our experience and the psychological language we use to describe it and not language *per se* that imprisons us. By immersing ourselves in a language that stays with our experience, "sticks to the image," "dreams the dream on," and that does not seek to interpret and thereby assimilate the "underworld," the "monstrous," and the "real" to the schemas of what is already known, we can penetrate beyond conventional discourse and reach beyond a linguistic prison of our own creation.

## *NOTES*

[1] James Hillman, *The Force of Character and the Lasting Life* (New York: Random House, 1999), p. xxiv.

[2] James Hillman, *Kinds of Power* (New York: Doubleday, 1995), p. 12.

[3] Friedrich Nietzsche, *The Will to Power* (New York: Random House, 1967), No. 522.

[4] Jacques Derrida, *Of Grammatology*, trans. G. C. Spivak (Baltimore, MD: Johns Hopkins Press, 1974), p. 49.

[5] Jacques Lacan, *Ecrits: The First Complete Edition in English*, trans. Bruce Fink (New York: W. W. Norton & Company, 2007), p. 229.

[6] Ludwig Wittgenstein, *Philosophical Investigations*, trans. G. E. M. Anscombe (New York: MacMillan, 1953).

[7] For example, over the years there has been a vigorous debate amongst cognitive psychologists regarding several versions of the so-

called "Whorf Hypothesis," the idea that language is not only the vehicle but the determinant of thought. For a recent discussion, see Steven Pinker, *The Stuff of Language: Language as a Window into Human Nature* (New York: Viking, 2007), pp. 124-151.

[8] Lacan writes in *Ecrits*, that "no signification can be sustained except by reference to another signification" (p. 415).

[9] Norman Malcolm, *Dreaming* (London: Routledge and Kegan Paul, 1959).

[10] Derrida, *Grammatology*, p. 50.

[11] Derrida, for example, denies that he is a linguistic idealist. His position is not to deny either "reference" or the "extra-linguistic" but rather to explore critically what these terms mean. He holds that what we ordinarily refer to as "reference" does not lead to anything completely extra-linguistic, but like all other words is in fact governed by the term's place in the quasi-systems of linguistic, political, social, and economic difference that govern its use.

[12] Wittgenstein, par. 261.

[13] Hillman himself has emphasized over and over that there is no singular "text" of reality, and no single interpretation of such a text that can claim to grasp truth. "Babel," Hillman writes, "may be a religious decline from one point of view and it may be a psychological improvement, since through the many tongues a fuller discordant psychic reality is reflected" ("Psychology: Monotheistic or Polytheistic?" in *The New Polytheism*, ed. D. Miller [Dallas, TX: Spring Publications, 1981], p. 116). There is an interesting tension between Hillman's "Babel" view of language and his claim that words evoke a "universal resonance" in our souls. See J. Hillman, *Re-Visioning Psychology* (New York: Harper Perrenial, 1977), p. 9. The discussion of this tension is beyond the scope of this essay.

[14] Hillman, *Re-Visioning Psychology*, p. 8.

[15] *Ibid.*, p. 9.

[16] *Ibid.*

[17] *Ibid.*, p. 8.

[18] *Ibid.*

[19] James Hillman, *The Myth of Analysis: Three Essays in Archetypal Psychology* (New York: Harper & Row, 1978), p. 205.

[20] *Ibid.*, p. 18.

[21] James Hillman, *The Dream and the Underworld* (New York: Harper Perrenial, 1979), p. 44.

[22] *Ibid.*, p. 50.

[23] *Ibid.*, p. 66.

[24] *Ibid.*, p. 55.

[25] *Ibid.*

[26] *Ibid.*, p. 193.

[27] Hillman, *Myth of Analysis*, p. 119.

[28] *Ibid.*, p. 120.

[29] *Ibid.*, pp. 121-122.

[30] *Ibid.*, p. 122.

[31] *Ibid.*, p. 118.

[32] *Ibid.*

[33] Hillman, *Kinds of Power*, p. 8.

[34] *Ibid.*, pp. 103-104.

[35] Hillman, *Myth of Analysis*, p. 121.

[36] *Ibid.*, p. 123.

[37] *Ibid.*, p. 130.

[38] *Ibid.*, p. 206.

[39] Hillman, *Kinds of Power*, p. 23.

[40] Hillman, *Re-Visioning Psychology*, p. 8.

[41] James Hillman, *Inter Views: Conversations Between James Hillman and Laura Pozzo on Therapy, Biography, Love, Soul, Dream, Work, Imagination and the State of the Culture* (New York: Harper & Row, 1983), p. 53.

[42] Hillman, *Re-Visioning Psychology*, p. 8.

[43] Hillman, *Dream and the Underworld*, p. 193.

[44] *Ibid.*, p. 194.

[45] James Hillman, *Insearch, Psychology and Religion,* 2nd ed. (Woodstock, CT: Spring Publications, 1994), p. 59.

[46] Hillman, *Dream and the Underworld*, p. 200.

[47] Mary Hesse, "The Cognitive Claims of Metaphor," in *Metaphor and Religion*, ed. J. P. van Noppen (Brussels: Universiteit Brussel, 1983).

[48] Richard Rorty, "Unfamiliar Noises: Hesse and Davidson on Metaphor," in *Objectivism, Relativism, and Truth: Philosophical Papers,* vol. 1 (Cambridge, UK: Cambridge University Press, 1991), pp. 162-174.

[49] The Davidson-Rorty view suggests that metaphors invite action rather than represent truths and ideas. On the other hand, such thinkers as Hegel, Ricoeur, and more recently, Wolfgang Giegerich, have held that "symbols invite thought." While I have no intention of

attempting to resolve this issue here, my own view is that metaphor is both a call to action *and* a revelation of meaning, wisdom and *gnosos*, and that a dialectical relationship exists between these two modes (the ethical and the epistemological). Each is prior to and foundational for the other. Action, will, and desire are both prior to and dependent upon truth and knowledge.

[50] Jacques Derrida, *Points ... Interviews, 1974-94*, ed. Elizabeth Weber, trans. Peggy Kamuf *et al.* (Stanford, CA: Stanford University Press, 1995), pp. 386-387. See also, Jacques Derrida, "Deconstruction and the Other," in *Dialogues with Contemporary Continental Thinkers*, ed. R. Kearney (Manchester, UK: Manchester University Press, 1984), p. 123.

[51] See Jacques Lacan, *The Seminar of Jacques Lacan, Book II: The Ego in Freud's Theory and in the Technique of Psychoanalysis 1954-1955*, ed. Jacques-Alain Miller, trans. Sylvana Tomaselli (New York: W. W. Norton, 1998), p. 164.

[52] Hillman, *Myth of Analysis*, p. 5.

[53] Hillman, *Re-Visioning Psychology*, p. 9.

[54] Hillman's view suggests, however, that engaging in, appreciating, and meditating upon (as opposed to analyzing and interpreting) music, art, and nature, may also be paths out of the prison of linguistic and ideational convention, and strong vehicles for deepening soul.

GREG MOGENSON is a Jungian psychoanalyst practicing in London, Ontario, Canada and the editor of the Studies in Archetypal Psychology Series of Spring Journal Books. The author of many articles in the field of analytical psychology, his books include *A Most Accursed Religion*, *The Dove in the Consulting Room*, *Northern Gnosis*, *Greeting the Angels*, and (with David Miller and Wolfgang Giegerich) *Dialectics & Analytical Psychology*.

# 12

# Hillman and the Syzygy

GREG MOGENSON

> Shahrazad turned to King Shahrayar and said,
> "May I have your permission to tell a story?"

When I think of the thousand and one articles and books, lectures and interviews that the honoree of this volume has created, I am immediately put in mind of that most sumptuous example of the syzygy motif, the Shahrazad/King Shahrayar relation, which is featured in the frame story of *The Arabian Nights.*[1] It is a worthy comparison. Imaginative and writerly, Hillman's work not only lends itself to being read in the light of the love-relation which is figured in that Persian tale, it also returns the favor, shedding a light of its own upon the storied conversations of that imaginal couple even as it continues their pillow-talk by other means. This, at any rate, it will be my task to show here. But first that word "syzygy." We need to have an understanding of this term, and of the motif that bears its name, before turning to our topic proper, the Shahrazad/King Shahrayar-like relation that plays through the pages of *The Hillmanian Nights.*

## S-G-Z-Y-Y-Y ?

Recently introduced into popular parlance by Scrabble players who would make an extreme sport of that board game, the word S-Y-Z-Y-

G-Y has had a long and venerable history. In astronomy and astrology, for example, it has been used since ancient times to refer to celestial configurations in which two planetary bodies orbit as a pair in relation to a third. Elaborating upon this tradition, the Gnostics used the term to refer to complementary male-female pairs of aeons or emanations of God such as Truth & Love, Thought & Power, Grace & Silence. And they were by no means the only ones to present the complex relations by which Being is structured in a personified and gendered manner. The gods in Greek mythology were also represented as interacting with one another according to a syzygial logic of gendered tandems—as Hera and Zeus, Aphrodite and Ares, Artemis and Apollo, and so on. Personified precursors of what in later history become the categories of metaphysics and the concepts of philosophy, the essence of these deities lay in the relations that the stories of their pairings disclosed. Also worth mentioning here are those cosmogonic principles of classical Chinese philosophy, the masculine *Yang* and feminine *Yin*. According to this Eastern worldview, everything may be understood in terms of the complementary interplay of these powers and principalities. And then there is the plenitude, the profusion even, of literary references: Anthony and Cleopatra, Romeo and Juliet, Aeneas and Dido, Tristan and Isolde, Professor Higgins and Eliza Doolittle—et cetera, et cetera, on and on.

It was Jung, of course, who first introduced the term "syzygy" into psychology. Impressed by the ubiquity of the motif, Jung ascribed to it the status of an archetype. "We can safely assert," he writes, "that these syzygies are as universal as the existence of man and woman. … [M]an's imagination is bound by this motif, so that he [has been] largely compelled to project it again and again, at all times in all places."[2]

Now, what Jung states here with respect to the imagination generally is true as well of *psychology's* imagination in particular. It, too, is bound by the syzygy motif. One expression of this, of course, is the emphasis in the depth psychologies upon the phenomenon of the transference and even the birth of these psychologies from the depths of this phenomenon. We may think in this connection of those most famous exemplars of the motif from the annals of our analytic tradition—Breuer & Anna O., Freud & Dora, Jung & Spielrein. Psychoanalysis, as I have argued elsewhere,[3] may readily be regarded as the love-child of these and still other syzygial pairings, right down to the present day.

But how, it may be asked, must the psyche be constituted for analysts and their patients to be drawn into such passions in the first place? Are the syzygial dialectics of the consulting room really to be accounted for by our being subject to the Oedipus complex and its parental pair, as Freud opined, or by the asymmetrical interiorization, along gender-political lines, of the aforementioned "universal ... existence of man and woman," as Jung maintained?

With this question, asked in a manner that sets aside the most ready and clichéd answers, an even more fundamental syzygy is brought to light. Logically prior to the transferences that act it out, this syzygy operates at the theoretical level, the level of psychology itself. I refer here to what might be called *the syzygial manner in which the relation between perspective and phenomenon, interpretation and "fact," self and other must be figured in a discipline for which an objective, Archimedean vantage point is unavailable.*

As Jung repeatedly emphasized, psychology's constituting conundrum resides in the fact that it does not possess an objective or external standpoint from which the psyche may be viewed.[4] "Subject" and "object," "observer" and "observed," far from being abstractly separable, stand in an internal, interchangeable, one-in-the-other (or better, one-as-the-other) relation. When, for example, psychology as subject speaks about the psyche, its manner of doing so has always the character, and embarrassingly so, of a slip of the tongue or a parapraxis of the pen. And this is the case even when the most exacting efforts have been made to observe objectively and reason soundly. Even then the discipline's foot lands in its mouth inasmuch as the theories it proposes and the interpretations it expounds are themselves but the further expression of the psychic process they were adduced to explain. As Jung put it in an early notebook entry, "I failed to consider that the soul cannot be the object of my judgement and knowledge; rather, my judgement and knowledge are the objects of my soul."[5]

Jung's humbling insight here into the slippery reversals and hermeneutic circlings that psychological reflection is both prone to and produced by is of immense importance for the discipline he helped to found. Succinctly stated, it is indispensable that psychology, giving up all illusions about objectivity, embrace the recursive, table-turning logic of its self-relation, for only in this way—with its teeth set deeply in its own tail—can it plumb the soulful interiority in which its lack of Archimedean distance and remove opens and engulfs it.

This is not to say, however, that the discipline has done so. On the contrary, keeping Jung's insight in the status of the proverbial stone that the builders rejected, most psychologies, down to the present day, cling to a naïvely empirical mindset by making an ersatz Archimedean position out of this or that psychic phenomenon that they deem to be of especial importance. Ironically, while having learned from Freud and his rejection of the seduction theory that trauma and abuse are not the basis of hysteria, psychology continues to hystericize its subject matter, seduced by any number of other theories of what psychic life is based upon. Is it any wonder, given psychology's resistance to its own recursiveness, that this—its self-ravishing/self-subverting, "he said/she said" dialectic—is displaced into the consulting room to be enacted by that latest of syzygial pairs, the analyst and patient?[6]

## Anima and Animus

But what about those most famous figures that Jung refers to in relation to the syzygy motif, those personified notions, as Hillman has referred to them,[7] the anima and animus? As the living composites of all that we have discussed thus far, these figures are part and parcel of Jung's *psychological* conception of the syzygy. Why then have we not mentioned them until now?

In keeping with the deferral strategy we will discuss below in connection with Shahrazad and the King, explicit reference to Jung's notion of the anima and animus has been left until this point so that our sense of these, and of the syzygy that they constitute, will not be foreclosed upon by their popular definition.

Popularly understood, the anima and animus are contra-sexual aspects of the human personality, the anima designating the inner woman in a man, the animus the complementary inner masculine figure in a woman. Trading in such clichés, many men today refer to their "feminine side," many women to their "masculine side." And this is to say nothing of the pivotal role that this gender-blending heuristic plays in the New Age spirituality and boutique psychotherapies of our day.

The merit of this fashion (if merit there is) is that gender stereotypes are challenged and our self-identicalness as the persons we take ourselves to be is thrown into question in a basic way. But this said, it must also be pointed out that as far as the *notion* of the anima/animus is concerned, the larger aspect of this syzygial concept is terribly short-changed when its gender metaphor is taken literally, as if men's and women's issues were what it is about.[8]

The rub here is readily understood when we think of the aforementioned Gnostic aeons, the Chinese *Yin* and Y*ang* principles, and the Gods and Goddesses that are paired together in myth. When these syzygies are reduced to parts of us, psychology's conception of the soul falls victim to the euhemerist fallacy. Drastically down-sized, the once great figures of the syzygy are regarded as residing in the human breast. The mystery of Being is forgotten.

True, this too-reductive, too-personalistic conception of the anima and animus has its source in Jung, who frequently talked in this manner himself; however, it was also Jung, with the above-mentioned epistemological considerations and phenomenological wealth in mind, who expressly advised against such a conception when he stated, "it often seems advisable to speak less of *my* anima or *my* animus and more of *the* anima and *the* animus."[9] Overcoming this apparent contradiction, we could say with Hillman that far from being *ours*, anima and animus are that which makes the impersonal (whatever that may be in any particular instance) feel personal even as they mediate for us, as creatures of desire, what Jung called the compensatory potential of the archetypal psyche. As Hillman writes,

> To speak of *my* anima and *my* soul expresses the personalistic fallacy. Although these archetypal experiences of the personal give salt and substance to my personal individuality, making me feel that there is indeed a soul, this "me-ness" is not mine. To take such experiences literally as mine puts the anima inside me and makes her mine. The more profoundly archetypal my experiences of soul, the more I recognize how they are beyond me, presented to me, a present, a gift, even while they feel my most personal possession. Under the domination of the anima our soulfulness makes us feel unique, special, meant—yet paradoxically this is when we are least individual and most collective. For such experiences derive from the archetype of the personal, making us feel both archetypal and personal at the same instant.[10]

## The Killer and the Story-Teller

We now come to our topic proper, the comparison that was drawn at the outset between Hillman's writings and the frame story of *The Arabian Nights*.

The principal anima/animus syzygy in that story is given in the figures of the highly educated and refined Vizier's daughter, Shahrazad, and the mad king, Shahrayar. In barest summary, we are informed that the King was driven to a murderous rage by a most ungodly spectacle: the sight of his wife cavorting in the arms of an enormous Black slave! Incensed by his wife's wanton infidelity, Shahrayar had her put to death. But this action was by no means sufficient to assuage his wrath. Having convinced himself in the immediate aftermath of this event that "there is not a single chaste woman anywhere on the entire face of the earth,"[11] the wounded king broadened the reach of his fury, marrying each night another woman, having his way with her, and then killing her the following day. Many women met their end in this way, the daughters of merchants and the intended brides of common men. Night after night it was the same routine, another marriage, another murder. But one day the daughter of the King's Vizier, the aforementioned maiden, Shahrazad, astonished her father by *volunteering* to marry the murderous Shahrayar! Worried for his daughter's life, the Vizier attempted to dissuade her. But the young woman was determined; there could be no stopping her. And besides, the King had by then learned of Shahrazad's seemingly mad request. His curiosity was piqued, his interest aroused!

We may be put in mind by what happened next of a familiar colloquial expression. When someone has survived an ordeal or come through a calamity we commonly speak of their having "lived to tell the tale." In Shahrazad's case this expression resounds with a surpassing vibrancy. For not only did she, intrepid maiden that she was, survive to tell her tale; already and in advance of this, while in the very midst of her ordeal, she survived by telling tales, the many tales that make up the canon of *The Arabian Nights*!

It was a brilliant strategy. Retiring to bed with the King, Shahrazad wept as he fondled her. Wondering what had become of her earlier enthusiasm, the King demanded an explanation. "I have a sister, and wish to bid her goodbye before daybreak," Shahrazad explained. Accommodating this request, Shahrayar had the sister, Dinarzad, summoned to the marriage chamber, where she was made to wait beneath the bed. Pleased that her sister was with them (as this was vital to her plan) Shahrazad surrendered to the violent amor of her husband. All night long she lay with him, her prowess and beauty stoking his fury to a feverish intensity. Never before had Shahrayar known such wantonness in a woman! Never, that is to say, except when, *horribile dictu,* he had seen his wife, the Queen, with her eyes rolling back and her toes curled, calling out to her slave-lover to enter her and not to stop!

Whore! Slut! Prostitute!—the text does not tell us the expletives that the King called out as the lash-stroke of these terrible images cut into his mind. Nor does it give us the details of how the comely Shahrazad rollicked beneath her cursing lord as he rode her like some war-horse of revenge. But we can easily imagine the tumult of that night!—the people outside, frightened as the sounds of a slaughterhouse or battlefield reached them from the marriage-chamber, and the couple inside, fucking like a house on fire!

But Shahrazad had not given herself in vain, neither then with King Shahrayar in the pages of *The Arabian Nights*, nor here in these pages as a figure through whom Hillman's writings may be insighted.

Just before dawn, when the commotion above her head had finally grown still, Dinarzad called out from beneath the bed, "Sister, if you are not sleepy, tell us one of your lovely little tales to while away the night, before I bid you good-bye at daybreak, for I don't know what will happen to you tomorrow."[12] This, of course, was according to Shahrazad's plan. Days before she had instructed her sister to make this request when the moment came.

Fortunately for all concerned, the King consented. A story could be told. Seizing the opportunity, Shahrazad chose an especially intriguing one from out of her vast repertoire and warmed to its telling. Content-wise the story had a certain analogical pertinence to her situation with the king. It concerned a prosperous merchant who was accosted while on a business trip by a great demon who was intent upon killing him. Blaming the merchant for the death of his son (even as Shahrayar blamed all women for his wife's infidelity), the demon held his sword over him, poised to strike. But at this point in the story, which she had built up to with much suspense, Shahrazad lapsed into silence. Morning had arrived; it was now her execution that was to be the order of the day! The King, however, was burning with curiosity.

And as he continued to be filled with rage, this presented him with a dilemma. If he killed Shahrazad as had been planned, why, he would not find out what happened with the merchant and the demon!

Wanting to hear the rest of the tale, Shahrayar postponed the execution. Another night of love-making and story-telling was agreed upon. And this in its turn was followed by many others, for each night Shahrazad made sure that there was still more to tell by daybreak. As legend has it, it was in this way—by fascinating the king with her thousand and one tales—that Shahrazad eventually effected his healing, saving her life and the lives of many others as well.

## The Hillmanian Nights

With titles such as "The Fisherman and the Demon," "The Enchanted King," and "The Porter and the Three Ladies," Shahrazad told tales of envious bewitchments, mad jealousies, sexual caprice, and many other topics of age-old psychological interest. Like dreams within a dream, each of these tales leads into another while at the same time partaking in that quintessential story, the story I have just recounted of Shahrazad's own death-defying marriage to the King.

A very similar dynamic is at play in Hillman's writings. In books and essays with such titles as *Re-Visioning Psychology*, *Suicide and the Soul*, "Silver and the White Earth," and *Loose Ends* (to name only a few of my favorites), Hillman has explored such wide-ranging topics as suicide, masturbation, abandonment, and betrayal; nightmare, paranoia, pornography, and schism; incest, transgression, nostalgia, and recovery; war, beauty, ecology, and citizenship; alchemy, animals, and the narcissism of analysis, etc. Inclusive of each other, this pantheon of topics is part and parcel of a highly imaginative, and at the same time, highly iconoclastic turn in Jungian thought, to which Hillman has given the name, "Archetypal Psychology." And herein lies the comparison that I am drawing in this paper. As the "frame story" in which Hillman's works have been written, archetypal psychology has also had to do with the Shahrazad-like efforts of its founder to survive as a writer and to stay psychological by again and again turning the tables upon the Shahrayar that he finds in the literalism, positivism, and monocular vision that so readily attaches itself to these topics and themes in psychology and culture today.

## AMBIVALENT BEGINNINGS

Many passages from Hillman's writings could be cited here to substantiate the characterization of his work that I have just given. I offer, instead, a personal story.

Decades ago, when I was in my early twenties, I happened upon Hillman's 1979 book, *The Dream and the Underworld.*[13] I well remember the uncanny feeling that crept over me as I gazed upon its deathly cover-image. It was a feeling of revulsion mingled with attraction, excitement with dread. Steeped in Jung's writings, I knew very little at that time of other Jungian authors, and nothing at all of "post-Jungians" such as Hillman. Like a crotchety old man (or angry young one[14]), I railed against that epithet, "post-Jungian." Why, if I remember correctly, I think I may have even spat!

To my credit, though, I bought the book.

When subsequently I came round to reading it, I found that with each page my ambivalent feelings became more and more unwieldy. While I was immediately taken by the intelligence and poetic style of the book, I was also threatened by Hillman's critique of various Jungian ideas to which I was happily wedded at that time.

Finally, it was all too much for me. Spitting again, I wrote a poison letter to its author (a letter not unlike some of those that I now occasionally receive from readers of my books!). Although I did not keep a copy of this missive, I vaguely recall having chastized Hillman for contesting the merits of Jung's notion of compensation, and perhaps also for his dismissive view of Jung's psychology of the Self that I had there sniffed out. How could he dispute these things? I irritably complained.

Looking back from the present vantage point, I can fairly say that Shahrayar's horror at seeing his wife in the love-grip of that Black slave could not have been more than my ire with Hillman for playing so fast and loose with *my* Jung! And yet, vexed as I was, I was attracted all the same. Who was this analyst-author who was making off with *my* anima even as I, with fascinated horror, bought and read another of his books?

A few weeks later, a letter from Dallas arrived in the mail. Hillman had written back! "It's all right to have troubles of mind: certainties are luxuries that should come from the animal base of our lives and not from truths, proposition, and beliefs, else we too easily get delusional. Hence I work so hard at deliteralizing ... then what's left is that animal sense."[15]

"Deliteralizing"—that, I believe, is what Shahrazad did for the mad King, and what Hillman had now begun to do with me. Consulting my recently purchased copy of *Re-Visioning Psychology*, I easily connected this term up with what is there referred to as "Psychologizing or Seeing Through." Pen in hand, I underlined the following passage:

> *Psychologizing goes on whenever reflection takes place in terms other than those presented.* It suspects an interior, not evident intention; it searches for a hidden clockwork, a ghost in the machine, an etymological root, something more than meets the eye; or it sees with another eye. It goes on whenever we move to a deeper level.[16]

Another passage from the same chapter struck me and I marked it, too:

> ... [A]n adequate psychology must be one that cannot take itself or any of its ideas literally. Its fantasy of itself must be one that allows psychologizing to continue as an open process of ideation. It may not be based upon axioms and laws, or even rely upon hypotheses. Instead it will have to consist of fictions [cf. the tales of Shahrazad!].[17]

There was more to my letter to Hillman and more to his response to me as well. At the end of my letter I had also recounted a dream that I had recently had. In the dream, an attractive unknown woman put the question to me, "Would you treat your life like work or like a woman?" Without the slightest hesitation, I answered proudly, "Like work!" But upon hearing these words the woman looked sad and disappointed.

It was a disconcerting dream. Though I had espoused one of my highest values, my pride in this, evidently, was the woman's shame. Puzzled by this contradiction (and thinking it might also reflect somehow my engagement with Hillman's texts), I wondered what light he might have to shed upon it.

Responding with a brevity comparable to that of the dream itself, Hillman advised, "... [E]njoy your day as work and as a woman, both. No need to cut woman from work or work from woman, is there?"[18]

Pleased that my cry from the wilderness had been heard, I became an avid reader of Hillman's works, paying especial attention to the themes he had touched upon in his letter.

The first of these themes—deliteralizing—has already been discussed. As for the woman of my dream and Hillman's comment about the exchange I'd had with her, I found sections on anima in the chapter, "Personifying and Imagining Things" of *Re-Visioning Psychology* to be especially pertinent.

> The movement through the constructed world of concepts and dead things into an animistic, subjective, mythical consciousness, where fantasy is alive in a world alive and means 'me,' follows anima. She teaches personifying, and the very first lesson of her teaching is the reality of her independent personality over and against the habitual modes of experiencing with which we are so identified that they are called, ego, I.[19]

There was another passage that I marked:

> To experience imaginal reality, a psychic function—the specific function of the imaginative soul—must be active. This soul person is the person of our moods, self-reflections, and reveries, of our sensuous longing beyond the sensately concrete, the spinner of fantasy who is the personification of all unknown psychic capacities that lie waiting, drawing us seductively, uncannily inward to the dark of the uncut forest and the deeps below the waves.[20]

It did not take long before my ire with Hillman left me and I became an aficionado of his work. But even with this development, the dialectic of deliteralizing continued. Sometimes in my dreams his image would appear. In my first years as a reader of his work, I dreamt that Hillman was wearing a long pleated skirt. Whenever I approached him, he quickly stood aside, skirting my advances as deftly as a matador whisking his cape away before a charging bull! Much later, when I was in the midst of my analytic training, I dreamt that he was at one of our Society conferences, while I, like some Jacob attempting to steal his father's blessing (Gen. 27: 1-46), walked around the lecture hall with animal hides lashed to my forearms! Reflectively mediated by a tricksterish, Shahrazad-like anima, a syzygy of puer and senex was played out for many years between writer and reader, analyst and analyst-candidate, publisher and would-be author.

## Imagistic Iconoclasm

Having indicated with these few youthful anecdotes of mine something of what it means, after Hillman, to "learn psychoanalysis on oneself" (Freud[21]), I now return to more strictly theoretical issues.

The adequacy of a psychology—we have heard this already from Hillman—resides in its capacity to interpret the phenomena with which it is concerned while seeing through itself at the same time.[22] In archetypal psychology, this capacity is manifest in the syzygial interplay of those constituting moments of psychological reflection that I introduced with my personal story, the ANIMA of "Personifying or Imagining Things" and the ANIMUS of "Psychologizing," "Deliteralizing" and "Seeing-Through."[23]

Now it is one thing to insist upon this interplay, pointing out as I have its ubiquity in man's cultural products; it is quite another to be up to what such a relation requires. Indeed, like the children discussed by Freud, who had developed a sadistic conception of parental love-making, we may lag behind our psychology, finding it difficult to see the *play* in it at all.[24]

Much of our resistance here has to do with clinging to illusions. Fearing what would happen if what we imagine soul to be were to be contradicted in some way, we are as troubled by this prospect as was Freud's beloved patient, the Wolf Man, by the spectacle of his parents in coitus. The syzygy at the back of things, we fretfully wonder, is it erasing us or making us?

These anxieties have also a deeper resonance. I refer here to the fact that on the face of it at least, imagining and deliteralizing are contradictory gestures, even as the title of this section, "Imagistic Iconoclasm," is an oxymoron. Meeting up with this strange angel, we are likely to veer sideways. Aligning ourselves now with its one side, now with its other, we would stave off the transgressive, category-defying threat that its self-sameness/self-difference brings to the reality sense of the ego—Oedipal anxieties serving as a handy defence against the poetic fright and even metaphysical horror through which a truly *psychological* psychology announces its, not our, arrival.[25]

But as Hillman goes on to propose, what I here am calling the syzygy of "Imagining Things" and "Deliteralizing" can also be conceptualized in terms of those related, even simultaneous moments of the soul's making, "Pathologizing or Falling Apart" and "De-humanizing or Soul-Making."[26] Defined as "the psyche's autonomous ability to create illness, morbidity, disorder, abnormality, and suffering in any aspect of its behavior and to experience and imagine life through this deformed and afflicted perspective,"[27] pathologizing is a process that undermines and disassembles the defensive, self-identical ego at the behest of psychic possibilities and archetypal imperatives that it had hitherto effaced or neglected. Also known as "De-humanizing," this imaginatively deliteralizing movement into depth leads at the same time out beyond the human even as in times of illness or calamity the Greeks of antiquity inquired of their oracles, "To what God or hero should I sacrifice?"[28]

As Hillman has expressed this in a passage that gives us further insight into what is healing about Shahrazad's fictions and Shahrazad-like about archetypal psychology's therapeutic return to myth,

> When I am in despair, I do not want to be told of re-birth; when I am aging and decaying and the civilization around me is collapsing from its over-growth that is over-kill, I cannot tolerate that word "growth", and when I am falling to bits in my complexities, I cannot abide the defensive simplistics of mandalas, nor the sentimentalities of individuation as unity and wholeness. These are formulae presented through a fantasy of opposites—the disintegration shall be compensated by integration. But what of cure through likeness where like takes care of like? I want the right background to the failure of life; I want to hear with precision of those Gods who are served by and thrive upon and can hence provide an archetypal background to and even an eros connection with the defeat, decay, and dismemberment, because these dominants would reflect the *experienced* psyche (not in its Aristotelian conceptualization as belonging to life), but in the actuality of its only known goal which is also both its way and its substance, death.[29]

## Reflecting Simultaneity into Itself

I stated at the outset that Hillman's work not only lends itself to being read in the light of the story of Shahrazad and the King, but sheds a light of its own upon their syzygial relation even as it continues this by other means. With this claim for a palimpsest, we then touched briefly upon those key gestures of Hillman's re-visioning of psychology project—"Personifying or Imagining Things," "Psychologizing or Seeing-Through," "Pathologizing," and "De-humanizing." As animating as they are deliteralizing, these concepts, it is important to stress, far from being abstract, are always the result of a story's being turned around upon itself. For only in this way, through the reiteration of what is given in a story, can the torch that Hillman brings to bear (which is never a light from outside) be kindled in the first place.

But what *is* the given story? Or, to get to the level of reflection that we need to reach here, what is the *given* in *any* story? The details—is that the answer? Well, yes, of course, we must "stick to the image." But still it must be asked: *how* are these details given by the forest of which they are the trees?

The question I raise here is prompted by a basic consideration of dream interpretation—the difference between our dreams as they were dreamt and our recollection of them. While dreams, to be sure, are the very stuff of soul, the way we recall them upon waking, record them in our journals, or tell them to a friend or analyst is always and inevitably a function of the defences and affinities of the ego. It is the same with myths and stories.[30] With them, too, the narrative form is the egoic version of the irrepresentable (but by no means unfathomable) image that is their life and depth and soul.[31]

Quickly indicating what is at stake here, I need only mention that mono-myth or mono-interpretation that is all too frequently bandied about in Jungian publications and training programs, the one that sees in almost every dream, story, or life scenario the abuse, denigration, or neglect of the Feminine principle at the hands of a supposedly malevolent Patriarchy, even as, conversely, it regards the Feminine to be the panacea for every individual and collective ill.[32] Applying this formula to the frame story of *The Arabian Nights*, "Da-Vinci-Code Jungians," as I have come to call the purveyors of this supposedly world re-enchanting narrative, would surely claim to find in it an historical precursor of the Dan Brown bestseller!

But psychology is betrayed when interpretation and image-work follow the ego (or *create* ego) by taking sides in this dissociative, undialectical, and gender-literalizing manner. Commenting upon this tendency, Hillman has referred to Jung's observation that in "psychic actuality 'the two figures [anima and animus] are always tempting the ego to identify itself with them.'"[33]

A psychology that is *truly* psychological, by contrast, begins with the recognition that the two sides, for all their difference, are moments of each other, one and the same. Echoing Jung's early notebook entry about the soul not being the object of our judgment and knowledge (except as, at the same time, our judgment and knowledge are the objects of the soul), Hillman avers, "We cannot take any stand regarding anima without … taking up an animus position. There is no *other* vantage point toward either than the other."[34] "*To be engaged with anima is to be engaged simultaneously with animus in some way or another.*"[35]

A crucial insight, this. As the bringing together of *psyche* (anima) and *logos* (animus), psychology, for Hillman, is the syzygial relation itself. And this, moreover, in free-fall manner, psychology beginning (for lack of an Archimedean point of anchorage) as its own headlong plunge right under the covers with Shahrazad and the King!

Illustrating the dynamics of this "syzygy consciousness," as he calls it, Hillman writes,

> During anima imagining of whatever sort … an animus spirit rises up and begins to criticize. Precisely here is the origin of the critical spirit as that part of fantasy that detaches itself, abstracts, makes comparison, and looks down. The animus serves soul by separating mind from mood to gain distance. However, as an animus bound in tandem with anima, this critical spirit still retains traces of moodiness, now "objectified" into opinion. So it is not altogether free of subjectivism. (Little wonder that critics seem anima-ridden and opinionated, both.) The objective spirit, that goal of our Western intellectual endeavor, is an attempt of the soul to free itself by means of the animus from the valley of its attachments. And the figure in dreams who judges is the one who both frees us from anima imprisonments and sentences us with his opinions.[36]

## Brotherly Cuckolds All

Pages being few, we must limit ourselves to only one further reflection, though many more would be possible.

In the abbreviated account that I gave of the story of Shahrazad and the King, I neglected to mention that the King had a brother. The sovereign of a neighboring state, Shahzaman, as this brother was called, shared something of Shahrayar's fate, for he too was a cuckold!

Narratively speaking, it happened like this. Longing to have Shahzaman visit, Shahrayar sent his Vizier to fetch him. Delighted by the invitation, Shahzaman set about readying himself for the journey. It was then, while in the course of making these preparations, that he stumbled upon his wife in the arms of a kitchen boy!

Shahzaman's shock was great and a depression ensued. Travelling to his brother's kingdom, he pondered dispiritedly the depravity of women. When finally he arrived at Shahrayar's palace, he found that his happiness at being with his brother did nothing to lighten his mood. Glum and wasting away, he could not always accompany Shahrayar on the daily hunting expeditions. And it was on one of these days, while he was home alone in his quarters, that Shahzaman witnessed his sister-in-law's infidelity with the slave. Of course, he was affronted by what he saw and concerned for this brother, but strangely he also found that his own mood immediately improved. His fate, evidently, was not his alone![37]

When Shahrayar returned from his hunting trip, he noticed Shahzaman's happier demeanor and pressed him to explain (even as at another moment of the story he pressed Shahrazad to account for her tears). With great reluctance, Shahzaman told him what he had witnessed. And so it was that Shahrayar's suspicions regarding his own wife were aroused, which subsequently led to his seeing her wanton infidelity with his own eyes.

Now for readers of *The Arabian Nights* these early details of the frame story are a first indication that the story as a whole may be turned around upon itself and read in a reflexive manner. For in the same way that the hands in the well-known M. C. Escher drawing produce themselves by sketching each other, so the brothers Shahzaman and Shahrayar are the source of each other's awareness of having been cuckolded by their wives. Their relation is a syzygial relation, just as much so as is the relation between Shahrayar and Shahrazad. It fact, it is already the Shahrayar/Shahrazad relation in another of its aspects, there being, as we heard from Hillman, "no *other* vantage point toward either than the other."

But what of archetypal psychology? With its concepts of "syzygy consciousness" (Hillman), "full simultaneity of the image" (Berry[38]), and "the tautological presupposition of myth interpretation" (Giegerich[39]), archetypal psychology is well equipped to appreciate that this story, far from being a mere narrative of the ego, is a multifaceted and inwardly self-mirroring document of the soul. Is there then something Shahzaman-and-Shahrayar-like about it, too?

Again I confine myself to a single example, an exchange between James Hillman and Wolfgang Giegerich that began in 1988 in the pages of *Spring Journal*.[40] Longtime friends and colleagues, Hillman and Giegerich engaged with each other in a dispute having to do with the important question of how the discourse of psychology (JH) must be logically constituted (WG) for it to adequately serve the soul's needs (JH) through a mode of reflection that is truly psychological (WG).

"Joust[ing] with Giegerich," Hillman challenges his friend's view that psychological consciousness must undertake a weighty, logic-transforming labor if it is to overcome the subject-object split that contradictorily continues to inhere in the very insights and ideas through which psychology supposes itself to have overcome that split—ideas such as the *unus mundus*, the oneness of psyche and matter, synchronicity, and, most precious of all to Hillman, *anima mundi*. Wittily dishing his colleague's plea for more Hegel, Hillman argues that with his "stubborn ascetic insistence on getting through [the subject here, object there problem] without fraud," Giegerich has gotten himself caught in that very split, since whatever one regards as being the "real problem" (in Giegerich's case the *logic* of psychology) is the "best clue to where we are literal ...."[41]

A mind as subtle as Giegerich's, however, cannot be so easily skirted. And we can suspect that Hillman's charging him with literalism is playfully intended as a provocation to bring Giegerich, the author of *Animus-Psychologie*, more forcefully into the fray. And this it does, but not before Hillman tosses down another gauntlet in the form of the happy declaration, "Aren't we all so smart in seeing through one another!"[42]

Translated into the terms of our Persian tale, this gleeful statement of Hillman's is the "unity of the unity and difference" (Hegel) of Shahrayar's invitation to his brother to come visit him (which immediately led to Shahzaman's discovery of his wife's unfaithfulness) *and* his brother's subsequent relief in learning that not just he, Shahzaman, but Shahrayar, too, is a cuckold! And this is not all. A Shahrazad/Shahrayar-like relation also figures in the mix. When, for example, Hillman goes on to propose his American approach to psychology via vision-stimulating, anima-inspired rhetoric ("speech before thought, rhetoric before logic" as he calls it[43]), the story-telling

Shahrazad once again sweet-talks the King out of his murderous fury even as she stokes it.

But Giegerich, too, writes as much under the aegis of Shahrazad as under that of Shahrayar! Indeed, as the quintessence of the vanquished (i.e., the sublated, dialectical negation of the wives that Shahrayar killed), a Shahrazad-like anima boldly asserts herself in and through his Shahrayar-like insistence that it is only in the violent embrace of the imagination's absolute exposure to itself that the many moments of an image or situation are fully *fathomed*, fully *thought*. Expressing this in terms that he rightly regards as being in accord with Hillman's usual stance, Giegerich concludes, "Psyche must not be split off from her own logic, logic not from soul: psychology must remain one word. And we must suffer the complication, if not contradiction, that psyche is subjected to an analysis of the logical status she is in, and logic moistened by psyche."[44]

So what then of Hillman's line about our seeing through each other? The key idea here is of a process that cuts both ways. As foils of one another, Hillman and Giegerich both hit their mark and take one for the team. This, however, is how it must be. For prior to the disputes that arise within psychology is the psychologizing action of the discipline itself. None of us escapes that syzygy.[45]

---

When morning came Dinarzad complimented Shahrazad on the story she had told. Speaking as much to the King as to her sister, Shahrazad replied, "What is this compared with what I shall tell you tomorrow night if I stay alive!"[46]

Throughout the course of his long and productive career, Hillman has said much the same to his readers: "What is this compared with what I will tell you in my next book, my next essay!" And as with Shahrazad, so too in his case there has always been another addressee. I refer here to that contemporary version of the wife-strangling Shahrayar, the discipline, the science, of Psychology itself. Responding to the insult that the language of psychology has in our day dealt the soul (through the rationalism and nominalism of its social-science speak),[47] Hillman's long years in his writer's cell have been as inspired as were Shahrazad's in the bedroom of King. Eloquently turning the prose of the tyrant around upon itself, Hillman has shown us, again and again, through the risks he has taken as a writer, how the soul is truly served. May this, his legacy to us—let's call it "Hillman's Syzygy," be as a challenge to all who honor him, that we may bring to our psychologizing efforts as much as he, through the Shahrazad of a lively imagination and the Shahrayar of an equally critical intelligence, has always brought to his.

## NOTES

[1] *The Arabian Nights*, based on the text of the fourteenth-century Syrian manuscript, ed. Muhsin Mahdi, trans. Husain Haddawy (New York: Alfred A. Knopf, 1992).

[2] C. G. Jung, *The Collected Works of C. G. Jung*, trans. R. F. C. Hull, vol. 9i (Princeton, NJ: Princeton University Press, 1969), § 120; hereafter abbreviated to *CW* followed by volume number and paragraph (§) number.

[3] Greg Mogenson, *The Dove in the Consulting Room: Hysteria and the Anima in Bollas and Jung* (Hove, UK: Brunner-Routledge, 2003).

[4] Jung, *CW* 8, § 421; *CW* 16, § 254; *CW* 17, § 163.

[5] Cited in Paul J. Stern, C. G. Jung, *The Haunted Prophet* (New York: Dell Publishing, 1976), p. 121.

[6] Mogenson, *Dove in the Consulting Room*, pp. 26-29.

[7] James Hillman, *Anima: An Anatomy of a Personified Notion* (Dallas, TX: Spring Publications, 1985).

[8] Cf. Hillman, *Anima*, p. 65: "Paradoxically, the very archetype of the feminine may not itself be feminine." This in reference to Jung's statement, "When projected, the anima always has a feminine form with definite characteristics. This empirical finding does not mean that the archetype is constituted like that *in itself*" (*CW* 9i, § 142).

[9] Jung, *CW* 16, § 469.

[10] James Hillman, *Re-Visioning Psychology* (New York: Harper & Row, 1975), p. 49.

[11] *Arabian Nights*, p. 10.

[12] *Arabian Nights*, p. 16.

[13] James Hillman, *The Dream and the Underworld* (New York: Harper & Row, 1978).

[14] Cf. Hillman's reference to me as an angry young man from Canada in an interview with Clarissa Pinkola Estés, "The Erotics of Publishing," *Bloomsbury Review* 9, no. 5 (Sept./Oct. 1989): 7.

[15] James Hillman, personal letter, February 25, 1981.

[16] Hillman, *Re-Visioning Psychology*, pp. 134-135.

[17] *Ibid*, p. 150.

[18] Hillman, personal letter, February 25, 1981.

[19] Hillman, *Re-Visioning Psychology*, p. 43.

[20] *Ibid*, p. 42.

[21] Sigmund Freud, *Introductory Lectures on Psycho-Analysis, S.E.* XV, p. 19.

[22] See note 17 above.

[23] Hillman, *Re-Visioning Psychology*, chapters 1 & 3.

[24] I allude here to psychological approaches and theories that wittingly or unwitting set up new versions of the seduction or trauma theory inasmuch as they conceptualize psychology in terms of some substrate or extra-psychic foundation.

[25] We know this anxiety, fright, and horror from our dreams. Beset by new and unsettling insights, the dream-ego flees from these as from some terrible other. Our terrors pass, however, as we come to realize that it is not us, but our psychology, that is being addressed by the soul and join the soul in speculating beyond our person. Cf. Wolfgang Giegerich, "The Dream in Psychotherapy, Its Role and Significance," unpublished paper.

[26] Hillman, *Re-Visioning Psychology*, chapters 2 & 4.

[27] *Ibid*, p. 57.

[28] *Ibid*, p. 139.

[29] James Hillman, "Three Ways of Failure and Analysis" in *Loose Ends: Primary Papers in Archetypal Psychology* (Irving, TX: Spring Publications, 1975), p. 104.

[30] A point made by Wolfgang Giegerich in his paper, "The Animus as Negation and as the Soul's Own Other," forthcoming.

[31] For an important discussion of the ego as the form that animus takes when it has lost its anima connection in the syzygy see Hillman's *Anima*, pp. 179-180.

[32] For Hillman's own more sophisticated treatment of this topic see the chapter "On Psychological Femininity" of his *The Myth of Analysis: Three Essays in Archetypal Psychology* (New York: Harper Perennial, 1992).

[33] Hillman, *Anima*, p. 181. The interior quote is from Jung, *CW* 16, § 469.

[34] *Ibid*, p. 171.

[35] *Ibid.*, (italics in original).

[36] *Ibid.*, p. 177.

[37] *Arabian Nights*, pp. 6-7.

[38] Patricia Berry, *Echo's Subtle Body* (Dallas, TX: Spring Publications, 1982), pp. 59-61.

[39] Wolfgang Giegerich, *The Soul's Logical Life: Towards a Rigorous Notion of Psychology* (Frankfurt am Main: Peter Lang GmbH, 1998), pp. 119-123.

[40] James Hillman's paper, "Hegel, Giegerich and the U.S.A." and Wolfgang Giegerich's response, "Effort? Yes, Effort!" *Spring* (1988): 177-180 and 181-188 respectively.

[41] Hillman, "Hegel, Giegerich, and the U.S.A.," p.179.

[42] *Ibid.*

[43] *Ibid.* p. 177.

[44] Giegerich, "Effort? Yes, Effort!" p. 183.

[45] For Giegerich, the syzygy can be expressed logically as the "unity *of* the unity *and* the opposition of the opposites." Relating this to Hillman and himself he asks, "Could it be that it is the syzygy that manifests in our strife at once uniting and dividing us with/from each other?" See his "Once More the Reality/Irreality Issue: A Reply to Hillman's Reply,"< http://www.rubedo.psc.br/reply.htm>

[46] *Arabian Nights*, p. 90.

[47] For Hillman's discussion on the insufficiency of psychological language see his *The Myth of Analysis* (New York: Harper Perennial, 1978), pp. 117-212. See also *Re-Visioning Psychology*, pp. 213-218.

Wolfgang Giegerich is a Jungian psychoanalyst in private practice near Munich, Germany. He has taught and lectured widely. Of his more than 150 publications in numerous languages, his latest books in English include: *The Soul's Logical Life* (2001); *Dialectics and Analytical Psychology*, co-authored with David Miller and Greg Mogenson, (2005); *The Neurosis of Psychology: Primary Papers towards a Critical Psychology*, Collected English Papers, Vol. 1 ( 2006), and *Technology and the Soul*, Collected English Papers, Vol. 2 (2007).

# 13

# "The Unassimilable Remnant" —What Is at Stake?

## A Dispute with Stanton Marlan

WOLFGANG GIEGERICH

In the "Alchemy" issue of *Spring Journal*, Stanton Marlan published his remarkable essay "From the Black Sun to the Philosopher's Stone."[1] It includes a discussion of the differing views that James Hillman and I hold on the alchemical Philosopher's Stone and related issues central to the basic conception of psychology, most notably the issue of "image" versus dialectic thought. His discussion is remarkable because of the diligence and fairness of his presentation, his learnedness and in-depth perception, his careful weighing of the differences as well as the affinities of the standpoints reviewed. In addition, one is struck by the sincere commitment that one can sense throughout his article. His presentation is also gracious because it displays a spirit of appreciation rather than derision. Despite reservations and misgivings concerning certain views, I wholeheartedly welcome his essay. I am grateful for it, because it puts very important issues on the table in an intelligent way that provides a sound basis for further discussion.

Meanwhile, I have clarified for myself my earlier still vague reservations and present the result of my reflections in this paper. I am only sorry that my article inevitably has to have the character of dispute and controversy rather than the reconciliatory character that Marlan's paper has. In his own interesting stance, he performs a kind of literal at-one-ment of the two compared and contrasted stances, saying that "[i]n Hillman and Giegerich we have two moments of the Stone that not only can live together but also belong together in the same mosaic," a statement to which he, however, feels compelled to add the doubtful question, "or do they?" He also mentions in this connection the alchemists' *solve et coagula*. It is curious to what different interpretations this dictum can lead. Marlan sees the need to complement my formula of "the union of the unity and difference" with another formula, "the difference of the unity and difference," and he insists on an *unassimilable* "not," thereby giving even more prominence to fundamental difference. So we see that *in* his theory, that is, on the semantic level, he emphasizes difference and discrepancy, while on the syntactical level he aims for a side-by-side complementary relation of the opposites.

In accordance with my view that the actual place of action for psychology is the level of logical form or syntax rather than the level of semantic contents, the weights are for me distributed the other way around. The emphasis on difference and negation appears on the syntactical level, between the different standpoints, whereas semantically I stress the union of unity and difference. It seems that in either case you get union as well as difference. They are a pair, and as such inescapable. But it makes a great difference where they appear.

Although I would certainly hope that in practical reality, in the sphere of collegiality, "the two moments of the Stone" alluded to by Stanton Marlan (and, in addition, also Marlan's own standpoint of no mean merit) can live together and maybe even belong together in the same mosaic, I will have the task of showing in the following that and how logically, *on the level of theorizing*, they are in essential regards downright incompatible: two mosaics, indeed two different levels, not one.

I begin with a discussion of Marlan's appreciative assessment of Jung's historical significance, which finds expression in his view that Jung's resuscitation of images amounts to a reversal of the dominant historical process.

## "Jung's Resuscitation of Images: A Reversal of the Dominant Historical Process"

To me, "a reversal of the dominant historical process" is a strange idea from the outset: is there, can there be, such a thing? Is the historical process not essentially irreversible? It seems to me that I have to relentlessly accept the history of personal life as well as of civilization at large and have to acknowledge it as my base and starting point. Rather than letting it be, I may wish to push off from this base, but I cannot reverse it. If I have truly accepted my personal history, I can perhaps change the direction of my personal life, but even so I have to build my future life on that base. Any idea that I or somebody else could change the historical process on the cultural level will turn out to be illusory, because we are all ourselves exponents of our history; the historical impulse is already in us and works through us, even through our illusions, resistance, revolution, or revival attempts. Apart from when real disruptions of the cultural process happen through absolute catastrophes, there will be only a continuation of history, either a sterile perpetuation of more or less the same, or, if "all the bills have been paid," its own further development.

In what Marlan says, I hear a contribution to the construction of a popular myth of history: the path of history as pathological and in need of correction or salvation. We hear in this text of "the shadow of Western thought ... since Plato," of the "hatred for image," "the fear of the power of image," the age-old "battle between spirit and soul." Something, so the implication is, has gone wrong. And over against all this, Jung and Hillman brought, Marlan thinks, a "reversal" that amounts to "a major advance of consciousness." Ultimately, this assessment of history faintly echoes a Manichean *ressentiment.*

Are we in that magisterial position to decide that the development that *was* is the shadow of the West, that the turn away from image was wrong, and that history should have been different? Quite apart from the question of whether the diagnosis of a prevailing "hatred for image" is factually borne out or not (what a rich history of art and imaginative literature has there been and how much love for all this!), is it the job of psychology to reverse a given "pathological" development, or not much rather to see it the way it was and to attend to the existing pathology by penetrating to its depth, to the soul in it? Can we allow ourselves, as therapists, to take sides against the way things are?

Be that as it may, I deny this alleged major advance of consciousness brought about by Jung's revival of image. No doubt, I am deeply indebted to the work of Jung (and Hillman, but here I am primarily concerned with Jung), especially to Jung's giving us a concept of "soul" as the basis of true psychological thinking. But I do not think that this amounts either to an advance of consciousness or to a real contribution to the historical process. It is only a contribution to a particular area or field within the present stage of consciousness. It is a semantic, not a structural or syntactical contribution. Jungian psychology does not contribute to the historical process, but it established a niche, an oasis, within it. Precisely when one takes seriously the concept of soul bestowed upon us by Jung, one has to admit that Jungian psychology is a sideline and does not engage the soul of the historical process. The basic motivation behind Jung's psychology, insofar as it *wants* to make a contribution to the historical process (Jung's work has other aspects, too), is a defense against his own time. Jung shares this quasi-Manichean rejection of the dominant historical process as being pathological and in need of a cure. As such, his basic stance is, at least in these regards, actually regressive and ideological, notwithstanding all the many marvelous insights that his psychology has given us.

Paradoxically, despite this subjective salvationist intent, Jung's psychology is *objectively* not even meant to engage the historical process or the dominant consciousness: his resuscitation of images is reserved for a logically segregated space, cut off from the historical process. The archetypes are defined as archetypes of the collective unconscious. This is like safe sex. The notion of the unconscious is, so to speak, the condom around the archetypes and archetypal images. Safe sex means you can have intercourse and the subjective enjoyment and feelings brought by it, but you prevent anything objective from happening, both your own possible infection and the act's becoming in fact productive through the impregnation of the female partner. Inasmuch as Jung's invention of the collective unconscious (or "the unconscious" in general) set up a clearly demarcated second ahistorical compartment over against the collective consciousness and the historical process, and inasmuch as he assigned the archetypal images to this unconscious, he ensured that, *per definitionem*, the images would not be infected by the dominant consciousness of today's world, nor consciousness be logically impregnated by the archetypal images.

Of course, you can have your numinous experiences of archetypal images and perhaps be subjectively shaken by them, but this is much like we can have our feeling experience of lions in a zoo or on television. They cannot possibly bite us. In the same way, the subjective archetypal experiences of private individuals cannot possibly reach the soul of the historical process, that is, the prevailing logical constitution of consciousness. The fundamental dissociation between consciousness and the unconscious functions like the bars of the lion's cage. The lion could make a difference only if he were let loose. For the images and the archetypes, this letting loose would mean that they would not be logically confined to the unconscious, to a "psychic reality" as a special, separate reality side by side with ordinary reality, but that they would share one and the same space, one and the same consciousness with all our other (for example, modern scientific) knowledge.

But this would of course mean that you could no longer merely imagine and experience them; you would have to think them, that is to say, engage them, their contents, on the same level of truth on which we entertain all our other notions about reality.

Since Jung did not want his thinking to become speculative and metaphysical on the one hand, and insisted, on the other hand, that the images have an immediate present reality (rather than only an historical presence, a presence in Mnemosyne), the price he had to pay was to segregate the images in a special fenced-in space, "the unconscious," and thereby systematically immunize them from consciousness. Now one might say that imaginal psychology is better off, since it does not compartmentalize in the same way. Nevertheless, when it does not compartmentalize any more, it is for the sole reason that it sublimated the fence, integrating it into its very style of thinking. The immunization of the imaginal from the historical process has become inherent in its very form. This notion of form takes me to the next topic.

## "The Image Understood in Its Most Radical Way"

Marlan states that "Giegerich actually misconstrues the way Hillman defines image." He comes to this assessment because he sees a discrepancy between my charge that the imaginal stance is based on "sensory intuition" and a form of "picture thinking," on the one hand, and Hillman's "more radical understanding of 'image,'" according to which "we don't see images but see through them," on the other hand. But Marlan here himself misunderstands my critique in the sense of an underdetermination. It is more radical. He thinks that I see "images as pictures" and that this "might be considered to be a remnant of a sensationist psychology that understands images and even the imagination as epiphenomenal to actual things." However, my argument is not on the level of images as contents of consciousness or as "copies" in the mind of the phenomenal at all. Rather than the image in the narrower sense, I am critiquing the imaginal style of thought as picture thinking. I take for granted that image is understood by Hillman as "a metaphor without a referent." The notion of a depiction of actual things has never entered my mind in such contexts.

My point is that as to the charge of picture thinking, it does not make any difference whether an image is "what you see" or whether it is—"understood in its most radical way"—"the way you see," that is, whether you stay with the image as content of consciousness or see it as a perspective with which we see. In either case, the sphere of sensory intuition (*sinnliche Anschauung*) is not left. The image merely recedes from the foreground into the hidden background, from the place in front of consciousness into the very structure of consciousness itself and in this way preserves the visual orientation (but also conceals this, its visual character, safely from the empirical ego). This imaginal form of the structure of consciousness is the sublimated successor formation to Jung's still concretistic "the unconscious" as a separate container of the images. The new sublimated container is "the imagination," that is, *space as such* (together with the vis-à-vis of one's seeing and what is seen [subject-object], the narrative-temporal succession, and the need to substantiate and personify), whereas "the unconscious" was still imagined as a distinct realm *in space* separate from the other "spatial" realm of "consciousness" located "above" the unconscious. To be sure, the image has now, through this quasi-transcendental-philosophical move, been deliteralized; it may no longer be visual in the empirical sense, but it stays *logically* visual: "Re-Visioning" (not just a revision), archetypal "perspectives," "seeing through" to the gods or myths. It may have become metaphorical seeing, but it does not advance to *sublated* seeing as thought or conceptual comprehension: "insight," "*intellegere*."

Marlan quotes Hillman as saying, "We do not literally see images." True, not we as empirical persons, but "the soul" or the mind in us *sees* the images (which is the precondition of the possibility of our empirical seeing through image). If "the soul" does not see the image, there is no image at all, and also not a seeing through images. The move from the literal to the metaphorical is *psychically* a great refinement, to be sure, but *psychologically* it does not alter the basic naturalism of this stance.

It is naïve to think that the image in imaginal psychology is not representational simply because it does not have an external referent and is not to be understood in sensationist terms as epiphenomenal to actual things. It is representational just the same—because it represents *itself*. The point here is that it does not make any difference whether there is a literal external referent or whether the "referent" has been totally internalized into the structure of image or imaginal seeing itself so that the image is now its own referent: the structure or form of representation has not been overcome merely by overcoming the externally existent referent. The *form* of representation would be overcome only with a transcendence of the form of image as such, that is, with *thought*. Thought does not see or imagine; it thinks. Here one sees how important it is to become aware of the dimension of logical form or "syntax." A merely semantic approach is naturally already satisfied with the difference between "image without external referent" and "epiphenomenal representation of an external referent."

## "How Is Giegerich's Idea of the Alchemical 'Gold' to be Differentiated from Hillman's Idea?"

"Once we have Giegerich's subtle view of 'gold' as totally liquefied Mercurius, can we still distinguish it from lead, silver, or mercury?" This is, of course, a vital question. If one claims (and I now deliteralize this question) that the imaginal approach is structurally insufficient, that it does not go all the way, then one has to show how an approach based on the idea of the soul's logical life can in fact go further, deeper, or achieve results that on principle grounds cannot be reached by the metaphorical or imaginal approach. Such a demonstration must, however, not be performed in thin air, on the abstract level of talking about the symbol or metaphor of gold. One has to get down to brass tacks, to concrete instances of the work performed on specific matters.

Although I do not claim ever to have actually reached the ultimately desired final result of true gold with my work, I think I have repeatedly shown what my style of work can do. And if you look at any of these examples, you will easily see the difference, that is, you will find that with the imaginal approach you could not have gone as far. I refer, by way of a few pertinent examples, to my treatment of Heraclitus's dictum about the depth of the soul, my chapter on the Actaeon myth, my discussion of the motif of the slippery or glass mountain, my work on the bottled spirit in alchemy and psychology.[2] Here you can see my dialectical approach in action and what it means to *think* an image all the way through (hopefully) rather than imagining it. It means letting the image decompose, letting it go under into itself, *distilling substance into logical form, semantics into syntax.*

And this is what the imaginal approach cannot and will not do. But this is also why it cannot truly leave behind the physical in the material. The imaginal stance is insensitive, indeed blind, to form-distinctions, and *systemically* blind. It takes semantic similarities of different phenomena for imaginal identity and ignores the fact that the logic or syntax (that is, the soul) of the phenomena and the respective status or function they have within the logical constitution of consciousness may make them incomparable. For it, Zeus, for example, is still alive today and we still today, in the context of our *modern* mode of being-in-the-world, offer bull sacrifices to him, even if only in a metaphorical way. It can think so simply because it looks for certain external likenesses. It is helpless vis-à-vis the psychology of modern phenomena such as the media, today's most advanced form of capitalism, or nanotechnology, because these are from the outset *in themselves* (in their logical form) syntactical rather than semantic or substantial, so that a thinking guided by images, myths, gods is *a priori* out of place. The imaginal stance knows of only three alternatives for dealing with material: taking it literally, making metaphorical use of it, or deserting the matter in the direction of the "poisonous state of splendid solar isolation." There is no place for the fourth possibility, the alchemical decomposition, sublimation, vaporization of the naturalistic form of image into syntactical form ("the Mercurius").

Marlan states, "While Hillman's move takes him beyond the physical, he stays with the material, the concrete, what I have called here the pigment, a certain impurity that for him saves gold from the 'poisonous state of splendid solar isolation.'" Hillman's work is so rich, he has given us so many studies on a multitude of subjects, that it would be a serious mistake to lump all his work together. He has said certain things now, and other things at other times; there are instances in which his work conveys much more "the negativity of the image" (Greg Mogenson) and comes much closer to a sublation of the image, whereas in other cases, the silvery nature of the imaginal approach is much stronger. Any global assessment of his work would go amiss. There are many Hillmans, not only one. So in what I have to say next I will restrict myself to those instances where the approach stays clearly within the confines of the imaginal-metaphorical approach.

But with respect to those instances, I deny that his move takes him beyond what is physical in the material. This is precisely what it does not do. His move takes him beyond the literal and to the metaphorical, but in this way precisely retains the physical, for which from a *psychological* point of view it is all the same whether it appears in literal or metaphorical form. Whether "simple physicality" (Marlan) or metaphorical physicality—it is physicality; it is naturalistic. And this is what counts psychologically. It is in some ways similar to how Jung believed himself to have left behind the "physical" of his mother fixation by going beyond his literal mother to the mother archetype. True, there is a great difference, empirically, between the former and the latter form of the mother complex. However, this great difference is only semantic. Psychologically, structurally, syntactically, the mother fixation has not changed.[3] I repeat: the move from the literal to the metaphorical does not take us beyond the "physical" in the material, if "the physical" is itself understood psychologically, that is to say, beyond the basic naturalism that inevitably informs the imaginal style of consciousness.

The phrase "poisonous state of splendid solar isolation" is not mine. For Hillman, it is the certain impurity that he allows his "gold" to have that saves gold from that isolation. Does it really? My critique of imaginal psychology had precisely always been that it cocoons itself in the unreality of a kind of "Platonism," as I once termed it. I had challenged psychology with the thesis that a real cut into the naturalism of the imaginal and metaphoric is indispensable to reach actuality.[4] And I believe that it is precisely by trying to save his "gold" by means of those so-called impurities (that is, through the logically unbroken tie to naturalistic apperception) that this cocooning in unreality takes place.

The fear of the "poison" is, I think, the problem. This is what makes consciousness shrink from going all the way forward and instead makes it turn back again to what it was itself, after all, intent upon leaving through its very move away from the physical in the material. It makes this move, but halfway there (namely after having moved from the literal to the *metaphorical*), it stops. Of course, the danger of splendid solar isolation exists. But the point is that it must be met, not avoided. You have to try to get to the top of the glass mountain. If you avoid the danger, you have psychologically succumbed to it unawares. You truly avoid it only by facing it. As Hegel said, in a statement quoted by Marlan in another connection, "only by looking the negative in the face, and tarrying with it …."

## "Brokenness, Incision, Wound, Cut"

The blackness of *sol niger* brought with it for Marlan "the *mortificatio* of brokenness, incision, and wound, castration, cut, negation, with an ultimate 'No' to the ego, with what felt unassimilable." He expands on this theme by first of all amplifying it with a host of experiences and images from different areas of life and culture and by including a section on "Mystical Death" (of the ego). He reminds us that his strategy in his book *The Black Sun*

> … was to hesitate before this darkness, to pause and then to enter its realm of corpses and coffins, of monsters and monstrous complexity, and to engage its most literal and destructive demons: narcissistic mortification, humiliation, delusion, despair, depression, physiological and psychological decay, cancer, psychosis, suicide, murder, and death.[5]

He rightly emphasizes that "the *mortificatio* drives the psyche to an ontological pivot point, to a desubstantiation of the ego, … leading to a gateway that is both a dying and a new life."[6] And even if only very briefly, he connects this with a shamanic-like initiation and describes by way of analogy the absolutely gruesome Tantric rites of Kali.

All these are experiences and images of negation. But the problem I have with them is that the negation remains decidedly naturalistic: experiential, sensible image, ritual behavior, *mystical* death of the ego. The negation does not come home to itself and cut itself loose from its tie to and immersion in immediate experience and natural(istic) image. So there is a cut, but it does not cut all the way through.

The desubstantiation of the ego is not enough. Where is the desubstantiation of substantiation itself (of the form of substantiation and personification)?

Our thinking is here tied to ancient modes of experience, shamanic initiation, Tantric ritual. But it is clear that we cannot go back to them (though this is, of course, not suggested by Marlan). My question is: Is it enough to use these references as *metaphoric* ones? Does it make a difference psychologically if we literally go back to ancient modes or only imagine our experiences metaphorically along the lines of archaic psychic realities? The soul remains in the spell of those images, which, however, do not provide a concrete way for the modern soul to go. The soul is lured imaginally back into the modes of the past and down into the experiential field. It is held captive there because the metaphor, which after all does not have a referent, does not open up to anything that could have a real meaning for a modern person. And this is also why the death of the ego has to be seen as a *mystical* death and why Marlan's paper, the closer it draws to a close, moves into the mysterious. The problem with the "mystical" is that you cannot say what it really is. You cannot account for it. You talk about it, but you cannot take responsibility for what you say—because in the last analysis it reveals itself, for Marlan, as being "the unthinkable" and "unspeakable." With "the unthinkable" we each have carte blanche. It is anything and nothing, a void. In the notion of the unthinkable, the imaginal style of thought imagines, and betrays, its own innermost nature, its total freedom from any real restraints, its free-floatingness.

We also hear, for example, of a move toward "a Zen-like perception of the ordinary, the 'sheer mereness of things.'" Things? Things today, in the age of television, advertising, the throw-away society, advanced capitalism? Of course, we still have the word "thing" in our language and use this word, but things in the strict sense (in the sense of their "sheer mereness"), and along with it the ontology of things, have been extinct for two hundred years, at least as far as the reality of the psyche is concerned. The *mortificatio* may have driven the psyche to the ontological pivot point, but it obviously did not drive it to the other side. The imaginal approach is the hidden recess into which the old ontology of "things" informed by "perception and imagination" has withdrawn and made itself less discernible. The cut did not really cut.

Marlan feels the need "to raise a number of concerns about any move that relegates images to a status secondary to thought." I connect this, his concern, with a desire not to have the cut cut the cut itself. The most terrible perturbations of the ego are permitted, but not the perturbation of the logic (or, if you wish, ontology) of the naturalistic orientation, of the image and of things.

Actually, it is not meaningful to say that image is secondary to thought. This is a wrong pairing. It is the imaginal *approach* that is secondary to thought. Image itself, by contrast, is itself thought, garbed in sensible form, much like animals are thoughts or concepts garbed in a physical body.

The mystical turns easily into mystification. When I once wrote in connection with the theme of the death of the ego that "[t]he art of psychological discourse is to speak as someone who is already deceased," this should not be construed as referring to the result of a mysterious existential death experience, as a kind of personal rebirth into a higher state of existence like that of a shaman, a sage, someone illumined or "individuated," one who has been in contact with the unthinkable and unspeakable or has had a satori experience. All these mystifying ideas have to be kept away. What I said has a very concrete practical, that is, strictly *methodological*, meaning. It is very much down to earth. Very sober. Nothing unspeakable. It can be described. It is not a statement about the state reached by a person, not about a human being, but about the logical subject that wants to do psychology or the logical constitution of consciousness necessary for psychology, a methodological stance to be taken by the psychologist *if* and *when* he or she wants to do psychology. That's all. The empirical person remains in his or her private life the same ordinary person.

Owing to its naturalism, to its unbroken connection to the *form* of the visible (in the sense indicated above), the imaginal approach is ultimately a resistance to "the death of the ego." It is the resistance to "let *intellectually, logically* go" without reserve, to "go under" into thought (thinking). Thought proper is the result of the full-fledged cut. As I pointed out elsewhere,[7] following Hegel's insight, we think, *if* we think, in names, in the words of language, not in images, and words are contingent sound clusters with no relation to the looks of the things that they "mean," sound clusters freely *produced* by the thinking mind itself.[8] In thought, therefore, the cut with the natural and sensible has really and fully happened.

## "The Unassimilable"

Time and again, Marlan insists on there being something unassimilable. The blackness of *sol niger* is his proof and paradigm. Here he says he encountered a darkness that refuses conscious assimilation. But is this really true? No doubt, this blackness was initially "*felt* unassimilable" (my italics). But did it not in fact become "assimilated"? First of all, by his tarrying with it, it revealed itself to be in itself the opposite of itself, light, "the light of darkness itself," "the *lumen naturae*." The eyes of consciousness must have become adjusted to the darkness to be able to see the light of this darkness, which in itself is already an assimilation of this darkness into consciousness. But above all, Marlan wrote a whole book on the black sun and the darkness of *sol niger*, with rich amplifications and deep insights. He himself proved the assimilability of the black sun through his own achievement. What more could be expected, what better conscious assimilation could we get? What else could assimilation possibly mean?

This question points precisely to the problem. Marlan elucidates the meaning of conscious assimilation that he has in mind with the following formulations: a black sun "that would not yield or be incorporated by an ego stance. It would not dissolve, go away, or be lifted up ...." It "did not allow itself to be possessed by ego ...." What is special about that? If this is the sense of "conscious assimilation," there cannot be any conscious assimilation of anything at all, because this applies to all psychic reality, all symbols and archetypal images. Does the image of a lion or of the philosophical tree dissolve, the motif of dismemberment go away, the symbol of virgin birth become possessed by ego, the glass mountain yield, the image of the Crucified become incorporated by an ego stance? Can Apollo or Zeus be assimilated in an ego sense of assimilation? They all are and remain what they are, even if the darkness reveals its inner nature to be light, if the crucifixion leads to resurrection, if dismemberment leads to restitution of wholeness. And of course in all these cases the ego could, conversely, possibly be possessed by them.

But the fact that the psychic images have their own internal solidity, integrity, and intactness and do not go away even when assimilated in no way means that there is an "unassimilable remainder" in the emphatic sense. If "unassimilable remainder" is supposed to mean more and something else than the basic Jungian insight that psychic reality is really real, Marlan has not proven his point. The reality of the darkness of *sol niger* is the same ordinary reality of all psychic images and different only with respect to its specific content.

Even the very image of consciousness, the sun, the *light* of the sun, cannot be possessed by ego, inasmuch as it is "*Sol et eius umbra*: light without and darkness within. In the source of light there is darkness enough ..."[9] The clear consciousness of something does not see this *consciousness's* own unconsciousness. What I am driving at is that the notion of "conscious assimilation" *in the sense of* incorporation by an ego stance, of going away or dissolving, does not apply in any case. It is utopian, fictitious, has no basis in reality. Conscious assimilation means something else, much more sober, concrete, and simple, for example, writing a book about the black sun (with all the psychic and mental labor that goes along with this). But that fiction is the ground for the dogma of the "unassimilable remainder." The "remainder" exists only for that position that expects assimilation to mean that everything should be incorporated by an ego stance. Marlan, it seems to me, confuses the "ultimate 'No' to the ego" (which logically is inherent in anything truly psychological) with a remainder. But psychological work is, from the outset, not defined as attempted incorporation by ego: it is, rather, the attempt to allow the psychic phenomena to self-unfold their inner complexity, to reveal their (soul) meaning, their "truth." And such an attempt is what I call *thinking* the phenomenon or image.

This is why I have trouble with statements like the ones quoted from Hillman that the Stone "does not allow itself to be held in meaning," "[i]t does not yield to understanding," or when he says of a particular alchemical process that it is "designed to obliterate a psychological *episteme* ...." Transferring this from the Stone to the black sun, I can agree that it does not allow itself to be held *in* meaning. But what is implied or suggested betrays much more, namely, a general anti-meaning, anti-understanding, anti-knowledge stance. My thesis, by contrast, is that each psychic phenomenon, each symbol or archetypal image *is* its own meaning, *is episteme*, *is* its own concept, *is* a thought. The blackness of *sol niger*, thus, does not have a meaning, it is meaning and it is only the meaning or thought *as which* it *exists*. This fact, namely, that psychic phenomena *are* meaning or concept, is the reason why we have to *think* them. Thinking means to think "the *soul's*" thoughts that "it" thinks in the phenomena in which it manifests itself for us.

All the problems here with darkness, unassimilability, the remainder, and meaning seem to arise because "the ego" is the hidden standard and measure, the secret ruler inside the intellectual stance, or, to use an earlier formulation, because the cut has not really happened and one's thinking does not begin on the other side of the "ontological pivot." If you define "conscious assimilation" as assimilation to an ego stance, I agree there is something unassimilable. But why define it so?

To be sure, despite this ego stance the defeat is supposed to happen for the ego; it is, as it were, "preached" and celebrated. Perhaps I could also say it is merely circumambulated. But it has not already happened. The death of the ego is here on the one hand a threshold before which one's theoretical stance tarries and thus it is constantly deferred to a (possibly imminent, but never gotten-over-with) future; on the other hand it is *imagined* and *ipso facto* pushed down into and held down in the sphere of the merely psychic (the subjective, emotional *experience* of *mortificatio*, the *mystical* idea of death, etc.). It is never the accomplished starting-point, the ground and background from which psychology proceeds.

The point about the death of the ego and its strange nature is that it can never happen. It is not such that it could happen. It is such that it can be only if it always already has happened; it comes into being as its own perfect tense. This one cannot imagine. It can only be thought. And this is why it is never an "experience." Any experience of the death of the ego inevitably confirms the very ego whose death it is supposed to bring. Emotional states solidify the personalistic prejudice; they tie back the notions of the death of the ego, of individuation, or of transformation in general to "me" as person. As long as one thinks in terms of a personal process, one cannot get beyond the mystical, beyond an "ought," beyond hoping, and vague divinations. One does not get beyond the stage of merely "dreaming" about the goal. Psychology does not become *real.* Real psychology has the goal behind itself as its pre-sup-position, as the condition of its own possibility. And real psychology is possible only if the purpose of *soul life* is understood to be *psychology-making* and not *our* "process," the realization of psychology and not our self-realization. The soul wants to become real, and psychology is its realization.

When Jung stated that "[t]he goal is important only as an idea; the essential thing is the *opus* which leads to the goal: *that* is the goal of a lifetime"[10] he showed two things. First, at least here, he opted for merely "dreaming" about and striving for the goal throughout one's life, that is, for never reaching it and for a linear, vector-like conception, although the soul is by definition uroboric, having its *telos* always behind itself as its *arche*. Second, he stays stuck in a personalistic conception of the work, the idea of the goal of *our* life. The two aspects require each other. It is clear that the moment that you are identified with the soul process, thinking that it is about you and that the goal is the goal for you, the moment that you are incapable of distinguishing yourself from the soul, it would be a case of inflation and hubris to claim that you either had already reached the goal or could possibly reach it. Jung simply had to go "linear" and defer the goal into a never-reached future, once he confused the soul process with our development as people. And the other way around: with his linear thinking, he precluded that psychology as psychology could begin, because it could begin only if it had already its goal behind itself as its beginning.

I know that for most people it is very disappointing, but the death of the ego is *logical* death, a *mortificatio* on the cold, "objective" level of soul and its logical life. It is the birth of psychology as a *methodologically* based enterprise. Nothing spectacular, emotional, mysterious, numinous. Only if the death of the ego is comprehended as a logical death can it become real. Nay, this comprehension, if it is real, *is* the reality of this death. It is the breakthrough through the imaginal stance into thought, through the ego's personalism, emotionalism, enthrallment by sensible intuition, through its need to substantiate.

Different archetypal images have different "meanings," are the manifestation of different concepts or truths. It is clear that an idea like *sol et eius umbra*, for example, has a totally different *telos* from that of *sol niger*. Now it might well be that the particular *telos* of the appearance of the latter idea is precisely that of initiating the mind to which it appears into thought and dialectics. The blackness is the objective negation of all imaginal seeing. But it is not negation in the sense of point-blank elimination. Rather, the blackness forces on consciousness the realization that it, the blackness, negates *itself* and reveals itself to be light. Marlan thus rightly wonders, "Could this darkness be called sublated?" The thought, which sets in only once the blackness has radically cut off any way back to the imagination, shows itself to be *sol niger's* own thought (or the thought of "the soul" as *sol niger*). It is not a human concoction, an ego activity. It is the self-thinking, self-movement of the matter at hand. The appearance of *sol niger* is also an attempt to initiate into the notion of soul as uroboric self-reflection. No otherness. The blackness is not in need of an external light source. No lack. It has everything it needs within itself.

But the *telos* of the initiatory appearance of the black sun is reached, the initiation has taken place, only if the black sun does not merely stay an experience affecting subjective consciousness (the ego), but becomes logical, theoretical, that is, radically changes the intellectual stance, its logical constitution, one's "ontology," I could also say, if it becomes an objective method of psychology. The appearance of the black sun has to come home to itself. It has to negate itself *as emotional or imaginal experience.*

From here it is possible to understand what the function is of such ideas in Marlan's paper as the unassimilable, the remnant, the unthinkable. We have to be very clear about this: all these ideas are not phenomena, not observed facts, impressing themselves on the mind of their own accord. The blackness of the black sun is by no means unassimilable, although of course not in the sense of assimilation as being incorporated by an ego stance. The point of psychological thinking is anyway to let each phenomenon think itself. The phenomenon is not supposed to be assimilated to the ego in the first place, but to "the soul," whose own thought, for example, this blackness is.

The latter is also by no means unthinkable. We can think it as the soul's need to negate the ego stance, the imaginal approach, the perception-governed mind. It does not by any means "drive the soul toward the unthinkable." On the contrary, it drives, if one dwells with it and follows its lead, "the soul" to the *lumen naturae*, that is, to its, "the soul's," own light (because "the soul" always talks about itself, thinks, displays its own truths and wants to bring *itself* as human consciousness to comprehend these, its own truths). The blackness does not resist consciousness, but illumines it with its own (rather than with an ego) light. And why should we call *sol niger* a remnant? A remnant of what? Is it not just one soul phenomenon, one prime matter, like all the myriad of other phenomena that may come up? The fact that its particular quality or property is blackness is on exactly the same level as that the ordinary *sol's* character is light, or that the character of dismemberment is dismemberment.

In the ideas of the unassimilable and the unthinkable, unspeakable, the blackness of *sol niger* is literalized. The initial experience and appearance of it is singled out of the entire process and frozen. The unthinkable, unspeakable is pure blackness. But *sol niger* is precisely not purely black. It is blacker than black, namely light. The self-movement of the black sun beyond its blackness is noted in Marlan's paper, but does not enter into and transform the style of thinking about it. Semantically, we are informed about the shining light of nature, but the syntax of consciousness or the theoretical standpoint holds fast and solidifies the initial absolute blackness.

The ideas of the insurmountable "not," the unassimilable remnant, and the unthinkable are *posited*. They are theoretical constructs and dogmatic prejudices. They are not the result of experience, but the outcome of a decision, a will or interest in having them: postulates. And their function is, I think, to give to psychology an *a priori reservatio mentalis*. Not a mental reservation as a personal behavior, but one built into the structure of one's theoretical stance itself. And a mental reservation not about particular contents or ideas, but the empty general (logical, methodological) *form* of a reservation. In the ideas of the unassimilable "not" and the unthinkable, the theoretical standpoint that entertains these ideas beholds the semantic reflection of its own logical refractoriness, its syntactical decision not to allow this standpoint without reserve to go under into the dynamics and fluidity of the theoretical process. In the apodictic idea that there is *necessarily* and *on principle* something that "resists conscious assimilation" and does not "dissolve" and "yield," we can see the projection, objectification, hypostatizing of a fundamental resistance to yielding.

The blackness of *sol niger* amounts to a *mortificatio* of the ego. But there are many ways the ego can be mortified (other examples are Dionysian dismemberment, Christian crucifixion, even passionate love). What is the specific type of ego death brought by the black sun? Here I have to come back to what I already hinted at above: absolute blackness, by cutting off all avenues back to any seeing and envisioning, to images and perspectives, and by furthermore *dialectically* revealing itself as its own opposite, light, could be interpreted as that particular "death of the ego" experience through which "the soul" wants to initiate a consciousness under the sway of the imaginal mode into veritable thought and dialectical thinking. And if this experience is said to "drive the soul toward the un*think*able," we see that consciousness has indeed somehow already got the message. It understands and admits that now it would actually be a matter of thinking rather than seeing or imagining. But we also see that it refuses to go on, to move across the threshold separating the imaginal from thought and into the sphere of thought proper. "The *un*thinkable" means that a real entrance into the realm of *thought* is declared to be off limits. The limits have been reached, but must not be crossed. The mental reservation, rather than being a reservation with respect to a particular content, is indeed a *mental* reservation in the strict sense, a reservation with respect to nothing but mind or thought itself: the *form* of thought.

Again, it must be stressed that this resistance to yielding or to going all the way must not be misunderstood as belonging to personal psychology. It is not on the level of personal development, experience, or subjective attitude. It is inherent in the objective *logical form* of the theoretical stance. The alchemists had a saying that one should not begin with the work before everything has turned into water. In our context we could also add: or into flame or vapor, at any rate in all cases into a non-solid, non-positive state, a state of negativity. I mention this alchemical dictum because of the "everything" in it. The alchemists did not say: do not start before *you* have reached such and such a state. They talked about the state of the objective contents, the matter, which, according to this statement, must first be transformed in its totality, with no remainder. But in our text, it is decreed in advance that there has to be a resisting remainder. This stance wants something absolutely hard, firm, impenetrable, unreachable and untouchable, something that is by definition exempt from the "alchemical" process.

"The unassimilable" is thus a kind of *fundamentum inconcussum*, but other than that of Descartes it is not a real content or a substantial truth, but rather merely the empty, hollow form (of an indestructible substance or fundament): a "not," an "un-"—or rather *resistance per se*. And it is, of course, not really a *fundamentum*, something known to be the ground of all that follows, but what once was ground has here been pushed to the edges, the border: as mere remainder. We would probably not go wrong if we stated that this standpoint is the hollowed-out and inverted Cartesian one: the Cartesian "doubt" absolutized and precisely as such turned into a (not ontological, but psychological) "foundation."

We could also describe the dogma of "the unassimilable" as a reified categorical imperative, "Don't yield all the way," where, however, this imperative is again not directed at the human subject, but at the logical form of the contents. It means: resist total liquefaction or transmutation into the state of absolute negativity. More concretely, it means that the contents are allowed to move only from the literal to the metaphorical or the imaginal, but not beyond. Psychology's (subtle, sublimated) naturalism, the imaginal (thing-like, personified) form of the content of images must be protected. In other words, the ego. The assimilation that Marlan himself has already performed is not owned up to; what is already a fact is not allowed to also be released into its being *true* and thus to become the very standpoint and starting-point of consciousness. Marlan does not theoretically catch up with the position already reached by him factually. He holds on to an alleged "insurmountable 'not'" that he himself has already surmounted, having long arrived at the *lumen naturae*. The death of the ego remains "mystical," although consciousness has long gone through the concrete experience of it.

The idea of "the unthinkable" is the point where any theory that entertains this idea becomes a metaphysical one in the pejorative sense of the word. How could we possibly know that there is an unthinkable? We would have to have transcended our own mind. But in this, its concept of the unthinkable, because of the categorical prohibition built into this concept, such a theory has brought its own metaphysicizing under its own control. It has completely surrounded and neutralized it, much like viruses in our body are sometimes encircled and rendered harmless by our immune system. In this way, such a theory can indulge in its metaphysicizing as its *general* logical outlook while seemingly not making itself guilty of it in a practical sense, since it, after all, precisely abstains from thinking "the unthinkable" and from making a metaphysical system of it. It celebrates this, its metaphysical orientation, merely by reverently circumambulating "the unthinkable" like a tabooed invisible fetish and maybe once in a while, like Paul Kugler, by making "Raids on the Unthinkable" (whatever that is supposed to mean): the *zero stage* of metaphysics.

Jung, at *his* historical locus, saw himself confronted with a "barrier across the mental world which made it impossible for even the boldest flight of speculation to" get beyond. It was for him a "wall at which human inquisitiveness turns back."[11] The result of this turning back was the duality or dissociation of the non-speculative, not-thinking empiricist observer here and "the unconscious" to be carefully observed over there. At the historical loci at which Hillman and Marlan have their place, this duality, that is, the whole Jungian *relation* between empiricist observer and the unconscious, has been sublated into "the imaginal stance." The imaginal no longer operates with an observing mind vis-à-vis its object, "the unconscious." It is logically much more refined, more subtle, because it is both at once, having collapsed and integrated them both into itself: it is both the seeing *and* what is seen at the same time.

What for Jung was still imagined as an external obstacle, a wall that forces human inquisitiveness from its striving forward towards knowledge back into itself, into "the *un*conscious" as the result of inquisitiveness's (*consciousness's*) logical about-turn, is for the imaginal stance no longer an external barrier. This stance has the brake that prevents it from moving into thought built into its own style of operation. It *is* the tarrying at the threshold, the "ontological pivot." And the idea of the unassimilable and unthinkable is the explicit objectification of this internalized, integrated brake, an objectification, in which the imaginal approach provides itself with the logical justification for not going under. It now *cannot* go under because there *is* something unassimilable and unthinkable.

But the imaginal approach has a *semantic* equivalent to Jung's logical barrier, something to be avoided at all cost. It is the "poisonous state of splendid solar isolation," the peaks of spirit, at one end, and literalism at the other.

Inasmuch as the Jungian observer and the numinous archetypal symbols that he observed have in imaginal psychology become collapsed and *interiorized* into the very logic of image as such, and, as perspectives, have become more or less indistinguishable (cf. "We do not literally see images." "An image is not what you see but the way you see."), the cocooning effect of the imaginal approach is obviously much greater than in the case of Jung's setup. It is due to the high degree of interiority and comes out in the emphasis that is put on the aesthetic and "sense-certainty" quality. The image in imaginal thinking bestows much more anima-like innocence, unwoundedness by the animus, even immunization against any such wounding, than the "symbol" did for Jung, which was, after all, beheld (as well as intellectually "understood" and "put into ethical practice") by an "external" observer, the ego. The logical fusion of symbol and observer into one has a suction effect and tends to prevent "alienation" (the intrusion of the animus) on principle.

Just as "the image" is the (much more subtle) successor of (the far cruder *combination* of) symbol + observer, so the enthralling aesthetics of the imaginal is the successor of the Jungian "numinous experience." The numinous experience is a special massively emotional event. It happens at certain times to certain people. The "beauty" of the images is no longer a particular event and not literal beauty. It is, again much more subtly, the general objective *mystique* of image as such. And in the postulates of the unassimilable and unspeakable, this mystique, so to speak, exudes from the imaginal and crystallizes into the theoretical construct of a (quasi-ontological) absolute mystery existing in its own right, as an unknown and unknowable object to be reverently "gazed" at, or to be more precise: merely divined, in silent wonder. Rather than forcing an about-turn and a logical shrink-wrapping of psychic contents in "the unconscious," as was the case with Jung's barrier, the "unassimilable unthinkable" invites and attracts consciousness, but attracts into nothing, into its void or darkness. It is the *hypostatized* mysticism (abstract mystical quality) of the imaginal.

Jung's constitutive move to, and bouncing back off, the barrier across the mental world and Marlan's move to an "insurmountable 'not'" invite a comparison with the kind of move suggested in Heraclitus's dictum: "You would not find out the boundaries of soul, even by traveling along every path: so deep a logos does it have."[12] Heraclitus sends us forward all the way; we have to keep moving without reserve. And instead of then letting us bounce against a solid barrier or an insurmountable "not," *his* "not" negates the very idea of our ever coming to a limit. Heraclitus precisely frustrates our expectation of a stop sign. You can go as far as you want, you will never end up at an "unthinkable." Instead of presenting us with a reified negation, *his* negation interiorizes the forward move *itself* into itself and only in this self-contradictory way causes this decided forward move to be a recursive move into soul and its depth. Or should we say: for the first time creates the space of soul at all? Because soul is nothing ontological. It exists only if and when and for as long as it is *made*, and it is made through the *opus* of absolute-negative inwardization. The forward move began as a move in spatial imagination. Through his "not," Heraclitus forces this move out of spatial imagination and its naturalism altogether into thought, into the logos of soul. The forward move becomes self-contradictory: *recursive* progression, an active move forward into its own going under.

If, as Heraclitus claimed, you can never come to a boundary of soul, no matter which road you take and how far you travel, how then did Jung get to his barrier and Marlan, with all the philosophers he cites behind him, to the insurmountable "not"? Did they disprove Heraclitus and show that there *is* a limit, after all—or is what they found perhaps something very different from a boundary of soul and its deep logos? Or is it their own putting a stop to the movement suggested by Heraclitus, that is, to the unreserved movement into this movement's own self-negation, into its further and further going under into itself? The barrier and the remainder are ultimately the reified "not." And whereas this reified "not" allowed Jung to turn his back on it, when it has the form of the unassimilable remainder it allows one to always keep it at the same safe distance in front of oneself while one is moving, instead of oneself moving deeper and deeper into, and exposing oneself to the work of the *living* negation (where "oneself" does not of course refer to the person, but to the logic of consciousness). Could it be that both Jung's empiricist observer and his "the unconscious" are located outside the sphere of soul, in the land of positivity? The soul all right, but displaced from its native state and translated into the foreign language of positivity and naturalism?

Freud once said, "It is a most remarkable thing that the whole undertaking [of analysis] becomes lost labour if a single concession is made to secrecy. If at any spot in a town the right of sanctuary existed, one can well imagine that it would not be long before all the riff-raff of the town would gather there."[13] The notion of "the remainder" is the theoretical equivalent of that concession to secrecy in the practice of psychoanalysis and that right of sanctuary in a town. The negation is safely shelved. Consciousness can wash its hands of it.

"The unassimilable," the "unthinkable," and the "remainder" that we are talking about here must be distinguished from the common (*vulgi* version of the) experience of something unassimilable. The former unassimilable is a building block of psychological theory and a postulate, a principle apart from concrete practical experience or work. The latter unassimilable, by contrast, is phenomenal. It is the not infrequent experience that one cannot make sense of this particular dream image today, this pathology, this symbol or this detail in a myth or fairy tale. Here the remainder that resists understanding is not a general principle any more. It is due to a personal limitation, a lack of intelligence or knowledge. Also, it may not stay un-understood forever, because at some later time what it means may dawn on one, or somebody else may be able to make sense of it. In my work, both in the consulting room and in my study, I go to work and try my best. My best may, however, not be good enough so that there will be a resisting remainder. I have no difficulty accepting the idea of this (practical, phenomenal) type of "remainder," but this is not what has been our topic here.

## "A Critical Stance toward the Hegelian Dialectic"

Hegel *per se* is of course not a topic for us. We cannot be Hegelians in the 21st century, just as we cannot be Thomists or Cartesians or neo-Platonists in good conscience today. It would be ideological. Hegel was a philosopher of his time. There is no way back. We have to make our own bed. When I nonetheless stress the importance of Hegel, it is mainly for two reasons. It is, to my mind, an obligatory part of cultural education and a general training of the mind to have gone through the process of studying Hegel. It is part of one's homework and indispensable for being able to understand at least part of the modern world. And secondly, psychology in particular needs the capability of thinking dialectically in order to do justice to "the soul." Hegel is a great help in acquiring and strengthening a sense of absolute-negative inwardness. But in both regards, we do not "buy" his philosophy as a whole.

Marlan does not turn to Hegel directly, but reviews the critiques of a number of thinkers of the 20th century of Hegelian dialectic. We have to be very clear about it that in this way we do not really approach Hegel. We have lectures by Hegel himself about the history of philosophy. But nobody in his right mind would read those lectures in order to learn something, for example, about Plato. You have to read Plato (and perhaps Plato scholars) for that purpose. Similarly, it would be an error to think that in reading what Heidegger or Derrida said about Hegel you would really address the topic of Hegel. Heidegger and Derrida are philosophers in their own right, not ordinary scholars. And true philosophers always talk about their own philosophy even when discussing other philosophers.

Besides, Heidegger and most of the major French philosophers of the 20th century were divided from Hegel and classical metaphysics by a gulf. They are *modern* thinkers, and all in one way or another started out and pushed off from Husserl's phenomenology, which from the outset obstructed any avenue to a real understanding of Hegel. When they criticized Western metaphysics, they projected (retrojected) fundamental problems of the modern situation into it, problems that metaphysics did not have. The label "metaphysics" in their discussions has the character of a kind of screen-memory.

It is furthermore clear that a thinking committed to deconstruction, deferral, a sliding of signifiers is diametrically opposed to and precludes an understanding of dialectics, of absolute-negative interiorization, or of alchemical decomposition and distillation. Deconstruction is a style of (intellectual-theoretical) acting out and going away, on and on; a method of how the form of consciousness reserves *itself* over against the process of the deconstruction of "the text." Dialectics and alchemy, by contrast, stay with the one (hermetically enclosed) matter at hand and in both it is always so that the form of the dialectically or alchemically thinking consciousness *itself is subjected to the same process of the matter that is dialectically decomposed.* The distillation of the one is at the same time the distillation of the other.

Goethe wrote: "At first one goes into the water believing one wants to wade through it, until it gets deeper and deeper and one is forced to swim."[14] But the point of both the modern philosophical and the imaginal approach is not to go into the water in the first place. They maintain the fundamental (logical) difference, their own distance to the water. They walk along the river bank, letting the water move on, the signifiers slide, or following the "polytheistic" impulse.

The notion that emerges most prominently from Marlan's review of the philosophers who faulted Hegel for his dialectic is that of engulfment, of an all-embracing tendency, a restricted, "speculative" philosophical economy, and of an incorporation of all contradiction. The spirit and fantasy underlying this conception comes out best in those views of Derrida according to which "trying to undo Hegel is like trying to decapitate the hydra" and "that every attempt to refuse such engulfment is seen as error ...." "How do we escape the perpetual reversal entailed in any oppositional system of thought?" Hegel, it emerges, is a terrible, nearly invincible monster. One can only hope to escape from or, like Hercules, undo this monster. Hegel's philosophy is a dynamically growing prison. Any move you make will just enlarge this prison. To my mind this is a rather paranoid fantasy.

This type of reaction could perhaps be compared to an imaginary reaction to paintings like those of Mantegna, Leonardo da Vinci,

Dürer, Claude Lorrain, a reaction that would consist in the will to undo them because everything in them is subject to and restrained by central perspective. Even if one is a modern abstract painter, can one not truly appreciate those old masters too?

But this interpretation of *Hegel's* dialectic as being an instrument for incorporating, engulfing, and assimilating everything is very odd indeed. The dialectic is not aiming for a totalitarian system. It starts with a concrete particular notion or reality and unfolds the logical life contained in it. It is not a trick or technique to capture or engulf more and more other *views*. Hegel's thought is not operating on the level of views in the first place. Views are the views of people; they belong to human discourse. But Hegel works with or on *concepts* as quasi-alchemical objective matters (cf. "the matter's cold march of necessity").

But even if *Hegel's* intent were indeed such an engulfment, it would be obvious that *in psychology* dialectics could not possibly have this effect inasmuch as the psychological *opus* is concerned only with a particular matter in its "eachness" and has no interest in an all-embracing system. The methodological maxim of the psychological approach is, as I stated numerous times, that the image or psychic phenomenon at hand has everything it needs within itself. The goal is interiority, the inward depth of the same, not extension, accumulation, or hoarding.

About Heidegger's critique of Hegel Marlan states, "The 'not' is more than a dialectical alienation on the way to a sublation." But such a "not" is not a dialectical one in the first place. It is a hypostatized or *positivized* "not," one extracted from the real process. It is now something in its own right and has therefore, allegedly, become subject to an illegitimate attempt on the part of Hegel to "assimilate" it. But for dialectics there is no "not" that could be, or would have to be, *assimilated*. Let's take a simple practical example, one I constructed. An orchestra, in which many musicians play their particular instruments, is in turn the instrument upon which the conductor plays. The musicians have become sublated moments in the new instrument, the orchestra. There is no "not" here that would be a separate reality which could either be assimilated or "resist assimilation." The negation is inherent in the musicians as real members of the orchestra. Dialectical thought reveals to us the negation or "not" that already exists in the real phenomenon, namely the orchestra musicians' self-negation as former soloists playing on their instruments.

I suspect that the charge of an *assimilation* of the allegedly self-sufficient "not" and the setting up of the "not" as self-sufficient is actually and unwittingly a reflection of the fact that both the modern philosophical and the imaginal-psychological stances keep their own logical form of consciousness out of *what* they discuss. The fact that Hegelian dialectics does not maintain this neat difference, but exposes its own form of consciousness to examination at each stage is sensed by those critics of Hegel, but this *coniunctio* is misconstrued as an illegitimate assimilation of the "not." The alleged independent reality of the "not" that Hegel is supposed to have ignored is actually the "not" of the modern stance's (logically) *not* going into the water.

Especially with what Marlan cites from Derrida's critique of Hegel, the impression is created that dialectics is an almost imperialistic endeavor, an attempt to conquer more and more ground and to subdue every objection, every other view. The result of this view is that "Absolute Knowing" becomes almost comparable to an all-comprehensive world government. The perspective guiding this interpretation is power, domination (and its obverse, the fight against domination), that is, an ego interest. But we already know that dialectics is nearly the opposite, the self-exposure to and self-immersion in the process of the conscious standpoint's going under, its self-distillation. Inwardization and *recursive* progression instead of engulfment. In the case of Hegel's *Phenomenology of Spirit* and *Science of Logic*, it is the self-distillation, self-liquefaction of all semantics of the metaphysical tradition into syntactical or logical *form*.

Sublation is not a *goal* towards which one could be on the way. The "not" is neither a remainder nor "a momentary hiatus in the dialectic." It is not something separate or in between two statuses or phenomena, not what happens to, is done to, or is inflicted upon a given stance. It is the realization that the matter has all along *not* been what it had seemed to be. And this is at once the (first immediacy of the) recognition of the new form of the matter.

The inclusion in Marlan's discussion of the critique of dialectics by modern thinkers and their idea of a positivized "not" serves to prepare the ground for and to underpin the psychological ideas of the unassimilable remnant and the unthinkable, which, as we already found out, safeguard the imaginal stance (the form of consciousness of this stance) from itself having to go under into the "alchemical" process and to be itself exposed to the transformations of the matter.

## Conclusion: The Needs and Demands of Psychology

Quite apart from what the merits may be of a general philosophy that insists on a "'general' economy," fights logocentrism, and celebrates otherness and difference, the needs of psychology are precisely to cultivate "a restricted economy," for which the closed, hermetically sealed vessel is our alchemical symbol. Psychology, despite being committed to the soul of whatever is, is nevertheless, or precisely because of this, aware of having only modest aspirations and modest relevance and of on principle belonging only in an out-of-the-way corner of modern life as a whole. Psychology does not compete with philosophy. It is not, as philosophy is, so to speak, a global player; it does not have a grand mission to better the world. This empirical or semantic modesty concerning the sense of its own importance is, on the logical or syntactical level, reflected in the fact that its general stance and particular theses do not come with the claim to be ontologically relevant, but to be merely methodological: *if* one wants to do psychology one has to approach, treat, and interpret things in the way specified. But nobody needs to want to do psychology.

The closed vessel demands a commitment to absolute interiority. Because the vessel systematically *excludes* the whole ego-world (*mundus vulgi*)—all external "positive" reality and thus externality as such—what is in the vessel is not only inside it, but in itself (in its own logical form) "inner, inward," that is to say, a self; it has self nature, is uroborically self-reflective, self-contained, without a real (external) Other and without absolute difference. As a self it has its other within itself. And this, its own other, is in principle transparent for it. It can—in principle—be known and thought, because it has been generated by itself.

Psychology boldly *privileges* unity by preferring *coniunctio* over dissociation and therefore also by preferring "the unity of unity and difference" over "the difference of the unity and difference."

And because it is committed to the alchemical warnings against the physical in the material, psychology *professes* its decided (but methodological) logocentrism and essentialism (*anima naturaliter essentialistica*).[15] Its business is to deal with (existing) meanings, that is, only with "matters" that *are* in themselves meaning, nothing but meaning ("thoughts," "the soul's" thoughts); in other words, that are in the status of absolute-negativity (rather than positivities). Its business is to deal with the *logos eôn* (the subsisting logos, Heraclitus), or rather the particular subsisting *logoi* of all the diverse prime matters in their eachness as the soul that lives in them.

In its work, therefore, psychology strives toward an inwardization of the matter at hand into itself, which, if it succeeds, amounts to the matter's deepening, liquefying, and distillation: the freeing of its mercurial soul from its imprisonment in the positive-factual, the thinking the thought or existing concept as which the particular soul phenomenon *is*.

How else could it be psychology? How could there be psychology if one faddishly insisted on fundamental difference and otherness, anti-essentialism, and the unthinkable? "No man can serve two masters." Or rather, a *man* can perfectly well serve several masters, because he can be a psychologist, politically active, scientifically interested, a lover, a believer, a sportsman, a philosopher, all in personal union. But psychology cannot serve two masters. If it does not want to become a mongrel, a chimera, it has to abide by its principle, its definition.

---

[***Editor's note:*** Wolfgang Giegerich first sent me his interesting and important paper, "'The Unassimilable Remnant'—What Is at Stake? A Dispute with Stanton Marlan," as a response to my paper, "From the Black Sun to the Philosophers' Stone," published in *Spring 74—Alchemy* (2006). Our exchanges were mutually thought provoking and led to the further refinement, differentiation, and clarification of a number of ideas that we both believe are relevant to Jungian as well as Archetypal Psychology. For this reason, I asked Wolfgang if I could include his paper in this collection and he agreed. My own further reflections on Wolfgang's response will be published elsewhere.]

## *NOTES*

[1] Stanton Marlan, "From the Black Sun to the Philosopher's Stone," *Spring 74—Alchemy* (Spring 2006): 1-30.

[2] Wolfgang Giegerich, "Is the Soul 'Deep?'—Entering and Following the Logical Movement of Heraclitus' 'Fragment 45'," *Spring 64* (Fall and Winter 1998): 1–32; *The Soul's Logical Life: Towards a Rigorous Notion of Psychology* (Frankfurt am Main: Peter Lang, 1998/

3rd rev. ed. 2001), pp. 203–275; *Dialectics and Analytical Psychology: The El Capitan Canyon Seminar,* with David L. Miller and Greg Mogenson (New Orleans. LA: Spring Journal Books, 2005), pp. 1–24; "Closure and Setting Free, or The Bottled Spirit of Alchemy and Psychology," *Spring 74—Alchemy* (Spring 2006): 31–62.

[3] Wolfgang Giegerich, "Irrelevantification, or On the Death of Nature, the Construction of 'the Archetype,' and the Birth of Man," unpublished paper.

[4] Wolfgang Giegerich, "Killings: Psychology's Platonism and the Missing Link to Reality," *Spring 54* (1993): 5–18.

[5] Marlan, "From the Black Sun," p. 14.

[6] *Ibid.*

[7] Wolfgang Giegerich, "Psychology—The Study of the Soul's Logical Life," in *Who Owns Jung?* ed. Ann Casement (London: Karnac, 2007), p. 256.

[8] Although fully aware of the decidedly arbitrary connection between sound and meaning, Paul Kugler advanced the very different thesis that "on a synchronic level" the sound patterns are "nonarbitrarily tied through phonetic parity to a cluster of archetypally related meanings" (*The Alchemy of Discourse: An Archetypal Approach to Language* [Lewisburg, PA: Bucknell University Press, 1982], p. 103). It may well be true that this is valid for reduced or pathological states of the psyche, where it functions merely mindlessly like an automat. But I don't think psychology should *base* its own theory on such observations. Chickens whose heads have just been cut off are said to sometimes still run around for a while. Should this be one's basis for a theory of chicken behavior? "In geometry, if I may use a remote comparison, it is possible to arrive at Euclidean parallels by reducing the curvature of a non-Euclidean space to zero, but it is impossible to arrive at a non-Euclidean space by starting out with Euclidean parallels. In the same way, it seems to be a lesson of history that the commonplace may be understood as a reduction of the exceptional, but that the exceptional cannot be understood by amplifying the commonplace. Both logically and causally the exceptional is crucial, because it introduces … the more comprehensive category" (Edgar Wind, *Pagan Mysteries in the Renaissance* [New York: Norton, 1968], p. 238).

[9] C. G. Jung, *The Collected Works of C. G. Jung,* trans. R. F. C. Hull, vol. 14 (Princeton, NJ: Princeton University Press, 1970), § 129; hereafter abbreviated to *CW* followed by volume number and paragraph (§) number.

[10] Jung, *CW* 16, § 400

[11] Jung, *CW* 18, § 1734 (translation modified).

[12] Fragment 45 (Diels).

[13] Sigmund Freud, "Further Recommendations in the Technique of Psycho-analysis," *Collected Papers, Vol. II* (London: Hogarth Press, 1953), p. 356n.

[14] In a letter to Schiller, dated 21 December 1804, my translation.

[15] We must not take exception to the fact that logocentrism and essentialism are historically obsolete. "The soul" is the *historical* presence of what is no longer a present reality. Psychology is to some extent comparable to the modern institution of museums, which, too, house archeological finds and cultural treasures of the past in the middle of our modern technological civilization. Like museums, psychology provides a kind of oasis in modern life. Objective symbols of this oasis are the consulting room in physical or rather social reality and "the interior of man" as an idea or fantasy. Psychology is thoroughly modern because it is conscious of the decidedly pre-modern ("archeological") nature of what it is dealing with as well as of the pre-modern logic with which it approaches its subject-matter. It is modern because in it the pre-modern has been sublated so as to have merely methodological validity. It is, after all, nothing but psychology, not metaphysics, religion, physics, not poetry or art. Jung, of course, saw the archeological nature of "psychic reality" quite clearly, but nevertheless, forgetting all modesty, claimed present reality and immediate meaning significance for the archeological. "The archetypes are timeless and ever-present." That is not only a fiddle; it also does not do justice to psychology, for which obsolescence, deceasedness, disdain (cf. the *lapis in via ejectus*) are constitutive (they are psychology's *home*) and by no means corrigible or to be overcome. Where the obsolescence is obliterated or obscured instead of respected as belonging, and where psychology claims to be immediately relevant for today, psychology becomes inevitably nostalgic and/or ideological, which in psychology's present-day reality is already the case to a large extent.

Michael Vannoy Adams is a Jungian psychoanalyst in New York City. He is a clinical associate professor at the New York University Postdoctoral Program in Psychotherapy and Psychoanalysis. He is a faculty member at the Jungian Psychoanalytic Association, the Object Relations Institute, and Eugene Lang College of the New School, where he was previously Associate Provost. He is the author of three books: *The Multicultural Imagination: "Race," Color, and the Unconscious* (1996), *The Mythological Unconscious* (2001), and *The Fantasy Principle: Psychoanalysis of the Imagination* (2004). He is the recipient of three Gradiva Awards from the National Association for the Advancement of Psychoanalysis. He has been a Marshall scholar in England and a Fulbright senior lecturer in India.

14

# Imaginology: The Jungian Study of the Imagination[1]

MICHAEL VANNOY ADAMS

In *The Fantasy Principle: Psychoanalysis of the Imagination*, I state that "Jungian psychology is what I call imaginology, and Jungian psychologists are imaginologists."[2] Imaginology is the study of the imagination, and imaginologists are students of the imagination. Other psychologists study drives, the ego, objects, or the self. Jungian psychologists study images. The emphasis on the imagination is what is unique about Jungian psychology, which is an imaginal psychology.

"Anxiety" is one of the most important technical terms in psychoanalysis. "The ego," Freud says, "is the actual seat of anxiety."[3] According to Freud, "It is always the ego's attitude of anxiety which is the primary thing and which sets repression going"[4]—or, more generally, I would say, which sets defenses going. Freud says that "anxiety is a reaction of the ego to danger."[5] That is, the ego reacts anxiously—and then repressively or defensively—to what it regards as dangerous. Jung says: "In this way, as Freud rightly says, we turn the ego into a 'seat of anxiety,' which it would never be if we did not defend ourselves against ourselves so neurotically."[6] In a very real sense, every neurosis is an anxiety neurosis.

What Jung means when he says that "we defend ourselves against ourselves" is that the anxious ego neurotically defends itself against the unconscious. As a practitioner of imaginal psychology, I prefer to say, instead, that the anxious ego-image neurotically defends itself against non-ego images. As James Hillman says of the ego, "it too is an image."[7] "Ego" means "I." The ego-image is the "I"-image. It is who or how "I" imagine myself to be. The psyche—or the imagination—comprises an ego-image and a variety of non-ego images.

In effect, I advocate that Jungians adopt a new terminology, which I believe would be advantageous. The terms *ego-image* and *non-ego images* emphasize that, as Jung says, "the psyche consists essentially of images."[8] As I define "unconscious," it is what the ego-image is unconscious *of. Ironically, it is not the unconscious that is unconscious. Rather, it is the ego-image that is unconscious, and what it is unconscious of are non-ego images.* To the extent that the ego-image is unconscious of non-ego images, it tends to react anxiously and defensively because it regards them as dangerous.

The function of non-ego images is transformative. Non-ego images are what I call "images of transformation." They attempt to contact and impact the ego-image in an effort to transform it. The ego-image, however, regards non-ego images as dangerous precisely because they are transformative. That is, non-ego images are only ostensibly dangerous, from the perspective of the ego-image. The ostensible danger that non-ego images pose is to the partial, prejudicial, or defective attitudes of the ego-image. Non-ego images present alternative perspectives on the attitudes of the ego-image. If the ego-image is not defensive but receptive, it may entertain these alternative perspectives seriously, consider them critically, and then either accept or reject them. How might the ego-image be less defensive and more receptive? It would have to be less anxious and, I would say, more curious about non-ego images.

"Curiosity," in contrast to "anxiety," is not a technical term in psychoanalysis. Freud does, however, discuss curiosity. True to form, he derives it from and reduces it to sexuality. Civilization, Freud says, progressively conceals the body and, as a result, provokes "sexual curiosity." He says: "This curiosity seeks to complete the sexual object by revealing its hidden parts."[9] Sexual curiosity, Freud says, is perfectly normal, although it may also be prurient or even perverse, as in voyeurism. It is ultimately, he says, "curiosity to see other people's genitals."[10] According to Freud, sexual curiosity in particular is the very origin of curiosity in general. From this perspective, curiosity is originally an urge to see the unseen—and, more specifically, what I might call the "sexual unseen," the hidden parts of the body, the genitals of other people. I would say, however, that curiosity is neither derivable from nor reducible to sexuality. Sexual curiosity in particular is merely one variety of curiosity in general. In this respect, I would say that curiosity is an urge to know the unknown—and, more specifically, what I might call the "imaginal unknown"—the non-ego images, of which the ego-image is unconscious. From this perspective, a defensive ego-image is an anxious ego-image, and a receptive ego-image is a curious ego-image.

It is a notorious fact that the ego-image rarely exhibits any initiative in regard to non-ego images. Seldom does the ego-image approach non-ego images. Most frequently it is non-ego images that approach the ego-image, that attempt to contact and impact the ego-image in an effort to transform it. Rather than approach non-ego images, all too often the ego-image avoids them, or, when non-ego images approach it, attacks them—demonstrates just how neurotically defensive it is and exactly how it is defensive, in an effort to protect the ego-image. The ego-image employs the familiar, famous defenses of "flight" or "fight." An anxious ego-image is a suspicious ego-image—even, at the extreme, a paranoid ego-image. In contrast, a curious ego-image would be an inquisitive ego-image. It would inquire into non-ego images.

Jung declares that it does not matter—or matters very little—what the image is. What matters to Jung is not the image but the concept—for example, the concept of the treasure or the monster. Jung says that "it does not matter" if the treasure is a ring, a crown, a pearl, or a hoard.[11] Similarly, Jung says: "It matters little if the mythological hero conquers now a dragon, now a fish or some other monster."[12]

Gregory Bateson notes that in formal logic a class is "on a *different level of abstraction*" from the members of the class.[13] As a result, the class cannot be a member of the class, and a member cannot be the class. In this respect, the concept "treasure" is a class, and the images "ring, "crown," pearl," and "hoard" are members of the class; the concept "monster" is a class, and the images "dragon" and "fish" are members of the class. Logically, a treasure is on a different level of abstraction from a ring, crown, pearl, or hoard, and a monster is on a different level of abstraction from a dragon or fish. In effect, Jung privileges the class over the members of the class. What matters to Jung is the class (or concept). The members (or images), he says, do not matter or matter little. Jung commits a version of what Alfred North Whitehead calls the "fallacy of misplaced concreteness." Whitehead defines this fallacy as "mistaking the abstract for the concrete."[14] When Jung says that the concept of a treasure matters more than the image of a ring, a crown, a pearl, or a hoard, and when he says that the concept of a monster matters more than the image of a dragon or a fish, he regards the abstract concept as more important—in effect, more "concrete"—than the concrete image.

On the contrary, I would argue that it matters a great deal if the treasure is a ring, a crown, a pearl, or a hoard—or if it is, in fact, a treasure at all—and if it is a dragon, a fish, or some other monster—or if it is a monster at all—and that it matters a great deal if the hero attempts to conquer the dragon, fish, or monster or engage it in some other way. Why it matters—and why it matters so much—is that, in contrast to a concept, which is an abstract form, an image is a concrete content. The concept is nondescript; it possesses no distinctive qualities. In contrast, the image possesses quite distinctive qualities that imply, with exquisite exactitude, an essence. It is in and through those distinctive qualities that it is possible accurately to ascertain what is essentially implicit in the image.

Consider a dream that Fritz Perls cites. The dream is of a lake with water that is drying up. The dreamer says:

> And I think that there's one good point about the water drying up, I think—well, at least at the bottom, when all the water dries up, there will probably be some sort of treasure there, because at the bottom of the lake there should be things that have fallen in, like coins or something, but I look carefully and all that I can find is an old license plate.[15]

The dreamer anticipates that she will find at the bottom of the lake a treasure, but all that she finds is an old license plate. In contrast to a treasure, which as an abstract concept possesses no distinctive qualities, an old license plate, as a concrete image, possesses quite distinctive qualities. The dreamer says that the license plate is "outdated." She notes that the essential function of a license plate is "to allow—give a car permission to go."[16] An out-of-date license plate is, in this respect, essentially dysfunctional. What this image essentially implies is that even if the dreamer has a car and may want or need to go somewhere in it, she does not effectively possess the wherewithal, the means to that end—an up-to-date license plate that would allow or give that car permission to go there. This image is, truly, the license plate "hard to attain."

Jung is what I call a *conceptual essentialist*. He privileges the concept over the image. He derives the image from and reduces it to a concept. He replaces the image with a concept. For Jung, the image is incidental—relatively trivial, even utterly irrelevant. What is ultimately important to Jung is the concept, for "some other monster," as he says, would serve the same purpose just as well as a dragon or a fish. From this perspective, a dragon might as well be a fish, and a fish might as well be a dragon, for both are monsters. The dragon and the fish are merely examples of the monster. They are images that exemplify a concept. For Jung, the images of the dragon and the fish possess the same essence, and that is the concept of the monster.

I, too, am an essentialist, but I am what I call an *imaginal essentialist*. I maintain that images have essences, implicit ones, and that the Jungian methods of interpretation and active imagination can render these essences explicit. Although it is extremely difficult—I would say, impossible—to define the essence of a concept, because a concept is an abstract form, I argue that it is possible, as Hillman says, to "stick to the image"[17] and accurately define the essence of an image, because an image is a concrete content with distinctive qualities. Hillman emphasizes "the actual qualities of the image."[18] It is the actual qualities of the image that enable the elaboration of a definitional consensus through the Jungian methods of interpretation and active imagination. Conceptual essentialism is futile, for it results in incessant, vain definitional conflict over concepts that are intrinsically vague. In contrast, imaginal essentialism is feasible, for it relies on the distinctive qualities implicit in images.

The images of the dragon and the fish possess very different essences that are neither derivable from nor reducible to the concept of the monster. These different essences are a function of the distinctive qualities of these images. *Functionally, an image is a qualitative distinction with an essential difference.* A dragon is a dragon is a dragon—and not a fish. A fish is a fish is a fish—and not a dragon. The one is not equivalent to the other, and neither the image of the dragon nor the image of the fish is commensurable with the concept of the monster. Different images serve different—often vastly different—purposes.

I do not merely prefer concrete contents to abstract forms. I do not just have a predilection for images over concepts. For me, the decisive consideration is purely pragmatic. Images simply have more practical value than concepts. What is so practically valuable about images is that they are more informative than concepts. The images of a dragon and a fish possess more information than the concept of a monster. Concepts are generalizations; images are particularizations. In this respect, it is the unique nuances, the details, of a specific image that eloquently articulate and heuristically indicate what it essentially implies and that pragmatically inform the conduct of any analysis.

Of course, from a certain perspective, a dragon and a fish are also concepts and not images. "Dragon" and "fish" are classes with members—for example, Richard Wagner's "Fafner" and Steven Spielberg's "Jaws." As concepts, dragon and fish are not as abstract as monster, but they are not as concrete as the images of Fafner and Jaws, which are *a* dragon and *a* fish with not only distinctive qualities but also proper names and very specific narratives.

"What others call neuroses," Ginette Paris says, "let's call a 'monster.'"[19] She says that a monster is an image, in contrast to a neurosis, which is an "abstract concept."[20] I agree with Paris that a neurosis is an abstract concept, but I disagree with her that a monster is an image. A monster is also a concept. It is no more a concrete image than a neurosis is. Catherine Atherton notes that the concept of the monster is "vague, malleable, and inconsistent" and that, as a result, "any general theory about what monsters are and what they do" must acknowledge "this uncertainty." Atherton says that "it is we who decide—in some sense of 'decide'—what counts as monstrous." She says that different definitions of monster are a function of "different times, places, and cultures" or of different perspectives within a culture.[21] That is, in teratology, or the general theory of monsters, the definition of monster, as a concept, is indefinite. I would say that it is the ego-image that decides what counts as monstrous. What the ego-image counts as monstrous are non-ego images, which it tends to regard as dangerous. A monster is just a non-ego image that an anxious and defensive—or neurotic—ego-image considers a danger.

In this regard, Jung mentions "the totally erroneous supposition that the unconscious is a monster." This notion, he says, is just "fear of nature and the realities of life."[22] The unconscious, Jung asserts, is not a "monster" but a "natural entity" that is "completely neutral."

He contends that the unconscious "only becomes dangerous when our conscious attitude to it is hopelessly wrong." He says of the unconscious: "To the degree that we repress it, its danger increases."[23] Or, as I prefer to say, non-ego images from the unconscious become dangerous only when the anxious and defensive—or repressive—attitude of the ego-image wrongly regards them as monstrous.

"Monster" is an epithet by which the ego-image disparages the non-ego image. This is an example of the process that Bateson calls "teratogenic," which he defines as "a creating of monsters."[24] A teratogenic ego-image creates a "monster" merely by calling it so. The non-ego image is a "so-called" monster. Calling it so "monsterizes" the non-ego image and immediately restricts the options at the disposal of the ego-image. For example, calling it so may excuse killing the non-ego image.

Among the seven types of plot that Christopher Booker identifies as basic, the very first is what he calls "Overcoming the Monster." I might say that the hero does not "undergo" the monster but "overcomes" it. Booker says that the monster is what "the hero must confront in a fight to the death."[25] From this perspective, overcoming the monster entails slaying the monster. The contemporary monster, Booker says, is the "monster of global terrorism."[26] He notes that the first war in Iraq, in 1991, did not "overcome Saddam Hussein," did not "slay the monster." Thus, the second war against Iraq, which began in 2003, was an effort by America and George W. Bush to complete the plot, but, as Booker says, "the plot was not quite so simple," for even if Saddam Hussein was to a certain extent a monster, he was not as monstrous as all that. He did not possess weapons of mass destruction, and, from another perspective, Booker says, "of course, it was not Saddam who was the monster" but "America and Bush."[27]

Monster-slaying is a recurrent but not, as Jungians tend to assume, a universal theme. Of the fifty cultures that Clyde Kluckhohn surveyed, the monster-slaying theme is indigenous to only thirty-seven.[28] Although by definition killing is a putting to death in any manner, while slaying is a putting to death in a deliberate, violent, even wanton manner, slaying has a more heroic connotation than killing—hence the Jungian preference for monster-slaying over monster-killing. To "slay" is more poetic—and, I might say, more euphemistic—than to "kill." Slaying justifies, dignifies, even glorifies killing.

When the ego-image regards a non-ego image as a monster, however, it tends to commit what I call *imagicide*. The tendency is for the ego-image to "kill" the non-ego image, the "monster." Consider, in this regard, the ego-image and non-ego image in the following dream:

> I'm walking in the dark. A very strange animal arrives. The body is of a big dog. The face is of a rabbit with two very big teeth like a snake's. The animal keeps biting me and literally taking part of my flesh. I grab the animal, twirl it in the air, and throw it away. At that moment, I'm thinking: "Yes, it's dead." I've killed it.

In dreams, Anthony Stevens says, "from a psychological perspective, the monster is the 'monster within.'"[29] Edward C. Whitmont and Sylvia Brinton Perera assert that monsters "are not uncommon in dreams." Such images, they contend, epitomize "energy that is, in actuality, or felt to be, 'monstrous.'" Frequently, they say, the image of the monster is "an unnatural combination of qualities."[30] In this dream, the ego-image does not explicitly identify the non-ego image as a monster. It describes the non-ego image as a "very strange animal." David Williams notes, however, that prominent among "monsters of earthly form" are those that are "combinations of various animal forms."[31] The animal in this dream is just such an unnatural combination of qualities. It is a combination of three animal forms—a dog's body, a rabbit's face, and a snake's teeth. After the dreamer recounted the dream to me, I asked him why he had killed the animal. "When you asked me why I killed it," he replied, "I was lost—I had no answer." Then he said: "In the dream, I felt that I had to protect myself, that I had to kill it." The non-ego image bites the ego-image and literally takes part of its flesh. The ego-image responds defensively, as ego-images tend to do, and kills the non-ego image. It does not occur to the ego-image to engage the non-ego image in any other way. The ego-image just reacts; it does not pause and reflect and consider that there might be any viable alternatives but to kill the non-ego image.

Not only is it impossible, in a strict sense, to kill the monsters that emerge from the unconscious—as Paris says, they "can never entirely be eliminated"[32]—but it is also imprudent even to attempt to kill them. In the first place, the non-ego image may not be a monster at all but only a "monster" in the paranoid projection of an anxious, excessively protective ego-image. In the second place, even if the non-ego image is, in some respect, a monster, to kill it is to obviate any necessity—and any opportunity—for the ego-image to engage it in some other way. For example, a curious ego-image might inquire into the non-ego image—might inquire of it why it is such a very strange animal, a combination of a dog's body, a rabbit's face, and a snake's teeth, and why it bites the ego-image and literally takes part of its flesh—why the non-ego image contacts and impacts the ego-image in just this way in an effort to transform it. Engaging the non-ego image in "some other way" than, for example, killing it (or censoring it) requires an ego-image capable of seriously entertaining, with no bias, a variety of options.

Not only in dreams does the ego-image kill non-ego images. England and America also kill non-ego images—dragons and fish. England has St. George and the dragon; America has Captain Ahab and the fish. St. George lances the dragon; Captain Ahab harpoons the fish. Jung says that, topographically, the unconscious is "something below your feet, and you are St. George standing upon the dragon." This image, he says, "is the medieval ambition, to kill the dragon and stand on top of it."[33]

I would say that this image is not only the medieval ambition but also the contemporary ambition, and it is not only, I would emphasize, a male ambition but also a female one. Consider, for example, the account that Williams provides of St. Margaret and the dragon.[34] Margaret is a convert from paganism to Christianity. A local prefect attempts to seduce her and force her to worship pagan gods, but she refuses. From prison, she prays to God. Instantly, the enemy manifests as a dragon, which swallows her. In the belly of the dragon, she makes the sign of the cross. The dragon explodes, and Margaret emerges. Then, however, the enemy manifests again, this time as a handsome young man, who attempts to seduce her. "But," Jacobus de Voragine says, "Margaret laid hold of him by the head, stretched him on the ground, and put her right foot upon him, saying: 'Proud demon, lie prostrate beneath a woman's foot!'"[35] Like Kali the Hindu goddess, Margaret the Christian saint stands on top of a prostrate man. This is feminist—or "genderist"—triumphalism with a vengeance. What an ambition! To kill the dragon, to kill the unconscious, to kill the enemy, to kill the handsome young man, to kill the demon, to kill the non-ego image, and then to stand on top of it!

In this iconography, it is not only female figures who stand on top of prostrate men but also male figures who stand on top of prostrate women—as, for example, in the statue "Civic Virtue" in New York. This statue is a marble sculpture, originally situated near City Hall in Manhattan, but eventually relocated near Borough Hall in Queens. As Jeff Vandam describes the statue, it is "a muscular nude male youth with two vanquished women representing corruption and vice at his feet" and "with a sword over his shoulder."[36] The statue has never been popular. Fiorella La Guardia and Robert Moses loathed the statue, and feminists despise it as a politically incorrect, sexist image because it depicts civic virtue as a man and corruption and vice as women.

"The implacable mutual hostility between man and dragon, as exemplified in the myth of St. George," Carl Sagan says, "is strongest in the West." It is not, however, "a Western anomaly," he says, but "a worldwide phenomenon."[37] Although in the motif-index that Stith Thompson provides, "*Fight with dragon*" is type B11.11,[38] the theme is not, in spite of what Sagan says, universal. The Western tradition, of course, equates the dragon with the devil. Rather than analyze the dragon, the Western tradition moralizes the dragon. Moralistically equating the dragon with the devil, the very epitome of evil, conveniently excuses killing the dragon. St. George is a variation on St. Michael, who fights the dragon in the Apocalypse: "There was war in heaven: Michael and his angels fought against the dragon; and the dragon fought and his angels, And prevailed not; neither was their place found any more in heaven. And the great dragon was cast out" (Rev. 12: 7-8). June Allen and Jeanne Griffiths say that "St. Michael threw the dragon out of heaven and left St. George to deal with him once he landed on earth."[39] As a result, it is easier, they say, to identify with the down-to-earth St. George than the up-in-heaven St. Michael.

Hillman notes that the tradition of St. George and the dragon is "the major Western paradigm" of the hero myth. "Killing the dragon in the hero myth," he declares, "is nothing less than killing the imagination."[40] Hillman recounts how in the 1950s he was present when Esther Harding delivered a presentation "in favor of killing the dragon." Harding was, he exclaims, "so moralistic!"[41] The hero may have, as Joseph Campbell says, a thousand faces,[42] but the face of the hero in the Western tradition is that of a killer. The implications are absolutely incredible: culturally, socially, politically, militarily, religiously, sexually, ecologically—and, of course, psychoanalytically.

Jung considers *Moby-Dick* "to be the greatest American novel."[43] Why is the novel so great? I would say that it is great because Melville so radically deconstructs the hero myth. Captain Ahab does not kill the fish. The fish kills Captain Ahab—and all the sailors except Ishmael, who survives only by accident. In an attempt to commit imagicide, or kill the image, Captain Ahab, in effect, commits suicide and homicide. Melville explicitly diagnoses Captain Ahab as a case of monomania. Captain Ahab is not neurotically defensive; he is psychotically offensive. As Melville deconstructs the hero myth, it is insane. Of course, this deconstruction does not prevent America from chasing the "White Whale"—however elusive, even illusory, it may be—and then harpooning it. America kills the fish first and asks questions later, if ever.

Thus, when Karl Rove, former Deputy Chief of Staff and Senior Advisor to the president, resigns from the administration of George W. Bush, he cynically appropriates the image of the White Whale for partisan political purposes. He quotes opponents who say, "Rove is the big fish." In this case, the harpoon is a subpoena that the Democrats might issue to a Republican with a grandiose persecution complex to compel him to testify before Congress. "You know," Rove says, "I feel like I'm Moby Dick and we've got a couple of people on Capitol Hill auditioning for the role of Captain Ahab." In this paranoid projection, Rove does not know whether he is the hero or the dragon. "Let's face it," he says, "I mean, I'm a myth, and they're—you know, I'm Beowulf. You know, I'm Grendel. I don't know who I am. But they're after me."[44]

Many villages and towns in England have traditions of dragon-killing heroes. These traditions recount local details about the hero and the dragon. For example, the version that Jacqueline Simpson provides of Jim Pulk and the Knucker of Lyminster even includes which pub the hero visits after he kills the dragon:

> Jim Pulk was a farmer's boy, who baked a huge Sussex pie and put poison inside it, and drew it on a farm cart to the Knucker Hole [at Lyminster], while he himself hid behind a hedge. The Dragon came out, ate the pie, died, and Jim Pulk then emerged and cut off his head with his scythe. He then went down to the Six Bells Inn, had a drink to celebrate his victory, and fell down dead. Presumably, he had got some poison on his hand, which, no doubt, very properly, he drew across his mouth after downing his pint.[45]

Apparently, the ironically hygenic moral of this tradition is that however civil the manners of the dragon-killing hero may be, in order to survive a beer perhaps he should also be an obsessive-compulsive hand-washing hero.

In *The Mythological Unconscious*, I acknowledge that I committed an egregious error when I interpreted a dream that a young man had about a dragon. I erred when I assumed that the ego-image must kill the non-ego image—that in order to become a hero, the young man must slay the dragon. The young man cautioned me that the dream did not stipulate that "the dragon must be slain." There was no dragon-slaying indication in the dream. The young man pondered the image of dragons and quite properly wondered: "Why does everyone want to *kill* them?"[46] At least on that occasion, he was a much more astute psychoanalyst than I was. I deserved a rebuke. Rather than "stick to the image," I had unconsciously—and uncritically—projected onto the dream the Jungian concept of the dragon-slaying hero. I had killed the image. The dream, I had to admit, did not indicate that the young man must slay the dragon but, at most, only that he "must effectively engage the dragon *in some way*."[47]

"Those of us who are students of psychology," Mary Watkins says, "have become heirs to a potential arsenal of ways to kill the image." The effect is to lead "away from a direct experience of the image," she says, "towards a concept."[48] Psychoanalysts—among them, Jungian psychoanalysts—routinely kill images. Hillman says that this killing occurs by interpreting images—that is, by deriving them from and reducing them to concepts. As Hillman defines interpretation, it is a conceptualization of the imagination. Interpreting a dream, he says, is "killing its images with interpretative concepts."[49] Replacing images with concepts—for example, interpreting a snake as "fear," "sexuality," or the "mother-complex"—is, Hillman says, "killing the snake."[50] A black snake may be an image in a dream, and in an analytic session an individual "can spend a whole hour with this black snake, talking about the devouring mother, talking about the anxiety, talking about the repressed sexuality, talking about the natural mind," Hillman says, and then the individual "leaves the hour with a concept about my repressed sexuality or my cold black passions or my mother or whatever it is."[51] From this perspective, any concept is the very death of any image. Not all interpretation, however, is conceptual. There is also what I call imaginal interpretation. Interpretation need not kill the image with a concept. Rather than replacing the image with a concept, it may respect the image and, by meticulous attention to the distinctive qualities of the image, render explicit the essence that is implicit in the image.

Of course, interpretation is not the only Jungian method. There is also active imagination. Active imagination requires an ego-image that is curious and inquisitive. The ego-image actively engages the non-ego image in a dialogue. Active imagination is a conversation between the ego-image and the non-ego image. It is not a dictation but a negotiation. In this sense, active imagination is a form of diplomacy. It is not only a "talking cure" but also a "listening cure." In active imagination, the ego-image talks to the non-ego image and listens to it, and the non-ego image talks to the ego-image and listens to it. Active imagination is *interactive imagination*. Both the ego-image and the non-ego image pose questions, and both provide answers. There is no imperative, I would emphasize, for the ego-image to capitulate to the non-ego image. In active imagination, the only obligation is for the ego-image to entertain seriously and consider critically what the non-ego image has to say. What the non-ego image has to say is not necessarily the "truth." It is an *opinion* that the ego-image may either accept or reject. In the process, not only may the non-ego image persuade the ego-image, but also the ego-image may convince the non-ego image. The non-ego image may transform the ego-image, and the ego-image may transform the non-ego image. In active imagination, the ego-image is just as much an "image of transformation" as the non-ego image is. Actively imagine a dialogue between St. George and the dragon or between Captain Ahab and the fish: not St. George lancing the dragon or Captain Ahab harpooning the fish—not a concept killing the image—but St. George and the dragon and Captain Ahab and the fish conducting a reciprocal conversation and experiencing a mutual transformation. Or actively imagine a dinner and a drink, a pie and a pint, with no poison, between Jim Pulk and the Knucker of Lyminster at a pub. Or actively imagine, as Nicholas D. Kristof does, a direct negotiation between America and North Korea over the issue of nuclear proliferation. "We sometimes," Kristof says, "do better talking to monsters than trying to slay them or wish them away."[52]

Whether in contemporary American culture the hero has to slay monsters in order to be a hero is a most important political issue in the 2008 American presidential election. Maureen Dowd asserts that Barack Obama "doesn't pay attention to the mythic nature of campaigns, but if he did, he would recognize the narrative of the classic hero myth." In order to attain the treasure—whether it is "a golden fleece or an Oval Office"—the hero, Dowd says, "has to kill monsters."[53] In this case, the allusion is to Jeremiah Wright, the African-American minister whom many white Americans consider a "monster." Wright has noted that historically America has perpetrated many abominations—among them, the racist atrocities of slavery and segregation. He has described the terrorist attacks of "9/11" as retribution for terrorist acts that America has committed. He has said that America may have employed AIDS for genocidal purposes. He has said, "God damn America" rather than "God bless America." Many Americans, especially white Americans, consider such comments "monstrous." They insisted that Obama not only denounce these remarks but also renounce Wright—or, in psychoanalytic terms, "dissociate" Wright—and Obama finally did so. The alternative to dissociation was persistent guilt by association. From a psychoanalytic perspective, Wright is a non-ego image that the ego-image of many Americans would prefer to repress and remain unconscious of. Obama may or may not be a "monster-slaying hero," but he is now a "minister-slaying hero." When Obama repudiated Wright, he "killed the monster"—or at least attempted to do so. (Whether the repudiation was rhetorically forceful enough to be persuasively "heroic" for white Americans was a question for which there was no immediately conclusive answer.)

I would say that what has distinguished Obama as a presidential candidate is an effort to be a new style of hero. For example, rather than "bomb, bomb, bomb" Iran, as John McCain would, or "obliterate" Iran, as Hillary Clinton would, Obama says that he would engage Iran in a direct negotiation over the issue of nuclear proliferation. In this sense, the alternatives in the 2008 American presidential election are between different styles of hero. Stylistically, Obama presents a challenge to the narrative of the classic hero myth in the Western tradition. In contrast to McCain and Clinton, Obama has an ego-image that does not immediately "monsterize" a non-ego image and "kill" it, but attempts to engage it in some other, more effective way—dialogically and diplomatically. Whether in contemporary American culture, at this stage in the history of consciousness, this new style of hero is politically plausible is the issue.

Why does the ego-image tend to kill non-ego images rather than engage them in some other way? I would argue that it does so because it regards non-ego images as "opposite" rather than "different." The neurotic reaction of the ego-image to the non-ego image is a function of what I call moralistic, scientific, and aesthetic oppositions—good versus evil, true versus false, and beautiful versus ugly. These oppositions provide the ego-image with a convenient excuse to repress—or "kill"—non-ego images that it considers evil, false, or ugly—and, as a result, dangerous. "Evil," "false," and "ugly" are, of course, concepts. When the ego-image applies these concepts to non-ego images, these oppositions eradicate the differences, the distinctive qualities that are intrinsic to non-ego images.

If Jungian psychology were an imaginology, it would be deconstructive rather than repressive. Such an imaginology would be a combination of Jungian psychology and Derridean philosophy. It would emphasize "differences," as Jacques Derrida does.[54] The ego-image would not repress non-ego images. Non-ego images would deconstruct the ego-image. The ego-image would not be "opposite" to non-ego images. Non-ego images would be "different" from the ego-image. An ego-image that non-ego images have deconstructed would be an ego-image that does not regard non-ego images as an array of oppositions that it must repress (evil, false, or ugly non-ego images as a danger to the good, true, and beautiful ego-image), but as a profusion of differences that it may contemplate and then engage in appropriate ways. This project would not be a conceptualization of the imagination but what Hillman argues is "*the major task*" of contemporary psychology: "the differentiation of the imagination."[55]

## *NOTES*

[1] This is a revised version of a paper presented at the "Psyche and Imagination" conference of the International Association for Jungian Studies at the University of Greenwich, London, July 6, 2006.

[2] Michael Vannoy Adams, *The Fantasy Principle: Psychoanalysis of the Imagination* (Hove and New York: Brunner-Routledge, 2004), p. 7.

[3] Sigmund Freud, *The Standard Edition of the Complete Psychological Works of Sigmund Freud*, trans. and ed. James Strachey, vol. 19 (London: Hogarth Press, 1961), p. 57. (Hereafter abbreviated to *SE* followed by volume and page number.)

[4] Freud, *SE* 20, p. 109.

[5] *Ibid.*, p. 129.

[6] C. G. Jung, *The Collected Works of C. G. Jung*, trans. R. F. C. Hull, vol. 10 (Princeton, NJ: Princeton University Press, 1970), p. 170,

par. 360. (Hereafter abbreviated to *CW* followed by volume number, page number, and paragraph [§] number.)

[7] James Hillman, *The Dream and the Underworld* (New York: Harper & Row, 1979), p. 102.

[8] Jung, *CW* 8, p. 325, § 618.

[9] Freud, *SE* 7, p. 156.

[10] *Ibid.*, p. 192.

[11] Jung *CW* 8, p. 112,§ 229.

[12] *Ibid.*, p. 372, § 718.

[13] Gregory Bateson, *Steps to an Ecology of Mind: Collected Essays in Anthropology, Psychiatry, Evolution, and Epistemology* (Northvale, NJ, and London: Jason Aronson, 1987), p. 201.

[14] Alfred North Whitehead, *Science and the Modern World* (New York: Free Press, 1967), p. 51.

[15] Fritz Perls, *Gestalt Therapy Verbatim*, ed. J. O. Stevens (Lafayette, CA: Real People Press, (1969), p. 81.

[16] *Ibid.*

[17] James Hillman, *Inter Views: Conversations with Laura Pozzo on Psychotherapy, Biography, Love, Soul, Dreams, Work, Imagination, and the State of the Culture* (New York: Harper & Row, 1983), p. 54; James Hillman, *Archetypal Psychology,* Uniform Edition of the Writings of James Hillman, vol. 1 (Putnam, CT: Spring Publications, 2004), p. 21.

[18]James Hillman, "An Inquiry into Image," *Spring* (1977): 69.

[19] Ginette Paris, *Wisdom of the Psyche: Depth Psychology after Neuroscience* (London and New York: Routledge, 2007), p. 68.

[20] *Ibid.*, p. 69.

[21] Catherine Atherton, "Introduction," in *Monsters and Monstrosity in Greek and Roman Culture*, ed. Catherine Atherton (Bari: Levante Editori, 1998), p. x.

[22] Jung *CW* 16, p. 152, § 328.

[23] *Ibid.*, § 329.

[24] Gregory Bateson, *Sacred Unity: Further Steps to an Ecology of Mind*, ed. R. E. Donaldson (New York: HarperCollins, 1991), p. 292.

[25] Christopher Booker, *The Seven Basic Plots: Why We Tell Stories* (London and New York: Continuum, 2004), p. 22.

[26] *Ibid.*, p. 695.

[27] *Ibid.*, p. 696.

[28] Clyde Kluckhohn, "Recurrent Themes in Myths and Mythmaking," in *Myth and Mythmaking*, ed. H. A. Murray (New York: George Braziller, 1960), p. 51.

[29] Anthony Stevens, *Private Myths: Dreams and Dreaming* (Cambridge, MA: Harvard University Press, 1995), p. 188.

[30] Edward C. Whitmont, and Sylvia Brinton Perera, *Dreams, a Portal to the Source* (London and New York: Routledge, 1989), p. 109.

[31] David Williams, *Deformed Discourse: The Function of the Monster in Mediaeval Thought and Literature* (Montreal: McGill-Queen's Press, 1996), p. 178.

[32] Paris, p. 69.

[33] C. G. Jung, *Nietzsche's Zarathustra: Notes of the Seminar Given in 1934-1939*, ed. J. L. Jarrett, vol. 1 (Princeton, NJ: Princeton University Press, 1988), p. 155.

[34] Williams, pp. 317-318.

[35] Jacobus de Voragine, *The Golden Legend*, trans. G. Ryan and H. Ripperger (Salem, NH: Ayer, 1991), p. 353.

[36] Jeff Vandam, "Hard Times Fall on an Ill-Loved Hero," *New York Times*, February 11, 2007, City Section, p. 8.

[37] Carl Sagan, *The Dragons of Eden: Speculations on the Evolution of Human Intelligence* (New York: Random House, 1977), pp. 140-141.

[38] Stith Thompson, *Motif-Index of Folk Literature*, vol. 1 (Bloomington, IN: Indiana University Press, 1955), p. 354.

[39] June Allen and Jeanne Griffiths, *The Book of the Dragon* (Secaucus, NJ: Chartwell Books 1979), p. 51.

[40] James Hillman, "The Great Mother, Her Son, Her Hero, and the Puer," in *Fathers and Mothers*, ed. Patricia Berry (Dallas, TX: Spring Publications, 1991), p. 169.

[41] J. Marlan, "Jan Marlan Interviews James Hillman," *IAAP Newsletter*, 26 (2006): 192. (Marlan: 192).

[42] Joseph Campbell, *The Hero with a Thousand Faces* (Princeton, NJ: Princeton University Press, 1968).

[43] Jung, *CW* 15, p. 88, § 137.

[44] Karl Rove, "FOX News Sunday with Chris Wallace," August 19, 2007.

[45] Jacqueline Simpson, *British Dragons* (London: B. T. Batsford, 1980), p. 45.

[46] Michael Vannoy Adams, *The Mythological Unconscious* (New York and London: Karnac, 2001), pp. 426-427.

[47] *Ibid.*, p. 430.

[48] Mary Watkins, *Waking Dreams* (Dallas, TX: Spring Publications, 1984), p. 135.

[49] Hillman, *Dream and the Underworld*, p. 116.

[50] James Hillman, *Re-Visioning Psychology* (New York: Harper & Row 1975), p. 39.

[51] Hillman, *Inter Views*, pp. 53-54.

[52] Nicholas D. Kristof, "Talking with the Monsters," *New York Times*, October 10, 2006, p. A25.

[53] Maureen Dowd, "Praying and Preying," *New York Times*, April 30, 2008, p. A19.

[54] Jacques Derrida, "Differance," in *Speech and Phenomena, and Other Essays on Husserl's Theory of Signs*, trans. D. B. Allison and N. Garver (Evanston, IL: Northwestern University Press, 1973), pp. 129-60.

[55] Hillman, *Re-Visioning Psychology*, p. 37.

# Poetry, Myth, Art, and Religion

... [F]ollowing Jung I use the word fantasy-image in the poetic sense, considering images to be the basic givens of psychic life, self-originating, inventive, spontaneous, complete, and organized in archetypal patterns. ... I am working toward a psychology of soul that is based in a psychology of image ... suggesting both a *poetic basis of mind* and a psychology that starts ... in the processes of imagination.

—James Hillman, *Re-Visioning Psychology*, p. xi

This move toward mythical accounts as a psychological language locates psychology in the cultural imagination. ... Archetypal psychology grounds itself in a fantasy that cannot be taken historically, physically, literally ....

—James Hillman, *Archetypal Psychology*, p. 28

Even if the recollection of mythology is perhaps the single most characteristic move shared by all "archetypalists," the myths themselves are understood as metaphors—never as transcendental metaphysics whose categories are divine figures. "Myths do not ground, they open."

—James Hillman, *Archetypal Psychology*, 3rd ed., p. 31

DAVID L. MILLER is Watson-Ledden Professor of Religion, Emeritus, at Syracuse University and is a retired Core Faculty Member at Pacifica Graduate Institute. He was made an Associate Member of the Inter-Regional Society of Jungian Analysts in 2002 and an honorary member of the International Association of Analytical Psychology in 2004. He is the author of five books and over one hundred articles and book chapters. For more information about Dr. Miller's work and publications, see: http://web.syr.edu/~dlmiller/

# 15

# Psyche's Poetry

DAVID L. MILLER

"I am working toward a psychology of soul that is ... a *poetic basis of mind.*"

—James Hillman

## Introduction: "Only a Poet ..."

On May 5, 1959, when he was 84, just two years before his death, C. G. Jung said to Miguel Serrano, the Chilean writer and diplomat: "Nobody understands what I mean, only a poet could begin to understand."[1] This could come as bad news to anyone who is not a poet and who at the same time wishes to understand Jung's psychology. However, a perspective of Ananda Coomaraswamy may help. He once wrote: "The artist [which surely includes the poet] is not a special kind of person, but every person a special kind of artist."[2] One might imagine, then, that it is the interior "poet" in every person that has a psychological sensibility. But, be that as it may, the question remains as to Jung's meaning concerning the relationship of depth psychology to a poetic perspective or a poetic logic. The answer to this question may well depend on which Jung one is petitioning, since Jung was by no means consistent about the matter of poetry.

## EARLY JUNG: THE POETS ARE CRAZY AND SICK

In the early years of his writing and thinking, Jung does not give much help about what he may have meant in his 80s when speaking with Serrano. On the contrary, in 1902, when Jung was 27 and writing on occult phenomena, he gave poets as an example of inflation due to hysteria or compensatory psychopathic inferiority. These are "persons with habitual hallucinations [who] ... draw attention to themselves, [like] ... poets, artists, saviors, prophets or founders of new sects."[3] A year later, writing about a case of manic mood disorder, Jung is reminded of "the miserable lives lived by poets and artists who, with small talent and indestructible optimism, eke out a hungry existence despite the fact that they possess quite enough intelligence to do good work in an ordinary profession."[4] And when Jung was thirty, in 1905, writing on cryptomnesia and wish-fulfillment, he spoke about poets being beguiled by their own ideas and believing their notions to be novel and new, which is just an expression of their wishing that they were novel and new.[5]

This is the young Jung who protested (perhaps too much): *Ich bin ein Empirischer*,[6] and who wrote to Maud Oakes, looking back on this period, and admitting: "I no longer lie. Once, perhaps, I had to, as a young scientist without a reputation."[7] So it is that the early Jung does not help with the question regarding depth psychology and poetry.

## MIDDLE JUNG: POETRY AS PSYCHOLOGY

However, when Jung was in his 40s and 50s, he seems to have changed his mind. In 1916, in a lecture on the structure of the unconscious, Jung wrote, much like Freud on the occasion of his 70th birthday: "The poets ... have supplied a good deal of evidence" regarding anima and the soul of psychology.[8] And even more strongly, five years later, when Jung was 46, he wrote: "They [the poets] are always the first to divine the darkly moving mysterious currents and to express them as best they can, in symbols that speak to us. They make known, like true prophets, the stirrings of the collective unconscious ... which in the course of time must inevitably come to the surface as a collective phenomenon .... We cannot therefore, afford to be indifferent to the poets, since in their principle works and deepest inspirations they create from the very depths of the unconscious voicing aloud what others only dream."[9] In 1924, three years later in a lecture in London on education, Jung said: "Primordial images in poetry ... are a mine of archetypal lore."[10] And six years later when Jung was in his mid-50s, in an article on psychology and literature, he wrote: "Psychology and aesthetics will always have to turn to one another for help."[11]

But this effusive turnabout, affirming the psychological importance and relevance of poetry, smacks of Romantic assertiveness, especially in the light of the context of the last quotation, which reads as follows: "The creative act, being rooted in the immensity of the unconscious, will forever elude our attempts at understanding. ... [I]t can be guessed at, but never wholly grasped."[12] Not only does this sound Romanticist—splitting thinking and poetry, putting them in opposition, like mind and heart—but it is odd since 29 years later he will say to Serrano that *understanding* is possible only poetically. This about-face of Jung's may be reminiscent of Freud's *Gedankenschreck*, "fear of thinking," of Heidegger's *der Flucht vor dem Denken*, and Wolfgang Giegerich's criticism of Jung as making a "flight into the unconscious" or a *sacrificium intellectus*.[13] Being one-sidedly positive may not be any more useful psychologically than being one-sidedly negative. Perhaps, finally, Jung cannot himself help us with the question that his comment to Serrano poses.

## Late Jung: Psychology as Poetry

However, there is one other matter that comes late in Jung's life, just seven years before the conversation with the Chilean poet. When Jung was 77, in 1952, he had a contentious exchange with Martin Buber in the journal, *Merkur.* Buber had written a critique of Jung's "Seven Sermons of the Dead" and his *Answer to Job*, accusing Jung of being Gnostic and of psychologizing religious content. Jung's response was that Buber did not understand a depth psychological perspective concerning the reality of the psyche as being objective, and that his, Jung's, approach to religious phenomenology was from the perspective, not of the divine, but of the soul. Jung's view was that his remarks about religion were taken theologically (metaphysically) rather than psychologically (phenomenologically). But in this essay responding to Buber, Jung did allow an exception to his usual approach. He wrote in German: *"Ich will hier einmal—ausnahmweise—transzendent spekulieren beziehungsweise 'dichten.'"*[14] This has been translated in two different ways in two issues of *Spring Journal—Spring 1957* and *Spring 1973* (the latter version being the one used in the *Collected Works*): "Here just once, and as an exception, I will speculate, transcendentally; that is, I will poetize"[15]; or: "Here, just for once, and as an exception, I shall indulge in transcendental speculation and even in 'poetry.'"[16] But perhaps Jung "poetized" more than "once" (*einmal*); perhaps this is not an "exception" (*ausnahmweise*). Perhaps, in some sense, all of his psychology is poetry. Did not Jung write: "Every psychology—my own included—has the character of a subjective confession .... Even when I deal with empirical data, I am necessarily speaking about myself .... Every psychology which is the work of one man is subjectively colored"[17]? He also said: "Every interpretation is an hypothesis."[18] It is not a far leap from all psychology as subjective and confession, to all psychology is poetry. Jung did write: "Our science is a language of metaphor."[19] And then there is that strange business about Jung imagining a personal connection to the poet, Goethe.

According to testimony in *Memories, Dreams, Reflections*, Jung's mother said to the boy, Jung: "You must read [Goethe's] *Faust* some day."[20] And, having subsequently read *Faust,* Jung later confessed: "*Faust,* I now realized, meant more to me than my beloved Gospel according to St. John."[21] And, even later, Jung observed: "I regard my work on alchemy as a sign of my inner relationship to Goethe."[22]

There seems to be something in Jung that desired, in the logic of psychology, a poetic nature. At the beginning of a creative period, he wrote: "I had not yet found the right language ... the matrix of a mythopoeic imagination has vanished from our age ...."[23] Similarly, Jung noted: "I realized the concordance between this poetic myth [The Grail Legend] and what alchemy had to say about the *unum vas,* the *una medicina*, and the *unus lapis.*"[24] Jung did not win the Goethe prize for literature. Freud did. But Jung did assert an intimate, even if false and fantastic, connection to Goethe, an archetypal poet. Perhaps he imagined—as he implied to Serrano—that it was the only way that he could himself understand his own psychologizing. In any case, Jung seems to have wanted it both ways: psychology as science (empiricism) and as poetry. As Yogi Berra said: "When you come to a fork in the road, take it." Jung did.

On the other hand, in his radical revisioning of Jung's psychology, James Hillman wanted it one way only: the way of poetry and image, metaphor and multiple meanings. Ironically, Hillman insisted on the one way of multiplicity. So it is that Hillman's archetypal psychology seems to have provided more of a reason for Jung's saying to Serrano: "Only a poet can understand."

## James Hillman: A Poetic Basis of Psychology

In the major articulation of archetypal psychology—the Terry Lectures at Yale in 1972, published as *Re-Visioning Psychology* in 1975—James Hillman says clearly at the outset that in order to make of life and the world a "vale of soul-making" (a phrase of the poet Keats) it will take a psychology whose logic and nature is "a poetic basis of mind."[25]

Like Lacan attempting to return to Freud's most deep and radical insights, against the prevailing trends of Freudian psychology in the direction of ego developmentalism and away from a depth psychology, Hillman wanted to pick up on Jung's most radical edge, and fight against what he saw as a weakening of *depth* psychological insight in the Jungian community. He was clearly on a mission. In *Inter Views*, he would write: "I trust my anger. It's my favorite demon."[26] "It's polemical."[27] "So many hatreds boiling up."[28] And recently, in an interview with Jan Marlan in the 2006 issue of the *Newsletter* of the International Association for Analytical Psychology, he said: "I work from anger."[29] I think of this as being like the anger of the Hebrew prophets (after all, Hillman's grandfather was a rabbi). Just as the prophets' anger was on behalf of the soul of the Hebrew faith, Hillman's anger has been on behalf of the soul of his patients. In his interview with Jan Marlan, he fears—as he did in *We've Had a Hundred Years of Psychotherapy—and the World's Getting Worse*—that psychological theory and practice "has become … a kind of New Age substitute for life …; a substitute for rigorous education in culture, philosophy and religion …; and a 'helping profession,'" i.e., to help the ego and its perspectives, itself a sort of narcissistic character disorder. Hillman says to Jan Marlan, "I just think Giegerich is right—and Ziegler was, too—the whole thing has lost its way. Something is deeply missing …. It's become too humanized, feminized, personalized, and its language feels dead. … The psyche has to keep working its *logos*, i.e., making psychology."[30]

In *Re-Visioning Psychology*, Hillman was angry about four fundamental things: a new emphasis on person and personalism; a salvific and quasi-religious emphasis on health and wholeness; a neglect of ideas and thinking in favor of emotion and feeling; and a humanism that ignores the archetypal and transpersonal. Hillman's antidote—the antidote of the poetic basis of soul-making archetypally—was to personify rather than to personalize, to pathologize and to go down and in rather than to spiritualize and to go up and out, to see and think through, and transpersonally to dehumanize in the manner of Renaissance Neo-Platonism.

The point in all of this was to deliteralize psychological theory, to differentiate it polytheistically, to nonobjectify and dissolve and defixate the insight of psychological practice and experience. He said in the Terry Lectures: "Here I join Norman O. Brown and Owen Barfield in a mafia of metaphor to save plain men from literalism."[31] That is, poetry shows the logic of the way to soul-making. A poetic logic allows a depth—as opposed to ego—to psychological understanding. This was also the point of Hillman's saying, even before the Terry Lectures, that in order to be radically faithful to Jung, even in ways that Jung was not faithful to his own deepest insights, it was necessary to abandon the word "archetypes," which substantialized and concretized essentialistically and universalistically Jungian insights, and rather to use the term "archetypal," meaning a way of seeing or seeing through.[32] This was also his strategy with myth, with the many gods and goddesses. As he put it: "By relying on myths as its primary rhetoric, archetypal psychology grounds itself in a fantasy that cannot be taken historically, physically, literally."[33] In emphasizing the non-literal nature of psychological language and notions,[34] Hillman was insisting that a soul psychology, whether in theory or practice, does not refer to ego, to human behavior, or to a person's personal attitudes, perspectives, and beliefs. It is not a humanistic psychology. As Hillman said forthrightly in *The Dream and the Underworld*:

> Every resurrection fantasy ... may be a defense against death; every rebirth fantasy in psychology may be a defense against depth; and every dream interpretation that translates into daily life and its concerns is a defense against soul.[35]

## A Poetics of Dying

Hillman's mention of death in relation to depth and soul is psychologically crucial. Jung, at the end of his life, wrote: "The experience of the self is always a defeat for the ego."[36] This is to say that every advance, in theory or in the practice of analysis, from an ego perspective to a soul perspective, is experienced by the ego as a death of its cherished attitudes, standpoints, and beliefs, not to mention its behavior. This also is the force of Hillman's entire book, *The Dream and the Underworld.* And, more recently, it has been the *leitmotif* of the psychological theorizing of Wolfgang Giegerich.

In his book *Animus-Psychologie,* Giegerich demonstrates this depth psychological insight by reference to the poet Hölderlin. This poet kept himself realistically in the contemporary mythless world, staying in the night (*nigredo*) of the Occident, where the gods have fled, but continuing to raise the question of how one can be a poet in a time of dearth. Rainer Maria Rilke had written about Hölderlin: "His poetic line closes itself as a destiny so that a death occurs even in the gentlest diction." This poet, Giegerich avers, speaks in a lively way as one already deceased, i.e., soulfully.[37]

Giegerich, like Jung and Hillman before him, insists that "the person who does psychology must be the new or *other* personality. The daimon, the Self, the soul: they are the ones who alone can produce a psychology that deserves the name [i.e., psyche-ology]."[38] So—from ego's perspective—"entering [psychology] cannot be done without some violence."[39] Or, as Giegerich put it forcefully: "Psychological discourse … has to *be as* the negation of the ego, and the psychologist … has to speak as one who has long died as ego personality. The art of psychological discourse is to speak as someone already deceased,"[40] i.e., like the poet (Hölderlin). These views by Giegerich and Hillman are close to Jung's saying: "Those who mouth my name have fundamentally no idea of what it's all about."[41] And again: "It looks as if only those who are relatively close to death are serious or mature enough to grasp some of the essentials in our psychology."[42]

Philosophers have talked this way for some time. For example, Montaigne wrote: "… [T]o philosophize is to learn to die. … It is uncertain where death awaits us; let us await it everywhere. Premeditation of death is premeditation of freedom. The one who has learned how to die has unlearned how to be a slave. … The constant work of life is to build death."[43] And Plato's Socrates is famous for having said: "Those who do philosophy correctly are preparing themselves for death."[44] Perhaps one can say the same about doing psychology, whether in theory or in practice. But what does this have to do with poetry? Perhaps everything. Indeed, the testimonies are many.

Santayana, in *The Life of Reason*, wrote: "Nothing is so poor and melancholy as art that is interested in itself [i.e., the ego] and not in its subject."[45] Ovid, in the *Ars amatoria*, said: *Si late ars, prodest,* "Art, if hidden [i.e., dying], avails."[46] Oscar Wilde is more blunt: "All bad poetry springs from genuine feeling [i.e., personal ego feelings]."[47] The contemporary poet, John Ashberry, concurs: "There is a view that poetry should improve your life [i.e., ego]. I think people confuse it with the Salvation Army."[48] And there is the stunning instance of this perspective in John Keats' letter to George and Thomas Keats, in which the poet defines poetry and poetic perspective as "Negative Capability." This means, he says, that "a person is capable of being in uncertainties, mysteries, doubts without any irritable reaching after fact and reason."[49] There is in this a dying of ego certitude, epistemological arrogance, and narcissism.

## End of Meaning

Poetry and psychoanalysis, like philosophy and religion, are a learning how to die. No, they are a dying. Not only is there implied in poetry and psychology a dialectical thinking that is also a dying, not so much of ego, but of egoic perspective, but there is also a letting be, a releasement, a non-attachment to meaning. This is indicated in a somewhat surprising statement by Jung about poetry and art. "We have talked so much about the meaning of works of art that one can hardly suppress a doubt as to whether art really 'means' anything at all. Perhaps art has no 'meaning,' at least not as we understand meaning. Perhaps it is like nature, which simply *is* and 'means' nothing beyond that. .... It needs no meaning, for meaning has nothing to do with art."[50]

To be sure, Jung is not consistent about this, since he seems to reverse himself, saying: "We must interpret, we must find meanings in things, otherwise we would be quite unable to think about them."[51] So, Jung goes both ways on meaning, as Wolfgang Giegerich points out that he does with myth, saying that no myth is available to us, that this is a mythless time, and that no myth can save us, but then adding that we need to go in search of the myth of a mythless time.[52] But read most radically, Jung seems to be saying: Psyche needs no meaning, for meaning has nothing to do with soul. This could be seen as a reason why only a poet—who is not interested in meaning—could understand depth psychology—which also is not interested in meanings that are attached to ego and its sensibilities.

Giegerich is clear about this. He writes: "There is no need for 'meaning,' for the state of in-ness, for myth or religion as a present reality. On the contrary, we can, now that the gods have become memories, devote ourselves to all the riches of Mnemosyne freely without having to hold our breath in awe. ... The feeling that there should be a higher meaning of life and that it *is* missing is the illness."[53]

This is by no means an affirmation of meaninglessness. An announcement of meaninglessness would be a positive negative. It would be positing something one-sidedly and would therefore not be dialectical or depth psychological. It would still be ego-syntonic, something negative that ego experiences. Rather, this is a call for a revision of our notion of the meaning of so-called "meaning," as Ogden and Richards did many years ago in their book *The Meaning of Meaning* (1956).[54] It is a reversal of T. S. Eliot, as I once heard William Lynch say: not "we had the experience but missed the meaning,"[55] but rather, we had the meanings—too many of them over the years—and missed the experience. Those meanings, so-called, need to die.

Joseph Campbell spoke compellingly about this in 1957 at the Eranos Conference in Switzerland: "The Symbol without Meaning." He said: "The world, the entire universe, its god and all, has become a symbol—signifying nothing: a symbol without meaning. For to attribute meaning to any part of it would be to relax its force as a bow, and the arrow of the soul then would lodge only in the sphere of meaning .... The bow, in order to function as a bow and not as a snare, must have no meaning whatsoever in itself—or in any part of itself—beyond that of being an agent for disengagement—from itself: no more meaning than the impact of the doctor's little hammer when it hits your knee, to make it jerk."[56] Then he quoted Christian scripture: "Consider the lilies of the field, how they grow; they toil not, neither do they spin!'"[57] And he commented, as he did in the Bill Moyers' interview: "What—I ask—is the meaning of a flower? And having no meaning, should the flower, then, not be?"[58] "Our meaning is now the meaning that is no meaning."[59] "And if we are ... to participate joyfully in the world without meaning, we must allow our spirits to become ... wild ganders, and fly in timeless, spaceless flight ... not into any fixed heaven beyond the firmament (for there is no heaven out there), but that seat of experience simultaneously without and within, where ... the meaninglessness of the sense of existence and the meaninglessness of the meanings of the world are one."[60]

This is reminiscent of Angelus Silesius (1624-1677). His words: *Sonder waeromme* are Middle High German for *Sonder Warum*, "without why," and they were one of the basic formulae of medieval mysticism. Silesius's lines are: "The rose is without why; it blooms because it blooms, / Forgetful of itself, oblivious to our vision."[61] And these lines are made contemporary by Archibald MacLeish in his famous poem "Ars Poetica":

> A poem should be palpable and mute
> As a globed fruit,
>
> Dumb
> As old medallions to the thumb,
>
> Silent as the sleeve-worn stone
> Of casement ledges where the moss has grown—
>
> A poem should be wordless
> As the flight of birds.
>
> A poem should be motionless in time
> As the moon climbs,
>
> Leaving, as the moon releases
> Twig by Twig the night-entangled trees.
>
> ...
>
> For all the history of grief
> An empty doorway and a maple leaf.
>
> For love
> The leaning grasses and two lights above the sea—
>
> A poem should not mean
> But be.[62]

The soul, like poetry, should not mean, but be.

## ENDING: ONLY A POETRY …

The issue here has to do with what Jung intended by his phrase "only a poet could understand." And the matter seems to be complex. The complexity of the relation between depth psychology and the logic of poetry is possibly expressed in the German of Jung's odd statement, "I poetize," which Jung put in quotation marks, and with which translators seem to have a problem. The German is: "Ich will … dichten." The noun connected to this verb, *Dichtung*, means "poetry," as one would guess. But it also means "seal," "gasket," and "packing." *Dichtheit* means "thickness" or "density." By a wild stretch of the imagination, in the overtones of the language itself, Jung's words might be saying that in his psychologizing he is thickening, complexifying, making dense and rich, dialectizing.

Patricia Berry and James Hillman have picked up on this possible pun. In *Echo's Subtle Body*, Berry writes: "We might image the dream as a series of superimpositions, each event adding texture and thickening to the rest. … Dreams are like knots of condensed implications."[63] And Hillman, in *The Dream and the Underworld,* wrote: "Dreams are made by a coagulative process: condensation, intensification (over-determination), reduction (abbreviation), iteration (repetition), concretizing. The synthetic cooking operation of the dream-work … brings disparate ingredients together and concocts them into new things. They are made, or given, as densities, and the German word *Dicht* ("dense," "thick," "tight") occurs both in *Verdichtung* (Freud's term, which we translate as "condensation") and in *Dictung* ("poetry"), *Dichter* ("poet")."[64]

Poetry and psychoanalysis make things complex … with them our ego plots thicken. Only poetry can understand psychology, because it knows about thickening. But, then, this suggests that Jung may have made a fundamental error in his comment to Serrano, or perhaps Serrano did not get the point or remembered inaccurately. With Jung and Hillman and Giegerich agreeing on the death of the ego in soul-making, perhaps Jung should have said: "No one, no body, no person, understands psychology, the logic of the soul; only poetry, not a poet, understands."

It is not the poet who thickens and understands; it is the poetry that thickens and understands. The poem seems to know better what constitutes it than does the poet. This may be why Lacan said: "I repudiate my birth certificate; I am not a poet, but a poem."[65] And it may account for a strange saying by the poet Lawrence Ferlinghetti.

Ferlinghetti was asked in a video interview: What is poetry? In response, he looked searchingly straight into the camera, and said firmly and loudly: "Poetry? ... Poetry is the voice of the fourth person singular!"[66] If one were to say to Ferlinghetti, but there is no fourth person singular. I can imagine him shouting back: "Right!" Not the poet. Poetry.

## *NOTES*

[1] Miguel Serrano, *C. G. Jung & Hermann Hesse: A Record of Two Friendships*, trans. Frank MacShane (New York: Schocken Books, 1966), p. 60. Jung was not alone in this sentiment concerning depth psychology. For example, Michel Foucault concluded the public defense of his dissertation on madness (*Histoire de la folie*) with the statement: "In order to speak about madness, one should have the talents of a poet." George Canguilhem, a member of the committee, said: "But you have, Sir, you have." This is recollected in Geert Lernout's book, *The Poet as Thinker: Hölderlin in France* (Columbia, SC: Camden House, 1994), p. 70.

[2] Ananda Coomaraswamy, *Coomaraswamy: Selected Papers*, ed. R. Lipsey, vol. 2 (Princeton, NJ: Princeton University Press, 1977), p. 349, n. 55. This statement has also been attributed to Meister Eckhart and to the British sculptor, Eric Gill. Coomaraswamy wrote an essay on Eckhart and he was a good friend of Gill's. So, the source of the idea is difficult to determine.

[3] C. G. Jung, *Psychiatric Studies, The Collected Works of C. G. Jung*, trans. R. F. C. Hull, vol. 1, (Princeton, NJ: Princeton University Press, 1970), § 34; hereafter abbreviated to *CW* followed by volume number and paragraph (§) number.

[4] *Ibid.*, § 219.

[5] *Ibid.*, § 174.

[6] Jung, *CW* 9i, § 149.

[7] Maud Oakes, *The Stone Speaks* (Wilmette, IL: Chiron Books, 1987), p. 15.

[8] Jung, *CW* 7, § 508.

[9] Jung, *CW* 6, § 321, 323.

[10] Jung, *CW* 17, § 210.

[11] Jung, *CW* 15, § 135.

[12] *Ibid.*

[13] Wolfgang Giegerich, "The Flight into the Unconscious," International Symposium of Archetypal Psychology, Santa Barbara, California, September 2000, audiotape, Sounds True Recording, Louisville, CO, 2000.

[14] C. G. Jung, *Das symbolische Leben, Gesammelte Werke, Bd. 18.2* (Freiburg: Walter Verlag, 1981), § 1508.

[15] C. G. Jung, "Reply to Buber," *Spring* (1957): 7.

[16] Jung, *CW* 18, § 1508. On this, see: Stanley R. Hopper, "Symbolic Reality and the Poet's Task" (1967 Eranos Lecture), in *The Way of Transfiguration: Religious Imagination as Theopoiesis*, ed. R. M. Keiser and T. Stoneburner (Louisville, KY: Westminster/John Knox Press, 1992), p. 110f.

[17] Jung, *CW* 4, § 774f.

[18] Jung, *CW* 16, § 322.

[19] Jung, *CW* 6, § 255.

[20] C. G. Jung, *Memories, Dreams, Reflections*, ed. A. Jaffé, trans. R. and C. Winston (New York: Vintage Books, 1965), p. 60.

[21] *Ibid.*, p. 87,

[22] *Ibid.*, p. 206.

[23] *Ibid.*, p. 188.

[24] *Ibid.*, p. 282.

[25] James Hillman, *Re-Visioning Psychology* (New York: Harper Colophon, 1977), p. xi.

[26] James Hillman, *Inter Views: Conversations With Laura Pozzo on Psychotherapy, Biography, Love, Soul, Dreams, Work, Imagination, and the State of the Culture* (New York: Harper and Row, 1983), p. 147.

[27] *Ibid.*, p. 150.

[28] *Ibid.*, p. 159.

[29] "Jan Marlan Interviews James Hillman," *The IAAP Newsletter,* 26 (March 2006): 193.

[30] *Ibid.*, p. 194.

[31] Hillman, *Re-Visioning Psychology*, p. 149.

[32] James Hillman, "Why 'Archetypal' Psychology?" *Spring* (1970): 212-217.

[33] James Hillman, *Archetypal Psychology: A Brief Account* (Woodstock, CT: Spring Publications, 1997), p. 28.

[34] James Hillman, *The Myth of Analysis* (New York: Harper Colophon, 1978), "Part Two: On Psychological Language."

[35] James Hillman, *The Dream and the Underworld* (New York: Harper Colophon, 1979), p. 283.

[36] Jung, *CW* 18, § 778.

[37] Wolfgang Giegerich, *Animus-Psychologie* (Frankfurt: Peter Lang, 1994), pp. 170-72. Cf. Giegerich's argument concerning the fact that "Jung's attitude [concerning psychological referents] is … close to that of a poet …. Myth and archetypes have for Jung a poetic, or as he would say, *psychological* truth, but thus, to be sure, a psychological *truth*" ("The Provenance of Jung's Psychological Findings," *The Neurosis of Psychology* [New Orleans, LA: Spring Journal Books, 2005], p. 133).

[38] Wolfgang Giegerich, *The Soul's Logical Life* (Frankfurt: Peter Lang, 1998), p. 17.

[39] *Ibid.*, p. 19.

[40] *Ibid.*, p. 24.

[41] C. G. Jung, *Letters, Vol. 2*, ed. G. Adler, trans. R. F. C. Hull (Princeton, NJ: Princeton University Press, 1975), p. 530.

[42] *Ibid.*, p. 536.

[43] Michel de Montaigne, *The Complete Essays of Montaigne*, trans. D. Frame, vol. 1 (Garden City, NY: Anchor Books, 1960), pp. 74, 81, 88.

[44] Plato, *Phaedo*, 64a 4-6, cf. 81a 1-2.

[45] George Santayana, *The Life of Reason, Vol. 4: Reason in Art* (New York: Scribners, 1922), p. 152.

[46] Ovid, *The Art of Love and Other Poems,* trans. J. G. Mozley (Cambridge, MA: Harvard University Press, 1969), pp. 86-87 (2.1.313).

[47] Oscar Wilde, *Intentions* (Portland, ME: Thomas B. Mosher, 1904), p. 181

[48] Cited by Francis X. Clines, "Inaugural Poetry: The Ode not Taken," *New York Times*, editorial section, January 19, 1997, p. 5.

[49] John Keats, *The Letters*, ed. M. B. Forman (London: Oxford University Press, 1952), p. 71 (December 21, 1817).

[50] Jung, *CW* 15, § 121.

[51] *Ibid.*

[52] Wolfgang Giegerich, "The End of Meaning and the Birth of Man," *Journal of Jungian Theory and Practice* 6, no.2 (2004): 1-66.

[53] *Ibid.*, p. 28f.

[54] David L. Miller, "Prometheus, St. Peter and the Rock: Identity and Difference in Modern Literature," *Eranos 57-1988* (Frankfurt: Insel Verlag, 1989), p. 76, n. 5.

[55] T. S. Eliot, *The Complete Poems and Plays: 1909-1950* (New York: Harcourt Brace and Co., 1952), p. 133 (*Four Quartets,* "The Dry Salvages," II).

[56] Joseph Campbell, "The Symbol without Meaning," in *The Flight of the Wild Gander* (New York: The Viking Press, 1969), pp. 177f.

[57] *Ibid.*, p. 183.

[58] *Ibid.*, p. 188.

[59] *Ibid.*, p. 190.

[60] *Ibid.*, p. 92.

[61] Angelus Silesius, *The Cherubinic Wanderer,* trans. Maria Shrady (New York: Paulist Press, 1986), p. 54 (translation modified).

[62] Archibald MacLeish, "Ars Poetica," in John Ciardi, *How Does a Poem Mean* (Boston: Houghton Mifflin Company, 1959), p. 909.

[63] Patricia Berry, "An Approach to the Dream," *Echo's Subtle Body* (Dallas, TX: Spring Publications, 1982), p. 59.

[64] Hillman, *Dream and the Underworld*, p. 134.

[65] Jacques Lacan, *Four Fundamental Concepts of Psychoanalysis*, ed. J.-A. Miller, trans. A. Sheridan (New York: W. W. Norton, 1981), p. viii.

[66] Lawrence Ferlinghetti, on George Quasha, "Poetry Is," DVD, version 1.2, vol. 1 (Barrytown, NY: Station Hill Press, 2006). I am grateful to Nor Hall for first drawing this to my attention, and to George Quasha for providing me with a copy of this interview.

NOR HALL is a writer, psychotherapist, and theatre-collaborator. She works with Pantheatre (Paris), Archipelago Theatre (Chapel Hill), and Shawn McConneloug's Orchestra (Minneapolis) in the development of new pieces that give imaginal work a stage. Author of *Irons in the Fire* (2002), *Broodmales* (1989), *Those Women* (1988), *The Moon and the Virgin: Images of the Archetypal Feminine* (1980), she also writes reviews, catalog essays, and articles on a variety of topics inspired by art and artists. She has lectured at the Eranos Institute on gender, at the Minneapolis College of Art and Design on Lou Andreas-Salome, at the College of St. Catherine on salt, and at the Walker Art Center on artists Jess Collins and Robert Gober. She lives with her extended family on both sides of the Mississippi in the Twin Cities.

# 16

# White Riding: Milking a Legend[1]

NOR HALL

## Cofa's Tree

Once there was a *Cofantree* in Coventry standing by a cove on the river bend somewhere between Barrs Hill and Broadgate at the crux of an early settlement in the vale. The old word *cofa*, as in "cove," is related to "covey," "cave," and *"couvere"*—recesses providing cover. The genitive case of *cofa* is "cofan," hence "cofantreo" is "the cove's tree." The *Cofantree* (which is thought to have given rise to the name "Coventry") marked a meeting place—not like nearby Mounds or Motslow Hill, where crowds gathered because voices carried on hilltops, but a more intimate leafy covered place for quiet word exchange, gossip, transacting sacred and profane business, listening. Word history is world history and the hidden *couvare* in Cofa connects us to an ancient practice of going inside or going under in order to find information covered up by time.

Despite the thin veneer of Christianity and its attempt to change the meaning of "crossing" to "a place where a cross stands," trees have long marked crossings and were regarded as flourishing intersections between the temporal and the eternal. Powerful trees have powerful presences and their function in bringing people together for a purpose could easily be threatening to a Christian priest or King. In the year 936

C.E., one hundred years before the legendary ride of Lady Godiva through Coventry, an edict was issued prohibiting the worship of such trees. Trees were so numerous and Coventry so surrounded by woods that a tree had to be special to be so named. In remembering these powerful roots of place, putting an ear to the ground around Cofantreo, we are likely to hear the gallop of horses' hoofs long before we see them coming.

## Good Riddance

Sacrifice is a radical exchange of energy for renewal. Classical scholars embraced a come-and-go concept of sacrificial rites, which tipped between two ends: the *do ut es* ("I give that you might give") practice, and the *do ut abeas* ("I give that you might go away") practice. On the one hand, we sacrifice in order to receive some good thing, to increase life's abundance. Giving to get. Or we give in order to make bad things go away: famine, illness, ghosts, poverty, drought, death.[2] Giving out of fear to make the bad go away is what is literally meant by "good riddance." Ceremonies of riddance (scapegoating being the most familiar) took shape regularly in the imagination of most cultures—and continue to do so.

Ancient processions of riddance become modern demonstrations: walking on the sacred road for a political purpose.[3]

Early images suggestive of sacrifice pulse in the fingers of folk history, reaching for Godiva/Godgifu/Good-Eve's reins—especially as depicted in paintings kept at the Herbert, a small jewel of a museum in Coventry. In a late iconographic painting by John Collier (1898) the soft budding virgin on the royally dressed horse looks to be headed out of town, alone, to a somber destination. Her white horse's head inclines upwards, ears pricked.

The custom of riding the town circuit, chasing out one thing to usher in another—season change, life change, regime change—is still followed in shires all over England, and nowhere more significantly than in Coventry, where the procession has been taking place for nearly four hundred years. Collier's painting and its important predecessors extend the imagination even farther back, to mythic origins in archaic Olympian sacrifices, made by day using white animals, whose garlanded heads were tipped towards the sky, in contrast to chthonic or underworld sacrifices, made with dark animals at night, whose heads were pointed down. Her posture and trappings recall Vedic horse sacrifices, Brahmanic fruit-gift observances, Hebraic offerings to Yahweh to remedy the problem of having been born of the body of woman, first field offerings, honey libations to Aphrodite, wineless sacrifices to Mnemosyne the mother of the muses, silent showings of the Earth goddess's ear of wheat, Mithraic transubstantiated offerings of bodies and blood in sacramental rites of expiation. Some were made on altars of stone, some at the foot of great trees, but in all cases there is an inherent request being made to something larger than oneself.

The request behind Godiva's gesture—riding naked on her horse through the town of Coventry at noon—was made to appeal to the chronic imbalance between rich and poor, as well as to her husband's sense of shame. He served a warring King who constantly raised taxes to support his soldiers and sailors. After persistent questioning, Godiva's husband, Leofric, Earl of Coventry in Mercia county, finally said he would stop collecting the oppressive toll if she dared perform the outrageous ride. Evil worldly leanings, greedy careerism, and perverse pleasure represented by the split-off shadowy figure of Peeping Tom, who appears at the noonday climax, were assigned in time to Leofric, whose oppressive levies threatened the village.

The Domesday Book indicates that Leofric underwent a conversion from rapacious to saintly around the time of his wife's mid-11th-century ride. His obituary in 1057 declares him to have been a virtuous statesman and generous partner to Godiva, who gave much of her holdings to support the needy. It was she who held Coventry, including five hides (each equivalent to 1,000 farmed acres) and land for twenty ploughs (a plough holding eight oxen). Also in the demesne, three ploughs with seven serfs, fifty villeins with twelve boarders, and twenty ploughs worth twelve pounds of weighed money in 1066.[4] This after forfeiting lands to the new King and making major gifts to the local monastery.

## Getting Dressed to Kill

Whether following a trajectory of riddance or of invitation, sacrifice always dances with the same partner—Necessity—and follows a particular three-step routine: selecting, adorning, separating.

Selection is simply the choice of representative. The sacrificed can be victim, martyr, model. One who is sacrificed, given up on, or abandoned to fate. Sacrifice without choice makes victims, whereas the choice to make a personal sacrifice sets the agent on a branching path towards possible martyrdom or transformation.

Adornment requires the putting on of symbols of authority, usually a ceremonial tradition of investing a person or object with meaning, as with the robes of a priest or the crown of the Queen. Accessory options for the chosen one: golden horns, a crown of thorns, a mantle, a jeweled girdle, a wedding gown, a coat of rags, calfskin boots, and so on. In addition to the dressing of the person, a substitute sacrificial animal can also be dressed—with garlands of roses, for example, or, in the case of the scapegoat, a crimson thread, tied round the head, like the crimson bridle on the white horse of Godiva.

The third stage in traditional sacrifice involves rites of contact and separation. Boundaries have to be established between what is inside and what is outside. A boundary crossing must then occur in order for the ritual enactment to cross the threshold of the daily. Some intimate thing from the inside, where it is safe, has to be taken over to the victim's side, the outside, where there is no longer any protection. Thus, the sacrifice functions to identify and draw out the secret dark life of the community, to take it beyond the pale.

Medieval architecture employed an intimacy gradient that is relevant to our attempt to understand sacrifice, especially as it pertains to women. Designs show the house enclosures with a gate facing the street. An anteroom functioned as a place of reception and business, an exchange between householders and the street. One step further into the interior is the great room, where the family cooked and ate and interacted among themselves, occasionally inviting in representatives of the street—such as couriers or players. The axis of intimacy extends more deeply inwards to the sleeping quarters, and then farther still to the total privacy of the scented closet, where Queen Gertrude famously entertained Hamlet.[5]

## Naked Power

Woman, who is considered to speak the language of the *domus*, risks her position alongside those in authority when she takes the inside outside, exposing herself. Even if she is a Queen. Godiva reverses the intimacy gradient in a way that is unheard of. Drawing a man in is all right—that's called seduction—but taking nakedness out into the streets is promiscuity. An unclothed woman would be entirely "out of (legal) hand." If a woman appeared naked on the road, she was subject to condemnation and even rape, unless she could, by some miracle, claim that her body belonged to God (i.e., she was a mad nun).

Once a year, however, taking nakedness to the streets and out to the fields was not only permissible but a hallowed act. In ceremonial processions, a social group swung into movement with intent—to mobilize and compel. Processional rites exhibit sacred things in order to distribute their potency—a book, an ear of corn, a naked girl. The traditional circumambulation of the town on St. George's Day may preserve a pre-Christian tradition of carrying an efficacious object, such as a girl, around the edges of a field to draw all new and nubile energy to the ground for seeding.

Myth attaches itself to the moment when an act strikes an archetypal chord in human experience.

To be naked is to be stripped of one's ordinary persona. Naked on a horse, the woman becomes the Lady of Wild Things, who experiences her body and animal power as one. As a horse-loving friend observed, Lady Godiva *becomes* her horse. "The legend would never have made it into the 21st century if the Lady had *walked* through town naked—which, apart from marking her as a woman without virtue, uncontrollable, and certainly a bad wife, would have only made her presence vulnerable, whereas riding a horse, especially a white horse in full regalia, she becomes a figure of tremendous power, uncorrupted, fecund, and goddess-like."[6]

Painters of Godiva's ride gradually moved her into goddess territory by adding doves, roses, vines, and garlanded attendants. Red and gold tones and the white of furs, cloth, birds are all aphroditic accouterments, though she needs none because her white nakedness is sign enough. "... [B]y loosening the braids of hair on her head, [she] veiled her whole body except her brilliantly white legs."[7]

Venusian sculpture was undraped, Virgins at least partially draped. Sometimes the image of our Lady Godiva reads as the goddess of love, sometimes as Mother Mary, Moon of the Church, sometimes the Virgin Diana, with flowery branch, or Artemis, sporting the powerful haunches of the animal huntress. The church spire in Landseer's canvas, *Godiva's Prayer* (1865), points towards her divinity. Her eyes are raised to heaven, though the pious old maid's eyes are closed. Godiva could be Aphroditic, Artemisian, or Marian in this much imitated moment.

Godiva's annual procession eventually became a semi-ecclesiastical municipal rite that symbolically carries nakedness and nature into Coventry city center. A centuries-long roster of riders, including a boy (perhaps the year William Shakespeare watched), adolescent girls, and women, have interpreted Godiva in every conceivable gestural mount. Nonetheless, the same question is repeated each time, over and over: will she ride naked?

## Monumental Rebellion

In an essay, "*Nuda Veritas*" (Naked Truth), Marina Warner describes the omnipresent nude in urban statuary. "The nude lies on architraves, holds up portals, ministers to great achievers in the streets of cities from London to Vienna to New York and we are rarely asked to care for what she is feeling, rather to feel better because of what she makes us feel."[8] What looks like tribute is actually sad commentary on how the body of woman has been idealized, linked to nature, and therefore dominated by culture. "She very rarely commands the drama in which she takes part; she is raped or at least arrested, uncovered, done to rather than doing. She is 'a negative imprint of domination' [Adorno] whose own erotic drives do not matter, only those she excites."[9]

Must we consign Godiva, "the new Eve come to retrieve what she had lost" (H.D.), to the same frozen state of monuments and naked maidens—or can we milk the living legend for a moving message? Doesn't a naked woman in procession keep imagination more alive than a statue? I like the suggestion that we ask how the power object feels. If we insist on staying with our subject inside the displayed object as she moves around the city circuit, concentrating energy at the center of our inquiry, we notice a few questions: Is she riding or being ridden, carrying or carried, silently displaying or displayed? What is *her* desire? If it is *her* announcement, "I'm here to get back what was taken," she could be offering rather than being offered.

A virgin without blemish (which she was not, but came to resemble) would make a pleasing gift to the gods—a fitting image for carrying away a people's mortal ills in the manner of archaic *pharmakoi* figures driven out of town so as to drive out evil. They wore white and bore budding branches on their mounts, not for decoration, but for thrashing,[10] as is customary in folk rites that beat out the bad and beat in the good—a literal form of moral stimulus. A woman so selected functions as object of both desire and abuse, as did girls who once suffered springtime beatings with forced flowering branches in ritual play.

From a later era, when Lady Godiva had become a heroine, Victorian women writers and activists prized her willingness to risk public scandal for moral good. "Her movement proceeds from the home out into the public arena and back again with her virtue intact and society improved. And yet in spite of a man's authoritative control and the perils of public exposure, she projects a spellbinding erotic appeal."[11] Godiva's bid contains both the anxiety and the desire for public exposure felt by women who had means to give and something to say.

It would suit such a woman to appear to be chosen rather than be the one to do the choosing, as happened with Mary the maiden standing on the temple steps at the moment when Joseph set his staff silently next to her and it burst into bloom.

## Where *Did* She Get Her Orders?

A woman who makes a personal sacrifice on behalf of others may not consciously know what motivates her. She knows only that she must do something, and this certainty grounds her act in instinct and passion, where she finds a reservoir of previously unknown resolve that supplements her own, which then becomes her own. But, still, we want to know where she gets her orders—in particular the order to risk everything.

I take the word "orders" from poets—the poet Robert Duncan, for example, who felt a kinship to Joan-who-talked-with-Angels. He said the first experience of the artist is obedience.[12] Orders are laid on you like a mantle by the cosmos, *incurred*, as when the poet becomes subject to an arriving poem. It comes demanding intense response. Instructions arrive in recognitions—offers you can't refuse. He often found himself called to order, as H.D. (Hilda Doolittle) did in London in 1944 when Our Lady appeared to her quite unexpectedly.

> [28]
> I had been thinking of Gabriel,
> . . .
>
> how could I imagine
> the Lady herself would come instead?

[32]
...
her veils were *white* as *snow*,

so as no fuller on earth
*can white them* ...

[29]
We have seen her
the world over;

...
Our Lady of the Chair;

we have seen her, an empress,
magnificent in pomp and grace,

and we have seen her
with a single flower

...

[31]
But none of these, none of these
suggest her as I saw her ...[13]

H.D. says the Lady appeared to her—to *them* actually, the straggling company of brush and quill (artists whose creativity was fire-strafed and starved)—in the miraculous vision of "a half-burnt-out apple-tree blossoming."[14]

The poet's description of the new Eve could be written under the window at the Church of the Holy Trinity in Coventry today. Preserved fragments of richly colored glass show a small figure on horseback riding between the portraits of Godiva and Leofric. She is carrying a blossoming branch for eternity—"a sign unto us"[15] (H.D.), a kind of blessing?

## Blessings of Boredom

We are no less in need of Good Eve's blessing today than in the 11th century. Medieval monastic teaching stated the problem precisely; *acedia*, the sin of sloth, has its three-toed talons in us. This vice is not normal everyday laziness, but rather, sloth of the spirit. A nearly comic allegorical image of *acedia* shows someone coming to ring a monk's doorbell. He startles up to see who it is but does not even complete the gesture of looking. Instead, he sinks back down into his chair returning to a listless reading of text. Midday torpor comes over him. He counts words, rifles through pages, fantasizes about a better monastic community somewhere, vaguely curses his companions for not being more intelligent and conversant, thinks he is getting hungry, but is increasingly inert until his head sags onto the book in a fitful sleep.[16] Puritanism co-opted this particular vice and turned it into resistance to the work ethic, but its roots are much more interesting.

*Acedia* meant "without caring." "Caring-not" had seven daughters: Malice, Small Soul, Stupor, Wandering Thought, Verbosity, Instability of Purpose, and *Importunitas Mentis*, which is something like Spiritual Attention Deficit Disorder. Importunity of mind is a fascinating bit of medieval psychology that shoots its wobbly arrow to the heart of our topic. To *importune* is to make repeated insistent requests, to vex or annoy without any sense of the *port.* The port or harbored point of the persistent demand is inaccessible even to the one who keeps asking. (A condition understood by the *I Ching* when it says, "One is furthered by having somewhere to go.")

Those familiar with accounts of Godiva's ride will recognize the refrain "repeated requests, annoying and persistent petitions," because these words are so frequently used to describe Godiva's appeal to Leofric. Her words have no port until she acts. Her energy needed to be met by his challenge, and his hardball challenge needed to be met by her courage before it could soften and transform.

The Lady's stubbornness turned certain of its aim. Queen of *Cedia* we could call her, the Woman Who Cared, Lady of Awesome Purpose. She was under orders as surely as any knight or poet or religious adept, driven by holy purpose. A living antidote to lazy spirit.

Seen from this angle, Godiva's story has a significant act of rebellion embedded in it—subversive, or actually *reversive*, because her performance reverses the traditional pattern of sacrifice. Tradition brings people to the parade route, but invention keeps them coming, especially women who are attracted to an old many-faceted story hidden in the municipal agenda and borne in the bones of those who attend. Throngs of followers want to lift the veil and see the goddess naked. Thousands more would like to be on the horse riding through the market at noon in direct confrontation with Sloth, the Demon of Noonday Sun.

## Activating Woman

When Godiva takes the reins in her own hands on that legendary but fateful day, she puts art in the saddle and creates an inspired new performance piece on sacrifice:

Instead of being selected, *she selects herself.*
Instead of investiture, *she divests.*
Instead of being made to separate, *she chooses to leave.*
Instead of being shown, *she shows herself.*

### She Selects Herself

"Spirit is life which itself cutteth into life" (Nietzsche). Woman knows how to live detachment. She cuts through, runs her risks and inserts herself.[17] Hélène Cixous in her classic article "The Laugh of the Medusa" says that women *must* express them*selves*—in writing, speaking, performance: "Muffled throughout their history, they [women] have lived in dreams, in bodies (though muted), in silences, in aphonic revolts."[18] *Aphonic* as in "without a voice." You will not find a text of Godiva's request anywhere. She carries off an aphonic performance that noiselessly, except for the neighing of a horse, shatters the vise grip of tax on the town. Her horizontal move from the closet, which is the only place a woman would be uncovered (since she most likely slept and made love and had children in her nightgown), slices like a knife across town to the market and back. Life called her to order and she risked responding.

### She Divests

Instead of investiture she divests herself of status, adornment, jewels, her garments of gold, all layers of clothing and regalia that constitute the complex signs of rank and social position—her robes, her retinue, coins, and companions.[19] She strips her persona bare, except for her hair.

We know that Godiva as the Good Eve was already living under the sign of the Blessed Virgin in 1043. She was devout and generous to the religious cause. Her nakedness, whether it was a stripping of status or actual clothing, had sanctified precedent in images of worldly renunciation, as in St. Francis stripped and running away from this world and its goods, or the Magdalene's sacrifice of acceptable identity when she retreated to the desert and lived as a penitent, covered by the dress of her matted hair.

Godiva's image repertoire would not have gone so far back as to include the Sumerian Queen Inanna. Nonetheless, she had a soul-sister in her who "lived above but turned her ear to below." Inanna's descent into the world as underworld was marked by the most dramatic story of divesting in recorded literature. Seven bolts on seven gates are opened one by one. At each gate she has to drop a piece of royal identity. At the first gate it is her crown of pure cloth, followed by her necklace, breastplate, ring, and precious stones. By the time she reaches the final gate, "someone unwraps the Lady's royal robe / someone strips away the Ladyship's royal robe."[20] She is naked and bowed low.

Piece by painful piece, the goddess discards elements of her power, her signs of achievement and garments of respect. She undertakes the ultimate transgression of turning the inside outside—instead of keeping to the chambers of women, inside the royal enclosure, she sacrifices her cover and faces the world unandorned, simply as everywoman.

Her husband thinks she is nothing, now that she is not identified as his, and that she cannot possibly succeed on her own. But a strange thing happens as the woman's identity shifts beyond the last gate. As she becomes common property rather than private property, her sense of herself expands along the entire plane of the earth. She entrusts herself to the people and is sure of their being-in-it-with-her, even as she must distrust the man in this instance because his understanding is narrowed by the values he has chosen to support.

### She Chooses to Leave

This is not the action of a young woman. Pain needs to be severe already before one approaches the threshold of sacrifice voluntarily. A young woman's psyche is rarely willing to abandon life to go and sit alone on a crag. I am referring to the story of Cupid and Psyche, in which the oracle tells the king to leave his beautiful daughter on a mountain crag—another sacrifice story with ties to the practice of riddance. A young woman is not likely to choose to leave her wealth behind, of whatever kind—her beauty, her family's protection, her resources. An authority figure still has to urge her "to get out there."

An older woman is differently capable of spiritual choice—of marrying herself to something unseen for the sake of the whole community, especially women who have already carried some creative life or project or child to fruition.

"Young" and "old" do not depend on age, but on experience. By "young" I mean pre-ordeal, before the transformative trials of relationship and bodily change. Older women are women who have known at least the first three blood mysteries in their bodies—how we bleed monthly without dying, how blood can change into womb-life, and then into breast milk to feed the newly born.[21] The fourth blood mystery in a woman's body is the cessation—when the blood flow turns inward to feed the spirit. Perhaps literally, perhaps in the way of the poet who said that memories of what you take in from the world turn to blood within you (Rilke).

In acts of self-sacrifice, women are forced to offer what they hold most dear, knowing that the balance of the entire system will change. Breaking up an old pattern means death to a way of life, a relinquishing of the person you have been until now.

Godiva had reached a point of ease in her life, with wealth and landholdings aplenty. She was a mother and a friend—a friend of reflection (later in life, she moved to be near Aefric, her husband's Confessor, and in one of the stories was buried alongside him). She was also a friend of the arts by virtue of her connection to Mannie, the famous Abbot of Evesham, who signed the charters relating to the monastery she funded. Clearly the best goldsmith in the country, he was an artistic soul, familiar with sacred literature, a master of chant and song, a writer, a painter, a man of many charms, who is said to have crafted Godiva's gifts of gold and jewels into adornments to hang on the mantle of the Blessed Mother.

But until she chose to separate from the worldly power center of Leofric by riding straight into the heart of the people, Godiva had not risked acting on her own desire. Paradoxically, the moment she assumes her own capability, she ends up riding *for* her husband—as well as for the townspeople, who also stand for the hardworking voiceless characters who people the soul.

## She Shows Herself

William Butler Yeats said of the moon, "Before the full / It sought itself and afterwards the world." Every time I look at one of the oldest paintings of Lady Godiva, (the one by Adam van Noort, dating to 1586), with Godiva sitting side-saddle on her formally festooned white horse, I am struck by how much like the full moon she sits, gloriously exposed, in full-bellied, lunar-breasted curves that cross our visual path as she passes through the shuttered town (see Fig. 1).

> The old wisdom says that he who has attained to the realm of the complete moon has attained knowledge of the past, source, and origin; he has power in this present world; and insight into the realm of the future.[22]

In the van Noort canvas, there is a barely discernible face of a man in one of the windows, like the man in the moon, who belongs to the

**Fig. 1:** This painting by Ellis the Limner is a copy of the original by Adam van Noort, commissioned in 1586 by the Coventry City Council. As Mr. Ellis's canvas has not been cleaned, it is difficult to detect the face in the window in the upper right-hand corner of the painting. (Reproduced by permission of The Herbert Art Gallery and Museum, Coventry, England; image courtesy of Ron Clarke.)

whole picture—perhaps the amazed Leofric, as some have suggested. But also like Peeping Tom, who appeared in the literary narrative a century later. Yet his presence is implied from the beginning in the shadow of the Earl's challenge. Richard Grafton's account, written about twenty years before the first painting, includes this lovely phrasing upon the conclusion of Godiva's ride: "... [H]er purpose obtained, her wisdom much commended, and her husband's imagination much disappointed."[23]

And *her* imagination? What did she think when he said, "Mount your horse naked!" Was she challenged? Aroused? Mortified? Had she known about instances of ordained exhibitionism instigated by kings, who showed their lady's naked beauty in annual pageants, parading her before their vassals (as in *The Lay of Graelent*)[24]? Or was she upheld by repetition of prayers to God in unintended but ironic imitation of the male viewing game—a purer exhibition meant for the eyes of her heavenly Lord only.

Virginitas shifts to Voluptas with the inclusion of the voyeur. We have been given a Godiva who is virginal, sensitive, compassionate—as well one voluptuous and seductive. Peeping Tom gets caught in the long shadow of the pure woman, sticking his head into the picture inevitably like the phallus. From a particular male point of view, it is an erotic moment, which also inevitably has an effect on the woman in her nakedness, generating an instant confusion of power. Women want to be powerful in an erotic manner—to attract the male gaze and arouse Tom. At the same time, a woman might want *not* to be caught by such an arrangement (Godiva bade the townspeople close all their doors and shutters), choosing to sleep like the virginal Artemis with one foot outside the covers, resisting the "masochistic prostitution of her body to a desire not her own [which] leaves her in a familiar state of dependency on a man for knowing what she wants."[25]

If, as Luce Irigaray observes, Woman takes pleasure more from touching than from looking, she will grow tired of "consignment to passivity, of being the beautiful object of contemplation,"[26] and she will long to ride.

*Her* pleasure then will be had in mounting the horse naked, in taking the reins of the magnificent animal in her own hands instead of being strung along by attending nuns, who think they know her desire. She is passionate and compassionate at once when she and the animal body become one body, quivering to ride and covered only in gleaming hair. Her hair unbound would signify erotic abandon—no woman leaves home without her hair bound and covered. Her ride is a sacramental act, as D. H. Lawrence understood religion to be—coming into sheer naked contact with Nature, experiencing a rush of fear transposed by hope into ecstasy.

## She Enters History

Godiva's ride is "a thing done," like the *dromenon* element of a ritual, a silent showing that has precedent in the realm of mystery religions and sets a precedent surfacing again in contemporary culture. Listen to Cixous[27] urging women to act in full daylight, full disclosure:

> Woman *seizing* the moment *shatters history* by *entering* it. Women must speak woman, *write woman*, act woman—*start scoring their feats in written and oral language, ... breaking out of the snare of silence. Every woman has known the torment of getting up to speak in public, her heart racing, at times* utterly *lost for words, ground and language slipping away. That's how daring a feat, how great a transgression it is for a woman to speak. Listen to a woman* express herself in public. *She doesn't speak, she throws her trembling body forward; she lets go of herself; she flies; all of her passes into her voice; and it's with her body that she vitally supports the "logic" of her speech. Her flesh speaks true. She lays* her body *bare. In fact, she physically materializes what she's thinking; she signifies it with her body. Her speech, even when "theoretical" or political, is never simple or linear, "objectified," or generalized: she draws her story into history.*[28]

## Writing a White Horse

There is a sacramental element in Godiva's "riding"—or *being ridden*—a kind of possession in the procession, a takeover that makes her act. Sacred action is urgent service. Something more is being done than that which we see performed.

Cixous again:

> *There always remains in woman that force which produces/is produced by the other—in particular, the other woman, in her. ... [M]atrix, cradler: herself ... as her* [own] *mother. ... It is necessary ... that the best of herself be given to her by another woman for her to be able to love herself ...—I don't mean the overbearing clutchy*

> *mother but, rather, what touches you* … [what] *fills your breast with an urge to come into language and launches your force* ….
>
> *In women there is always more or less of the mother who makes everything all right, who nourishes, and who stands up against separation: a force that will not be cut off but will knock the wind out of the codes.*
>
> … [*A*] *woman is never far from this "mother"—as matrix. There is always within her at least a little of that good mother's milk.* Every woman who acts herself thus in accordance with the divine cradler within, every woman who writes out of her body laid bare, *writes in white ink.*[29]

As our Lady rides her milk white steed with love exceeding,[30] "she cannot fail … to transform directly and indirectly *all* systems of exchange based on masculine thrift."[31] Her passion produces the longed-for change.

Before the full it sought itself, afterwards the world (Yeats). The "woman of a thousand summers back" (Tennyson) points us to the moon to read her message anew—at first blush we seek ourselves and reflections of ourselves in the world, but afterwards, in the waning phase of life, before going down into darkness, a burst of love for the world compels strange acts and unlikely processions.

Perhaps you have heard the rumor that men's sexuality shifts later in life upwards from the base chakra towards the heart? Godiva's ride seems to have had that effect on Leofric, whom history records as leaving his worldly goods to spiritual purposes. For women, her ride relays a message about the conversion of self-centeredness into a sacrifice of the self on behalf of all the constrained voices that, once freed, clamor to speak. This is no renunciation, but a liberation, a dam burst, a breakthrough—of love and wealth and beauty and passion that has the potential to transform *us* and the communities we care about by knocking Sloth (old Caring-Not) off his high horse.

## *NOTES*

[1] Originally conceived for *Women Undercover*, "Women and Sacrifice," at Carran Waterfield's Triangle Theatre conference in Coventry, England held in the Herbert Art Gallery and Museum on the eve of the annual Godiva Procession, June 3, 2002.

[2] Jane Ellen Harrison, *Prolegomena to the Study of Greek Religion* (New York: Arno Press, 1975), pp. 3-7.

[3] Lecture III, "Processional," in Norman O. Brown and Nor Hall, *Book of Ours: Student Manual to Accompany "To Greet the Return of the Gods"* (University of California Santa Cruz, 1971).

[4] Ronald Aquilla Clarke and Patrick A. E. Day, *Lady Godiva: Images of a Legend in Art & Society* (Coventry: Herbert Art Gallery and Museum, 1982), p. 8. References to Godiva procession lore and specific images in painting are drawn from this scholarly and charming source.

[5] Yi-Fu Tuan, *Segmented Worlds and Self: Group Life and Individual Consciousness* (Minneapolis, MN: University of Minnesota Press, 1982), pp. 68-72.

[6] Exchange with Lyn Cowan, author of "Seabiscuit: The Little Horse That Could, and Did, and Still Does," unpublished lecture first presented in 2005.

[7] From *Chronica Majora,* ca. 1250; quoted in Daniel Donoghue, *Lady Godiva: A Literary History of the Legend* (Oxford: Blackwell, 2003), pp. 26-27. See also discussion of Godiva's salvific signification in the story of a 17th-century attempt to replace the body of Christ on a town cross with an image of the naked Godiva, p. 55.

[8] Marina Warner, "*Nuda Veritas,*" in *Monuments & Maidens: The Allegory of the Female Form* (New York: Atheneum, 1985), p. 325.

[9] *Ibid.*

[10] Harrison, p. 100.

[11] Donoghue, p. 92.

[12] These ideas about incurring orders were discussed in class with Robert Duncan at Santa Cruz in the History of Consciousness seminar, 1970. See also his *Truth and Life of Myth: An Essay in Essential Autobiography* (Fremont, MI: Sumac Press, 1968), p. 46.

[13] H.D. [Hilda Doolittle], "Tribute to the Angels," *Collected Poems 1912-1944* (New York: New Directions Books, 1983), pp. 563-566.

[14] *Ibid.*, p. 561.

[15] *Ibid.*, p. 558.

[16] Giorgio Agamben, *Stanzas, Word and Phantasm in Western Culture* (Minneapolis, MN: University of Minnesota Press, 1993), p. 3.

[17] Hélène Cixous, "The Laugh of the Medusa," trans. Keith and Paula Cohen, originally published in *Signs* 1, no. 4 (Summer 1976): 875-893. The quotes woven together in what follows are taken from "The Laugh of the Medusa," in *The Woman and Language Debate*, ed. Camille Roman, Suzanne Juhasz, Cristanne Miller (New Brunswick, NJ: Rutgers University Press, 1994), pp. 78-93.

[18] *Ibid.*, p. 86.

[19] Danielle Regnier-Bohler, "Imagining the Self," in *A History of Private Life, Vol. II: Revelations of the Medieval World*, ed. Georges Duby, trans. Arthur Goldhammer (Cambridge, MA: Harvard University Press, 1988), p. 370.

[20] Several sources with different translations have been helpful with the Inanna material: Diane Wolkstein and Samuel Noah Kramer, *Inanna Queen of Heaven and Earth* (New York: Harper & Row, 1983); Sylvia Brinton Perera, *Descent to the Goddess* (Toronto: Inner City Books, 1981); Betty De Shong Meador, *Uncursing the Dark: Treasures from the Underworld* (Wilmette, IL: Chiron Publications, 1992).

[21] See Erich Neumann's discussion of the first three blood-transformation mysteries in *The Great Mother* (Princeton, NJ: Princeton University Press, 1963), p. 31.

[22] Mary Esther Harding, *Women's Mysteries* (New York: Putnam, 1971), p. 212.

[23] Clarke and Day, p. 8. Quoted from Grafton's version of the Godiva legend published in 1569. (Grafton was a printer and M.P. for Coventry in 1562-63.)

[24] Regnier-Bohler, p. 372.

[25] Luce Irigaray, "This Sex Which Is Not One," in *The Woman and Language Debate: A Sourcebook*, ed. Camille Roman, Suzanne Juhasz, Cristanne Miller (New Brunswick, NJ: Rutgers University Press, 1994), p. 95.

[26] *Ibid.*

[27] The impetus for a poetic marriage of Cixous's famous white writing notion with the Godiva material is entirely mine with tribute intended.

[28] Cixous, pp. 81-82. The words in italics are taken from various places in Cixous's text.

[29] *Ibid.*, p. 83. Various parts of Cixous's text have been combined. Her words are in italics.

[30] In a 1634 account of his visit to Coventry, a captain of the military company of Norwich commented that Lady Godiva freed the city from heavy tributes "by undertaking a hard and unseemly task, which was to ride naked openly at high noone day through the city upon a milk white steed, which she willingly performed according to her lord's strict injunction. It may be very well discussed here whether his hatred, or her love exceeded." (The Lansdowne MSS, in the British Museum, cited in E. Sidney Hartland, "Peeping Tom and Lady Godiva," *Folklore* 1, no. 2 [June 1890]: 217. See also, Donoghue, p. 70.)

[31] Cixous, p. 83 (italics in original).

Rafael López-Pedraza was born in Cuba in 1920. He settled in Venezuela in 1949. Eventually, he went to Zürich, where he studied at the C. G. Jung Institute for eleven years, working at the Zürichberg Klinik and developing his ideas on the study of the archetypes. In 1974, he returned to Venezuela, where he set up a private practice (in which he is still engaged) and lectured on mythology for thirteen years in the Department of Literature at the Central University of Venezuela. He also has a group of psychiatrists and psychotherapist for regular sessions of supervision and coaches at SOCSAL, an association involved in providing help and support for underprivileged Venezuelans. He has lectured widely in Europe and the United States, and has published dozens of papers and books in English (many translated into Italian). However, in the past few years he has limited himself to writing in Spanish, specifically for the Venezuelan reader. He remains active and continues writing, particularly pursuing his interest in art and psychology.

# 17

# On Art and Psychology[1]

RAFAEL LÓPEZ-PEDRAZA

Modern psychology has tended to approach the arts from a position that seems untenable in the face of the possibilities that art can offer to psychology. It has projected too many psychological theories onto the artist and his work, and applied too much interpretation. Psychology does not seem to have acknowledged yet that throughout history, art has always been the unparalleled expression of man's psyche, culture, and religion. Psychology has become a new body of knowledge, called by some a science and by others an art. Furthermore, it is supposed to be the study of the most difficult, unconscious, and irrational part of human nature, the fathomless psyche; however, when it is confronted by a work of art, its attitude mostly changes into a rationalistic interpretative approach.

E. R. Gombrich brings some reflection to such psychological approaches in his paper "Freud's Aesthetics," in which, among other things, he discusses Freud's monograph on Leonardo da Vinci: Freud "approaches at least two of Leonardo's paintings, the Mona Lisa and the St. Anne, as if they were the phantasies of a patient."[2] For me, Freud's monograph is an example of a psychologist using his own theories as a tool for understanding an artist and his work. Freud focused on his psychoanalytic theories for his vision of Leonardo. The result was a tremendous reduction. Freud was too taken up with the notion of trauma in a person's early years and that it was crucial for any insight into the personality, thus creating the illusion of having a thorough knowledge of that personality.[3] How a person responds to and overcomes the conflicts of life were of little consequence. As far as I am concerned, Freud's imaginative reconstruction of Leonardo's infancy reveals a very rich childhood. In the series of paintings depicting the grandmother, the virgin, and the child (St. Anne, the Virgin, and the Child), especially the Cartoon at the National Gallery in London, we can perceive that Leonardo's artistic conception redefined the archetype of the mother and son. The painting is a "maternity" and, for me, it is through the imagery of maternity that the psyche finds the way to express what is ineffable: psyche expressing its own essence or producing psyche. Moreover, the painting suggests that Leonardo had assimilated his infancy. At the same time, in the same breath, so to speak, he depicted the archetype of the mother and the daughter (St. Anne and the Virgin Mary), an archetype which carries a very obscure aspect of human nature. And one sees Leonardo's respect for the mystery of the union and separation of the mother and the daughter, and how he expressed it at an artistic level unmatched in Western culture.[4] It was an extraordinary psychological and historical achievement.

Gombrich also analyzes Freud's reaction to modern art as expressed in his correspondence. As far as Freud was concerned, Expressionism and Surrealism were the product of madmen and lunatics.[5] In a rather contemptuous manner, he dismissed the expressionists and surrealists who, as he himself acknowledged, had, in many ways, been influenced by his own revolutionary ideas. In any event, Freud's reaction is quite surprising, considering that for him psychology ought to be concerned mainly with lunacy and madness.

Freud's aesthetics were based on the German *Bildung* of the $19^{th}$ century and his classical perspective on art. However, his psychoanalytic theories imposed limitations and hindered his approach to man's psyche as expressed through art. He was unable to accept man's new historical expression, as was shown in his response to expressionist and surrealist artists. Nevertheless, we must not forget that Freud was a great lover of art and made good use of his artistic education: his trips to Athens and Rome, and the numerous essays he wrote with reference to art attest to this.

My own attitude, backed by many years in the study and practice of Jungian psychology, is to learn psychology from art. I suspect my position in this respect is historical, in that it is many years since Freud wrote his monograph on Leonardo (1912). A historical perspective is borne out by the rather similar attitude of another Jungian psychologist who is also an art historian, Christian Gaillard, when he writes in his paper "Leonardo's Mother Revisited": "For we deliberately started, not from the psychology of the man Leonardo, but from his work."[6] Psychology should take a position from which it can value and learn from the artist's achievement.

In 1932, Jung was invited to comment on Picasso's retrospective exhibition at the Kunsthaus in Zürich. Jung visited the exhibition twice. In his commentary, he wrote: "Had it not been suggested to me from an authoritative quarter, I should probably never have taken up my pen on the subject."[7] Jung goes on to apologize for covering such a huge subject in a short article: "I have nothing to say on the question of Picasso's 'art' but only on its psychology."[8] He thus made a split. There is a feeling of discomfort in Jung's visit to Picasso's retrospective at the Kunsthaus in that he was pushed into commenting on the exhibition as a psychiatrist, probably feeling that he should please that "authoritative quarter." Zürich, the cradle of modern psychiatry, was at that time a very psychiatric city. Jung took up the challenge and immediately saw that the many blues of the Blue Period were the expression of a *Nekyia*: "the journey to Hades, the descent into the unconscious, and the leave-taking from the upper world; who follows not the accepted ideals of goodness and beauty, but demoniacal attraction of ugliness and evil."[9] We can now appreciate that this was a remarkable observation about some Blue Period paintings. Jung refers to the blues of the Blue Period, to "the blue of night, of moonlight and water, the Tuat-blue of the Egyptian underworld."[10] Furthermore, he sees an important characteristic in Picasso's personality: "I mean that personality in Picasso which suffers the underworld fate—the man in him who does not turn towards the day-world, but is fatefully drawn into the dark."[11] So there is no doubt that Jung saw an aspect of a genius whose consciousness was very close to the forces of the underworld.

Although he was acquainted with the paintings of schizophrenic and psychotic patients, [12] Jung's formulation did not include any major knowledge of or interest in art. That is to say, he had no antecedents for perceiving the plastic arts as contributing to the process of psychological knowledge.[13] Jung's view of painting was limited by a psychiatric culture. As we have seen, Jung seems to have known very little of the artistic movements of the 19th century, or more precisely, the history of art from Goya onwards. He knew even less about modern painting, which to some extent is characterized by the artist's use of painting as a way to explore the inner life. In the latter case, it compensates the collective consciousness of the epoch, for example, the way Goya's works of his Black Period, so irrational and emotional, compensated the excessive rationalism of the Enlightenment. Today, I feel that art has its deepest value when it compensates the one-sidedness of collective values.[14]

Jung's essay "On Picasso" continues:

> From a purely formal point of view, the main characteristic is one of fragmentation, which expresses itself in the so-called "lines of fracture"—that is, a series of psychic "faults" (in the geological sense) which run right through the picture.[15]

Jung seems to be referring to analytical Cubism, a pictorial movement that revolutionized the history of art. I can only imagine that the creative energy for such a revolution was mobilized from a very repressed level of the unconscious and expressed through those "lines of fracture" and psychic "faults." Historically, Cubism was the pictorial way to express the schism in Western culture just before the First World War.[16]

My own appreciation of Cubism has to do with the theory of the complexes, one of the greatest achievements of this century's psychology, which Jung developed at the same time as Picasso developed Cubism. It brings a complex view of human nature and history, meaning that there can be no reductive descent into cause and effect. In reality, our first view of the people and the world around us is complex psychologically or, we could say, "Cubist." Our first impression of another person, for example, is full of "lines of fracture" and "faults," like Picasso's analytical Cubist portraits. Likewise, to comprehend the world around us, we gather its scattered pieces, like those wonderful synthetic Cubist paintings of a guitar, a bottle of anis, a piece of wood, a torn-off bit of newspaper, or the suggested title of a poem. Nevertheless, it is still very difficult to think in terms of the complexes, just as it is difficult for those most versed in art to see the psychological implications of Cubism, the movement that turned art upside down. Gertrude Stein's view of Cubism as a Spanish product has been more or less accepted. I can also say that the theory of the complexes is a Swiss product and one that, in spite of its difficulty, compels us to think in terms of complexities.

When Jung wrote: "Seldom or never have I had a patient who did not go back to neolithic art forms or revel in evocations of Dionysian orgies,"[17] he was actually describing two trends in modern art. We can safely say Neolithic art forms and Dionysiac orgies have been the sources for the work of several modern artists. William Rubin, in his *"Primitivism" in 20th-Century Art*, demonstrates the presence of primitive art elements in modern art.[18] In his essay on Picasso, Rubin's first words are: "In no other artist's career has primitivism played so pivotal and historically consequential a role as in Picasso."[19] We could say that Picasso was a forerunner of this century's attempt to connect through art to man's primitive and archaic history. Our own times are especially marked by new studies on evolution that help us to connect to man's primitive past, to what has existed since long before recorded history, and to what we could call the "old soul."[20] In his search, Picasso went farther back than tribal art and, through his painting, connected to the legacy of Altamira and Lascaux.

We have also to give credit to the many painters who, in response to a psychic need, have made their work into a desperate attempt to connect to "Dionysian orgies." The orgy is a ritual that pertains to Dionysus, so their attempt can be seen as a reconnection to that which was the most repressed by Christianity, to a time in which the orgy was a sacred emotional act, not the carousal that Western tradition has made of it.[21] It seems to me, there is a great deal of modern art that strives to reconnect to repressed Dionysiac religiosity. However, much of it comes nowhere near the Dionysiac realm of the psyche, but pertains to what Christianity, after St. Paul, called "the flesh," meaning it pertains to a different psychological standpoint and so remains only an "evocation."[22] Probably Picasso was the only one to have felt at "ease" in that adventure, experiencing it in his own Dionysiac "body." He was the greatest Dionysiac exponent in modern painting, for in almost any period of his work Dionysus is present. From this point of view, his art is a testimony to painting as an inner religious dialogue, a *religare*, leaving aside its artistic achievement.

When reasonably cultured people read Jung for the first time, they often feel the same uneasiness one senses Jung felt when confronted with Picasso's paintings. This seems obvious enough, in view of the lack of references to Jung in current studies of psychiatry. Likewise, there is no art academy that holds up Picasso's work as a model. Because of the psychic one-sidedness of modern man, both geniuses would seem to travel in the same boat of attraction and misunderstanding, though they were both the greatest exponents of the attempt to compensate this century's rationalistic one-sidedness. Picasso himself remarked: "Everyone wants to understand art. Why not try to understand the songs of a bird?"[23] To try to understand with so-called understanding, that is to say, with collective rational powers, is simply foolish. As a matter of fact, to arrive at a communication with both Jung's psychology and Picasso's works, a continuous digging is required and the awareness that only an individual communication will serve. The bulk of Western culture's knowledge is simply not enough. Any collective view of these two giants will fail.

But there is more to Jung's uneasiness with Picasso's painting for, from my point of view, it pertains to what we would call trans-alpine psychology. It is the point where the psychological differences between North and South become an unbearable wound. Picasso, with his Dionysiac essence, is a paradigm of the difference. At best, Jung's religious background meant that for him Dionysiac religiosity and its way of life were very alien. I am trying to approach Jung's psychological attitude to Picasso's painting by taking into consideration some *lacunae* in his formulation with respect to the history of art, as well as, in my opinion, insurmountable historical and ethnic barriers. It seems that for the Swiss in general it is very difficult to understand and accept some aspects of Picasso's life and work. Between the Swiss Jung and the Andalusian Picasso, both great geniuses of this century, there remained an unbridgeable historical, cultural, and religious gulf. For example, it would have been unthinkable for Jung to appreciate bullfighting, one of Picasso's emotional sources. The appreciation of this sort of limitation is a more fruitful approach than having superficial notions that everything in both the fields of art and psychology can be understood.

It was not easy for Jung to sustain a reading of Picasso's paintings, and he jumped into the future:

> As to the future Picasso, I would rather not try my hand at prophecy, for this inner adventure is a hazardous affair and can

> lead at any moment to a standstill or to a catastrophic bursting asunder of the conjoined opposites.[24]

Such a catastrophic outcome did not happen. Picasso went on to produce great art until he was 92 years old. Jung, though a great revolutionary, was an inheritor of the 19th century's psychiatry. In *Whom Gods Destroy*, Ruth Padel writes that the idea that madness could be fearsomely latent was a new development from the characteristically 19th-century desire to claim secret insight into long-hidden madness.[25] This idea has left a lasting imprint on psychiatry, and Jung was not immune to it. But it implies that he lost the perspective of the here and now. His focus on the future makes for a Promethean psychology, the very opposite of a Dionysiac here-and-now attitude. For the psychiatrist, madness is to be treated; for the artist, madness is to be turned into art. It is a pity we are still unable to make a differentiation between the two, especially since Plato has already done it. Socrates, in referring to Dionysiac telestic madness, says, "And that there are two types of madness, one arising from human disease, the other when heaven sets us free from established convention."[26] Needless to say, I am interested in both types of madness, especially when a relation between the two can be noted.

The way in which Freud and Jung—the two pioneers of modern psychology—responded to this century's art, the opinions they held of it, have influenced art criticism and also psychology in its relation to art, resulting in a shortsighted view. The psychologists tend to concentrate on the artist rather than his work and the art critics tend to concentrate mostly on the outer influences in the art, two attitudes that belong to the inheritance of each discipline. In any event, just as in the psychoanalyst's technique of free association in connection with the patient's personal history, and the Jungian method of amplification[27] in connection with the history of culture and the collective unconscious, there is a similar movement of the psyche away from the image and its emotion. This tendency in both art criticism and psychology, the excessive intellectualism one feels, has been exacerbated in our times. I think it accounts for a gap in both art and psychology. Art makes psychic—whether it is in the work of Leonardo or Picasso—or to use Picasso's word, "exorcises" harmful unconscious contents. In reality, art and psyche cannot be so split.

My attitude in front of a work of art is to wait and see if a living relation to it happens. I try to "read" the work of art with the sort of awareness that I bring to the "reading" of a dream, for such awareness helps to keep my mind free of interpretative psychological theories. For instance, if a theory does come to my mind, it means that my individual values and feelings are not present, that I am off the mark and prone to project unconscious contents disguised as theories onto the dream or the art. Marie-Louise von Franz described Jung's theory of projection as follows: "Jung defined projection as an unconscious, that is, unperceived and unintentional, transfer of subjective psychic elements onto an outer object."[28] This means that projection is a natural psychic function. Jung, in a very colloquial way, showed the general mechanism of projection through a well known metaphor, speaking "of a 'hook' in the object on which one hangs a projection as one hangs a coat on a coat hanger."[29] We begin to suspect an unconscious projection when there is a notable disparity between the "coat" and the "hook."

So, as with the dream, my attempt to read a painting is as an image, and this sets a limit on my imagination. For me, an image is incommensurable, unknowable, and mysterious; nevertheless, in front of Leonardo's *Cartoon*, for example, or Picasso's *Demoiselles d'Avignon*, one feels the imagination is stimulated tremendously, and yet, at the same time, one feels one's limitations painfully. The image gives the painting its quality as a work of art, its force and emotion. The reading of the image in painting is, at best, a happening and it relies on the subjective factor of an emotional relationship to the artist and his work. Here I align myself with the poet José Lezama Lima, who said: "It is the image that makes possible the impossible."[30]

## *NOTES*

[1] This article was originally published in Spanish under the title "Sobre arte y psicología" in *Revista Venezolana de Psicología de los Arquetipos y Estudios Junguianos 2* (2007).

[2] E. R. Gombrich, "Freud's Aesthetics," *Encounter* 26, no. 1 (January 1966): 32.

[3] See Rafael Lopez-Pedraza, *Dionysus in Exile: on the Repression of Emotion and the Body* (New York: Chiron Publications, 2000) for a view of childhood trauma as a Dionysiac initiation and the danger of a non-traumatic childhood rendering a shallow soul, without depth.

[4] See Christian Gaillard, "Leonardo's Mother Revisited" in *The Transcendent Function: Individual and Collective Aspects* (Proceedings of

the Twelfth International Congress For Analytical Psychology, Chicago, 1992), ed. Mary Ann Mattoon (Einsiedeln: Daimon Verlag, 1993), in which he discusses Freud's view of Leonardo, seeing and respecting its reductivity from an historical perspective and contributing his own archetypal view of Leonardo's *The Virgin, Jesus, and St. Anne.*

[5] Gombrich, p. 34.

[6] Gaillard, p. 458.

[7] C. G. Jung, "On Picasso," in *The Collected Works of C.G. Jung,* trans. R. F. C. Hull, vol. 15 (London: Routledge & Kegan Paul, 1966), § 204; hereafter abbreviated to *CW* followed by volume number and paragraph (§) number.

[8] *Ibid.*

[9] *Ibid.*

[10] *Ibid.*, § 210.

[11] *Ibid.*

[12] Painting has remained a therapeutic tool in psychology. It is indeed an acute tool for diagnosis and a way to discern the patient's relation to his or her illness, but it is not art.

[13] On the other hand, Jung was interested in the psychological processes in artistic creativity and in its compensatory aspect. In such works as *Psychological Types*, he equated psychological and artistic creativity.

[14] See Rafael Lopez-Pedraza, *Anselm Kiefer: "After the Catastrophe"* (London: Thames & Hudson, 1997; New York: George Braziller, Inc., 1996), my first book on art and psychology, mainly devoted to a discussion of the madness of Western culture at the time of National Socialism and The Second World War, as depicted by Anselm Kiefer, the German painter.

[15] Jung, *CW* 15, § 208.

[16] Alexander Cirici Pellicer, in his book *Picasso Antes de Picasso* (Barcelona: Iberia-Joaquin Gil, Editores, S. A., 1946), praises both Jung and Picasso for bringing the insight of a split-off consciousness in Western culture. Cirici Pellicer seems to me to be a religious man who is able to recognize the schizophrenia in Western culture, that which Picasso, half consciously, displays in his Cubist paintings. Ciricci does not fall into the common aesthetic vision of Picasso's work. He has a deep feeling for the decline in Western culture

[17] Jung, *CW* 15, § 212.

[18] William Rubin, "*Primitivism" in 20th-Century Art: Affinity of the Tribal and the Modern,*" vols. 1 and 2 (New York: The Museum of Modern Art, 1988).

[19] *Ibid.*, vol. 1, p. 241.

[20] There is a marked difference between an artist's work that shows the presence of the "old soul," compensating the one-sidedness of the Western psyche, and work that shows only the presence of this century's "new soul," searching for novelty and resulting in shallowness and stupidity.

[21] See Lopez-Pedraza, *Dionysus in Exile*, in which there is a discussion of the Dionysiac orgy as a sacred ritual, as well as the historical repression of Dionysus, referring to E. R. Dodds's Introduction to Euripides, *The Bacchae* (Oxford: Clarendon Press Paperbacks, 1986).

[22] I want to differentiate between the psychology of what St. Paul called "the flesh," expressing complexities full of repression and guilt, and the psychology expressed through a Dionysiac body. It is very difficult in our culture to differentiate between a soul that lives in the body as its only habitat and the soul as depicted in the Scriptures. Of course, there is a great deal more to be said about the painting of "the flesh," from how it was painted in the Renaissance to how it is painted today.

[23] Picasso, *Picasso on Art: A Selection of Views*, ed. Dore Ashton (New York: Da Capo Press, 1972), p. 11.

[24] Jung, *CW* 10, § 214.

[25] Ruth Padel, *Whom Gods Destroy: Elements of Greek and Tragic Madness* (Princeton, NJ: Princeton University Press, 1995), p. 30.

[26] Plato, *Phaedrus and The Seventh and Eighth Letters*, trans. Walter Hamilton (Harmondsworth, UK: Penguin Books, 1973), § 265.

[27] Jung's "Tuat-blue of the Egyptian underworld" in his essay "On Picasso" (*CW* 15, § 210), is an example of the amplification method.

[28] Marie-Louise von Franz, *Projection and Re-Collection in Jungian Psychology*, trans. William Kennedy (La Salle and London: Open Court, 1980), p. 3. For further reading see also *CW* 9i, § 121f.

[29] *Ibid.*

[30] José Lezama Lima, "las imágenes posibles," in *Esferaimagen* (Barcelona: Tusquets Editor, 1970), p. 51.

SYLVESTER WOJTKOWSKI is a Jungian analyst in private practice in New York City. He is a founding member of the Jungian Psychoanalytic Association (JPA) and a graduate of the C. G. Jung Institute of New York. He received his doctorate in Clinical Psychology from the New School. He is a board member of the C. G. Jung Foundation for Analytical Psychology. He gives workshops throughout the country on Jungian and Archetypal Psychology, on imagination, mythology, psyche and culture, etc. He has presented at several National and International (IAAP) conferences for Analytical Psychology on various topics, including "Islamic Wound of the Western Psyche" (Barcelona, 2004), "Approaching the Unspeakable Regarding 9/11" (Chicago, 2005), and "Deconstructing the Monstrous" (San Francisco, 2006). He may be contacted at: s.wojtkowski@att.net.

18

# Deconstructing the Monstrous: An "Ecologically Correct" Approach

## From "What are Dragons for?" to "What do Dragons Want?"

SYLVESTER WOJTKOWSKI

> Dreams and Beasts are two keys by which we are to find out the secrets of our nature.
>
> —Ralph Waldo Emerson (1832)

> Could we become conscious without [the hero-dragon] struggle?
>
> —James Hillman (1973)

In this paper I will take another swing at the unconquerable motif of hero-slaying-the-dragon with the monstrous chutzpah of delivering the "final" blow. Of course, I exaggerate; I am just trying to be true to the discursive style of the archetype, while being aware that the frontal assault on the hero just strengthens him/it. I will consider the motif from the side of the monster in the ecological context of its appearance in the history of culture and Jungian theories about it. I will be biased, reversing the traditional point of view—that of the hero. Although that traditional perspective served us well for a long time, it tends, particularly in verbal descriptions, to privilege the hero. Visual depictions of the hero-monster battle have been more balanced, since one of the characteristics of the experience of the monster is that it captivates the imagination (and memory), so artists have devoted a lot of attention to rendering these marvelous creatures. I will emphasize the monster's contribution to re-education of the hero and the development of consciousness.

In the postmodern world, the heroic ego is the major problem both in the psyche and in the culture. The critique of the ego is eloquently present in Jungian literature of recent decades (Hillman, Giegerich, Adams). "Ego" has become conscious through the heroic process of confrontation with the unconscious, symbolized by the battle between the hero and the monster. However, the ego, a self-proclaimed center of consciousness, ended up as a defensive complex through identification with the hero archetype. The monster, like the hero, is intimately connected to the ego but always in the background. Western civilization has been developed through the power of ego, through its heroic conquest of the inner and outer monstrosities that have always been, and still are, in its way. Deeper understanding of the role that the monster plays in this development is crucial and timely for further deconstruction of the ego-complex.

Recently, there has been renewal of interest in monsters not just in cinema, computer games, politics, and Jungian psychology, but also in other scholarly studies.[1] David Gilmore opens his psycho-historical study of monsters with a revealing statement of enormous, if not monstrous, significance for imaginology, or the study of imagination[2]: "The mind needs monsters. Monsters embody all that is dangerous and horrible in human imagination."[3]

Depicted monsters are usually more interesting, more unique-looking than the heroic figures who fight them. The hero may have a thousand faces, but he has been rendered graphically in more stereotypical fashion than his opponent, who is represented with unique, if grotesque, features. Thus, as an image, a monster more closely represents individuality than the hero-image does. To illustrate this point, let me just mention several contemporary cinematic monsters—Frankenstein (Boris Karloff), Dracula, King Kong, or Alien—and vivid, particular images immediately enter our minds. Of course, the hero is there too, but not so distinct; he can be equally well played by different actors.

Let's look for initial insights into the etymology of the "monster."

The English "monster" derives from the Latin "*monstrum,*" which is a translation of the Greek *teras*, meaning "warning" or "portent," and stems from the root *monere*, meaning to "show" or "warn"; the Greek *mnasthai* (to remember), and *menos* (spirit) share the same root. The Latin *monstrum* refers to *monitus* (from which the English "admonition"), "that which reveals or warns," often a sign or an omen to be interpreted; that is to say, *monstrum* symbolizes something unknown. Ancient Romans spoke of *monstra* whenever they encountered an extraordinary or strange phenomenon, which they regarded as a warning or an omen from the gods, not just monsters, or demons. The term *monstrum* was often used in religion in the context of divining divine intentions from natural phenomena. "Monster" and "mental" share the same etymology, reflecting that both originate in the mind.

Monsters are represented as creatures immense in size, grotesquely repellent, gigantic, often reptilian, or horrible part-human hybrids with enormous jaws, superhuman in power, combining human and animal traits such as cruelty, malice, or cannibalism. In the narratives, their huge mouth is emphasized as an organ of predation and destruction, used to rip and tear bodies, to bite, rend and devour, sometimes emitting noise, smoke, and fire. They tend to inhabit wildernesses, dark corners of the earth, caves, dense forests; they often dwell in seas or lurk in deep lakes. They are fond of devouring virgins and youths.

Images of monsters are as old as the beginning of artistic human expression. Monstrous forms decorate the prehistoric caves of Lascaux and Altamira. Parietal art works (drawings and paintings on cave walls) recombine natural forms in bizarre and imaginative ways. The composite parietal figures have a human base with animal appendages (antlers, horns, paws) or animal heads (bird-man, bison-man, snake-man). Monster images existed in the earliest human civilizations. Composite creatures occur both as visual images and as descriptions in the earliest fragments of Mesopotamian and Egyptian art. In *The Epic of Gilgamesh*, we have depictions of dragons, ape-men, scorpion-men, and goblins. These Ur-monsters are co-creators of the human world. The earliest image of such "civilized" monster is the Egyptian sphinx. Its image is a female head with the body of lion, and lion's paws, or eagle's talons.

Andre Leroi-Gourhan,[4] a pre-eminent mid-20$^{th}$-century French anthropologist and art historian, argued that Stone-Age monsters had a symbolic nature and constituted initial evidence for the autonomy of the human imagination, and were therefore crucial to understanding our psychological nature. Cave paintings of monsters indicated for him that Cro-Magnon hunters were like us in their capacity for symbolic thought. They had the ability to imagine impossible combinations and create such ideas as images, that is, they possessed a free, i.e., not merely "natural," fantasy life. Some anthropologists, such as Mary Douglas,[5] viewed monsters as examples of interstitial concepts, that is, existing between, and in contrast to, ordinary categories. By conflating cognitive boundaries recognized as the basis of the order of things, images of monsters challenge the moral and cosmological order; this is the reason why monstrous deviations are so terrifying. For Victor Turner,[6] monstrous forms operate in liminal space, contradicting and subverting reality, and help deconstruct common sense, releasing humans from everyday constrains. For René Girard,[7] images of monsters traditionally assisted humans in the displacement and discharge of original violence into ritual violence, not unlike in our contemporary culture, where monsters depicted in horror movies and fiction allow us to discharge aggression imaginally.

An historian of religion, Norman Cohn,[8] argues that early religion rested on the allegorical myth-of-origin of a man fighting a monster. A harmony-and-order-defending hero battles a chaos monster that threatens the world. As a result of such apocalyptic confrontation, civilizations emerge and prosper, and humans become masters of the world. Cohn calls the narrative of man-versus-monster the universal "combat-myth" of the origin of civilization.

Psychoanalytically, the monster was seen as an example of condensation, a collective figure uniting the actual features of two or more people, animals, or objects into a single dream image. Freud[9] and Jones[10] interpreted "monsters" as a manifestation of id forces of sexual sadism, exemplifying the sadistic eroticism of human infants. As is typical of Freudian interpretation, the imagination is pathologized and located in the mind of a polymorphously perverse infant. It is no surprise that Melanie Klein, no stranger herself to the analysis of oral sadism, aggression, rage, disintegrations, annihilation, and other species of destruction beloved by our infantile self, discusses monsters:

> Man-eating wolf, the fire-spewing dragon, and all the evil monsters out of myths flourish and exert their unconscious influence in the phantasy of each child, and it feels itself persecuted and threatened by evil shapes.[11]

However, she concretizes and personalizes them, believing that the real objects behind monsters are the child's own parents, and those dreadful shapes reflect the features of its father and mother, seen as deformed by the child's autonomous fantasies of oral violence against its parents. They direct the death instinct towards the external object—the mother's body—and away from the ego as means of warding off the ego's disintegration.

To paraphrase Winnicott, one may say there is no such creature as a monster; there is only a monster-hero dyad. Like mother and infant, monster and hero are inseparable, and are often relatives as well. In myths, monsters and heroes occur together. Monsters are not totally alien, no matter how grotesque; they are, as Gilmore puts it, our lineal relatives,

> ... no matter what their cosmological provenance, the monsters constitute the older generation to the young heroes who vanquish them .... From the earliest we are confronted with an Oedipal theme: child against parent, monster and human one blood, linked by hatred and violence and patrimony—all the way to the present Frankenstein. But *men create monsters from nothing, from thought.*[12] (Italics added.)

Nevertheless, I would say that it is psyche that creates monsters.

Even this cursory historical overview of the monster-hero archetype role in the culture indicates to me that this archetype has been providing energy for the human imagination from the very beginning. We have been accompanied by the monster-slaying motif (of which dragon-slaying is a sub-genre) from parietal (cave) art to postmodern media-culture. At the infancy of ego-consciousness, as the mythopoesis aimed at creating a relatively stable consciousness, monsters may have provided the process with the psychic libido that this embryonic ego required to fight off the regressive pull of the unconscious.[13] However, as the will-power of the ego itself has reached monstrous proportions and threatened to destroy both "inner" and "outer" ecosystems (not unlike the dragons of yore), the continued emergence of monsters may indicate quite another *telos*. I call inquiry into this *telos* the search for the treasure-hard-to-find, since the ultimate value concealed in the motif has been so elusive.

## The Jungian View of Monsters

Prior to Hillman's questioning of the hero-dragon motif,[14] the Jungian interpretation of the motif seemed definitively and convincingly set (both by Jung himself[15] and by Neumann[16]) as symbolizing the ego destroying the regressive pull of the collective unconscious in the process of claiming the "treasure-hard-to-attain," or individuation. Jung perceived an intimate connection between the hero and the dragon early on as pro- and anti-individuation movements of the unconscious:

> ... [T]he hero who clings to the mother is the dragon, and when he is reborn from the mother he becomes the conqueror of the dragon. ... [T]aken purely as a psychologem the hero represents the positive favorable action of the unconscious, while the dragon is its negative and unfavorable action—not birth, but a devouring.[17]

Jung interpreted the dragon as "the negative mother-imago" which symbolized the fear of the monstrous consequences of breaking the incest taboo.[18] He came to this interpretation through relating the psychic experiences of his patients to comparative mythology. Through the extensive use of mythological amplifications, Jung was able to move the Oedipus complex from the personal level of Freud to the archetypal level (from incest to the rebirth archetype, for example, "Jonah in the whale") and thus opened the door to his psychology project. If we look at this process from the perspective of the dragons, the dragons can be seen as facilitating Jung's understanding of the dynamics of the collective unconscious, while at the same time representing it. However, Jung tended to interpret the predominantly masculine dragons as symbols of the devouring side of the feminine unconscious. The particularity of dragons, or other monsters, was of no interest to Jung, only the meaning they represented for the psyche.[19] They were safely classified as subspecies of the "devouring monsters" category,[20] symbolizing the "regressive pull of the unconscious." Jung realized that the battle with the monster is a continual, repetitive one. No matter how skilled the hero becomes at dispatching them, new monsters just keep coming. Jung concluded his early analysis with the idea that throughout an individual's lifetime, the ego has to struggle with the regressive pull of the unconscious:

> Unfortunately, however, this heroic deed has *no lasting effects. Again and again* the hero must renew the struggle, and always under the symbol of deliverance from the mother."[21] (Italics added.)

However, Jung stopped short of seeing this recurring process as a repetition-compulsion, a symptom in itself that needs to be seen through. Only in his concretization of the second half of life would Jung allow for the immersion in the unconscious for the purpose of rebirth.

The paradox of the center of consciousness being at the same time a defensive complex (i.e., also possibly blind, which in the case of consciousness has grave consequences) lies at the core of the Jungian theory of the "ego."[22] While the paradox is a common psychic phenomenon, and the alchemical Jung has become increasingly comfortable with it, a defensive ego-complex as the center of consciousness has produced countless theoretical difficulties: from the precise definition of the ego itself to specifying its relationship with consciousness, self, and other non-ego images.[23] While it is a common rhetorical device (and one not without merit) in Jungian thinking to pass over such conceptual problems by declaring a fuzzy concept in question a symbol, and as such escaping precise definition, it is also often an excuse to avoid rigorous critique of the fundamental elements of our theory.

I will argue that the "Jungian" ego consists of at least five components: (1) a subjective component of personal identity (ego as an identity complex); (2) ego as a center of consciousness (ego as consciousness complex); (3) ego as a seat of reason (ego as a reason complex); (4) ego as a will complex; and (5) a defensive component (ego as hero-complex, or an identification with the hero archetype)—all expressed and confounded in a singular ego-image. While identity includes what is essential to an individual, it implicitly excludes other characteristics. In itself identity is not necessarily a defensive structure; only when the ego perceives itself as threatened does it become defensive and respond from its heroic side. The ego as center of consciousness, theoretically at least, can be seen as the component that allows us to see things with a certain degree of objectivity (akin to what Wolfgang Giegerich has recently called "transcendental ego"[24]). Ego as a reason complex allows us to think logically through the experience. Ego as a will complex gives us a certain amount of libido at our disposal. All the components of the ego are strongly influenced by the hero archetype, from which they originated and differentiated. For all archetypal psychology's critique of and effort to relativize it, the heroic ego still seems to be going on strong, both in theory and in practice. I will argue that the massive resistance of the ego to change has to do with its, and our (as Jungians), identification with the hero archetype.

Following Jung, we have come to realize that all "images have a quality of consciousness"[25] and by extension that complexes have consciousness. However, it is harder to realize that consciousness itself is complexed. It is as if we have tried to preserve the Eastern ideal of pure consciousness, consciousness as transcendent light. In actual experience, consciousness is always under the influence of a particular archetypal dominant—it reveals the world to us as it appears through this archetypal structure (of which we are not immediately aware, and can realize only through reflection, or when the dominant shifts.) Different modes of consciousness are governed by different archetypes. Moreover, for embodied consciousness, the situation gets even more complicated and complexed, since complexes can be dominated by different archetypes, and at times the expression of a particular archetypal dominant can be distorted by a complex.[26] In spite of this, the hero complex features in our very definition of consciousness as

> the logos sword of discrimination in the hands of heroic ego in his mission to clean up the mother-benighted world. What we have taken for consciousness, this too has been determined by the mother. To be conscious has meant and continues to mean: to kill.[27]

The hero-slaying-the dragon constitutes the archetypal dominant of our Western consciousness. We split the hero off from the dragon and identify with the heroic drive, calling it consciousness, and repress the inertia of the devouring dragon, calling it unconscious and regressive.[28] However, by slaying the dragon (a personification of imaginal instinct, according to Hillman[29]) the hero is left without imagination, we are dissociated from our depths and our heroic ego has a hard time seeing itself as an imaginal figure: "To be a hero one must be dead. The hero is dead because he is an imaginal power, a fantasy. The hero is present not in actuality but as a psychic projection through his cult."[30] In our classic Jungian theory, we have identified with the hero part of the hero-dragon archetype and have become inflated with his will power; we have thus defined the consciousness complexed by the hero as the center of consciousness and banished the dragon to unconsciousness. For Hillman, there is no solution to these twisted heroic entanglements within the hero-dragon complex. The only salvation lies in shifting emphasis from hero-mother duality to the puer-senex dyad:

> For anyone in this culture at this time the battle with the mother and the heroic stance of the "first half" cannot but be archetypally wrong, regardless of one's age. This stance is anachronistic in the true sense of being out of tune with time, and every victory over the mother is a defeat for the fundamental task of the present culture: becoming aware of the senex in all its archetypal significance and relating puer phenomena to it.[31]

It seems that the logic of the hero has us in its grip one way or another, and there is no way out but to move to another archetypal dominant. Nevertheless, can we further explicate the hero-monster archetype from within its own rhetoric? Of course, with the inevitable heroic expectation of shifting the archetypal structure from within itself.

In his earlier analysis of the dragon-slaying archetype, Adams indicates that this archetype itself structures both the mythic motif and its Jungian interpretation.[32] That is, in the process of interpreting the motif some image has to be destroyed: either the dragon (Jung, Neumann), or the assertive masculine hero (Hillman), or the idealization of the Jungian Analyst (Adams himself). In *The Mythological Unconscious*,[33] Adams responds to a dreamer's question, "Why does everyone want to *kill* the dragons?" with the profound analytical self-critique of the hero's (and the analyst's) impulse to kill the monster. He ends his reflection by stating that instead of killing it, the dragon image in the dream only indicates the dreamer's need to engage it "*in some way*." For decades now the "ego" has been assaulted by its Jungian critics, who find it now the "real monster" to be slain and thus unconsciously propagating "the hero-slaying-the-monster" paradigm and paradoxically strengthening the very heroic ego they want to destroy. In other words "the Ego" cannot be transformed through the heroic critique, which on the content level slays the ego but on the process level promotes the ego of the critic. Since the hero-monster battle constitutes the core of the hero archetype, clarifying the role of the monster in the heroic ego is of utmost importance.

## Renouncing Dragon-Slaying

Here it will serve us well to remember Hillman's warning that "killing the dragon in the hero myth means nothing less than killing the imagination, the very spirit that is the way and the goal.[34] Killing the dragon deprives the hero of depth and vital, creative imagination. So in our imaginings of the hero-dragon dyad, we are handicapped if we approach it from the side of our heroic-ego, which simply does not have enough imagination to do the job and by definition has a propensity to take the hero's side and dissociate from the dragon. At this point we can engage another helpful story, one told by Wolfgang Giegerich, that in order to do any psychology at all, we need to speak as "dead psychologists," as non-egos, in this case from the side of the dragon.[35]

As Adams stresses in his recent work, "Imaginology: The Jungian Study of the Imagination," an anxious ego-image defends against non-ego-images. Monster is "an epithet by which the ego-image disparages the non-ego image."[36] He further calls the ego teratogenic, that is, creating monsters by "monsterizing" the non-ego images. Adams considers "monster" an indefinite concept not an image.[37] Monster consists of two components: an image of the ego's anxiety facing the unknown image and a non-ego image itself. The initial terror distorts the perceptual acuity of the ego and it perceives an unknown Other as a generic (and threatening) monster rather than a distinct Other with a host of individual characteristics. As ego loosens its defensive posture and becomes more receptive (or as Adams calls it "curious"), it can discern the specificity of the Other. It can still fear the Other, but now the Other gains the definiteness of a composite image, as opposed to the vagueness of a generic concept. Image, as Hillman has emphasized, is not only a specific psychic content, but also the way we approach it or perceive it.[38] We can treat "images" conceptually and regard "concepts" imaginally. This image-concept dynamic is necessary to consciousness, if not to the whole psyche. Throughout this discussion, I have been regarding "monster" imaginally, as a composite image, and a "symbol of symbolism" (in Nietzsche's phrase about the sphinx, which I will engage a bit later).

Alfred Ribi sees demons as personifications of emotions.[39] As a result, a monster, always a creature that evokes intense emotional response, is a spontaneous psychic formation personifying fear of the unknown. It is as if the monster-producing power of psyche is an engine of the imagination. This point is beautifully illustrated in alchemy:

> In the *blackness of a despair* which was not his own, and of which he was merely the witness, [the alchemist] experienced how *it* turned into the worm and the poisonous dragon.[40]

Originally, psyche is all other, almost all Monster, with only a scintilla of light of consciousness. Thus, consciousness is the son of the Monster, like Murduk in the Mesopotamian myth, who slays his mother Tiamat and constructs the world and its cosmic order out of her. The monster as the Other is the ground of consciousness. Monster is the *prima materia* of the world. The monster is real, and what is real cannot be eliminated. In spite of continual destruction, monsters have not become extinct. However, the purpose of their emergence may have evolved over time. Now, they may want us to engage them in a manner other than repetitive slaughter. Ego-image, as Adams says, is not only unconscious of non-ego-images, but also of its own monstrosity, its own Otherness.[41] The hero dissociated from its own other is dangerous to self and others. Without seeing the other as its own essence, in blind self-sacrifice to eliminate the last vestiges of otherness, the ego possessed by its murdering impulse is now posed to destroy the world and itself.

For all his emphasis on unity, Jung the writer is many Jungs, sometimes contradicting, sometimes complementing one another. Here the Jung of Visions (Seminars) offers some insights that can further us on our quest:

> The monster symbolizes or personifies the hidden meaning of a situation or an epoch of history, as well as of a human being. Every hero is at the same time a monster, as one sees by its inhuman attributes. ... So this monster seems to be the hidden meaning of a hero, or savior, a god. But it is a hidden aspect, we don't know what will come of it. ... So all we can say about this monstrous figure is that it is the hidden meaning of a god that is in the state of development.[42]

Here, more clearly than anywhere else, Jung sees monster as an essence of the Hero, both a developing god and a god of development. Hence derive all psychoanalytic ideas of ego-psychology, stages of ego-development, and the like. Both killing the monster and the monster-ego keep us in the grip of the ego-monster archetype and blind us to the developing aspect of the unknown "*mysterium tremendum et fascinosum*" (the designation that Jung gives monsters),[43] personified as monstrous. Monsters' images are composite, mysterious shapes, as if attempts at unification of different forms into one image. As images, they come closest to representing Jung's definition of the symbol, as "an intuitive idea that cannot yet be formulated in any other or better way."[44] "We may not be able to *unriddle* its meaning to our entire satisfaction. The symbol remains a *perpetual* challenge to our thoughts or feelings."[45] It is as if Jung sees the symbol as a sphinx that keeps calling upon Oedipus to penetrate its mystery. From this perspective, it makes sense that Nietzsche would consider the sphinx "the symbol of symbolism." Since the "symbolic process is an experience in images and of images,"[46] the images of monsters can be seen as symbolic of this symbolic process. It is as if monster images were "meta-images," still depicted in the form of (composite) image, since psyche has at its disposal only imagistic display, and not a discursive, logical conceptual language.

We have traditionally attributed to the ego our conceptualizing capacity. However, I will argue that monsters are essential to forming concepts and thus to thinking. It is because of monsters that we can engage in direct thinking, that is, in deliberately organizing chains of associations, gradually conquering the boundaries of the unthought unknown, protected by their monstrous guardians (monsters are traditionally creatures on the boundaries). As a result of the engagement, we can either move the border and extend our field of knowing or yield to the power of the monster and "become uncomfortable and stop thinking."[47] As monsters are targeted by the ego-image for the proverbial kill, so they aim at the ego-image to further its consciousness at their own expense. They willingly give themselves as food for thought, so to speak: "*In the age-old image of uroboros lies the thought* of devouring oneself and turning oneself into the circulatory process"[48] (italics added). It is as if the monsters, through their self-sacrifice, aim at the development of our minds:

> The dragon, or serpent, represents the initial state of unconsciousness. ... Unconsciousness has to be sacrificed; only then one can find the entrance into the head, and the way to conscious knowledge and understanding. Once again the universal struggle of the hero slaying the dragon is enacted, and each time at its victorious conclusion the sun rises: consciousness dawns, and it is perceived that the transformation process is taking place inside the temple, that is, in the head.[49]

Consciousness dawns as the monster is laid to rest, and we gain a new idea to see through, to understand our experience, and to further our thinking.

We can imagine that by devouring and assimilating a lot of feminine energy, masculine dragons when slain release their captive feminine essence into the ego, thus subverting its masculinity. Over time, they deposit more and more of the feminine in this masculine structure. When feminine energy absorbed from the monster reaches a "critical mass," the heroic, defensive ego can exhibit some feminine characteristics, like Hercules serving as a woman at the court of Queen Omphale. Thus, in a paradoxical way, defensiveness may lead to receptivity (or curiosity about the Other;[50] even the hero in the defensive position needs to have some curiosity about the enemy, if only to dispatch him more efficiently).

There is a radical shift in the imaging of dragons, from the huge creatures painted on the interior walls of Paleolithic caves, through antiquity (where they are represented as mythological figures, mostly guardians of treasures, devouring chained virgins and youths, to be slain by wannabe heroes) depicted mostly on the external walls of ceramic vessels, to the human-scale figures of alchemy, fond of dwelling in alembics, pelicans, and other vessels. It is as if dragons moved from cave walls to the exterior of Greek vases and then into the vessels themselves. This shift reflects an understanding of dragons as creatures of the imagination, as shown by their substantial reduction in scale and the gradual process of internalization. Alchemical material provides an access to a "not heroic, not literalized, and not viewed from ego consciousness"[51] view of dragons. Alchemical dragons are personified, seem to exhibit some form of consciousness, and gain the power of speech.

However, the transition from the mythical dragon to the alchemical one did not happen spontaneously: it was a cultural achievement, accomplished through interpretation. For example, Jung quotes an Arab alchemist, Kalid, who identifies the dragon as the first stage of transformation of *Sol redivivus.*[52] (Each stage symbolizes a different degree of insight, wisdom, and initiation, the others being the lion, the eagle and the hermaphrodite.) This being alchemy, though, the dragon seems to carry multiple, constantly shifting meanings:

> Sol as personification of consciousness is the father of the dragon, but the dragon begets itself as well and is increatum, and Sol is its own son and the dragon. Dragon is also close to Luna who as a mother is contained in the dragon, and when the dragon is slain it dies both with Sol and Luna, solar and lunar consciousness. The death of the dragon is thus the central mystery of transformation. At the same time dragon is the product of union of Sol and Luna.[53]

Alchemy itself speaks in sphinxian riddles, a language proper to monsters, and it presents the dragon as an enigmatic shapeshifter. Here the dragon is really a mercurial being that takes on the identity required by different moments in the process and thus appears to be a personification of the mysterious psychic transformative process itself. The image of the dragon takes on the identity of other images depending on the context in which it appears. The dragon is the son of the sun, who is itself its own son and its own father, and it contains its own mother, but somehow they share each other's essence since at the dragon's death, they all die, a death of metaphor, so to speak.

These alchemical dragons are seen as consisting of opposite elements: "The dragon [Uroboros] impregnates itself through biting its own tail (masculine tail in the feminine mouth) and devours itself, its body swallowed into his head."[54] The dragon is a *coniunctio oppositorum*, an image that compensates for the one-sidedness of ego consciousness. The dragon's head contains the precious stone, which Jung interprets as consciousness containing the symbolic image of the self. Here we have a different idea of consciousness from the heroic one, a holistic consciousness of the dragon—as a container of the symbolic image of the self.

Alchemical dragons are often found as protagonists undergoing operations of *mortificatio* and *putrifactio.* Some alchemical masculine dragons die a quite unheroic death, in the spasms of ecstatic agony, a *petite mort* indeed:

> Let the grave be dug for that dragon, and let that woman [who slays her husbands] be buried with him, he being chained fast to that woman; and the more he winds and coils himself about her, the more he will be cut to pieces by the female weapons which are fashioned in the body of the woman. And when he sees he is mingled with the limbs of the woman, he will be certain of death, and will be changed wholly into blood. But when the Philosophers see him changed into blood, they leave him a few days in the sun, until his softness is consumed and the blood dries, and they find that poison. What then appears is a hidden wind.[55]

A masculine dragon (*prima materia* itself)[56] through a gruesome intercourse with the woman (as another personification of *prima materia*) reveals himself as a hidden spirit. He is vaguely cognizant of his death; he can change into blood and dry into poisonous spirit. These images indicate that the alchemical dragon is far from his origins as a wild creature of murky caves and by this time has become pretty much domesticated. He does not need to be dragged into the grave, nor does he resist being chained to a woman. It is a considerable change from the depictions of youths in chains being led to a cave to be devoured (or be subjected to whatever else the dragon did to them). We can say that "women," "chains," and "dragons" constituted a particular constellation of psychic images that over time evolved into a different combination in alchemy: the dragon, who obviously lost his predilection for virgins, submits to chains, and instead of dismembering the woman is himself cut into pieces by her. This dragon consciously submits to death, or radical transformation, and then alters its form after death. Mythical dragons would disappear completely after being slain, or only some of their body parts, such as the skin, tongue, teeth, or ears, would be preserved by the hero as a testimonial to his deed. However, after its death, this alchemical dragon turns into blood. Here we can see the death of the image and the dissolution of its form as a dragon into the image of blood, a pure symbol for libido, which then, through the additional exposure to the light of consciousness, dries up and is transformed into poison, a substance that modifies the natural course of things, and reveals a hidden spirit. Thus, the dragon, through dismemberment, is liquefied into blood, which dries up into poison, which conceals the spirit, justifying its symbolic designation as *prima materia*, as a potential for all forms.

The libido, in the form of the dragon, is easily transmutable. It is as if the imagination clothes a certain amount of transformative libido in the image of the dragon, which is easily usable for the process of individuation. The psyche encapsulates the libido in the dragon envelope, so to speak, and this readies it for assimilation by the ego-image. Some contemporary videogames use pixelated dragons, exactly for the same reason; a pixelated hero fights the dragon and after slaying it, his energy increases by the amount provided by the dragon.

After traversing and gathering insights from all these dragonian stories and ecologies, we are now in a position to pose the title question: What do dragons want? In order to find the answer to this question we will not be interpreting the material or imputing the answer to the dragon, but actually listening to what the dragon has to say. Beatus in *Aurelia Occulta* has the dragon speak alchemically:

> Many from one and one from many, issue of a famous line, I rise from the lowest to the highest. The nethermost power of the whole earth is united with the highest. I therefore am the One and the Many within me.

Jung comments on this passage: "*the dragon makes it clear that he is the chthonic forerunner of the self*"[57] (emphasis added). It takes tremendous confidence in the autonomy of the psyche to cite the image as a reliable source of knowledge about the psyche. Such appreciation of the autonomy of images and respect for their voice took Jung himself a couple of decades to achieve: from the heroic confrontation with the unconscious after his break with Freud (compare his description of the initial descent into active imagination in *Memories, Dreams, Reflections*[58]) through the years of active imagination, to his alchemical writings. Jung learned to befriend the dragon and value it. He asserted that Uroboros has a wonderful quality of aseity (or coming into existence by self-origination), which makes it indistinguishable from the godhead.[59] Further, Jung saw Uroboros as a goal of the opus, the "serpent rejoicing in itself, ... *physis* embracing itself, ... an emblem of Mercurius, a symbol of the union of the opposites."[60] It is an image of self-generating being that has within it all that is necessary, "one of the attributes of God."[61]

Over the course of the alchemical opus, the dragon transforms from the lowest and inchoate, poisonous personification of the masculine form of Mercurius into an articulate *pharmakon*, who can accurately portray his own status in the psyche.[62] Let's pay heed to what else this dragon has to say (also from the *Aurelia Occulta*):

> I am an infirm and weak old man, surnamed the dragon; therefore I am shut up in a cave, that I may be ransomed by the kingly crown. ... A fiery sword inflicts great torments upon me; death makes weak my flesh and bones ... my soul and my spirit depart; a terrible poison, I am likened to the black raven, in dust and earth I die, that out of Three may come One. O soul and spirit, leave me not, that I may see again the light of day, and *the hero of peace whom the whole world shall behold may arise from me*.[63] (Italics added.)

The dragon seems quite comfortable with all these tortures, and even death, and prays for resurrection as *the hero of peace*. Here is the answer to our question. The dragon wants a new kind of hero, wants to be a new hero, the hero, the dragophontes by nature, who renounces killing and by implication opens the way to a peaceful engagement with the other, a different relationship between the hero and the dragon. This would be a worthy end to the millennia of hero-dragon warfare.[64] It would be a radical transformation in the nature of the hero and by implication in the structure of the heroic ego. This ego could negotiate with the non-ego others in a peaceful, respectful way.

For a long time we have assumed that through careful interpretation we can surmise what dragons are for. In the process we have treated the other as an object rather than subject. All along, the answer was out there, if only we had treated the dragon as a subject, engaged him in the imagination, asked him what he wants, and hearkened to him, in line with the late Jung's wisdom: "We have simply to listen to what the psyche spontaneously says to us."[65]

## *NOTES*

[1] Catherine Atherton, ed., *Monsters and Monstrosity in Greek and Roman Culture* (Bari: Levante Editori, 1998); Norman Cohn, *Cosmos, Chaos and the World to Come: The Ancient Roots of Apocalyptic Faith* (New Haven, CT: Yale University Press, 1993); David D. Gilmore, *Monsters: Evil Beings, Mythical Beasts, and All Manner of Imaginary Terrors* (Philadelphia, PA: University of Pennsylvania Press, 2003); David Williams, *Deformed Discourse: The Function of the Monster in Mediaeval Thought and Literature* (Montreal: McGill-Queen's Press, 1996).

[2] Michael Vannoy Adams, "Imaginology: The Jungian Study of the Imagination," paper presented at "Psyche and Imagination," Conference of the International Association for Jungian Studies, University of Greenwich, London, July 6, 2006, personal website of Michael Vannoy Adams, n.d., <http://www.jungnewyork.com/imaginology.shtml>

[3] Gilmore, p. 1.

[4] A. Leroi-Gourhan, *The Dawn of European Art: An Introduction to Paleolithic Cave Painting* (Cambridge, UK: Cambridge University Press, 1982).

[5] Mary Douglas, *Purity and Danger* (London: Routledge, 1966).

[6] Victor Turner, *The Ritual Process* (London: Routledge & Kegan Paul, 1969).

[7] René Girard, *Violence and the Sacred* (Baltimore, MD: The John Hopkins University Press, 1979).

[8] Cohn, *Cosmos, Chaos and the World to Come.*

[9] Sigmund Freud, *Interpretation of Dreams*, Standard Edition of the Complete Psychological Works of Sigmund Freud, vol. 4 and 5, 1900-1901, trans. James Strachey, *et al.* (London: Hogarth Press, 1958).

[10] Ernest Jones, *On the Nightmare* (New York: Liveright, 1951/1971).

[11] Melanie Klein, *Love, Hate and Reparation, and Other Works* (London: Hogarth Press, 1975), p. 249.

[12] Gilmore, p. 36.

[13] At this stage of the development of consciousness, the hero could ignore his death for the sake of posthumous fame. Mortality was a common fate and one could moderate it by dying honorably. Compare the Greek concept of "beautiful death."

[14] James Hillman, "The Great Mother, Her Son, Her Hero, and the Puer," in *Fathers and Mothers*, ed. P. Berry (Dallas, TX: Spring Publications, 1973/1991), pp. 166-209; *Re-Visioning Psychology* (New York: Harper & Row, 1975); *The Dream and the Underworld* (New York: Harper & Row, 1979).

[15] C. G. Jung, *Symbols of Transformation*, *The Collected Works of C. G. Jung*, trans. R. F. C. Hull, vol. 5 (Princeton, NJ: Princeton University Press, 1912/1956); hereafter abbreviated to *CW* followed by volume number and page number.

[16] Erich Neumann, *The Great Mother* (Princeton, NJ: Princeton University Press, 1955).

[17] Jung, *CW* 5, p. 374.

[18] *Ibid*, p. 259.

[19] See Adams, "Imaginology."

[20] Jung, *CW* 5, p. 248.

[21] *Ibid.*, p. 348.

[22] Compare Hillman: "The ego as base of consciousness has always been an anachronistic part of analytical psychology" (*Anima: An Anatomy of a Personified Notion* [Dallas, TX: Spring Publications, 1985], p. 87).

[23] As Joseph Redfearn points out, "Jung does not distinguish in his use of the term "ego" between the subjective "I" and the function of defense and adaptation" (*My Self, My Many Selves* [London: Karnac, 1985], p. 9).

[24] Wolfgang Giegerich, *The Soul's Logical Life* (Frankfurt am Main: Peter Lang, 1998).

[25] Jung, *CW* 8, p. 323.

[26] Hillman, *Re-Visioning Psychology*.

[27] Hillman, "The Great Mother," p. 194.

[28] *Ibid.*, p. 196.

[29] *Ibid.*, p. 169.

[30] *Ibid.*, p. 196.

[31] *Ibid.*, p. 202.

[32] Michael Vannoy Adams, *The Mythological Unconscious* (New York: Karnac, 2001).

[33] *Ibid.*, pp. 425-31.

[34] Hillman, "The Great Mother," p. 79.

[35] See: "The 'Who' of Psychological Discourse," in Giegerich, pp. 17-25.

[36] Adams, "Imaginology," p.5.

[37] *Ibid.*

[38] Hillman, *Re-Visioning Psychology.*

[39] Alfred Ribi, *Demons of the Inner World* (Boston, MA: Shambhala Publications, 1990).

[40] Jung, *CW* 14, p. 350.

[41] Adams, "Imaginology," p.1.

[42] C. G. Jung, *Visions Seminars* (Princeton, NJ: Princeton University Press, 1988), p. 849.

[43] *Ibid.*, p. 846.

[44] Jung, *CW* 15, p. 70.

[45] *Ibid.*, p. 77.

[46] Jung, *CW* 9i, p. 38.

[47] C. G. Jung, *Memories, Dreams, Reflections* (New York: Random House, 1961), p. 171 (hereafter abbreviated to *MDR*).

[48] Jung, *CW* 14, p. 365.

[49] Jung, *CW* 13, p. 89.

[50] Adams, "Imaginology."

[51] Hillman, "The Great Mother," p. 80.

[52] Jung, *CW* 14, p. 141.

[53] *Ibid.*, p.142.

[54] Jung, *CW* 14, p. 116.

[55] *Turba Philosophorum*, cited in Jung, *CW* 14, p. 21.

[56] *CW* 13, p. 139.

[57] *CW* 14, p. 224.

[58] Jung, *MDR*, pp. 178-179.

[59] *CW* 14, p. 293.

[60] *Ibid.*, p. 504.

[61] *CW* 13, p. 82.

[62] *CW* 14, pp. 335-336.

[63] *Ibid.*, p. 515.

[64] A similar conclusion has been reached by Michael Adams, who says: "An ego-image that non-ego images have deconstructed would be an ego-image … [that] regards non-ego images as a profusion of differences that it may contemplate and then engage in appropriate ways" (Adams, "Imaginology").

[65] C. G. Jung, *C. G. Jung Letters, Volume 2: 1951-1961*, ed. Gerhard Adler, trans. Jeffrey Hulen (Princeton, NJ: Princeton University Press, 1976), p. 591. (To Read, September 2, 1960.)

THOMAS MOORE is the author of the bestselling book *Care of the Soul* and fifteen other books on deepening spirituality and cultivating soul in every aspect of life. He has been a monk, a musician, a university professor, and a psychotherapist, and today he lectures widely on holistic medicine, spirituality, psychotherapy, and ecology. He also writes fiction and music and often works with his wife, artist and yoga instructor, Joan Hanley. He writes regular columns for *Resurgence*, *Spirituality & Health*, and Beliefnet.com. He has two children and lives in New England.

# 19

# Notes towards an Archetypal Theology of the Gospels

THOMAS MOORE

Several years ago I was visiting a large university in the South to give a series of lectures. I was looking forward to meeting members of the religious studies department there, since religion is my field. After the first lecture I asked my host if any were attending, and he told me that they had decided to boycott my lecture because I don't talk about Jesus—I focus only on the Greek gods and goddesses.

That comment seeded a desire in me to engage in some archetypal studies of the Gospels. In graduate school at Syracuse University in the early 1970s I studied ancient Greek classical texts, read Jung, and discovered James Hillman, and wrote a dissertation on Marsilio Ficino, who in the 15th century was busy at reconciling Greek religion with Christianity.

Ficino was an Orphic Catholic, who saw no problem being a priest at the cathedral in Florence and at the same time reviving pagan ritual and imagery. His philosophy, combining Greek mythology, Christian theology, and Hermetic magic inspired me to develop a blending of polytheism with a Christian myth as it is filtered through the writings of Teilhard de Chardin and Paul Tillich. After meeting James Hillman, my interest in Greek texts deepened, and I began to use Greek imagery as my primary starting point in most of my writing. Recently, I have turned back to the stories of my youth and have been doing work on the Gospel narratives and teachings.

Generally, archetypal psychology has not been favorable to Jesus. David Miller's excellent book *Christs* (1981/2005) is an outstanding exception. There he advocates "archetypal theology," which is one way I imagine my work. Here I propose to treat the Gospels as rich in implication and archetypal depth, equal in that way to any Greek tragedy or tale.

## Jesus without Christianity

James Hillman has pointed out the dangers of what he calls "Christianism," referring to the ideology, I assume, of Christian theology and practice. I have taken a different direction by focusing on the Gospel texts—not only the canonical New Testament books, but the extracanonical ones as well—without the biases and habits of thought of Christian theology. I work with the Gospels the way I do the Greek stories, looking for levels of resonance, noting the history of key words, and making connections to other mythologies. The common language of the Gospels and the Greek tales helps make connections through etymologies and the nuances of words.

When I was a novice in a religious order in my late teens, I read the Gospels in Greek every day for a year. In doing so, I developed a taste for Greek expression and even then saw wide gaps between the words I was reading and the meanings I had heard in church all my life. The Gospel is one thing; Christianity is another.

One easy example of a word commonly used with moralistic tones in churches but clearly more subtle and interesting in the texts is "sin." The word in Greek is *hamartia,* which, as many people know, means "missing the mark." In classical literature, it is used to mean a failure to live up to one's ideals or character. Today, some interpret Aristotle's discussion of drama to mean that *hamartia* is a disturbance in character and understanding that leads to a hero's downfall. It is not a calculated, knowing attempt to do something evil but rather self-destructive ignorance, like Oedipus not knowing his parentage, or some other deep and unconscious gap.

If you consult a Christian Greek lexicon, or even Liddell-Scott, you will find the word "sin" used for hamartia, simply because it became the official or traditional, unquestioned translation. But imagine what would happen to those who live by the Gospel if they shifted from a sense of sin to concern for character and psychological catharsis. Suddenly we would all be in the Greek soup, sorting out issues of character and psychology that lead us to failure and disaster, and we would be wondering how this confusion interferes with the work of the community and nation. Moral and psychological questions would deepen considerably.

The notion of "sin" creates a psychology of guiltiness, whereas a psychology of *hamartia* creates an awareness of guilt. These are two very different experiences. Guiltiness is a defense against the shadow elements in life and character. As long as you feel guilty, you can remain convinced of your innocence, but if you suddenly perceive your real guilt, you lose your innocence and take a step further into the human condition. Guilt is a maturing initiation; guiltiness is a means of staying fixed in an infantile state.

This small example, bringing Aristotle to bear on a Gospel word, not even at the core of the teaching, shows how a careful approach to language can have major consequences in spirituality and psychology.

## The Kingdom as *Mundus Imaginalis*

Four Greek terms form the understructure of the Gospel vision: *basilea, therapeia, metanoia,* and *agape*.

*Basilea* means kingdom. Some contemporary scholars translate it as domain or realm. I prefer the more concrete and traditional image of kingdom. In the Gospels, the word appears either in the phrase *basilea theou*, the kingdom of God, or *basilea ouranou*, the kingdom of heaven.

You may have heard this language all your life, and you may dismiss it as being naïve and uninteresting. Or you may take these terms literally and miss their resonance. I would like to revisit them with their classical history in mind.

Jesus says that the kingdom is among you or within you—the translation is ambiguous. But it is clearly not elsewhere. It is not in the afterlife, and it seems to have nothing to do with a church or a religion. These are later interpretations.

He says that this kingdom is not of this world, and yet it is in your midst. It seems clear to me that the kingdom he is talking about is a particular *mundus imaginalis*, a world of meaning and value defined by Jesus' stories and example. Jesus goes on to say much about the kingdom, emphasizing the importance of healing, wakening, purging (catharsis), and dealing with the demonic. Parables describe the kingdom as a tiny mustard seed that grows into a huge tree—a comic exaggeration. It's like a bit of yeast worked into bushels of flour causing bread to rise. Again, a comic hyperbole. The kingdom is a world of imagination in which the slightest shift in the life-defining eidos changes everything.

In the Gospels we find the phrase *basilea ouranou*, the kingdom of Ouranos, the sky god. The kingdom, the *mundus imaginalis*, is in your midst, but it is also in the sky. Freud criticized God being in the sky as a projected father figure, but Ouranos is the sky as father, not a neurotic projection but the discovery of a father spirit active in human life. As a god of the sky, he puts the focus on the spiritual, the cosmic, and the vast compass of a human life.

Jesus speaks of his father in terms that echo Ouranos. He is a father whose domain is the sky. He is a spiritual fathering and indeed the spiritual domain itself. Jesus models and recommends living in constant conversation with that sky father. "Our Father, who art in heaven ...." He does the will of the father. He lives by the logic of heaven as well as the demands of earth. "On earth as it is in heaven."

Jesus advocates two streams—my image, not his: the region of the sky spirit and the region of ordinary earthly life. He lives in these two realms and speaks favorably of both. He has dinner and dances with his friends and then prays in the garden to the father. He heals a blind man and then speaks about blindness of the heart.

The other relevant phrase in the Gospels is *basilea theou,* the kingdom of *theos*, God. But here, too, we need not be literal and naïve. The kingdom is theological or theocentric. Stanley Romaine Hopper would say, "theopoetic," meaning that a *theos* imagination shapes one's understanding and values. *Theos* need not represent a naïve belief but rather the perception of life's impenetrable mystery. *Theos* is a kind of *arche*, as in archetypal. *Theos* is the realm of the mysterious and the ineffable—this is the ancient *via negativa* tradition often ascribed to Pseudo-Dionysius and developed in a remarkable way by the early $15^{th}$-century theologian Nicolas of Cusa.

C. Kerényi links the words *theos*, theory, and theater under the general theme of spectacle or vision. He says that the word *theos* was used in two senses: having a vision of the gods or seeing as the gods see. If a Greek had a glimpse of the divine, he would utter the word "*theos*" as an exclamation. A god is present. The realm of the gods has broken through. So, when Jesus speaks of *basilea theou*, we might keep Kerényi's elucidation in mind: *basilea theou* is a kingdom or realm, a world or *mundus*, where the divine breaks through and is seen.[1]

*Basilea theou* is the kingdom of the divine, the place of the gods, the pagans would say, Olympus. It is that place in imagination where we can connect to the mysterious, the ineffable, and the more-than-human. Jesus does not speak of the gods, though the Gospels have many echoes of Greek polytheism, as David Miller has shown. But if you pull away the typical literalism that infects talk of the Gospels, Jesus can be seen to relate to divinity in a similar way. The distance between Gospel spirituality and Greek polytheism is not as great as the anti-pagans have presumed.

Jesus locates his spirituality in relation to the sky father God, *basilea ouranous*. You have to be able to lift your sights above the mundane, and you need a father spirit for governance in your life and of society and for procreativity, the power to inseminate your culture with your ideas and genius. A connection to the father divinity is necessary for human creativity and identity. Ficino adopted this father spirituality in his role as priest, but he added devotion to the goddess of the garden and the sea—Venus. He honored Sol, or the sun, as a spirit necessary to human life.

The problem with the sky God of Christianity is that he does not allow other expressions of *theos*, such as a holy spirit of the garden or sexuality. Jung was encouraged by the theological doctrine of the assumption of the Virgin Mary into heaven, because her presence there was the beginning of a solution to the problem. Heaven was being repopulated. A similar development is taking place today in the popular effort to link Jesus with Mary Magdalen, an avatar of Aphrodite.

*Basilea ouranou* and *basilea theou* are inspiring images for expanding the place from which you live and work. Without the greater dimensions to which these images point, you would be trapped in pure subjectivity and a limited kind of humanism. You would be bereft of an imagination needed for beholding the divine within the profane.

## The Dionysian Connection: A Gospel of Vitality

In the *Gospel of John*, the first action of Jesus signifying *basilea theou* was the sign of water and wine. I say "sign" rather than miracle because the consistent Greek word for such actions is *semeia*, as in semiotics. Jesus' actions ritualize or represent the character of the father's kingdom in contrast to default reality.

In the story, Jesus goes to a wedding party with some of his students and his mother. His mother notices that their hosts have run out of wine and mentions it to Jesus. He says, "My hour is not here yet." Nevertheless, he tells the wedding planner to taste the contents of some large jars used to hold water for ritual purification. The wedding planner is surprised. "Who would keep his best wine for the end of the party?" he says.

This is a short tale, but it is full of implications. You don't have to look far for a connection with Dionysus, the god of transformation, wine, and parties. We have to remember that Jesus was in the thick of Greek culture. It is thought that there was even a temple to Dionysus less than twenty miles from his center of operations.

The alchemy by which this particular water became this particular wine suggests a shift from purity to intoxication. In context, it refers to the change in state from the single life to marriage, a rite of passage creating a more complex and potentially vital phase. But in a larger sense, it gives image to a foundational shift from the ordinary pragmatic and literalistic view of life to life in the kingdom, the place of vision and poetics. Life in the kingdom is like wine, compared to the plain water of mundane existence. I am reminded of a sentence from Emerson: "The poet speaks with the flower of the mind … with the intellect inebriated by nectar." Jesus not only spoke as such a poet, but he advocated a way of life, a kingdom, in which one speaks regularly with the intoxication of the imagination.

Let's not overlook the anima instigation in this story: Jesus' mother noticing what is wrong at the party and cautiously urging some action. For all the extreme spiritualism that has evolved from the Gospels throughout history, Jesus is more a soul figure. Here again, recent work linking him to Mary Magdalen also reflects the intuition that he is not a purely spiritual character but is equally engaged with the soul.

Nothing about the story of the wedding seems to fit with the direction Christianity took in its departure from the Gospels. The churches are not known for their encouragement of a Dionysian way of life, for making sure that people have enough to drink and that the party goes on. More seriously, they seem not to have grasped the central idea: generating vitality and conviviality as identifying characteristics of the kingdom. Having a church social is far different from aiming at transforming world culture into one of intoxicating delight.

## Jesus Therapist

As you read the Gospels, you see over and over that Jesus tells people to live by the inverted laws of the kingdom, most of all by being healers. The word *therapeia*, in its various declensions and conjugations, appears again and again. The texts give the impression that the main concern of the Gospels is therapy.

Freud and Jung and all of us who practice the psychological arts follow a similar pattern: we have a vision of human life, and we are inspired to heal others of their suffering through the vision that we cherish. It is a point not often considered: the connection between therapy and vision. I see the pattern in clients: in the midst of their own therapy, having gained a new vision for their lives, they become inspired to be healers themselves. Archetypal psychology is largely an intellectual movement, but it is also a therapy.

Jesus, of course, does not heal the way modern medicine heals. He heals mainly through touch, word, and presence. We do not often think of images and touch, and yet touches of many kinds can send imagination into a spin. Touch can mean many things, but perhaps the most powerful is *eros*. Not sex, but *eros*. Jesus' touch represents the coming to each other of the human and the divine, for Jesus always says that he heals through the father. He is the conduit of mystery, and those who follow his way understand that healing always takes place mysteriously, and in a broad sense, erotically.

The soul yearns for touch, to sense the other who offers a sense of connection. It is an emotional, sensory assurance that you are in the human world and the life can proceed because of eros. Freud would call it analclitic—the feel of the mother's body, the knowledge of the world as matrix. Any restoring of this connection can be healing.

John's Gospel makes it clear that healing, too, is semiotics. Healing the blind man, Jesus comments on how everyone is blind and is need of a cure. In an extraordinary story from the *Acts of Peter and the Twelve*

*Apostles*, a non-canonical Gospel, Jesus goes by the name Lithargoel. The text explains the name as meaning "a light stone like the eyes of a gazelle." The word seems to be made up of *lithos* (stone), *argos* (light), and *el* (divine being). He appears as a physician who sells pearls, who actually is a pearl in some mystical sense. He has a key, hidden insight that is precious to anyone in search of vitality, and, though he is a merchant, he will give this precious thing to anyone who wants it. All they have to do is be in his presence. He is the pearl that heals. Towards the end of the story, he reveals that he is Jesus.

Jesus' words are healing and his teaching is primarily therapeutic. Again, with a shift away from belief to therapeutics, those who follow his way would shift dramatically in substance and style. We go to a therapist with our confusion and wounds, but typically we come to religion with anxiety about morals and the afterlife. The Gospels suggest going through a radical shift in vision to enjoy heaven on earth.

## A Change of Heart

In the festschrift for David Miller, *Disturbances in the Field*, I wrote a chapter about *metanoia*, Jesus, and Hermes. Here I will summarize.

Metanoia is a deep and radical shift in perception and imagination about how the world works and how to get along in it. In Greek, *meta* means after, between, or coming into. We speak of the meta-morphosis in which a worm becomes a butterfly. Here it suggests a radical transformation. In fact, a Latin translation for *meta* could be *trans*.

*Noia* is a form of *nous* or "mind." In the history of philosophy Nous is a key term, referring in Plotinus, for example, to the second emanation of being. The recently translated Gospel of Judas has Judas saying to Jesus, "I know that you are from the realm of Barbelo." Barbelo is similar to Nous but is a feminine form, like Sophia.

*Metanoia* is the action, a shift in imagination, that corresponds to *basilea*, the *mundus imaginalis* that is the object of Jesus' teaching. In the Gospel, Jesus stands in the river to be baptized, a ritual that signifies *metanoia*, where the water implies the stream of life, waters of birth and cleansing renewal, and perhaps death to the old form of imagination, the former *mundus*.

## Love and the Soul

Jungian and archetypal psychology are both interested in the connection between *eros* and *psyche*, but little if anything has been done with *agape* and *psyche*. *Agape* is the other key Greek word for love that emphasizes esteem, respect, and value. Liddel-Scott indicates that *agape* was used to describe an appreciation for precious stones. Jesus redefines *agape* to mean a love of other that is somehow discovered through love of self.

The Gospels define a kind of love that is sifted for any signs of narcissism and paranoia, is fully compatible with friendship and community, and has the added mysterious element by which that which is normally rejected as unworthy becomes a special object of love. Those people who find themselves outsiders to default society have a special welcome in the kingdom, as do those qualities in ourselves that we find objectionable. They are to be loved, accepted, and allowed to transmute into new powers of soul: sexual mistakes, for example, become the raw material for radical participation in community.

These sketchy ideas, based on the four key terms of the Gospels—*basilea, metanoia, therapeia,* and *agape*—are mere prologue to a full archetypal theology to be found in the teachings and stories of Jesus. That Jesus has been taken literally, sentimentally, and moralistically for two millennia does not mean that there is no depth of imagination in the sources. As we in archetypal psychology know through our work with classical mythology, questions of historicity are irrelevant. Theologians still argue about who Jesus actually was, but few inquire into the archetypal nature of his person and his story. Since so much of world culture has been affected by this mythology, it seems time to take the archetypal route/root seriously.

## *NOTES*

[1] C. Kerényi, *The Religion of the Greeks and Romans* (New York: E. P. Dutton & Co., 1962), pp. 141-154.

# *Practice*

Yes, I am critical of the "whole analytic discipline." I see it as a remarkable genius reflection of a period of history, and I think it has become years later a kind of … substitute for rigorous education in culture, philosophy and religion … and … a "helping profession."

—James Hillman, "Jan Marlan Interviews James Hillman," *IAAP Newsletter* 26, 2006, p. 193

Surprise! I want to defend therapy, your basic kind—inward-searching, long-term, insight therapy—and its goal of individuation.

—James Hillman, *We've Had a Hundred Years of Psychotherapy—and the World's Getting Worse*, p. 50

Patricia Berry was for many years James Hillman's student, companion, and wife. She has been active in the Jungian world for nearly half a century, serving on faculties and boards of training institutions, and as President of the Inter-Regional Society of Jungian Analysts, as well as of the New England Society of Jungian Analysts. She teaches and lectures internationally and is the author of many publications including *Echo's Subtle Body: Contributions to an Archetypal Psychology*. Currently, she lives and practices in West Bath, Maine.

# 20

# Rules of Thumb towards an Archetypal Psychology Practice

PATRICIA BERRY

The other day I was asked if I still considered myself an archetypal psychologist. The question astonished me. How could I not? I was in at the base level before archetypal psychology was named Archetypal Psychology—there first as student *adept*, later as *soror mystica*, leaning over the edge with those stirring this heady brew. Newts, lizards, our innards were all in the pot. Not only did I feel archetypal psychology was me, I was part it—in it for a toe or two, my whole head, and lots of spit.

Yet, it is true, in the last several years I have not hung out much with the folks talking Archetypal Psychology. One of the reasons for my absence is that as Archetypal discussion has become focused increasingly on ideas, I have become increasingly less so. I certainly honor ideation; theory is important. No school of anything would exist without it. But it is not for all of us—all the time. As I age, I become more often "hands on" about most things. This does not mean I don't think—only that when I do, the thoughts tend to appear clothed as psychological dynamics, mechanisms, etc., appearing in individuals, relationships, groups, or even situations. This practice of seeing ideas as they function is fun stuff for me, and that is where I have spent my time. Is that still Archetypal Psychology? Well, you tell me. Perhaps it is just *my* archetypal psychology, one of the many archetypal psychologies. Whatever the case, in the following pages I will lay out something of how I have come to think. These are my rules of thumb for practice, as well as I can describe them just now.

## Rule of Thumb #1: Any Idea Can Be Used Defensively

Here by "rule of thumb" I mean: approximately, or more or less. Seems to me there are no "right" ideas, more or less. The "less" part is that some ideas truly *are* more useful, rich, fruitful, interesting, promising. Ah, but that does not mean they are right—or wrong either, for that matter.

As a depth psychologist, my focus is on how the psyche works. One of the ways the psyche works, according to depth psychology, is by way of a fragile ego fending off what it perceives to be threats from within or without. To protect itself against these threats, the ego hauls from its arsenal all sorts of defensive weaponry.

Ideas are like the ramparts surrounding the castle. They are designed to keep other ideas from intruding. In times of peace, they may give lovers a safe place to meet, wise men a space to converse above the treetops without interruption, a place for women to spin in the fresh air, and wizards to conjure under the stars. But in times of war, ramparts are used to hide behind while arrows fly and boulders are catapulted. So too with ideas. Ideas can nurture life, or they can serve as defensive structures.

## Rule of Thumb #2: If a Sacred Cow Is Blocking the Path, Shoo It Off

The method of depth psychology is something of a *via negativa*. By that I mean we more often shoo away what is blocking the path than claim to know what the path ought actually to be. Nonetheless, there are some general values assumed, although they may vary in emphasis depending upon the context and from practitioner to practitioner. Some of these values are: the unknown, depth, resonance, complexity, interconnection, integration, richness, mastery. I am sure you could add more.

Values or value-laden concepts can provide orientation, but one must sense and consciously choose when a value or set of values is to be applied. When values are idealized and clung to, one tends to get blinded by their glow such that one can no longer discern more subtle, new, challenging, or, I would even say, real psychic events. When one or another shiny feeling is embraced such that the ego hides behind it, then we may need to put aside the value itself, for the moment at least, shoo that darn cow off the path, even if it represents Truth and Motherhood—or Soul, Psyche, and World. Whatever the sacred terms, the secret handclasps, such values can and will be used to occlude more interesting, challenging, or fecund possibilities.

## Rule of Thumb #3: Ideas Ought Not to Be Applied

The problem with the notion of *praxis* is that we tend to think of it as an application of theory. When we apply ideas to practical situations, I find it usually results in misapplication of one sort or another. In fact, the first few times around, misuse is almost a given. A new idea is like a new tool or toy one might try out in lots of places—most of which are inappropriate. In my experience, few life situations are such that a single idea does them justice anyway.

My view is that it is best to work from the event to the idea not the other way round: (1) begin with the living event, i.e., the image; (2) focus on the image/event, sensing into it; (3) track bits of resonance that begin to form out of the event. Whether these resonances are immediately like known ideas or mere fragments does not matter. Eventually, ideas will spring up like weeds around and through them. Ideas are organic. They live in things. Perhaps this is what William Carlos Williams meant when he insisted "no ideas but in things."[1]

so much depends
upon

a red wheel
barrow

glazed with rain
water

beside the white
chickens.

Perhaps the glaze in William Carlos Williams's poem is the shimmer of ideas?

## Rule of Thumb #4: Whenever Possible, Think Poetically

For Aristotle, practicality, or *praxis,* leads to action, whereas making, or *poeisis,* leads to production. Aside from praxis as in a spiritual practice, which, to my mind, is right on the money, *praxis* tends to lend itself more to political thinking. Marx regarded his dialectical materialism as *praxis*. Sometimes, however, one is more about making—simply making—than about politics. When that is the case, as it frequently is for me, the fantasy of making, creating—just the activity for the sake of itself—is quite appealing. For me, "making" psychological moves, interpretations, interventions, reflections, and moments seems more fitting than any other conceptualization for what I am about.

## Rule of Thumb #5: Go *Connatural*

*Connatural* is a term coined by the Catholic theologian Jacques Maritain. Maritain was interested in the interrelation between artistic processes and the processes of nature. In his view, the task of the artist or craftsman is to align mimetically with "nature's secret workings and inner ways."[2] He saw artistic activity, when working properly, as attempting to parallel nature's processes. Human creativity is like nature's creativity. The task is to work connaturally with nature on a very conscious level—to sense nature's operations, to feel them, see them, hear them. Attempting to look deeply into natural psychological processes and attuning with what is perceived is what depth psychology is all about.

## Rule of Thumb #6: Symbols Are Not Symbols *of* Anything but Symbolic *with* Many Things

Islamic scholar Henry Corbin characterized symbols as "symbolizing with" rather than "symbolic to" their referents.[3] The distinction is important in that no one symbol is regarded as necessarily prior to or more important than another. The kind of making implied here would develop by way of similarities, reverberations, and improvisations mimetic with, or paralleling natural movements and processes. In that same spirit, rather like the spirit of Maritain's connaturality, our depth psychological work proceeds with an ear to the ground of nature's reverberations, both natural and symbolic.

## Rule of Thumb #7: Stick to the Image

OK, so this is an old rule. We all know it. I have always attributed it to Rafael López-Pedraza,[4] since he was the guy I heard it from repeatedly. At this point in my life, however, my sense may have wandered a bit from Rafael's. Today I regard Image as a more supple notion than I once did. One way to understand its flexibility is to talk about framing.

## Rule of Thumb #8: To Know It Is to Frame It

Please, let me be clear. I am not saying things exist *only* because of their framing. I *am* saying that frames organize what we see. Organized well, what we see can become fresh, even breathtaking. The way in which a picture is framed becomes part of its effect and meaning. The frame of the window over my desk gives a particular view of the woods outside. When I frame a picture in my camera viewfinder, I am positioning the view in such a way as to enable something revelatory to come forth. In a moving image, many frames rushing one after another become the film that an editor then cuts and shapes—i.e., frames—into the final film. The purpose of framing is to put limits on the view so that what is within those limits can be focused on with greater clarity and freshness.

How we frame a story we tell to a friend or a case presentation to colleagues has to do with what we want to show (and perhaps how we want it and ourselves to be seen!?). How we frame something also conditions how others approach it, what they get from it, and what activities generate around it. This is not as obvious as it may seem. In a case colloquium, for example, someone presents a situation with a client with whom they are having difficulty. Generally speaking, what the participants in the group will see, being astute psychological participants, is not what the presenter "meant" for them to see but what the presenter has *not* presented and perhaps not known.

I consider the image here to be both what the presenter presented and what others saw, the unconscious workings behind the presentation and evoked by it. The conscious framing was the framing of the presentation, but that framing also brought other levels, other insights, and other points of view into the discussion.

If the practitioner had presented the story differently, what the participants perceived would have also been somewhat different. Let's say the practitioner had framed the story, beginning and end, with a statement about how annoyed he gets with this particular patient. The group would then tend to work on the case with this countertransference emotion in mind. My point is that situations framed differently *are* different, and the comments as well as the dynamics of the group will change accordingly—because the image is different.

Sometimes images are framed too small. When too little context is given a situation, working with it tends to get loose, projective, less fitting, and less meaningful in terms of the actual situation. On the other hand, sometimes psychological events get framed so large that it is difficult to work on them in depth or with anything but broad, sweeping strokes. On occasion, these large strokes are just what you want, as, for example, when taking on issues at a cultural or political level. At this level, particular and precise image work is not helpful or appropriate.

### Rule of Thumb #9: The Observer and the Observed May or May Not Be the Same

Our perceptual convention is to experience ourselves when we observe—e.g., the participants observing the case presentation (as discussed above)—as separate from what we are observing. We know from modern physics, phenomenology, and other disciplines, that we are, in one way or another, implicated in what we observe. But on a practical level, the positions we assume *vis-à-vis* "other"—whatever "other" is (dream, client, colleagues, the world of psychology) varies considerably.

Sometimes it is important to be close to the "other," so close as nearly to merge. With a client's dream, say, some therapists might want to be so close that they feel the dream's energies through their own muscles and organs. They might then speak to the dream via their own imagination. Their imaginings (or amplifications or associations, for that matter) may be as important to the process as the patient's imaginings.

Or one may assume a position at some distance from the patient and the material. It is not that one or another stance is correct; each has advantages and can be more or less fitting depending on the circumstances. Sometimes it is useful to get as close as you can to the experience. At other times it is crucial to put yourself out of the picture so you can see it more clearly. What's important here is to know that you are assuming positions, and to attempt to develop as large a repertoire as possible. In any situation, you can then consciously choose your stance, which includes of course knowing the effects of that position, its strengths, its limitations, and its dangers.

Sometimes one wishes to frame what is going on in, let's say, a therapeutic situation, in terms of "transference/countertransference dynamics." When one frames the situation within this conceptual fantasy, one can see everything as occurring within and because of those relations. To pass exams in many Jungian training institutes nowadays, one must be adept at this mode of framing and at use of the language that goes with it. As with any other frame, this transference enclosure both limits and reveals. To my mind, the danger of this model is that it is the currently accepted one, and so is usually assumed to be "true" and taken literally.

### Rule of Thumb #10: Contrast—It's a Set-Up

I find Hillman's notion of multiplicity to be not only a larger, more generous umbrella, but also a more interesting attitude than, for example, dualism. Yet at times one wants to point up strong contrasts. On such occasions one might sound "either/or" dualistic. Contrasts are ways of making points stand out clearly. Imagine a painting with a dark background and white figures in the foreground. The white figures stand out because of the contrasting background. When archetypal psychology sets up oppositions, it is important to remember that these oppositions are about contrast rather than literal exclusion. Think of some of archetypal psychology's oppositions: underworld versus the day world, imaginal versus heroic ego, world versus consulting room, and (my favorite) psychological versus literal. The good guys are set up at one end of the opposition and the bad guys at the other, good guys foreground, bad guys background.

Aesthetically speaking, these "either/or" exclusions create contrasts to make a point. But, let's not forget, these bad guys are merely straw men hauled in to be railed against. In drama, straw-men caricatures act as foils for the more complex principle characters. Some dramatists I know maintain that collective taste requires these figures. Maybe so, but as psychologists we need to remember that it is a set-up.

## Rule of Thumb #11: Steal Tools When Necessary

Hillman once characterized his method as being like that of a *bricoleur*[5] (an inventive do-it-yourselfer); I'd say mine is like that of a thief, though a good thief and for good reasons, I hope. Although Archetypal Psychology distinguishes itself philosophically from widespread collective psychologies such as Behaviorism or Cognitive Psychology, nonetheless as a practitioner one might on occasion lift a tool or two from their bright boxes. On occasion those toolboxes may contain something useful. The tool may be one that allows us to focus on behavior as such, or to advocate change in behavior before understanding what the behavior is about. This may sound quite unlike depth psychology, but it is sometimes necessary—as in situations of abuse or addiction. Since there are as many explanations of events as there are psychological perspectives for viewing them, sometimes a simple negative reinforcement (such as terminating the therapy) *is* the way to go.

If we take seriously the Maritain/Corbin image of parallel processes, then perhaps imaginal change can begin with behavioral change as well as the other way around. Sometimes grabbing the stick by the other end is easier. It seems to me, it is not other psychologies that are reductive, material, and literal—*it is we who are, whenever we view them without a psychological eye.*

If we stand on psychic ground, *in medias res*, maintaining our awareness from that position, what we do *will* be psychologically based. It is a matter of awareness. When we are psychologically aware, our means *will* be metaphorical, and our tools reflective.

## Rule of Thumb #12: Don't Take the Literal Literally

Earlier I said that the literal versus the psychological was my favorite opposition. But, you know, one ought not to take even the literal so literally. To do so is to become way too literal. That literal voice, insisting on "nothing but," is just one of many voices in the chorus. Sometimes it is useful for belting out strong, sure tones, but the point is to hear it as one voice—rather than the whole-truth, nothing-but-the-truth that it pretends to be.

### Rule of Thumb #13: Truth or Daimon

Sometimes I think of truth imagistically, as in the "true line" a carpenter might determine, a navigator reckon, or a Zen master draw in the sand. Truth is for me of highest value, but I do not capitalize the word. In terms of an individual psyche, I think of truth as the path of individuation. This old-fashioned Jungian term is vague, subjective, and interior enough to work for me. Some might speak of following one's daimon rather than Jung's notion of *individuation* as a guide, but daimons are flashy. Besides daimons are also demons, and so easy to identify with! So, too, notions like "psyche" and soul don't work for me as they once did. In the beginning of Archetypal Psychology, these words were truly alive, earth-shaking, electrifying, daring as heck. Now they are clichés in the titles of half the books on the Self-Help shelf. Is the notion (Psyche, Soul) true? Sure. But it is hard nowadays to inspire in someone like me much feeling of a true line from those words.

I tend to orient myself with more practical aesthetic notions, such as "what works." What "works" as a novel, film, painting, or piece of music is determined by the piece itself. Each piece sets up its own criteria. In this way, the work is measured against itself—sort of like what *individuation* implies in personal psychology, where the unique nature of the person is the goal.

### Rule of Thumb #14: Layard's Rule

I tend to view dreams through Layard's rule.[6] I may not always share this vision with my client. But I often do, because it is in fact how I see things. John Layard was an anthropologist and a first-generation Jungian analyst who resided in England. Jim Hillman passed along the maxim to me almost 40 years ago, crediting it to Layard, and so I do also. This rule of thumb has since served me and several generations of students well. It is my favorite tool.

The rule goes like this: "Everything in the dream is right except perhaps the dream-ego." The purpose of this rule of thumb is to turn awareness toward a realm beyond the ego. Its use deliteralizes the usual, ego point of view, enabling a change in perspective.

As with any other rule of thumb, this one applies only loosely and sometimes not at all. Always it is, I think, a helpful perspective for practitioners in deepening their own awareness. It is *not* always the right tool for therapy. In some cases—for example, when support or stabilization is a priority—moving against the ego perspective is not therapeutically wise. In such instances, Layard's rule is not the right tool. Pick up another. As with any other rule, this one is simply more or less useful and appropriate—one of many in the tool box.

As an example, let's look at the following dream:

> *I go into my bathroom. My dog, Max, is in the bathtub, under water. He is just lying there like he usually lies. I am horrified, knowing he is going to drown. He just looks up at me as if nothing is wrong.*

I know nothing about the woman who dreamt this dream—her situation in life, her complexes, where she is in her analytic process—nothing. But that does not mean I cannot get something from the dream.

From a naturalistic perspective (the ego perspective here), the dog seems as though he is going to drown, and that feels terrible to the dreamer. To apply the Layard rule, however (here, an underwater as well as "underworld" perspective), we bracket out the ego's feeling and look to the dog. Max acts as though nothing is wrong. Perhaps this is an underwater dog, able to survive under water. Or perhaps he is going to drown, to dissolve into the alchemical *solutio,* and that is part of the process. Whatever the case, we know clearly from the dog's point of view, according to Layard, that indeed "nothing is wrong." Everything is as it should be.

This point of view would seem horrific to an Ego- or Humanistically-oriented psychologist on several counts. For one thing, the situation is not natural. Dogs are not naturally content under water. Thus, there is something wrong with this woman's "dog." Her dog instinct is unaware, self-destructive. Another reason the dream would not sit well is that in humanistic psychology it is the human that is most highly valued. Human perspectives and values are identified with and taken literally.

To flip things such that we are looking from the dog's perspective, trusting the animal over the human viewpoint, can lead us into awarenesses that other, more usual perspectives do not allow. The Layard perspective deepens and enriches our understanding. If everything is right except the dream-ego, it is "right" that the dog dies.

Perhaps the dog is like an old instinct, effective for many years in sniffing out what was what, but no longer needed. Perhaps a new dog with new senses is in order.

## RULE OF THUMB #15: LISTEN TO YOUR FRIENDS; LOVE YOUR TEACHER

I regularly lead seminars for students in the final stages of depth psychological study. The drill is that each student takes several hours during the weekend to talk about his or her work with a client. As the participants interact around the images and processes that arise, I am astonished at how well they have come to understand one another. Of course, each arrives at the weekend with particular perspectives and favorite theories. They may not always agree, but eventually they all come to *appreciate* one another, to understand what is being said and where it is coming from. They listen to one another. And to me.

Do they know I am an archetypal psychologist? Do they know my background? I don't know. If they do know, certainly not in any detail. Yet they are doing what I consider to be archetypal psychology. They are focusing carefully on what appears as image, aware of their framing, the lenses they use. They bracket causal explanations and appreciate mimetic resonances. They have learned to steal. They make inventive use of available resources (the "*bricoleur*"!). To one degree or another, each has an eye for some "true" line. They recite Layard's Rule like a mantra. Is this archetypal psychology? Well, it is certainly one form of it.

In ending, I must say thank you, Jim Hillman. Those years in the mix with you were fundamental to my learning, glorious in reach and spread and lift, beyond inspiration. It was an extraordinary time. I remain deeply and forever grateful to you, my teacher.

### *NOTES*

[1] William Carlos Williams famously summarized his poetic method in the phrase "No idea but in things" (from his 1944 poem "A Sort of Song").

[2] Jacques Maritain, *Creative Intuition in Art and Poetry* (Princeton, NJ: Princeton University Press, 1953/1977), p. 127.

[3] Henry Corbin, *Avicenna and the Visionary Recital*, trans. Willard R. Trask (New York: Pantheon, 1960), p. 261. Cf. also p. 31 and

"*Mundus Imaginalis*, of the Imaginary and the Imaginal," trans. Ruth Horine, *Spring* (1972): 9.

[4] Patricia Berry, "An Approach to the Dream," in *Echo's Subtle Body: Contributions to an Archetypal Psychology* (Dallas, TX: Spring Publications, 1982), p. 57f.

[5] James Hillman, *The Dream and the Underworld* (New York: Harper & Row, 1979), p. 127f.

[6] Patricia Berry, "Defense and Telos in Dreams," in *Echo's Subtle Body: Contributions to an Archetypal Psychology* (Dallas, TX: Spring Publications, 1982), p. 83.

Stanton Marlan, Ph.D., ABPP, LP, is a Jungian psychoanalyst and archetypal psychologist in private practice in Pittsburgh, PA, and an adjunct Clinical Professor of Psychology at Duquesne University. He is a training and supervising analyst with the Inter-Regional Society of Jungian Analysts, a member of the C. G. Jung Institute of New York, and a licensed psychoanalyst in that state. He is also President of the Pittsburgh Society of Jungian Analysts. He holds diplomates in both clinical psychology and psychoanalysis from the American Board of Professional Psychology. Dr. Marlan has a long-time interest and involvement in archetypal psychology and the work of James Hillman, particularly in the area of dreams and alchemy.

# 21

# Mystical Light: Dream Images and the Alchemy of Psychic Momentum

STANTON MARLAN

... [I]mages are the fundamentals which make the movements of psychodynamics possible.

—James Hillman, *Archetypal Psychology*, p. 19

The appearance of mystical or primordial light is well-known in religious and philosophical literatures as well as in artistic canons worldwide. The theme is somewhat less known but prominent in alchemy as well, and it is an important feature in the world of modern dreamers and analysands. Mystical light appears, as does light and dark in general, in many manifestations and varieties.

Feshbach, for instance, distinguishes "a number of varieties of ordinary light from the sun, from the wood fire, from the burning wax of the candle, from the coal of the fire, from the kerosene, from incandescent, neon, fluorescent, and electrical lights, from the television screen, even from the digital clock at 3:33 a.m."[1] In short, the values of light and dark are highly contextual and dependent on the situation in which they appear. Consider the value of light and dark on a beach, or in a sunroom, in a laboratory, a restaurant, a bedroom, and the rich varieties of lights in dreams. In all of these examples, the context is critical to our understanding.

"Light is the grand archetype under which we gather a vast array of phenomena. ... Our language ... is suffused with metaphors of light, and ... empirical life is conducted with constant poetical reference to light."[2] Feshbach mentions a number of important texts in which mystical light is prominent and shows itself in different literary and religious contexts: Genesis, Plato's myth of the cave in *The Republic*, *The Zohar: The Book of Light or Splendor*, and Corbin's *Man of Light* in which Corbin articulates the notion of a primordial mental, spiritual, or imaginal light.[3] For Corbin, the imaginal light of the *mundus imaginalis* is linked to the search for self-knowledge and is a mark of spiritual realization. Likewise, for Mircea Eliade, inner light (*antar jyotih*) defines the essence of the atman and can signify an encounter with the Self, not only in yoga, but also in Tantrism, as well as in *The Tibetan Book of the Dead* and in many varieties of shamanism. Mystical light is said to enable [the shaman] "to see in the dark, both literally and metaphorically speaking."[4] In her book *The Alchemy of Light,* Urszula Szulakowska traces the importance of "the divinity and generative power of light" from the mid-16th to the late 17th century.[5] She notes that "scholarly research into the alchemical discourse on light is relatively little developed," and her study attempts to redress this absence.[6] She shows how the

> late Renaissance alchemists developed a conceptual structure which could be called an "alchemy of light," a syncretic philosophy integrating the discrete intellectual and mystical currents of Pythagorean geometry, neoplatonism, medieval optics, Paracelsian alchemy, and cabbalism.[7]

She follows the way the image of divine and mystical light emerged from ancient times and traces its development through Plotinus and various hermetic and Gnostic writers, including those of Hermes Trismegistus and the Christian writers Pseudo-Dionysius and St. Augustine. Tracking this line through Marsilio Ficino and Cornelius Agrippa's *Astral Magic*, Szulakowska arrives at the way the image of mystical light enters into a medical and psychological context and how it was used in Paracelsian medicine and beyond in the luministic cosmogenies of John Dee's cabbalistic theories.[8] Resonant with Corbin's notion of the Man of Light and the illuminated yogis and shamans noted by Eliade, there began to emerge with Dee an image of the Magus as an illuminated being whose "intellectual light mirrored, not only that of the stars and sun, but of God's own radiance."[9]

The power and importance of mystical light was also well known to Jung from many sources but perhaps most particularly from the alchemical treatise *The Secret of the Golden Flower*, in which the alchemical/yogic practice of the circulation of light was linked with the birth of a spiritual embryo and to the regeneration of the alchemist.

All of these texts and many others link mystical light to a process of transformation and self-realization. This linkage is also true in the dream texts of analysis. Here the stories of psychic transformation are more personal and often less grand, but nonetheless important to the phenomenology of psychic life.

The focus of this paper is to reflect on a couple of images of mystical light in the dreams of analytic patients and to consider some of the ways these archetypal images seem related to and accompany psychic momentum. It seems to me that even in a time when mystical experiences have been denigrated and the theme of inner light and vision has become suspect, images of mystical light remain an important factor in the healing and transformation of modern patients in analysis.

## Dr. Hill, the Unknown Poet

Dr. Hill, an accomplished psychiatrist, grew up in a small town. When his father passed away and afterwards, he was teased and tormented by other children. He was ridiculed and felt undesirable. He repressed his feelings and his capacity to show emotion receded into the dark. In a passionate overcompensation for his wounds, he worked hard to achieve success and in the end, his professional, intellectual, and cultural achievements far outstripped those of his childhood companions. He got married, but there was difficulty in the relationship, and he and his wife lost a child in childbirth. After a number of years of a difficult marriage, he and his wife got divorced. Dr. Hill entered analysis stating that he liked living alone, that it allowed him to be more efficient in accomplishing his goals, but that he was feeling an odd kind of dysphoria.

Dr. Hill presented a dream in which he was walking around his house, which sat on top of a mountain. He was with an appraiser and was considering selling the house. It overlooked the town where he grew up as a young boy and, as he walked around the house, he found it beautiful. It had many accouterments that signified high status: large windows, beautiful views, an outdoor veranda, and a large library. As he looked further, he discovered that the house even had a chapel in it. He knew that this was a mark of high status in old European homes of an earlier era. Wealthy people did not have to go down into town to mix with the commoners to practice their religion; the clergy would come to their homes to perform liturgical ceremonies.

While Dr. Hill felt some pleasure in what he had accomplished in his life, he also felt the house was barren. While he was professionally successful, he had trouble with relationships and had little social life. He spent much of his time working, and when he had any free time, he would spend it in solitary highbrow cultural activities and study. He loved opera and classical music, but not rock or country. He considered himself conservative and disparaged liberal causes. He liked and valued the Germans, though he was not German, and didn't like the Italians, though he had an Italian background. He preferred northern rather than southern food, and in literature, he preferred prose to poetry. He had a distaste for common activities, such as going to the movies and bowling, which felt like a waste of time. He disliked people who had no taste or culture and who participated in activities he deemed below him. This caused many problems in his marriage: while he loved his wife, he was critical of her "lower class tastes." Appraising his house, Dr. Hill found it beautiful, but it also had a hollow feeling as he walked around it.

In the dream, as Dr. Hill was looking out of a window down toward the small town where he grew up, he was shocked to see a "strange, heavenly, and mystical light" shining up from a gravesite on the side of the hill. He knew this light signified a divine presence, and associated it to the image of the burning bush, the sign from God that Moses saw when he was appointed by God to lead the Hebrews out of slavery from Egypt. At that moment, Dr. Hill felt a chill and was uncharacteristically filled with emotion. He recognized the grave out of which the light was shining as the place where his dead child was buried. As he looked at the grave, tears entered his eyes, and he spoke about the life he might have lived had his child survived. The anticipation of his child had promised new hope for a fuller life, a promise that was not fulfilled.

As the analysis continued, we explored how this gravesite marked not only the loss of his dead child, but also the loss of his father, his marriage, and in and through his unresolved grief, the loss of his inner child and the fullness of life that he had once anticipated. On the burial ground of this lost child, Dr. Hill had erected a life that he described as one of becoming a Nazi. He was referring to the harshness with which he had made demands on himself to live in a detached, cold, rational, and overly disciplined way, always in quest of further challenges in order to feel some moments of Promethean vitality—even though his quest took flight from this hollow ground of his buried child and from an emotional life that had receded into the dark recesses of the shadow. Dr. Hill's inner potential, like his dead child, never had a chance to come to life and was buried on the side of the mountain below where he lived.

Facing the divine light seems to require coming down from the mountain top, in the direction of his origins, and this was facilitated by the emergence of an archetypal and numinous image. This image called attention to the darkness of the grave, but simultaneously filled him with an experience of light, warmth, and religious feeling, as it pointed to what he most dreaded and to a way out of his Egyptian and Nazi-like slavery that had become the fabric of his daily life. The way out was the way into the darkness of the grave, which at the same time released a flood of feelings.

In the next session, Dr. Hill reported a short dream reminiscent of Hillman's recognition of the link between death and "the poetic basis of mind."[10] Dr. Hill was no longer on top of the mountain, but at a gravesite, as if he had followed the direction indicated in his prior dream. He now was writing poetry on the gravestone of an unknown man, in effect reflecting Hillman's insight that "[t]he underworld aspect of each complex, where it touches death, is also where … soul can be refound."[11] His dead father was now alive and with him; both were weeping. He told his father that he had made it, he had become a psychiatrist. He had to repeat this twice, but his father then heard him, smiled, and said, "It's good you told me." Both figures seemed relieved and grateful. Then Dr. Hill noticed a blond woman, an aunt who had died and whom he recalled as very supportive of him.

Dr. Hill, traditionally a man of logos and prose, was now uncharacteristically writing poetry at the gravesite of an unknown man—the unknown man that he was to himself—reflecting an inner development barely on the edge of his consciousness and working its way into awareness. As he inscribed this/his stone and his stony-ness with the poetics of his soul, he began to find life returning, to find a living connection to his father and to a supportive soul figure. He was able now to connect with what was lost and to find some of what he had been seeking.

## Mr. Block and the Light of the Dragon

Mr. Block is a successful communications specialist, though in his own life he reports feeling bogged down, wounded, and frozen in an impasse. He presented the following dream:

> A wounded elephant is in a battle with a prehistoric dinosaur, a raptor. The elephant strikes back and hits the raptor in the face, but the creature is totally unaffected and impervious to the blow. The elephant is deeply wounded and disappears. The dreamer is feeling a deep sense of pain, concern, and love for the elephant. He fears the animal may have gone off to die. The love he feels is powerful and fills him with motivation to go in search of the wounded animal to express his love and to see if he can save it.
>
> As he is beginning to set out to search for the elephant, he is approached by another man, who is in charge of the place where the animals are kept, a farm or reserve of some kind. He tells the man that he is in search of the wounded animal and the man casually offers him a relatively newborn green elephant as a substitute. This is not at all satisfying to the dreamer. He feels the animal keeper doesn't get it, that he loves the lost animal and can't simply substitute some other animal for the one he loves and for whom he is searching. The dreamer's desperation is growing and he begins to have a sense of impotence and frustration about not being able to do anything.
>
> The scene changes. The dreamer is now with his first-born daughter. She is about 10 years old and has been injured. The dreamer looks at her wounds. At first, it appears as if she has only superficial scrapes and bruises, but as he looks at her side he sees deep gashes that need serious attention. He calls to his wife to look at the wounds. The child is upbeat and buoyant, taking it all in stride, but his wife worries that these wounds may disfigure her and is concerned for the future welfare of their child.

The dream awakened him and Mr. Block became progressively aware of a deep feeling of woundedness. He began to realize not only that he had a tough elephant skin, but also that his long memory held onto hurts too long. In addition, his primitive and impervious raptor-like posture led him to the point of emotional isolation. As his anxiety about the future deepened, his growing awareness of pain was felt in relation to his scarred child. But no matter how much he focused on this pain, he remained blocked and nothing moved in psyche or soul.

As he was reflecting on and letting himself be gripped by his dream, the love and compassion he felt for the wounded and lost elephant, for his child and his wife, accompanied him as he started to fall back to sleep. On the threshold of consciousness, a powerful and visceral image of a huge dragon appeared in the sky. As he looked at it, it emitted a blast of fire and an intense light, which filled the horizon with almost blinding intensity. Mr. Block felt this energy run through his whole body. It instantly dissolved all his feelings of rigidity and left him feeling deeply relaxed. He fell into a deep sleep and awoke with the following dream:

> He is in the process of purchasing a new car. The car is parked on a hill. As he is talking to the dealer, the car is being brought down to him. He is very excited. The car is a convertible, shiny black. As it comes down, he has a moment of worrying if the engine is big enough, but he quickly realizes that the car is beautiful and light in weight and the midsize engine will have plenty of power to get him where he needs to go.

It would appear that the dragon image and its kundalini-like power directly penetrated the core of Mr. Block's impervious complexes. In this case, it was the direct power of the image and not its meaning that had the effect of loosening his literal and lived body and that seemed to activate the psychic momentum that led to the purchase of a new vehicle appearing in the above dream following his experience of deep relaxation. The new vehicle had a dark shine, was open and lighter, and had plenty of power to get him where he wanted to go.

In the experiences of both Dr. Hill and Mr. Block, the images of mystical light played an important role in each dreamer's psychological unfolding. In the case of Dr. Hill, the illumination of his dead child's gravesite filled him with emotions that had been split off because they were too intolerable to feel, and made it possible for him to face a whole series of important losses, inner and outer, that had remained buried. Beyond this, Dr. Hill's recognition of the divine and archetypal dimension of the image set in motion a *telos* that inspired a movement of soul beyond the psychic imprisonment he felt on his isolated mountain top. The progression of his dreams showed him to be following the call of the image of divine light, to have come down from the mountain and closer to the grave, to the place of death which turned out as well to be a place of poetry and of the discovery of the unknown man that he had become, a man in touch with the living presence of his father and of his soul. What is remarkable to me is the intelligence of the image, of the psychic light, of its knowing just where to point to bring about a renewal of life.

In the case of Mr. Block, it is likewise impressive not only that the image knows where to point, but that it exhibits the power to loosen embedded complexes and to free psyche's momentum directly. It appears that this quality of images was well known by the Buddhists, who spoke of the superhuman, beatific body of the Buddha as he enters *Parinirvâna*. It is said that the Buddha not only shines, but also emits "a light so intense that it fells the universe, a light more powerful than that of the gods which penetrate those regions plunged in eternal shadows beyond the rays of sun or moon."[12]

Analysis, of course, is an ongoing process, and in neither case did the experience of mystical light finally resolve the problems of the patient in question. Nevertheless, it is clear that powerful archetypal images continue to play an important role in healing, and often help to catalyze psychic momentum, instrumental to the teleological movement of psychic life. In both cases, the experience of archetypal images of mystical light and the momentum of the soul were evident. In both cases, we are reminded of Jung's conviction that it is the numinous that heals and of Hillman's avowal that it is in and through the power of images that the soul awakens and finds its way.

## *NOTES*

[1] Sidney Feshbach, "The Light at the End of the Tunnel Is Coming Right at Me, or, the Dialectic of Elemental Light and Elemental Dark," in *Analecta Husserliana: The Yearbook of Phenomenological Research*, Vol. XXXVIII, *The Elemental Dialectic of Light and Darkness: The Passions of the Soul in the Onto-poiesis of Life*, ed. Anna-Teresa Tymieniecka (Dordrecht: Kluwer Academic Publishers, 1992), pp. 56-57.

[2] Thomas Ryba, "Elemental Forms, Creativity and the Transformative Power of Literature, in A-T. Tymieniecka's *Tractatus Brevis*," in *Analecta Husserliana: The Yearbook of Phenomenological Research*, Vol. XXXVIII, *The Elemental Dialectic of Light and Darkness: The Passions of the Soul in the Onto-poiesis of Life*, ed. Anna-Teresa Tymieniecka (Dordrecht: Kluwer Academic Publishers, 1992), p. 17.

[3] Henry Corbin, *The Man of Light in Iranian Sufism* (Boulder, CO: Shambhala Publications, 1978), pp. 55-84.

[4] Mircea Eliade, *Shamanism: Archaic Techniques of Ecstasy* (Princeton, NJ: Princeton University Press, 1964), p. 61.

[5] Urszula Szulakowska, *The Alchemy of Light: Geometry and Optics in Late Renaissance Alchemical Illustration* (Leiden: Brill, 2000), p. xi.

[6] *Ibid.*, p. xiii.

[7] *Ibid.*

[8] *Ibid.*, p. 183.

[9] *Ibid.*

[10] James Hillman, *Archetypal Psychology* (Putnam, CT: Spring Publications, 1983/2004), p. 18.

[11] James Hillman, *The Dream and the Underworld* (New York: Harper& Row, 1979), p. 202.

[12] Andre Bareau, "The Superhuman Personality of the Buddha and Its Symbolism in the Mahâparinirvâna Sûtra of the Dharmaguptaka," in *Myths and Symbols: Studies in Honor of Mircea Eliade,* ed. J. M. Kitagawa and C.H. Long (Chicago: University of Chicago Press, 1969), p. 14.

GLEN SLATER is a core faculty member at Pacifica Graduate Institute, where he teaches in the Mythological Studies and Depth Psychology Programs. He has written several essays for *Spring Journal* and currently edits the journal's film reviews. He also served as editor for and wrote an introduction to Volume 3 of *The Uniform Edition of the Writings of James Hillman*.

# 22

# Numb

GLEN SLATER

The psyche's one sure-fire way of conveying its reality has always been through symptom. More than dream, fantasy, or projection, it is the symptom's ability to disrupt, disturb, and reroute psychic energy that makes the head turn and remind us of our inherent divisibility. Jung pointed out that the gods had devolved into neurotic symptoms, and Hillman underscored this insight by recognizing the pathologizing soul's proclivity to fall into its parts. To face symptom squarely is to know one is at least two, and this opens the door to knowing one is also many—or dependent upon the many. Although there are multiple ways to encounter this multiplicity, such as remembering ancestors, dialoging with inner figures, and engaging fantasy images, symptoms open the steepest paths to what lies beyond mere egoism. As the world has become increasingly fabricated, the symptom has kept us honest. Until recently, that is. After a century of following disturbances into the psyche, symptom may now be added to the endangered species list.

For multiple reasons, some of which I will describe here, psychological symptoms no longer appear the way they did to our predecessors around the turn of the last century, when neurosis arrived as a stark counterpoint to constricted Victorian minds and invited early psychoanalysts into rich inner landscapes. Since then, psychic terrain—or at least our description and conception of it—has become too familiar and its once exotic inhabitants over catalogued. Symptoms neither convey the sense of autonomy they once did, nor do they invite the same concern and consternation. Increasingly, they are not even perceived *as* symptom—as indicators of larger problems or maladies. Their call has grown faint. They are rarely followed *down* or *in* or *beyond* the preoccupations of everyday functioning. What symptoms have to say about the conditions of their arising, whether individual or collective, arouses little interest, reflecting a milieu in which expedient solutions, fear of introspection, and biological determinism hold sway. In such a milieu the neurotic mutterings of Woody Allen wandering through Manhattan appear quaint, for few spend time talking to their complexes or wrestling with their obsessions and mood swings in a world stacked with diversions and medications. Having once appeared to lead us into a new realm of psychic understanding, that harbinger of complex and creative lives we call "neurosis" now appears to have headed back underground. The sense of psyche *as psyche* is becoming unconscious.

In essence, in the culture at large and in mainstream psychology, the symptom is no longer held psychologically. The kind of psychic split around which depth psychology grew up and through which the psyche made itself known as such has been transcended and colonized by a more insidious kind of split: a dislocation of psychic disturbance from psychic ground. In this situation one is less inwardly conflicted and more outwardly disoriented, distracted, dazed, and not much aware of any soul state. A hundred years of psychotherapy with the world getting worse was just the beginning.[1] Now the capacity to actually feel what is wrong is fast eroding. Despite the surrounding psychological and social distress, considering the consequences and significance of this distress is now a rare pursuit. Amidst the diminished tolerance for discomfort, the Hollywood-style outing of psychopathologies, the ubiquitous psychobabble, and the acculturation of defense mechanisms, a different, more pervasive variety of unconsciousness and disconnection is apparent. It is a state of mind that is adept at keeping the psyche itself at bay, a state of mind best described as "numb."

Always being in the psyche in no way ensures that we are always in touch with the psyche. In a society more afflicted by psychological illness than any in history, there is a deep irony about the fact that it does not actually relate to its underlying distress on its own ground. The oft-cited self-absorption of today would seem to suggest an equal sensitivity to the psyche's communication of what is wrong. However, an opposite effect is actually more evident: the more psychological we become, the less psychological we are. The insulation of emotion, feeling, and instinct is being built into normative ways of knowing and modes of perception right alongside national campaigns for mental health awareness. Epidemic levels of depression and anxiety are read neither as calls for inner exploration, nor as indications of wayward lifestyles, nor as comments on the soulless contours of the world at large.

As we look ahead into the third millennium, this general numbing of the psyche places us in a precarious position. Saying a long goodbye to psychological symptom removes an essential channel for the self-regulating tendency of the psyche, via which we perceive the rhythms and promptings of cosmos and nature. The gods, requiring recognition, may have returned as diseases, but if the symptoms of these diseases are no longer felt, what becomes of the gods? What becomes of us without the gods? And what becomes of a planet inhabited by a people insulated from their natures?

Numbing is the absence of feeling response in the face of suffering, trauma, or general discontent. Its underlying process, which ushered in the age of dynamic psychiatry and depth psychology, is *dissociation*. Once described almost exclusively in relation to the hysterical response to pathogenic ideas and personal trauma, and as a process creating large divisions of conscious and unconscious contents—a so-called bifurcation of the self[2]—dissociation is present today as a more pervasive means of managing incompatible emotions and perceptions. Part social insularity, part defensive response to overwhelming amounts of information and stimulus, part apathy, and part susceptibility to spin, fabrication, and abstraction, dissociation seems to grow out of the contemporary scene. It is built upon hairline fractures that pervade everyday experiences, covering over the fault-lines once traced through the deep psyche and maintained by repression and suppression. It is a second layer of fragmentation, eclipsing more primary neurotic splits. This dynamic of dividing up, compartmentalizing, and insulating life exists as a common strategy of maintaining a stance above the fray, a strategy that mixes pieces of consciousness and unconsciousness rather than divides the psyche into two neat, distinct areas. Whereas *DSM*-validated dissociative disorders are associated with about 5% of the population, this other kind of dissociation is reflected in the tuning out, black-and-white thinking, and lack of in-the-worldness detectable at all levels of society.

This style of dissociation has become cultural, normative, evident in the mania of multitasking, in the disembodied cult of appearances, and in the fog of indifference to injustice and political manipulation. It is also evident in the behaviors and attitudes of prominent individuals from Wall Street to the White House. The traders at Enron were not just cut off from their greedy shadows, nor merely repressing a swollen complex: their behavior portrayed a psychopathic dissociation from civility. The "Bush Bubble" describes the intentional ignorance, solipsism, and insularity of an administration that is also a form of unconsciousness *built into* the workings of consciousness. This bubble exists only because of what lies outside it: a cultural tolerance for the willful avoidance of actual events, facts, and real-world consequences. The startling thing about this phenomenon is not so much the celebrated disinterest of its central occupant; it is the acquiescent populace watching the implications unfold. Everyone seems to be out to lunch. These processes of cultural dissociation thrive on the absence of common sense—common sensitivity and responsibility. Their common purpose is to avoid the discomfort and cognitive dissonance of immediate reality. Little wonder that "Second Life" is one of the fastest growing online diversions. When actual life is unpalatable, an alternate one is a mouse-click away.

Speculating on the roots of this condition, it is sobering to consider just how much a dissociative pattern may be built into the very foundations of American society. The idea that the nation has traumatic wounds yet to scar over is but one dimension of this. In the wake of killing off its native inhabitants, civil war, segregation, assassinations, Vietnam, and 9/11, it has mostly been unable to undertake the kind of reflection, imaging, and storying that Greg Mogenson calls "crust-making."[3] It has so often failed to enter into mourning following collective losses that it now follows every new affliction with the kind of control, contempt, and triumph known as the manic defense. In this way, collective traumas simply give rise to more dissociation. This phenomenon may be built upon an even more foundational one embedded in cultural values. James E. Block opens his 600-page treatise on *agency* in American history this way:

> A relative *absence* of serious political and cultural discourse amidst a *made-for-TV* public culture *belies the churning soul of contemporary American life*. As a nation, we've *lost* our way, *lulled*

> by the drifting stream, *unmindful* in Tocqueville's cautionary words of "the current" which "*hurries us away* and drags us ... *towards the abyss.*"[4]

I have underscored Block's expressions: A culture that is "made-for-TV," which "belies the churning soul;" a nation that is "lost," "lulled," "unmindful" and is heading "towards the abyss." Each term intimates dissociation. Perhaps the very concept of agency and the individual pursuit of happiness, combined with the technological means to keep the "churning soul" at bay, are a good recipe for cultural dissociation; perhaps a culture geared to manifest destiny is destined to finds itself at odds with manifest reality.

It may be that the predisposition for normative dissociation in the American context is built into the idealism, individualism, and frontierism of its character, all of which require acts of separation. Idealism is both part of the American character and a defense mechanism. Idealism requires a separation from actuality, which thwarts it at every turn, a move that so easily turns to denial and rationalization—two subsequent defensive strategies that are apparent in idealist renderings of recent and past American history. Although individualism is rarely "rugged" and usually cloaks an unconscious conformity, it is still lived out within the drive for mobility, obsession with liberty, and resistance to socialized supports that is singular in the Western world. Always looking to the future, always hopeful, always engaged with the new, America also retains its grip on the frontier vision, an incessant stepping forth wherein the movement itself eclipses the terrain traversed. The flex of American military power around the world may have many motivations, but one is to make sure the horizon stays open. "Spreading freedom and democracy" sounds noble; it is also a rationalization for a compulsive need to maintain the frontier and ignore social realities back home.

Dissociation is also a central feature of Robert J. Lifton's description of an emergent kind of personality that he calls "the protean self,"[5] reflective of the multiple modes of being required of persons moving into post-modernity. Though this personality is adaptive to the prevailing conditions, perhaps because it is so adaptive to these conditions, there is quite a downside. Lifton uses the term "dissociative field" to describe "an environment within which a collective pattern of dissociation is rendered not only 'normal' but 'expectable,' even required. Such a field is maintained by *psychic numbing* and by … *doubling*."[6] Doubling refers to the capacity to move in and out of two different concepts of self, seen for example in fundamentalism, where an ideal self is embraced alongside an everyday self, but the two operate independently. "Fundamentalism and other forms of totalism, embraced to overcome fragmentation, can intensify that fragmentation in turn."[7] There is little need to put this insight in context. Lifton goes on to note the phenomenon of the "static self," which "in its relation to technology and to the modern 'neutralization and disappearance of symbols' can proceed to a 'zero point' of immobilization."[8] Even in the case of those who find creative pathways beyond their traumatized past, he describes as "precarious" the "equilibrium between dissociation or numbing, on the one hand, and vitality of self on the other."[9] One comes away from Lifton with the distinct notion that dissociation dogs the postmodern, modular, multi-tasking personality at every turn. It is a normal coping mechanism. As another commentator noted back in 1970, "life is muted, experience filtered, emotion anesthetized, affective discharge incomplete."[10]

Another dimension of this collective condition: we are overwhelmed by our discontent, sick and tired of hearing about the woes of the world. It is all too much. Lifton quotes the novelist Penelope Lively describing the protagonist in one of her novels: "He is told so much, and from so many sources, that he has learned to disregard, to let information filter through the mind and vanish, leaving impressions—a phrase, a fact, an image. … He is an intelligent man, a man of compassion, but he can hear of a massacre on the other side of the globe and wonder as he listens if he remembered to switch on his answering machine." Lifton comments on the "late-twentieth-century self" and suggests "[w]hile that self invokes defenses of withdrawal and numbing, it remains continuously bombarded by ideas and images and is in some measure recast by them, made more fluid in response to the surrounding fluidity."[11] This fluidity has loosened rigid orthodoxies but has also drowned a generation, which no longer takes a position on the issues of the day.

Some of these foregoing themes are echoed in Allan Bloom's *The Closing of the American Mind*, where he writes, "the self is the modern substitute for soul,"[12] taking psychology to task for its egocentric focus within a broader discussion of ignorance, self-centeredness, and disconnection from life's larger concerns. The mind closes when it can no longer imagine past its own self-absorption and engage the ideas that make an epoch.

Some of this solipsism stems from flippant, superficial discussion of psychological symptoms. Psychopathology used to be studied under the heading of "abnormal psychology"; but now abnormal is pretty normal. No longer confined to the back ward, psychopathology is daily fodder for Oprah and Dr. Phil. One operative fantasy on these programs is to normalize the condition of the day, making both guest and audience feel like they are not alone in their maladies. Unfortunately, the malady is recast as a disease without meaning or purpose, to be overcome heroically. If everyone is depressed and anxious, then why spend time contemplating the significance of such conditions, either individually or collectively? Finding the spirit of neurotic kinship and fighting these undesirable visitations together is usually the order of business. Neurosis used to be accompanied by a profound feeling of isolation and alienation. Jung discovered that the recovery of a meaningful context for suffering or an internal narrative could alleviate this feeling and often undo a neurotic tangle. But *this* reversal of alienation is vertical, not horizontal. It occurs when one feels an echo of pathos in myth and poetry, joins the trials and tribulations of tragic and comic protagonists, and senses universality by moving into and through the peculiarity of the symptom and not by dissolving that peculiarity in a vat of vapid collectivized sound bites. The kind of psychobabble we are exposed to on a daily basis, which puts suffering into boxes with fashionable lids, works as an effective barrier to being more authentically psychological. Even Bloom in his curmudgeonly swipe at narrow-mindedness notes that today's concern with self has "grown into the highway of a ubiquitous psychology without the psyche (soul)."[13]

A large part of the ease with which psychological symptoms are thrown about in public discourse has to do with their being imagined as medical rather than psychological problems. Alleviating the sense of moral failure and self-blame may be a valuable move, but it always comes packaged with the failure to accept any felt sense of an autonomous psyche. For most, psychology falls into two camps: either it pumps the mind with motivational tricks and exercises in self-confidence, or it controls the capricious actions of neurons. Little lies between this Cartesian division of a willful mind and mechanistic body. Depression, anxiety, phobia, addiction, and a host of other conditions, once imagined as points of entry into complexes and histories, have become stand-alone, anomalous neural mishaps that do not point to anything beyond their own biological ground. Psychiatrists and mental health advocates, working under the guise of reducing the stigma of diagnosis, actively disconnect psychological symptoms from psychic situations, whether individual or societal. It is now more acceptable to regard physical symptoms as expressions of a holistic mind-body configuration than it is to perceive psychological symptoms in the same holistic context. Beneath the division of mainstream psychology into cognitive-behavioral reprogramming and neurological rerouting is a profound fear of the psyche, evident in the reaction one receives when suggesting anything but a physiological etiology for psychological symptoms. Avoiding the study of its own subject, psychology bends to collectivity rather than listening to the collective's unconscious.

In his book, *Artificial Happiness*, here is how Ronald W. Dworkin, an anesthesiologist with an eye for cultural anesthesia, describes the situation with attention deficit disorder:

> What neurologists had failed to establish with their scanners—a physical basis for ADHD—the primary care doctors accomplished through inference; a simple drug effect turned attention deficit into an engineering problem. The Ritalin effect became a subset of psychotropic drug ideology, causing attention deficit to join everyday unhappiness among the ranks of physical diseases.[14]

Dworkin suggests a halo effect of "psychotropic drug ideology," which is that "doctors have taken on the responsibility of curing unhappiness—not depression, but everyday unhappiness—through artificial means."[15] He argues that there now exists a whole class of people in the United States who live in a state of "Artificial Happiness," the "distinctive feature" of which "is its power to resist life." People who live in this state "manage to avoid feeling miserable when life is miserable."[16] The problem is that people who are artificially happy "don't feel the unhappiness they need to feel to move forward with their lives;" they "lose [the] impulse to change," they "stay in their old ruts, stagnate in a pool of sham happiness, and sacrifice any chance for the real thing."[17] In other words, those living in states of artificial happiness live in a way that is dissociated from the trials and challenges of everyday existence. They become comfortably numb.

Let's be clear: precise, targeted use of psychotropic medications can open an otherwise locked door to therapeutic intervention. However, indiscriminate prescription and use of these medications exchanges the conflict, tension, melancholy, and sensitivity required in soul-making, character building, and "crust-making" for an artificially-induced, culturally-condoned numbing. Avoiding everyday unhappiness simply swaps one kind of symptom for another—one socially-dystonic for another socially-syntonic. The latter may be read as a symptom of a whole configuration of social ills—as I am attempting to do here—but it is being turned into a way of life. When everyone has the same problem, it is no longer a problem, and the capitalist drive kicks in to keep it that way.

There is yet another strategy afoot for obscuring the condition of the psyche. A great deal of psychological distress has been absorbed into normal social discourse. Alongside the acculturation and medicalizing of psychological symptoms, we now have an array of conditions, the intrinsic nature of which concerns the concealment of pathology behind a façade of normality. The character disturbances that dominate today's psychoanalytic discussions are essentially ways of managing and covering over high levels of rage, sadness, and fear that are present beneath a mask of adaptation. It has been nearly thirty years since Lasch's claim that narcissism went cultural.[18] Even the now-pervasive borderline personality, with its multiple symptoms, high volatility, and chaotic relationships, is proving to be adaptable. Borderline conditions thrive on the discontinuity, volatility, and instant gratification rampant in certain social circles—qualities idealized in the world of hotel heiresses and adolescent stars in and out of rehab. The impulsivity and histrionics of borderline conditions find their home in such high-profile celebrity antics, where notoriety seems to legitimate all. Here the façade occurs through exposure, through turning the psyche inside out and letting mania and addiction pass for lifestyles of choice. When pathology is simply adopted by the persona, it no longer has any inner standing and becomes magically unhooked from a sense of character, identity, and responsibility. What remains hidden is the terror of annihilation and feeling of utter worthlessness. The drive to fill each moment with something sensational never fills the gap of true sensation, for there is always a background numbing that is only a quiet moment away.

Topping the list of such adaptive disorders of character is psychopathy, whose very nature it is to thrive in society by creating an oft-cited "mask of sanity."[19] Robert W. Rieber, whose work does for cultural psychopathy what Lasch's did for cultural narcissism, places dissociation at the very core of psychopathic behavior, noting "it is manifest in the psychopathological glibness, in the inability to feel guilt, in the inability to profit from experience, and in the semantic dementia, generally, of the psychopath."[20] Rieber argues that the psychopath has also become a cultural role model:

> In a world in which social institutions cannot function effectively, the best way to succeed is to dissociate oneself from value conflicts. The mechanisms by which this numbing is accomplished combine with prevailing social conditions to produce psychopathic behavior on a large scale. This phenomenon feeds on itself, driving out "good" as a bad moral currency, and welcoming the dark side of human nature.[21]

In particular, what the psychopath does is dissociate "the 'me' and the 'not me,'"[22] a trait explored in some depth by Adolf Guggenbühl-Craig in *The Emptied Soul*, where he suggests the absence of eros determines the nature of psychopathy.[23] Hillman had earlier pointed out that eros and psyche reach beyond their mythic relationship to constitute "two ends of every psychic process." Further, "they always imply and require each other."[24] But the psychopath splits these ends, and without eros there is no psyche. As Guggenbühl puts it, "only through Eros can gods or archetypes be loving."[25] These understandings point to the psychopath having no connection to psyche, no soul, and in this way reflecting the dissociation between a thoroughly isolated, defended mind and the psyche itself. The psychopath thus epitomizes the trend towards dissociation from the psyche itself.

The notion of leaving the psyche behind altogether is aided by Rafael López-Pedraza's description of Titanic psychology, which also provides another mythic entrance into cultural dissociation. He describes the "two basic elements of Titanism" as "emptiness on the one hand" and "excess on the other."[26] As the Titans always threaten to displace the Olympians, they may well be considered the archenemies of psychological life. Titanic impulses represent drives freed of all archetypal constraint, a theme I have addressed elsewhere.[27]

In a later work López-Pedraza juxtaposes the Titans and Dionysus, pivoting the collision of these forms on the moment in the Orphic hymn concerning the birth of Dionysus when the Titans tear the child-god to pieces, leaving only his heart, which Athena then saves and Zeus swallows, thus bringing about the child-god's second birth.[28] The descriptions of Dionysiac psychology that follow resuscitate a psychology of the heart and provide an apt counterpoint to Titanic dissociation. Such a psychology "is rooted in emotions and the living of life as destiny,"[29] "makes the connection between mind and body,"[30] and cultivates a "tragic consciousness."[31] In a recent article, Noel Cobb describes R. D. Laing's affinity with Dionysus and his sense of "*psychophobia*—'the fear of our own souls,'" which he considered "characterized our time more than anything else."[32] Above all, Dionysus keeps us close to our madness, holding this too within the pantheon, making this divinity as intrinsic to soul as the Titans are extrinsic.

What is unconscious today, more than ever, is psychology itself. Talk shows, self-help books, the spotlight on mental illness, and the acceptance of psychotherapy have created a veneer of pseudo-psychological awareness, which functions as another form of defense against psychic reality. Symptoms have not been conquered they have been assimilated—blended into normality. Sometimes we wear our illnesses on our sleeve and use them as we would use any other element of the persona field that regulates our relation to the collective; sometimes the symptoms are hidden behind slick, thick masks of sanity. At times, the immediacy of psychic life, embodied perceptions, symbolic thought, and the capacity to respond to social and political injustice seem farther from us than ever before. The heroic ego, to which Hillman has attributed many guises, may have lost its fighting spirit and turned to insulation, escapism, distraction, and avoidance.

Technology suggests a further concern: adaptation to the machines that surround us may both promote and require dissociation. The likely degree of future immersion in technology is reflected in science-fiction writer William Gibson's recent suggestion that within ten years the realm we refer to as "cyberspace" (a term he coined) will *invert* and begin to displace ordinary, everyday perceptions of living and being. Today cyberspace is deliberately entered by turning on a computer and directing attention towards the World Wide Web. However, this web will soon become a cocoon that surrounds us on all sides, and breaking out will require more deliberation than stepping in. For many, there will no longer be two worlds, just one world, filtered and organized by software technicians. The dissociation required by this new situation will result in a radically different phenomenology: being in time and *cyber*space. Leaving the body behind in technology has been well described by Robert Romanyshyn.[33] Yet along with the body also goes a sense of place, and with a sense of place goes a sense of limitation, which is intrinsic to every archetypal situation.

Recreational and relational experiences that are primarily web-based already fill the psychological horizon. "Second Life" has over nine million residents—"avatars" that users create when they enter this world. With such acclimatization present to a whole generation and on the increase for the next, actual disconnection from cyberspace may change the modality but not the *mode of adaptation* to that modality. This is what Gibson is pointing to. The phenomenal field will be perhaps irreversibly altered: the rhythms of instant access, multiple windows, hyper-visual stimulation, and information streams without context will accompany the cyber-oriented psyche back into the world, where it will bend the contours of lived experience into the shape of web-based discourse. Instead of the phenomenal world moving into the cyber world, the reverse will happen. A taste of this trend occurred recently when the Blackberry network went down for nearly four hours, sending its subscribers into a half-day panic attack. Users of the handheld devices reported various levels of discomfort upon being forced out of their habitual routine of checking information and making calls every few minutes. The streets of Manhattan were full of contemporary "Neos" unplugged from their matrix.

After Bernie Neville wrote a paper describing a world in the grip of a Hermes inflation,[34] Hillman responded by suggesting that the phenomenon to which Neville was referring was better considered in terms of the continued grip of monotheism. "Hermes and his computer is merely the fashionable front-man," writes Hillman,[35] who points out that the changing domination of one god over another on the cultural scene does not add up to a new Hermes-mediated polytheism. Of course, inflation already suggests a pseudo-archetypal situation, which presents as a stereotypical shell of a god without associated complexity or feeling of archetypal otherness. The Hermes who rules the Information Age is, as Hillman says, "one fallen from the brotherhood and sisterhood," without "the limits of divine company" and "only profane."[36] In other words, the Hermes of the

Information Era is dissociated from his true character, only mimicking interactions with the many, allowing scant connection to the pantheon or between levels of existence. Without the family system, the world of intersecting realities and relativized meanings becomes a web of dissociation. The "googled" information that appears alongside a vast array of links and *associated* material is mostly *dissociated* from author, lineage, place, and genre. Its only phenomenal context is that of the machine it appears on and the moment of its appearance.

A good indicator of Hermes inflation and related dissociation is the preponderance of manipulation present in all electronic media, and the different shades of the "we create our own reality"[37] ethic found in a wide spectrum of society from Washington to L.A. Instead of subtlety, nuance, and a sense of trickery, we have spin, double-talk, and what the philosopher Harry G. Frankfurt describes as "one of the most salient features of our culture": bullshit.[38] One way to distinguish between the deception of Hermes at work within the pantheon and the deception of bullshit is that the former is associated with trickster intentionality whereas the latter is inevitably tied to egocentric purposes. Hermes deceives as a means of keeping the gods in play, whereas the bullshit culture usurps divine sparks to daze, dazzle, and dupe for a lower purpose. Use of imagery is often the medium for this exercise. However, Hillman goes to some lengths to distinguish the images of this syndrome from the images of archetypal concern. Whereas Neville asserts we are afloat in a sea of images, Hillman argues that "these images are life preservers after the shipwreck of titanic modernism."[39]

The information age and its online world appear at this point to offer only an intimation of Hermes, not the archetypal field within which the gods might be met in their complexity—or depth. Internet Hermes shows a lot of horizontal connectivity, but little vertical movement. Importantly, however, this hermetic intimation is always *promising* depth. In our minds it is usually just the next web page away. Hillman writes, "[T]he gods have been deprived of images for so long that they have been going quite mad, finding only concepts and abstractions and formulae in which to settle down."[40] The gods, returning as diseases, have moved from symptom to stereotype. In such a way, dissociation offers a kind of pseudo-polytheism, a pantheon of empty shells, without actual gods, without the connective tissue of the *mundus imaginalis*. The stereotype itself offers only the horizontal not the vertical plane of existence. When mistaken for the real thing, stereotypes invite what Jung referred to as "mass-mindedness," the great counter pole of individuation and a differentiated relation to the psyche. More to the point, stereotypes leave one cold, deadened, flattened—numb?

The acute symptoms that appear in the consulting room are no longer our primary concern. To the contrary, these symptoms may be some of the last indications of a healthy psyche's ability to communicate its discomfort. In the same vein, Jung's formulation concerning the movement of neurotic suffering into meaningful suffering is no longer universally valid. A third state of suffering must be added: the realm of the numb. Although states of dissociation may fall under the heading of neurosis, when dissociation pervades culture and character, even neurotic suffering is avoided. By fitting one's neurotic conflict into some external frame of reference or by completely flattening affect, suffering is deflected from its unique, individual context and cannot be read or felt as a communication.

Neurosis used to be a holding pattern—a way station between raw symptom and the conscious, meaningful embrace of one's fate. In this light, neurosis might nowadays be considered an accomplishment, perhaps even an indication of psychological health. At least in direct engagement with neurotic suffering the conflict is present and graspable, and the psyche is speaking; the situation remains psychological. Such thoughts lead to another: psychology's new task may be to put people squarely back in their neurosis, to help them suffer honestly, in a way that reflects their actual circumstances.

The omnipresence of the autonomous psyche that we find in James Hillman's writings maintains a psychology with a psyche-logos dance. In this time of numbing and horizontal splitting, his polytheistic, in-the-world perspective is prescient. The shift from highly conceptual language and inner geographies of conscious and unconscious to a more phenomenological, aesthetically attuned perspective works to make psychological *sense* and counter the anaesthetized mind. Rooted as they are in *associational* processes that relate us to the depths, to history, myth, and timeless ideas, soul-making and imagination undo numbing. These processes return the psyche's innate vividness and provide a nose for the psychopathology that is concealed within so-called normal and well-adjusted lifestyles and in the standard operating procedures of corporations and communities. In *The Myth of Analysis*, Hillman discusses both the significance of developing an "imaginal ego" and re-entering Dionysian consciousness.[41] In turning the tide of dissociation we could do no better than go back to these reflections, which make vivid the very tissue of psychological life.

Dissociation operating at a cultural level invites a hard-to-reverse vicious circle. For one thing, dissociated states go hand in hand with suggestibility, which makes for an even greater vulnerability to media spin and political double talk. Closer to home, when dissociation becomes so pervasive and normative that it starts to dictate treatment, when symptoms are read without psychological or historical context, psychology proper ceases to exist. Currently psychology at large appears to be succumbing to this age of numbing and splitting. In so many literary and cinematic dystopias societies degenerate into automated or totalitarian support systems for the numb. Here at least the artistic imagination may be seen doing its work, responding to the signs, making the associations and showing soul concerns. But to where will we turn when the signs and symptoms become unreadable?

## *NOTES*

[1] James Hillman and Michael Ventura, *We've had a Hundred years of Psychotherapy—and the World's Getting Worse* (San Francisco, CA: Harper, 1992).

[2] Robert W. Rieber, *The Bifurcation of the Self* (New York: Springer, 2006).

[3] Greg Mogenson, *A Most Accursed Religion* (Putnam, CT: Spring Publications), pp. 111-138.

[4] James E. Block, *A Nation of Agents: The American Path to a Modern Self and Society* (Cambridge, MA: Harvard University Press, 2002), p. 1.

[5] Robert J. Lifton, *The Protean Self: Human Resilience in an Age of Fragmentation* (Chicago, IL: The University of Chicago Press, 1993).

[6] *Ibid.*, p. 208.

[7] *Ibid.*, p. 192.

[8] *Ibid.*

[9] *Ibid.*, p. 142.

[10] Philip Slater, *The Pursuit of Loneliness: American Culture at the Breaking Point* (Boston, MA: Beacon Press, 1970), pp. 24-25.

[11] *Ibid.*, pp. 20-21.

[12] Allan Bloom, *The Closing of the American Mind* (New York: Simon and Schuster, 1987), p. 173.

[13] *Ibid.*, p. 175.

[14] Ronald W. Dworkin, *Artificial Happiness: The Dark Side of the New Happy Class* (New York: Carol & Graf, 2006), p. 57.

[15] *Ibid.*, p. 2.

[16] *Ibid.*, p. 4.

[17] *Ibid.*, p. 8.

[18] Christopher Lasch, *The Culture of Narcissism* (New York: W. W. Norton & Company, 1979).

[19] Hervey Cleckley, *The Mask of Sanity: An Attempt to Clarify Some Issues about the So-Called Psychopathic Personality*, 5th Edition (Saint Louis, MO: C. V. Mosby Company, 1976).

[20] Robert W. Rieber, *Manufacturing Social Distress: Psychopathy in Everyday Life* (New York: Plenum Press, 1997), p. 52.

[21] *Ibid.*, p. 12.

[22] *Ibid.*, p. 52.

[23] Adolf Guggenbühl-Craig, *The Emptied Soul* (Woodstock, CT: Spring Publications, 1999), p. 27. [Formerly published as *Eros on Crutches*.]

[24] James Hillman, *The Myth of Analysis* (Evanston, IL: Northwestern University Press, 1972), p. 106.

[25] Guggenbühl-Craig, p. 26.

[26] Rafael Lopez-Pedraza, *Cultural Anxiety* (Einsiedeln, Switzerland: Diamon Verlag), p. 15.

[27] See Glen Slater, "Resink the Titanic," *Spring 62* (1998): 104-120; "Cyborgian Drift," *Spring 75* (2006): 171-195.

[28] Rafael López-Pedraza, *Dionysus in Exile* (Wilmette, IL: Chiron Publications, 2000).

[29] *Ibid.*, p. 36.

[30] *Ibid.*, p. 34.

[31] *Ibid.*, p. 67.

[32] Noel Cobb, "Dreams of God: R. D. Laing and Asklepios," *Spring 77* (2007): 237.

[33] Robert D. Romanyshyn, *Technology as Symptom and Dream* (New York: Routledge, 1989).

[34] Bernie Neville, "The Charm of Hermes: Hillman, Lyotard and the Postmodern Condition," *The Journal of Analytical Psychology* 37, no. 3 (1992): 337-353.

[35] James Hillman, "A Note on Hermes Inflation," *Spring 65* (1999): 9.

[36] *Ibid.*, p. 10.

[37] Comment attributed to a Bush White-House aide. "Faith, Certainty and the Presidency of George W. Bush," *New York Times*, October 17, 2004.

[38] Harry J. Frankfurt, *On Bullshit* (Princeton, NJ: Princeton University Press, 2005).

[39] Hillman, "Hermes," p. 12.

[40] *Ibid.*, p. 13.

[41] Hillman, *Myth of Analysis.*

Velimir B. Popović is a Jungian psychoanalyst, also trained in clinical psychology and Freudian psychoanalysis, who maintains a private practice in Belgrade, Serbia. He is a lecturer in the Department of Psychology of the University of Belgrade, Serbia, where he teaches clinical psychology, clinical assessment, and analytical and archetypal psychology. He is a faculty member and lecturer at the Gestalt Psychotherapy Training Institute on Malta. His current and long-standing intersts include archetypal psychology, phenomenology, hermeneutics, and Orthodox mystical theology. He has published a number of articles on archetypal and analytical psychology, including two books: *The Psychology of the Feminine* (1995) and *On Soul and Gods: Theory and Practice of Archetypal Psychology* (2001). Among his many responsibilities, he has recently been invited to teach at the International School for Analytical Psychology (ISAP) in Zürich, Switzerland.

# 23

# Hekate, or On Being Trivial in Psychotherapy[1]

VELIMIR B. POPOVIĆ

> ... [T]he metaphors we believe we choose for describing archetypal processes and ideas, ... are inherently part of those very processes and ideas themselves. It is as if the archetypal material chooses its own descriptive terms as one aspect of its self-expression. ... We might even submit that there is an archetypal selective factor involved in the invention of terms. Let us call this an archetypal semantics or phonetics on which archetypal hermeneutics is based. After all, to lead archetypal significance out of the language of psychology suggests that the significance is already "there" in the words, their root or their sounds.
>
> —James Hillman, *The Dream and the Underworld*, p. 25

## Introduction

In the following essay, I will reflect upon some of the manifold epiphanies of the goddess Hekate—the Mistress of the Soul—in our earthly lives and psychotherapeutic praxis. Following a fundamental tenet of archetypal psychology that "psychology is a mythology of modernity,"[2] I will try to explore some activities in which and through which Hekate manifests herself. The reason I am going back—via Hekate—to our Greek cultural heritage is not for historical or archeological reasons. As it was stated by Hillman:

> We return to Greece in order to rediscover the archetypes of our mind and of our culture. Fantasy returns there to become archetypal. By stepping back into the mythic, the nonfactual, and nonhistorical, the psyche can reimagine its factual, historical predicaments from another vantage point. Greece becomes the multiple magnifying mirror in which the psyche recognizes its persons and processes in configurations which are larger than life but which bear on the life of our secondary personalities.[3]

Also, I intend to show that this *Mistress of the Crossroads* is the self which stands at the crossroads of discourse and narration as a *who* of discourse in the guise of a narrating self—*Hekate narrans*—a peculiar storyteller who both finds herself in stories already told and strives for a self-constitution by emplotting herself in stories in the making. To be a self/subject is to be able to render a mythological account of oneself, to be able to tell the story of one's life. It was Jung who taught us that individuation is, first and foremost, a "personal myth," "... a *story* [my italics] of the self-realization of the unconscious ...."[4]

Yet, Hekate's discourse is highly peculiar, awkward, and trivial, never seen as an accomplishment or as an achievement. Her presence in our lives is seen as a problem, full of semantic ambiguities, lost in the multiple forms of speech and language games. However, it is my intention to show that this ominous divine creature, with her borderline/liminal dynamics, can produce the unity and identity of the self/subject. She manifests this unity and identity in narration, in the telling of her stories, emplotting the multiple and changing episodes of her (or our) communicative actions. In this I am following Renaissance philosopher, physician, and astrologer Girolamo Cardano, who was of the opinion that the human soul exist only insofar as it discovers, interprets, and responds to signs sent by "superior minds" (archetypes). I would say that according to Cardano, human identity or subjectivity is a process of (self-) interpretation. We humans exist as a hermeneutical response.[5]

My interest in Hekate (῾Εκάτη), a nightmarish threefold Titanic divinity, mistress of ghosts, demons, and bogies, the goddess of witchcraft and sorcery, is directed towards fulfilling a particular therapeutic task: I would like to shed some light on her and to clarify the influence she has over us in terms of our appeasing and assuaging her wrath. Even more, I see her as an agent who stimulates psychic reflection in the analyst and, at the same time, prevents the analysand from becoming the prey of his or her own stereotypic images of psychotherapy which will inevitably rob the client of his or her individuality.

## Scraps for an Imaginal Biography

In order to learn more about Hekate's qualities and to encourage our psychotherapeutic reflections, I will call upon Karl Kerényi and Martin Nilsson for help. The Hungarian classical scholar has offered us a rich description of Ἑκάτη κραταιίς—*Hekate krataiis*[6]: "Hekate … was always closest to us—although her name perhaps means 'the Distant One' …."[7] She is literally at a distance and far away from us, as her name, "Hekate," suggests (Ἑκάτη-βελέτης or ἑκατηβόλος—"She who is distant," "She who has power from far off," "She who shoots and hits at a distance"), and at the same time she is close to us as *Hekate Antia* (ἀντία—"she who confronts")—as Nilsson says: "[M]an needs gods who are near to him."[8] Also, she is the one whom we may meet as we journey, as her epithet *Enodia* (Ἐνόδια—"she of the roads") reveals.[9]

"She was literally 'close' to us," says Kerényi, "in the sense that she stood before the doors of most of our houses under the name of Prothyraia (Goddess of the Threshold), the goddess who helped women in childbirth or sometimes cruelly oppressed them,"[10] torturing women who were giving birth with the most horrid tricks. One may find the duality of her nature also in her relation to illness: she inflicts many diseases, especially madness and epilepsy; she brings bad dreams, apparitions, and nightmares. If a man had evil dreams, saw frightful creatures, and leapt up from his bed at night, the ancient Greeks would say that he had been attacked by Hekate. Concomitantly, she is the protectress who defends us against the very same evils she inflicts, and for this reason, her triple image was erected before every house in order to avert evils of any kind. In her negative aspect, she is responsible for lunacy, and, on the positive side, she is the Giver of Vision.[11] Her title *Prothyraia*—Goddess of the Threshold—also connotes two things at once: a Portal to the Deeps of Hades' realm of Soul, and a Gate to New Life, for in this epithet she is identified with *Eileithyia* (Εἰλείθυια—Goddess of Midwifery). Like Mother Earth or

Artemis herself, she was *kourotrophos* (κουροτρόφος)—a *nurse and nourisher* of all those born after her.

## Trinitarian Goddess

In both Hesiod's *Theogony* (411 ff.) and his *Orphic Hymns* (Hekate, I, 1-2), Hekate is called τρίοδιτιν (trioditin)—"One Goddess who is Three." The *triple form* is a fundamental characteristic of her nature. Hekate's association with the three phases of the moon have earned her the epithet "Three-Headed One" (τρικέφαλος—trikephalos). She is also described as "three-faced" (τριπροσωπος—triprosopos) and referred to as the "Three-Eyed One" (τρίγληνα—triglena). For the ancient Greeks, Hekate's triplicity connotes something underworldly.[12] Indeed they were right! Her triple form—three heads or faces, six arms, and snakes instead of legs—undoubtedly establish her as true Mistress of the Underworld.

Nicomachus of Gerasa took advantage of Hekate's threefold nature in his mathematical work *Theologumena arithmeticae* when he used her name for the number three. According to Nicomachus, one signifies the monad or "sameness," two signifies the dyad, which introduces "otherness," and three signifies the triad, which adds the "mean" between two things and is associated with "marriage," to which Hekate belongs by virtue of her triplicity.[13] Most noteworthy in Nichomachus's mystical mathematics is material that enables us to discern something more about Hekate's threefold nature than mythology allows. Hekate's threefold attributes imply that her essence is Trinitarian, so to speak; if we strip her of everything, of her character and movements, of her relationships and the realms where she rules, of her cultic practices and rites, what remains is her number: *three*.[14] This numeral three—Hekate as three—is the most basic thing, her most primitive and elementary manifestation.

It was C. G. Jung who taught us that number is the most primitive aspect of the archetype and its most elementary manifestation. Jung advanced the idea that *number is an archetype of order that is in the process of becoming conscious.*[15] Natural numbers possess *qualitative* properties, and they also, according to Jung, represent the most primitive self-manifestations of the spirit. Here, spirit is seen as *the dynamic, active, and ordering aspect* of the objective psyche, i.e., that "which inspires us, moves us, which spontaneously produces and orders images in the inner field of vision."[16] Seen from this angle, numbers are *temporal qualities* through which the individuation process unfolds.

Therefore, if we follow Jung and his Pythagorean predecessors, the number one would stand for the quality of origin, the beginning point, unity, non-duality; it is also the One, All-Oneness, the monad.[17] For the Pythagoreans, one is not a number at all; the first number is two. One is not a number because it does not yield itself to any form of calculation. Only two—the "Other"—makes counting possible; with it separation and multiplication begin.

Between the "One" and the "Other," there is a dialectical antagonism of archetypal proportions, which can be manifested in the realms of spirit and matter alike. If one is the monad (unity), and two stands for the "Other" (duality), for the sake of symmetry, we must ask: What about the number three? Or, what are the psychological aspects of Hekate when she is seen in terms of the number three? For Jung, a dialectical tension of opposites arises between the One and the Two/Other:[18]

> But every tension of opposites culminates in a release, out of which comes the "third." In the third, the tension is resolved and the lost unity is restored. … Three is an unfolding of the One to a condition where it can be known—unity become recognizable; … three therefore appears as a suitable synonym for *a process of development in time*, and thus forms a parallel to the self-revelation of the deity as the absolute One unfolded into three.[19] (Italics added.)

Hekate, thus, personifies the psychological processes of unfolding, unification, and becoming. Nicomachus taught that Hekate stands for "marriage" and "mean," i.e., she is the archetypal force that binds things together, which unites and holds elements that were split apart. Her Trinitarian numerical quality orders and connects psyche and matter. Hekate's temporal quality consists in *perfecting* and *completing* our psychological processes. Also, her threefold dynamic is a prerequisite of the process of becoming conscious. Divinity "governs things in three" and uses the ternary number to perfect beings of the phenomenal world, says Marsilio Ficino,[20] and therefore limits life experience in triangular fashion.[21] When we find ourselves in some triangular situation in life, Hekate is in our midst and intervenes as a binding image. Her Trinitarian form is itself an image or perspective and an imaginal (triangular) way of construing reality. As numeral three, she stands for directed action and movement. Let me put this differently—she/three is the *moving* and *dynamic* aspect of the psyche.[22]

## Mistress of Images

Hekate was also known as "Queen of the Dead"[23] and Mistress of the Underworld, who brings death and life, who is consort of Hades and Chthonian (Underworld) Hermes, a medium who connects images of Life and Death, who binds the worlds of our daily and nocturnal existence, who ties up our conscious and unconscious perspectives. Even more, this "child of the depths" (τά ρταροπαις—tartaropais), who possesses the ability to go deep and to return from below, bringing dreams and visions from this realm, is a true messenger, herald, or angel (ἄγγελος—*angelos*). And we all know that this chthonic realm of Shades (images) where she resides is a purely psychical world, where soul and psychic material come first. Hillman summed up this superbly: "… [U]nderworld is psyche. … Being in the underworld means psychic being, being psychological, where soul comes first. … Underworld images are ontological statements about the soul, how it exists in and for itself beyond life."[24] Hekate is, therefore, a psychic medium who brings a plethora of images (φάσματα πολλά—phasmata polla) from the Land of Shades. Euripides called her also the εἰνοδία θυγάτηρ Δήμητρος—"the queen of the phantom-world."[25] Psychologically speaking, "the phantom world" stands for the world of images, and this ominous creature is a harbinger who furnishes us with abundant images, which she expresses in a highly obscure, volatile, subversive, or trivial way. In Hekate, psychic images find their true abode, dwelling place, and peculiar way of narrative expression.

"The goddess who roves by night," who is the embodiment of movement, also represents the *mobility of images*,[26] and, at the same, as *angelos* she is a messenger who helps us understand their meaning. Gaston Bachelard gave us the insight that motion is the most important aspect of imagination through which we may be constituted as imaginal beings. "[I]magination is a becoming" says Bachelard.[27] Incessantly interpreting moving images offered by Hekate, the human subject increases its beingness.

From Martin Nilsson we learn that Hekate first came to Greece from the Orient, from the southwestern corner of Asia Minor—Caria—as early as the early archaic age:

> Man needs gods who are near to him. ... [A]nd as the Greek gods did not meet the needs of the Greek people, other gods were brought in from other peoples with whom the Greeks had intercourse. First came Hecate .... In Greece the attempt to make a great goddess of her did not succeed. She was always the goddess of witchcraft and sorcery.... At all events Hecate was accepted by the Greeks because there was a place for a goddess of witchcraft and ghosts.[28]

There is an important difference between Oriental and Greek cultic practice. While Greek cults find form more important than meaning, "it is the very essence of the Oriental cults, in fact, to 'sacrifice form to meaning.'"[29] If we apply this to Hekate's cult, which is Oriental in origin, we could say that it is not in her nature to transform images in abstract concepts. It is habitual in Greek/Western mentality to fix meaning, to organize and solidify it into monolithic ideas, abstract concepts, theories, ideologies, or theological idolatries. "There was a place for" Hekate means that we Westerners desperately need an archetypal perspective that would mediate forms of meaning into a vast panoply of moving metaphors and shifting and ever-changing images. Let me amplify this, once again, with the words of an expert on imagination—Gaston Bachelard—through whom Hekate obviously speaks:

> ... [I]mages do not adapt themselves very well to ... ideas, or above all, to definitive ideas. The imagination is ceaselessly imagining and enriching itself with new images ....[30]

The pure imagination designates its projected forms as the essence of its proper fulfillment. It delights naturally in imagining, and consequently in changing forms. Metamorphosis thus becomes the specific function of imagination. The imagination cannot comprehend a form except by transforming it, by dynamizing its becoming ....[31]

Hekate unifies via the imagination. She discloses us as imaginal beings. "The Queen of the Phantom World" can be seen as an imaginal container of coming-into-being, of becoming a particular something, of becoming imaginal subjectivity. She is the dynamizing agent who through wayward and erratic movements constitutes us as imaginal beings. As a Guide of Souls, she makes metaphors of our daily experience; as Angelos, she makes it possible to develop a perspective of meaning which is, though all too mundane and human, nonetheless far more beyond than personal. Without Hekate there could be no knowledge of transpersonal, transcendent, divine reality. She is the archetype that mediates other archetypes.

Yes, Hekate brings us images from the realm of Soul (the Underworld), but she also helps us to "read" or "see through" these hermetic elements. Let us not forget that she is *Eileithyia*—Goddess of Midwifery, who helped women in childbirth. It was Socrates, the son of a midwife, i.e., a servant of Eileithyia, who introduced a new therapeutic technique into midwifery—the so-called "Socratic dialogue"—as a method of inquiring into moral and philosophical questions by examining and refuting the opinions of his fellow discussants. Socratic midwifery is the basis of our contemporary hermeneutic —"talking cure"—procedures. In a manner of speaking, our analytical forefather, Socrates, is an offspring of this mighty goddess. If so, then we are all descendants of Hekate—via Socrates, Freud, Jung, and Hillman—and we can use her hermeneutic procedures in our analytical work.

## The Obscenity of Images

Hekate is the Moon Goddess, and as such closely connected with the Moon and therefore with the life of women. In ancient times, she was even called Bitch and She-wolf, "which, for the Greeks, symbolized the last word of obscenity,"[32] of something that is indecent, crass, and vulgar. According to Nilsson, in the Greek world it was the men who "fashioned the religion according their own ideas and … left too little room for emotionalism."[33] Their civic cults were very sober and well regulated. The women, therefore, "had a longing for an emotional religion,"[34] and they found a means of satisfying this longing by introducing Hekate to their predominantly masculine Greek world. Her Oriental cult was highly emotional, and through it Greek women were able to develop highly mystical and orgiastic forms of religion. Both Euripides in *Hippolytus* and Hippocrates in the *De morbo sacro* list her as deity who causes mental trouble and psychosomatic disturbances. Hekate is a goddess and protectress of all magic and sorcery; she was especially associated with necromancy, love magic, and love-potions. We may say that witchcraft and Hekate's orgiastic cult were the mythic prototypes of the homoeopathic cure. Their psychological function was to satisfy and relieve the repressed emotions and impulses, those urges that exist in all of us and can become, under certain social conditions, irresistible yearnings. From the aforementioned, we might imagine Hekate as a safe container that could hold all those repressed aspects of the Greek masculine mind (and our contemporary mind as well): irrationality, madness, obscene sexuality, anxiety, and various kinds of fears.[35]

Her image does not fail to contain and retain the bitchy, the sense of the sensual and the erotic, which is so important in our lives. Small wonder that she was also known under the title "Thrice Whirled" (*trigladine*), which to the Greek mind was an allusion to sexual intercourse, or, to be more specific, to various sexual acrobatics. In a manner of speaking, the Hekatean realm, which appears to us so crass and obscene, is the *temenos* where the union of the sexual, deviant, horny soul and the spirit seems imaginable. According to Lewis Richard Farnell, Hekate's "worship was without morality, and displayed energy only in sorcery and imposture."[36] It is precisely the most vulgar and mad, the most coarse and low that is the holiest and most spiritual in her realm. What is implied in her myth is that imagination is located, among other realms, in madness and sensuality, within the lunacy of our sexuality and the eroticism of amorality, within muddled and cheating motherliness and motherly indecency, within the obscenity of irrationalism and the pathology of deceptive rationalism. "The image has body. … Images don't work for us when we cannot sense their body,"[37] says Hillman. Therefore, imagining is always contained within the confines of a specific image or imaginal being. Hekate embodies, shapes, and limits the way amorality, sensuality, madness, and obscenity work. Through the "thrice-whirled" goddess, discarded, vulgar, pornographic, obscene images reincarnate their sensual and sexual bodies once again; they become imaginatively productive material that can be used as a means of de/con/structing our moralistic and naturalistic attitudes towards insanity, sexuality, and polymorphism. In her narrative (her *mythos*) one finds oneself at a threshold, or one starts developing boundaries and limits. Lulled by her obscene actions and discourse, we get guiding images that can move our lives onwards.

Hekate is seen as amoral, i.e., as one who does not bring his or her attitudes, actions, and ideas into line with prevailing mores, or one who is beyond all good-and-evil dichotomies. Therefore, her twisted, sensual, amoral, and perverted perspective is the very opposite of the ruling collective consciousness and the modern *Weltanschauung*. Becoming a "child of Hekate" means embracing and containing the pathologizing images and experiences she offers us. By embracing her amoral, sensual, or psychopathic material within a wider field of soulful space, we can tie her erratic nature to fantasy images. A similar view is presented by Hillman:

> If we are to fulfill the humanistic ideal by becoming fully human, then we are obliged to remember that the process of that becoming means saving the unforgivable. By saving, I mean remembering, keeping the pathologized experience and its images safe in memory. The process of individuation or the work of soul-making is the long therapeutic labor of lifting repression from the inhumane aspects of human nature. … Self-realization involves the realizing in consciousness of psychopathic potential one prefers to call inhuman.[38]

Her consciousness—*Hekatean consciousness*—is a twisted, sublated, distorted, or subverted one. When realized in analysis, Hekatean consciousness becomes a subversive and sublating perspective through which we are able to deconstruct and reconstruct images that are offered as food at our analytical table.

## Hekate as *Archetopos*

From Hekate we may learn that analysis is an interactive field in which a *plurality* of truths is available, and that these truths can be continuously "constructed" or "re-imagined" through the particular interactions and interpretations that arise in particular contexts. The interactive field that is constellated through the interplay of the two subjects in analysis makes the *third* possible. This third, which emerges from the intersection and interplay of two different organized subjectivities, forming "an indissoluble psychological system,"[39] is the intersubjective or interactive field as it is called in psychoanalysis. Psychoanalyst Donna Orange furnishes us with a description of intersubjectivity:

> ... [I]ntersubjectivity theory ... functions at a different level of discourse from that of self psychology. It describes the triadic system or field in *any* psychoanalytic treatment, classical or relational. The emotional organizing principles that each participant has distilled from relational experience form the two subjectivities. The interplay of these two subjectivities forms the third element of the intersubjective triad. ... [I]ntersubjectivity theory has clinical implications that require the analyst to be sensitive to the triad. ... [T]he concept of a "triad" highlights the capacity of the field itself to have both history and emotional qualities.[40]

Orange's words in this passage announce the presence of the threefold goddess Hekate—"the triadic system," "the intersubjective triad," or "triad." It seems as though the "thrice-whirled" deity stands behind all Trinitarian fantasies, including the psychoanalytic. If this triadic system is the working principle in "any psychoanalytic treatment," and furthermore, if it is present in any human relationship, as Jung described it in *The Psychology of the Transference,*[41] then it represents something that is *universal.* I consider threefold Hekate to represent *space* as a basic dimension in all our psychotherapeutic endeavors. Dreams, visions, and imagination all have their unique psychological locus, where their images come into being; the same holds true for therapy as such. According to Hillman, "Images are somewhere, and they have their own characteristic spatial quality. ... The fundamental language of depth is neither feelings, nor persons, nor time .... It is space. Depth presents itself foremost as psychic structures in spatial metaphors."[42]

In my imaginal perspective, Hekate stands for the interactive field, i.e., she personifies the archetypal basis or the space where interactive processes are going on. "No place is without archetypes," says Edward Casey.[43] Therefore, the interactive field is an archetypal place where Hekate resides. Or, to be more specific, she is the *archetopos*, which contains, covers, shelters, and subtends processes that are going on. Hekate as archetopos exerts an active force on the phenomena she situates. As an archetypal *locus*, she has power of her own to change the course of events within an analytical relationship. She has her own dynamics, which are separate from and independent of the subjects involved. Yet, the discovery of her dynamics is possible only by the imagination and by experiencing it emotionally through the personal and combined subjectivities of both participants. Experiences of this kind can be potentially deeply healing.

Hekate as an interactive archetopos is of a paradoxical nature, a process simultaneously out of time and situated in time. She is an ever-present reality, a particular imaginal realm that places us. Still, we make her presence palpable when we are ready to give up our ego control and abandon ourselves to the transpersonal, numinous, yet archaic and awesome processes of the field. Her paradoxical nature is based on the fact that she is not created by our intersubjective actions and yet our mutual presence and processes constellate her epiphany. The "three-faced goddess" as an incarnation of the interactive field—a "triad," a "third area," or "analytic third"—shares both the objective properties of the collective unconscious and the blended subjectivities of the participants in the analysis.

Each divinity as *archetopos* is, as Kerényi tells us, "the supra-individual source of a particular world-experience and world-configuration."[44] Gods are the world, modes of the world's presence, and they open the world to us. Yet Hekate is more than merely the archetypal image of a world. She is the source of the peculiar world, through whom that world originated and through whom it becomes comprehensible. To specify her world, we shall have to see how Hekate personifies it.

"The place before the gate of the temple, or city, or house was consecrated to Hekate," says Farnell.[45] In the *Aeneid* she is mentioned as standing by the gates of hell; she is often described as the keeper of the gates. Hekate's favorite abodes are crossroads, forked roads, and especially junctions of three roads, and this is the reason she was named *Hekate trioditis* (τριοδιτις—"of three roads," "one who is at the junction of three roads," or "the meeting place of three roads"). Wherever roads branched off or met, a wooden statue of Hekate, known as *Hekateia*, was erected on a triangle, and she was portrayed with three faces or three masks, carrying torches in her hands and wearing a bright headband. She was standing at the point of union, and each of her three faces was looking down one of those roads. Where roads run into each other or cross, there she is, symbolizing the union of opposites (*coincidentia oppositorum*). Hekate is the object and symbol of all union. Still she resides where roads divide, where separation, splitting, parting can happen. So, right there at the crossroads we find cleavage or division in her nature—"the Mighty One" is the symbol of all parting and splitting, farewell and separation.

The "Strong One" was also known as 'Ενόδια θεός (*Enodia theos*)—"goddess of the roads" and traveling. It was possible to see "the goddess that roves by night" at midnight on some road or junction of three roads, accompanied by a host of her ominous attendants—ghosts, demons, and apparitions—roaming around. Her arrival at some meeting point would be announced by the barking of her four-legged companions—dogs, hounds, and wolves. On other occasions, their howling would disclose her unnoticed and unheard presence at our doorway. At junctions or in front our doorsills, she would wait for a proper sacrifice. *Enodia Theos* (Goddess of the Road) is constantly on the move, on the tracks, constantly in motion, roaming here and there; she is Enodia ("by the road"), "a leader along the path," as well as *Antia* ('Αντιά—"she who confronts" or "she who meets"), one who encounters everyone on every path or road. Above all, she is true mistress of the Underworld, holder of the keys of Hades, the "night-wanderer of the underworld" (*nyktipolis chtonie*) and Queen of the Dead.[46] Evidently, we can say that roads, crossroads, different worlds are the archetypal images of this aptly-named almighty goddess. Hekate personifies our psychological junctions, meeting points, crossroads, as well as boundaries and limits. "Mistress of the Roads" indicates our psychological borders and frontiers and marks the place where, in our soul, the alien and the foreign touch the familiar and common. Finally, she is the traveler who wanders from here to yonder, between known and unknown. The *Goddess of the Road* forms a world in her own right, a border-domain where a person in this erratic and movable place has access to everything. Those who move about with familiarity in this "world of the road" have *Antia* for their goddess and patroness; for it is here that the most striking aspect of Hekate's cosmos is portrayed.

In the myths and traditions of various cultures, as well as in life, the "limit" or the "border" represents the spot where the action of the utmost importance is taking place. The border symbolizes discontinuity, parting, or separation; yet, at the same time, it is a place of union, a meeting place, a spot where formerly broken alliances are once again sealed. Hekate *the traveler* is at home while on the move, at home on the road itself, and at the crossroads or on the border as well. The border is here understood not as a connection between two definite points on the earth's surface, but as a particular world in itself. The border is a place or container that can hold experiences. Place is a matter of containment; therefore, to be in a given place is to be enclosed within a containing boundary, to be held there. This is why being at the border is a matter of holding, embracement, enclosure, or encapsulation—and also why images such as the crossroads, the junction, the bridge, and the river capture what is most crucial in the notion of border.

Martin Heidegger gives us a positive account of boundary: "A boundary is not that at which something stops but, as the Greeks recognized, the boundary is that from which something *begins its presenting*. That is why the concept is that of *horismos*, that is, the horizon, the boundary."[47] In fact, place is that for which somebody makes room, that which is allowed to dwell within its boundaries. Things for which we make place are at the same time things that are bound together, i.e., embraced by the very place they occupy. Hekate-as-boundary is the place where phenomena can come to being. In short, the border or crossroads is an archetypal image of exceptional importance; a *locus* where conscious and unconscious, Ego and Psyche, I and Thou, spirit and matter, body and soul, health and illness, personal and archetypal touch each other and unfold each other.

Is it possible to imagine analysis without the archetype that serves as a *temenos* or vessel, as a meeting place where one may encounter another human being (on the horizontal plane) or divinity (on the vertical one)? For me, she is the cornerstone of archetypal psychology, i.e., of psychology that goes into depth and the unconscious, into the Underworld and Soul. Like her, subjects of analysis are at home while on the move, at home on the road (of individuation) itself, the road being understood not as a connection between two definite points in one's life, but as a particular world where psyche unfolds itself. Her power of making connections concerns the inner life of the psyche; she makes possible connections with psychological complexes and archetypes grounded in other divinities. However, her competences cannot be restricted to the inner realm only; a threefold goddess has powers in all worlds, and she therefore stands for the nodal point where inner and outer intersect.

Her borderline aspect is dual. If we internalize the benevolent side of the "Mighty One," then it would be Hekate in us who encourages us to befriend different complexes and archetypes. Or, shall we say, it is her amiable and benevolent nature that promotes our individuation or psychological wholeness. On the other hand, her meeting points, junctions, or crossroads are not only locations where a *coincidentia oppositorum* is likely to take place, but also areas where separation, division, disjunction, or severance can be initiated. In her negative aspect, she personifies the psychological separation, fragmentation, and splitting that one may find, for example, in borderline personality disorder.

*Hecatē Lucifera* ("torch bearer") enables psychic life and analysis to unfold along diverse paths—junctions of three roads, where she was venerated, are reminders of our illusion that there exists one and only one road to follow. She introduces uncertainty into our lives and, at the same time, helps us learn that *uncertainty* is an inherent part of our existence. I agree that it is difficult to accept the idea that the basis of human subjectivity is so uncertain, volatile, and unstable, yet it seems that only what is flexible, erratic, and changeable can pave the way for future psychic development. In order to propitiate the "Queen of the Phantom World," each of us has to make an individual sacrifice to Πανδεἱνη (Pandeine), the "All-Terrible One,"[48] because the pathway she illuminates for one of us may be a blind alley for another.

## The Psychology of Sacrifice in the Cult of Hekate

Our Greek and Roman predecessors used sacrifice to secure the approval of the personal deities they believed in. The Olympian and Titanic gods and goddesses each had their own rituals of sacrifice. They differed from one another in the type of sacrifices that were acceptable. The particular oblations that were made to each of them indicate their diverse dispositions and qualities. The bulkiest and most acceptable sacrifices nearly always involved animal victims. Each divinity had his or her preferred oblation. However, slaughtered animals were just one type of oblation offered to gods and goddesses. It was also possible to win their favor by furnishing them with cookies, milk, oil, honey, cheese, beans, or eggs. Sometimes one could make a promise instead of a gift, and the gift would follow the favor received. But no matter what kind of oblation was preferred, the kind of victim denoted the peculiar characteristics of each particular deity. The essential traits and nature of a given deity are revealed in the way the rituals of sacrifice were performed, and in the kind of victim or food that was offered. According to classical scholar John Ferguson, "In all this there is a personal relation between worship and deity; the worshipper is establishing for himself the *pax deorum*, the favor of the gods."[49]

By all means, sacrifice represents a pivotal religious motif, yet it is also completely psychological. Through sacrificial ritual we once again re-connect (Latin, *re-ligare*) ourselves with our divine sources (archetypes). A proper oblation is a psychological link that establishes an assured relation with a given archetypal power.

According to Farnell, mysteries, cults, and rituals performed in the name of Hekate were quite different from those carried out in the name of other divinities of antiquity. Her sacrificial rituals and festivities deviated from prevailing moral standards, "her mysteries are not known to have had any moral or spiritual significance"[50] and her worship was without morality."[51] This may be seen in the specific nature of the oblations that were presented to her. In addition to dogs, cheese, eggs, and cookies, all food that was left uneaten on the table, all scraps and household garbage belonged to Hekate. Uneaten morsels, crumbs, or leftover scraps were ritually disposed of at midnight where roads cross or enter into one another. The "suppers of Hekate" seem to have been offerings made to the chthonic goddess, mistress of phantoms, in order to keep evil spirits away from the house. Such oblations were offered on the thirtieth day, which was sacred to the dead. On some occasions when the moon was new or full, the "banquets of Hekate" were offered by rich people; they would leave cookies or scraps and leftovers for the poor at the crossways. [52] Hence, the whole ritual was known under the name "Hekate's dinner."[53]

I am less interested in the social aspect of Hekate's cult, i.e., the fact that Greek and Roman societies looked after their marginalized citizens in this rather strange way. My attention is captured more by the *psychological* aspect of this cultic activity. The first thing that comes to my mind is the disparity between the sacrificial offerings (scraps, leftovers, discarded food, bites, junk, and garbage) on the one hand, and the numinous epiphany of the goddess on the other. How is it possible that the "Almighty" and the "Queen of the Dead" is pleased, not offended, by such lowly gifts? Shouldn't she be insulted by these humble offerings? Is it possible that she finds some value in waste, garbage, and leftovers? One thing is sure: our predecessors from Greece and Rome knew how to make contact with Hekate. Leftovers, scraps, garbage, trash, rubbish, or waste belonged to her, i.e., all these items represent unique and essential aspects of her image.

But what do those frivolous and trifling comments of mine regarding scraps and Hekate have to do with contemporary life and analysis? The most laconic answer I can offer you right now is that all I have said is no more than rubbish, a heap of worthless ideas—twaddle! I assume this explanation is not satisfactory, so let me offer an indirect explanation for being superficial and trivial.

Hekate belongs to the brood of Night (Νύξ—Nyx); the poets Sappho, Valerius Flaccus, and Nonnus all identified her with Nyx and called her "Queen of Night."[54] When Hekate becomes equated with Nyx—the goddess of night—as also in Maurice Scève,[55] Shakespeare,[56] and Dom Pernety,[57] then dreams made out of scraps, images based on rubbish, nightmares composed of trifles, or visions build on trash become her domain, and our interpretative ideas reflect her perspectives. The "black night" goddess conceived, without a mate, and gave birth to a multitudinous and lofty brood. From Nyx/Hekate were born some of the most powerful and portentous forces: ʺΟνειρος (Oneiros), ʽʹΥυπνος (Hypnos), Θανατος (Thanatos), ʼʹΕρος (Eros), Λήθη (Lethe), Μόρος (Moros), ʼʹΕρις (Eris), etc.[58] This fatherless archetypal cluster, brought forth solely from the mother, comprising dreams, sleep, death, love, oblivion, fate, and strife, belongs, according to very ancient tradition, to the world of Night and Hekate. They have no other home than beyond the gates of Hades in that dark realm where she rules.

Mythical family trees of the ancient gods and goddesses are the best means we have of observing various relations and emplotments of the archetypal powers. Through this particular mythical narrative we learn that the lofty brood has only one parent—Hekate, goddess of Night. We also discover that they are all bound by very strong blood and family ties, and no one among the brothers and sisters is superior to the rest, nor is anyone subjugated to anyone else. The mythical story of Nyx/ Hekate gives us a rather different perspective from those offered by depth psychologists. For example, Freud maintained that Eros is the builder of dreams, that Lethe (Oblivion) represses dreams, that Thanatos is at war/strife (Eris) with Eros (Love), that fatherly Dream (Oneiros) looks after Sleep (Hypnos), and so on. Describing their archetypal kinship, myth tells us where they really belong, namely, to Hekate (or Night), who is their sole originator, in what (horizontal) relations they are, and who supplies them with appetizing nourishment. Do not forget, Hekate is also κουροτρόφος, archetypal *nurse and nourisher.*

My story of Hekate and her children is nothing more than an attempt to build an imaginal background or dwelling place (*archetopos*) for those archetypal powers, where they may feel "at home." In a manner of speaking, I am trying to *emplot* them in a most suitable psychological narrative, or, to be more precise, Hekate *is* emplotting them in the best possible way. *Hekate narrans*, is a storyteller who both finds herself in archetypal stories already told and strives for self-constitution by emplotting herself and us in stories in the making. From Mark Johnson we learn that "[n]arrative is not just an explanatory device, but is actually constitutive of the way we experience things."[59] To be a subject or a self is to be able to furnish a story of oneself, to be able to tell the narrative of one's life. Here I also follow Donald Polkinghorne's definition of narrative as a "form of 'meaning making'" that organizes human experience into meaningful episodes, functioning as a "lens through which the apparently independent and disconnected elements of existence are seen as related parts of a whole."[60]

What Johnson and Polkinghorne both fail to keep in mind, however, is the fact that *mythology* is the *logos* of *mytheai* (μυθέαι—narrating, telling, speaking, recounting, and explaining). The reason for telling stories through which we emerge as subjects rests in myths. The "Queen of Phantom World," i.e., the Queen of Images, is the basis of our archetypal narrative. Each image she offers us is, at the same time, a story which begs to be recounted and interpreted. Every image tells a story! Each and every image possesses its own idiosyncratic narrative texture.[61] Hence, Hekate as a source of images is for me an imaginal *locus* or *archetopos* of a different kind from the one offered by Freud. Hekate's dual nature is manifested in the fact that she represents the archetypal ground or foundation of all our psychological material, and yet she is a weaver who emplots our perspectives and experiences.

Therefore, my archetypal hermeneutic investigation assumes that Hekate is the *archetopos* and emplotter of various powers that are unavoidable elements of any psychological endeavor or story. Hekate and her chthonic perspective represent the mythological style in narrating the psychological cosmos. If we are really so eager to work on and with the psyche we must descend to the Underworld in order to face the "Three-Faced One." Each of us who wishes to become an analyst must, willy-nilly, collaborate with the Ruler of Tartaros and her abundant progeny. Descent into the Underworld also implies that we are supposed to return to the upper world, empowered by the images we have encountered while down under. Traveling downwards and upwards (on the road as Hekate, or traveling upon her roads) will enable us to emplot our individual subjective histories as a dynamic coming from the past and moving into the future in such a manner that the past and the future figure as familiar features of the stories of ourselves as they unfold. Via Hekate, one shapes one's self and identity. By this I mean that the identity of the self consists in the degree to which the self is able to unify its past accomplishments and its future projects.

## *Hecatē Trivia*

We do not err to say that Hekate behaves as a "good-enough mother"; she is a soothing, warm, empathic caregiver who provides her children with the proper nourishment, holding, and protection. In a subtle yet firm way she safeguards their development. Like any other mother, she spends a lot of time securing proper food for her children, food that will give them optimal nourishment. The tasty sacrifices—the leftovers from the table or the household garbage—that we place at Hekate's altars are not something she selfishly enjoys all on her own; she sustains her nurslings with our votive presents. As a matter of fact, Freud corroborates my story with a description he left us in his book *The Interpretation of Dreams*, where he dealt with one of Hekate's children. In his effort to explain how dreams come into being, or with what kind of nutriments dreams are nourished, Freud wrote: "The day's residues in dreams are essential ingredients in the formation of dreams;"[62] the "residues of the previous day have been left over from the activity of waking life;"[63] "indifferent refuse left over from the previous day;"[64] "trivial elements,"[65] "this recent element is often of the most trivial kind;"[66] "the content of the dream itself … seems to be concerned with the most indifferent trivialities, which would be unworthy of our interest if we were awake;"[67] "the most trivial elements of a dream are indispensable to its interpretation."[68]

For Freud, then, the material that dreams are made of and their proper food are trivial and worthless "day-residues." Trifles, rubbish, or leftovers of scraps of every kind were sacrificed to Hekate, and Freud corroborates the accounts of ancient story tellers with scraps from his book on dreams.

For centuries the "Queen of Night" was implicated in dream interpretation, and we find her still working nowadays in our therapeutic premises. The goddess of magic applies her charms to transform the trash, morsels, scraps, and garbage of our daily life into holy nutriments. Ioan Couliano, an expert on Renaissance psychology, said in his great work *Eros and Magic in the Renaissance* that "the main entrance for all magic processes is fantasy."[69] Magic, Couliano explains, represents an imaginal process that bonds the individual soul to the *anima mundi*. "Magic is a phantasmatic process that makes use of the continuity of the individual pneuma and of the universal pneuma."[70] Psychic trash is saved by Hekate's magic, even transformed *via* the imagination into proper food for our soul. Now we can understand why she cherishes any kind of nutriment—junk food, tasteless meals, waste, rubbish, leftovers from the table, garbage: all of these are the necessary *ingredients* (Freud) of soul-making.

Dreams express themselves in images, through images, or as images, therefore I will extend my phantasmic observations on images as follows. Any image that is from the perspective of the upper world labeled insignificant, petty, trifling, or worthless might be placed on Hekate's altar. Through her blessing and magic, she saves flimsy, frivolous, or unsubstantial psychic material of various kinds, transforming it into highly potent images that will move our souls onwards. Through her magic, she makes an archetypal background for the residues of waking life, turning everything that is assessed as of no value or insignificant into narrative fragments by which we can weave our life stories further.

With this imaginal approach to Hekate, another of her essential characteristics makes its appearance. When advancing to her altar, one does not have to be clean, immaculate, spotless, or pure. Remember, she is *amoral*, unmindful of the virginally pure patterns of behavior so precious to our collective consciousness. The proper way of drawing near to her, of entering into her chthonic realm and her dark abodes is not by being pure and chaste; rather, it is *via* impurity, defilement, or messiness that one may approach the "Strong One" and the images she offers us. Truly, this communion with Hekate is marked by mutual indecency, lack of measure and honor. *Pax Hekateis* (*Pax deorum*) helps us in saving worthless, abandoned, or useless phenomena that would otherwise be projected or repressed. Hekate is not a bottomless *inferno* that swallows up everything; whatever has been eaten and digested will be returned as image spared from moralistic babble. Dirtiness, messiness, obscenity, lustfulness, and nastiness are avenues by which we may approach her realm and become a "child of Hekate."

As therapists we have to admit that psychologically speaking there is myth in junk and garbage, in defiled and base material; hence, the proper disposal of the leftovers of waking life in their rightful place—Hekate's altar—is nothing less than appropriate analytical intervention. In one ritual, the leftover scraps and waste were placed at midnight at a junction of three roads or at a crossroads where a statue of the threefold goddess had been erected, so that each of her three masks may lead off in at least three directions besides the one from which the refuse had been brought. By locating the mistress of the Underworld among other archetypal images, we will begin to develop another perspective in our therapeutic practice—a Hekatean perspective or consciousness.

A crucial psychological aspect of Hekate's character is represented by the places where she dwells—forked roads, crossways, or junctions of three roads. This is the reason why she was known among the ancient Greeks under the name Hekate *Trioditis* (Τριοδιτις—"one who is at the junction of three roads"). When she was absorbed into the Roman world, this epithet was translated into Latin, and she was invoked as *Hecatē Trivia*. Her title served as a root for the Latin word *trivialis*—of the street, common, usual, and everyday. In European languages *trivial* denotes—commonplace, common, trite, ordinary, rubbish, trifle, of little worth or importance, occupying oneself with trifles or unimportant matters, coarse, vulgar, banal, shabby, degraded, and base. In addition, it connotes a person standing at a crossroads such that he or she might be seen by everybody, or a thing or person not hidden from sight, or a fact that is known to everybody, and, last but not least, a person who is playful. This multiplicity of meanings, which situate her in a visible extraverted world, at the crossroad, in flirting and toying enactments, or in vulgar and playful activities, balance her one-sided introverted position. Through her introverted side, she places value on things outside of or below the *polis*, things shrouded in darkness, far away from our sight and knowledge, things that are mysterious or numinous; on the other hand, her trivial-extroverted aspect invests energy in *communitas*, in community, in what is common, in things visible by day, in what is happening in the marketplace, in foul language, in what is obvious, banal, or vulgar, or what is ready for play and fooling around. When her introverted side is offset by her extraverted one, Hekate may be constellated in people of whatever psychological type.

The mythical background and original significance of the trivial can entirely change our contemporary attitude to seemingly unimportant, banal, or worthless psychological phenomena. From now on, everything we perceive as common, shabby, inconsequential, degraded, or paltry may possess an archetypal ground as well. What is more, we realize that our daily trivialities and trifles are "descended" from the archetype, which is the source of basic psychic processes and powers (love, death, oblivion, sleeping, dreaming, strife, blame, friendship, etc.) which are so necessary in every possible therapy. Let us keep in mind that Hekate Trivia is first and foremost *psychopompos*! Thus, I will declare: There is no imagination that is not inherently trivial. By necessity, images are trivial. So are our stories. What shall we say about contemporary art? It is trivial and vulgar too, and yet provocative and creative. Likewise, evil can be banal, yet profound and unfathomable. Led by Hekatean consciousness, we can shape her peculiar psychotherapy. Hekate's therapy is not analysis of the trivial, but one led *by* the trivial. Her/our psychotherapy has to be trivial.

*Hekatean psychotherapy* concerns itself with finding connections between the trivialities of life and the psyche. Its trivial perspective is concomitantly superimposed and grounding, because she must reveal herself in every human project or activity. Psychological Puritanism is foreign to her, i.e., she saves images in their entire wealth and diversity. While the puritanical perspective visualizes the soul (or is it the puritan soul?) and psychic processes in pairs of opposites—clean-unclean, light-dark, mind-body, valuable-worthless, meaningful-meaningless—thus splitting images and narratives (and soul as well) apart, Hekate observes images as wholes and as divine yet playful and trivial phenomena. From her perspective, every narrative possesses value because its merit is contained in its polysemic and polyvalent character. As a matter of fact, the trivial is a psychic phenomenon perceptible only by means of the same psychic consciousness as it is itself composed of. We perceive trivial images with Hekatean eyes, or we hear banal stories through her imaginal ear. From her perspective, only the trivial has substance, only trifles truly matter.

The trivial is the very stuff of the psyche, the inner blackness that pulls downwards out of the light and life, keeping us in unrelenting bondage to the Underworld. At the same time, the trivial could be understood as indeterminable constancy in the psyche. Trivial imagery can pop up in the therapeutic here and now, can explode into the analytical process at any given moment, even in the first session, regardless of the circumstances, whether in a borderline rage or not, or in anaclictic depression, devoid of any emotion.

---

These scraps on triviality that I have offered here were shaped and interpreted mostly by my own trifling perspective, but support and encouragement in following this approach came from James Hillman, who said: "Because psychology is a hermeneutical discipline having to do with interpretative meaning, with significances, there are no objective data independent of the subjective vision of the gatherer. A psychologist will be bound to see his own myth in his material."[71] I hope that you now have an impression of the manifold ways in which Hekate can aid our psychotherapeutic undertakings. Through her unique psychic nature and numerous revelations, she compensates and balances soul. She has her erratic or borderline attitude to analysis: she is able to connect us to very foreign or trivial aspects of the psyche. Her elusive and twisted perspective can help us to make an image of each psychic happening that the analyst is confronted with. However, if you did not find a sound theoretical frame of reference in my paper, or meaningful and concise explanations, the fault is not mine; with her borderline aspect, her elusive nature, and her "true otherness," Hekate guided and directed the story of herself.

## *NOTES*

[1] This essay is abstracted from a larger work on Hekate and Artemis (in preparation for publication), and has been edited for the current volume. The material offered here is inspired by James Hillman's book *The Dream and the Underworld* (New York: Harper & Row, 1979).

[2] Hillman, *Dream and Underworld*, p. 23.

[3] James Hillman, "Image-sense" in *Working with Images: The Theoretical Base of Archetypal Psychology*, ed. B. Sells (Woodstock, CT: Spring Publications, 1979/2000), p. 7.

[4] C. G. Jung, *Memories, Dreams, Reflections* (London: Collins, 1967), p. 17, hereafter abbreviated to *MDR*.

[5] Works on Cardano that have helped me are: H. C. Lea, *Materials toward a History of Witchcraft*, vol. 2 (Philadelphia, PA: University of

Pennsylvania Press, 1939); A. Grafton, *Cardano's Cosmos* (Cambridge, MA: Harvard University Press, 1999); and A. Maggi, *Satan's Rhetoric: A Study of Renaissance Demonology* (Chicago, IL: University of Chicago Press, 2001).

[6] *Hekate krataiis*—Hekate of wide force or Hekate the strong one.

[7] Carl Kerényi, *The Gods of the Greeks* (London: Thames & Hudson, 1985), p. 35.

[8] Martin Nilsson, *Greek Popular Religion* (New York: Columbia University Press, 1940), p. 90.

[9] *Ibid.*, p. 91.

[10] Kerényi, p. 36.

[11] Marija Gimbutas, *The Goddesses and Gods of Old Europe* (London: Thames and Hudson, 1989), p. 198.

[12] C. G. Jung, and Carl Kerényi, *Essays on a Science of Mythology: The Myth of the Divine Child and the Mysteries of Eleusis*, Bollingen Series XXII (Princeton, NJ: Princeton University Press, 1969).

[13] Cf. David L. Miller, "Between God and the Gods—Trinity," *Eranos* 49 (1980) (Frankfurt: Insel Verlag, 1982), p. 129.

[14] In the astral-medicine system of Catalan philosopher Ramon Lull, the highest divine essence is Three. In his *Ars Magna*, three geometrical figures are involved: the triangle, the square and the circle. The triangle symbolizes the divine, the square stands for the four elements, and the circle symbolize the heavens. See Frances Yates, *The Occult Philosophy in the Elizabethan Age* (London: Routledge, 2001), pp. 11-18.

[15] Cf. Marie-Louise von Franz, *Psyche and Matter* (Boston, MA: Shambhala, 1992).

[16] *Ibid.*, p. 157.

[17] Jung, *MDR*, pp. 241-2.

[18] In her essay "Meaning and Order," von Franz describes how an archetype constellates itself through such time-phases in a process of reaching consciousness. See *Psyche and Matter*, pp. 283-4.

[19] C. G. Jung, "A Psychological Approach to the Dogma of the Trinity," *The Collected Works of C. G. Jung*, trans. R. F. C. Hull, vol. 11 (Princeton, NJ: Princeton University Press, 1969), p. 119; hereafter abbreviated to *CW* followed by volume number and page number.

[20] Marsilio Ficino, *Commentary on Plato's Symposium on Love* (Woodstock, CT: Spring Publications, 1985), p. 45.

[21] In Ramon Lull's *Ars Magna*, the triangle stands for the divine. For further details, see Yates, pp. 11-18.

[22] In Christian Trinitarian doctrine, *Personality* is the outcome of the relationship between the Three Persons in the Godhead.

[23] Apollonius Rhodius, *Argonautica* 3. 840.

[24] Hillman, *Dream and Underworld*, pp. 46-7.

[25] Eshil, Sofokle, Euripid, *Grèke tragedije*, trans. M. Djuric (Belgrade: Dereta, 1994), p. 612.

[26] Cf. Gaston Bachelard, *Air and Dreams: An Essay on the Imagination of Movement* (Dallas, TX: The Dallas Institute Publications, 1988), pp. 1-2.

[27] Gaston Bachelard, *Water and Dreams: An Essay on the Imagination of Matter* (Dallas, TX: The Pegasus Foundation, 1994), p. 103.

[28] Nilsson, pp. 90-91.

[29] J. Seznec, *The Survival of the Pagan Gods* (Princeton, NJ: Princeton University Press, 1972), p. 252.

[30] Gaston Bachelard, *The Poetics of Space* (Boston, MA: Beacon Press, 1994), p. xxxvii.

[31] Gaston Bachelard, *Lautréamont* (Dallas, TX: The Dallas Institute Publications, 1986), p. 89.

[32] Kerényi, *The Gods of the Greeks* (London: Thames & Hudson, 1985), p. 36.

[33] Nilsson, pp. 96.

[34] *Ibid.*

[35] For more on the role of primitive and irrational forces in Greek mentality, see E. R. Dodds, *The Greeks and the Irrational* (Berkeley, CA: University of California Press, 1991).

[36] Lewis Richard Farnell, *The Cults of the Greek States*, vol. 2 (New Rochelle, N.Y.: Caratzars Brothers, 1977), p. 519.

[37] James Hillman, *Pan and the Nightmare*, new rev. edition (Woodstock, CT: Spring Publications, 2000), p. 182.

[38] James Hillman, *Re-Visioning Psychology* (New York: Harper & Row, 1975), p. 188.

[39] George E. Atwood and Robert D. Stolorow, *Structures of Subjectivity: Explorations in Psychoanalytic Phenomenology* (Hillsdale, NJ: The Analytic Press, 1984), p. 64.

[40] Donna M. Orange, *Emotional Understanding: Studies in Psychoanalytic Epistemology* (New York and London: The Guilford Press, 1995), p. 9.

[41] C. G. Jung, *CW* 16, see especially p. 206, where Mercurius is described as a trinity, or pp. 215-6, where he is the *coniunctio* factor depicted as three living things: the queen, the king, and the dove of the Holy Ghost.

[42] Hillman, *Dream and Underworld*, p. 188.

[43] Edward S. Casey: "Getting Placed: Soul in Space," in *Spirit and Soul: Essays in Philosophical Psychology* (Dallas, TX: Spring Publications, 1991).

[44] Karl Kerényi, *Hermes: Guide of Souls* (Woodstock, CT: Spring Publications, 1996), p. 101.

[45] Farnell, p. 517.

[46] Apollonius of Rhodes, *Argonautica* 3. 840.

[47] Martin Heidegger, *Poetry, Language, Thought* (New York: Harper & Row, 1975), p. 154.

[48] Farnell, p. 514.

[49] John Ferguson, *The Religions of the Roman Empire* (London: Thames and Hudson, 1970), p. 157.

[50] Farnell, p. 514.

[51] *Ibid.*, p. 519.

[52] *Ibid.*, p. 511.

[53] V. Zamarovsky, (1985) *Junaci antièkih mitova* (Zagreb: Školska knjiga, 1985), p. 127.

[54] Sappho, *Greek Lyric* I, Valerius Flaccus, *Argonautica* 7. 515, and Nonnus, *Dionysiaca* 44. 198.

[55] Edwin M. Duval, "'Comme Hecaté': Mythography and the Macrocosm in an Epigramme by Maurice Scève," *Bibliothèque d'Humanisme et Renaissance* 40, no. 1 (1979): 7-22.

[56] "For, by the sacred radiance of the sun, / The mysteries of Hecate, and the night; ..."—William Shakespeare, *King Lear*, Act I, scene 1, lines 121-122.

[57] Dom Antoine Joseph Pernety, *Dictionnaire mytho-hermétique,* Paris, 1758/1787.

[58] She was the mother of other, no less psychologically important, children: Blame, Doom, Fate, Woe, Destinies, Indignation, Deceit, and Friendship. Hesiod, *Theogony*, 11. 211-225.

[59] Mark Johnson, *Moral Imagination: Implications of Cognitive Science for Ethics* (Chicago, IL: The University of Chicago Press, 1993), p. 11.

[60] Donald E. Polkinghorne, *Narrative Knowing and the Human Science* (Albany, NY: State University of New York Press, 1988), p. 36.

[61] Cf. James Hillman, "Further notes on Images," *Spring* (1978): pp. 152-182; see also James Hillman, "The Fiction of Case History," in *Healing Fiction* (Barrytown, N.Y.: Station Hill Press, 1983), pp. 1-49.

[62] Sigmund Freud, *The Interpretation of Dreams*, The Standard Edition of Complete Psychological Works of Sigmund Freud, ed. and trans. James Strachey *et al.*, vol. 5 (London: Hogarth Press, 1953), p. 562.

[63] *Ibid.*, p. 589.

[64] *Ibid.*, p. 589.

[65] *Ibid.*, p. 564.

[66] *Ibid.*, p. 563.

[67] *Ibid.*, p. 656.

[68] *Ibid.*, p. 513.

[69] Ioan P. Couliano, *Eros and Magic in the Renaissance* (Chicago, IL: The University of Chicago Press, 1987), p. 92.

[70] *Ibid.*, p. 88.

[71] Hillman, *Dream and Underworld*, p. 216.

ROBERT BOSNAK is a Jungian psychoanalyst who left his native Holland in 1971 to study in Zürich at the C. G. Jung Institute, where James Hillman was his primary training analyst. He had his psychoanalytic practice in Cambridge, MA from 1977 to 2003. He currently lives and works in Sydney, Australia. He also travels around the world training therapists, actors, and other artists in the *embodied imagination* method he has developed, based on the work of Jung, Hillman, Corbin, and Stanislavski. His methods have been used as a rehearsal technique by various theater companies, including the Royal Shakespeare Company in Stratford. In 1997, he co-founded the website www.cyberdreamwork.com, the first interactive site for real-time voice and video work with imagery. With Stephen Aizenstat he co-organized the 2007 conference *Imagination and Medicine*, aimed at the establishment of an integrative medical healing sanctuary in Santa Barbara. A book containing the proceedings of this conference will be published by Spring Journal Books in 2008. His most recent book, *Embodiment: Creative Imagination in Medicine, Art and Travel,* was published by Routledge in 2007.

# 24

# How a Character Embodies an Actor

ROBERT BOSNAK

In August 1993 it suddenly became glaringly apparent to me that my deeply held conviction that the dreams that I have are mine was a reflection of the beliefs of my culture and had nothing to do with the true nature of dreaming. I was sitting with Nganyinitja, an old tribal Aboriginal woman, who had lived the ancient uninterrupted nomadic Pitjantjatjara lifestyle in the bush before she first met white fellas at the mission as a teenager. Her English was very poor, and we talked dreams through a translator around a campfire in the middle of the red Australian desert. She told me that she had dreamed of a song she had never heard before and a dance in an ever-expanding circle around a campfire. I asked her if she felt the dream might be related to the work that was her passion: inviting numbers of white folk to her Outback lands, of which she was the traditional guardian, to teach them the old ways. I said that ever-expanding groups of people were dancing around her fire to a song that no one had heard before, because most *Anangu* keep their traditions private. It seemed obvious to me that the dream portrayed some aspect of her life. I was surprised that she could not understand the translator, who had to use ever more words. After several minutes of fruitless attempts, she said, "Maybe," just to be polite. Then she gave me an explanation of the dream that changed my understanding of dreaming. She said that she had to go back to her people and teach them the song and the dance so they could dance it for the landscape in order to keep its memory intact. The dream was generated by an ancient force which makes the Pitjantjatjara people sing the land in order for it to stay vibrantly alive. In short, Nganyinitja explained to me that the dream had a relationship to her but that it was not for her. It was a dream for the land. As the conversation ended, I realized that everything I had ever thought true about dreaming had in fact been thoughts about my culture. If Nganyinitja could experience the dream as not being for her, but as having been dreamed vicariously for the landscape, then my understanding that dreams are primarily about the life of the one who dreams them must be equally culturally biased. Such an understanding of dreams grows out of the Western dogma of individualism and is not a statement about dreaming itself.

In 2006, the Netherlands planned a year-long celebration in honor of Freud's 150$^{th}$ birthday, which would culminate in "Night of the Dream" at the Schouwburg, Amsterdam's oldest permanent theater. Having grown up in Holland, I regarded the Schouwburg as a great cultural landmark, like the Sydney Opera House or Carnegie Hall. So when I was asked to show my stuff before a sell-out audience in the intimate old-fashioned hall worthy of a romantic film, with its red velvet chairs rising up balcony after balcony to a domed ceiling painted with clouds, I was gripped by a hodgepodge of emotions difficult to disentangle.

I had flown in the week before from my home in Sydney, after having attended the Opera House opening of the Bell Shakespeare production of *The Tempest*, which we had dreamworked, as we had the two previous productions of the 2006 season. The show was equal to Prospero's magic; our work showed through in the performance of several actors, and I felt a profound satisfaction.

Janet Sonenberg and I had developed the method of dreamworking plays from the mid-90s on at M.I.T. in Cambridge, Mass., where she is a professor in the drama department. Our method takes the point of view that a character, when called to life in a theatrical production, takes possession of the actor. Such a character, we thought, behaves like a living being, and when it is fully in possession of the actor, it might have a dream life of its own. We proposed that when given the chance, the character might manifest itself clothed in the personal images of the actor. Time and again, our hypothesis proved fruitful. John Bell's Prospero's relation to Miranda, his daughter, came up in the actor's dreams as the innocent love of John for his young granddaughter; Miranda's complicated passion for young prince Ferdinand, apparently against her Father's wishes, arose in the actress's dream of two swans on a polluted lake; Ferdinand's maturation process—after being stranded on the island, thinking he had lost his father and thereby becoming king of Naples, but also meeting the love of his life—was portrayed in the actor's dream of a mature man on skates flying a kite in a tempestuous lightning storm, electrifying the body which had to contain all the diverging vectors—giving a distinct sense of the turmoil that coming-of-age brings in its wake. After the actors had allowed the dreams to embody them, their performance reached a depth of authenticity that had not previously been present.

The act of dreaming on behalf of someone else is called dreaming by proxy and had been practiced in classical antiquity, when it was possible to hire a dreamer at a healing temple to receive vicariously a healing dream on behalf of a patient who was not able to dream for himself for herself. As I found out while speaking with Nganyinytja, our contemporary Western certainty that our dreams are about us, an idea propounded with such implicit faith by Freud, is actually a cultural bias. Such cultural presuppositions do not say anything about dreams, but only repeat assumptions implicit in the ambient waking culture.

For years I had searched for a self-evident definition of dreaming on which we might all agree, a pre-cultural definition based on the dreamed phenomena themselves—a definition from the point of view of dreaming, not from the perspective of waking. Finally I came up with a formal definition, namely, that *a dream is a quasi-physical environment where events take place*. All else is waking bias subject to culture.

Fast forward to my work on Saturday, September 30, 2006, before an audience of Freudian psychoanalysts and other Western minds held firmly in the belief that dreams belong to the personal domain. In an interview on stage preceding my dreamwork with the actors, a well-known Dutch psychoanalyst had declared, without having to explain herself any further, that dreams are messages from ourselves to ourselves, thereby unconsciously asserting the hegemony of Western individualism.

Looking into the black hole created by the bright lights, I knew that the three minutes I had been allotted to explain my theoretical framework to an audience so utterly convinced of the individual nature of dreaming would be an exercise in futility. All I could do was focus on speaking Dutch correctly after having lived out of the country for 35 years, hoping it would not suddenly stall on me. I had to trust that our demonstration would speak for itself.

Flashback to the Monday before the Saturday event. The artists' entry to the Schouwburg is behind an unassuming door leading to a hall with glass doors posing as sliders but which, surprisingly, open up in your face. I almost fall over backwards to avoid a collision; then I get lost in a labyrinth of hallways leading to doors that open up to dead ends.

Finally I end up in the foyer where we are supposed to gather. There I meet the actors, Katja Schuurman and Pierre Bokma. Katja is an actress with a body of such languid feline fluidity and sensuous, shy innocence that it is immediately obvious why she is one of the leading media stars and sex symbols in the country. Pierre has a powerful presence, a brooding complexity, behind a serious frown and the low center of gravity of a man of a much larger physique. He is a renowned classical actor. Our task is to present a scene from their movie *Interview* by Theo van Gogh to the audience at the Schouwburg, then dreamwork it in public and have the actors play the scene again on stage so the audience may judge if there are striking differences between the two performances. Today we meet for the first phase of the dreamworked acting process, the incubation phase, the seeding of dreams.

Dream incubation is a method of intentional dreaming geared toward a response from the dreaming imagination. We attempt to elicit a dream that we can treat as a vicarious dream, dreamed for the character. Just as a professional dreamer for hire at a healing temple was to receive a dream incubated by the illness on behalf of a patient who could not host the dream herself, the actor makes his or her own material available for the character to wear like a costume. Even though the dream will manifestly consist of the personal images of the actor, we posit that the creative imagination of the character will inhabit them and shape them to its purposes. In my 2007 book *Embodiment: Creative Imagination in Medicine, Art and Travel*, I have described how, following Henry Corbin, I understand image-presences to be embodiments of their own intelligence. In the process of dreaming by proxy, we approach the dreamed images, embodied in the vernacular of the actor, *as if* they were suffused by the character's intelligence.

Classical antiquity had no problem with the fact that dream images are not who they seem. When Telemachus was encouraged to search for his father Odysseus, Athena came to him in the body of Mentor, Telemachus's teacher. She wore Mentor as a costume, so to speak. To Telemachus's mother, Penelope, the goddess presented herself as Penelope's waking-life sister. In other words, a dominant of the creative imagination, such as a goddess, was understood to adopt a person from daily life with which to embody itself.

Usually, we come in around the third week of the rehearsal process, when the actors have had a chance to inhabit the characters and their world, and the text is known by heart. Our process reverses the roles: before it, the actor strives to inhabit the character; after our work, the character takes possession of the actor, taking over his or her body within the limits of his or her craft and the author's text. As in a sonnet, creative forces press against preset forms. The pressure this evokes takes the actor by surprise, causing the text to sing afresh. At least, that is the result hoped for. One of the Royal Shakespeare Company actors, Naomi Frederick, describes the subsequent unfolding of such a dreamworked state as follows:

> After working with the dream, I was not in the body I anticipated. It was not what I had thought of for myself. It was very interesting, being displaced. It was an out-of-control thing that both fired me up and weakened me. I was in an unfamiliar body. I was relying entirely on the feelings you helped me find. I don't usually feel as much, particularly in the early stages of rehearsal. It was like a cradle. The moment you came upon a line, you suddenly found yourself *there*. And a new feeling would feed in, one of the feelings you [the dreamworker] had addressed, and that would then inform the next bit. It was not cerebral, it was physical.

*Interview* is a strange film. Van Gogh made it some time before he was assassinated by the kind of zealot despised by history, who kills because he has a direct line to a grand homicidal Truth. The movie was made with Katja Schuurman in mind, and the female character is called Katja Stuurman. Katja's character is a sex symbol soap star, the kind that those who believe in serious art look down upon and envy. Pierre's character is called Pierre Peters, and is *not* based on Pierre Bokma. Peters is an arrogant snob, a journalist who has been given the assignment to interview Katja the Star on the very night that the government in The Hague is falling and every self-respecting journalist in the country wants to be there—Pierre especially, since he had predicted the event weeks in advance and considers it his story. So here he is at Katja's place, doing an interview he hates doing, with a woman he despises to begin with. In his eyes, she is some kind of dumb tits-and-ass subject for a piece of work incomparable with the kind of journalism he did as a war correspondent in Yugoslavia. But instead of his interviewing her, she asks him questions, seducing him and at the same time keeping him at bay, as a kind of punishment for his insolence. She intuits that he is hiding something. While Katja is out of the room, Pierre finds a diary, and on reading it, he discovers that the writer of the diary has to have a mastectomy. Katja's breasts are famous all over the land, and this would be just the sort of scoop that he could report on. Katja is aghast that he has read the diary. Pierre promises that he will not use the information. They agree to exchange confidences. Katja reads from the diary, and Pierre reveals the skeleton in his own closet: he has murdered his alcoholic wife in such a manner that the crime cannot be traced, after she caused an accident while driving drunk near their Dutch home when he was in Yugoslavia, an accident in which their daughter was killed. Katja videotapes his confession in the same way that he had audiotaped her reading of the diary. She leaves the room and he takes out the tape, which Katja has surreptitiously replaced with another one beforehand. He walks down the stairs calling his editor with the scoop that Katja Stuurman is to have a mastectomy. Outside, he turns to see Katja standing on the balcony with the diary, which she now truthfully reveals to be that of a friend. With her other hand she waves the tape that contains his confession of murder. We hear the sirens of a police car on its way to arrest Pierre. He has been outmaneuvered in his vain underestimation of Katja the Star, whose superior performance has been his downfall.

In the scene that will be shown at the Schouwburg on Saturday, Katja provokes Pierre by saying that he has not been to Yugoslavia at all. That he is all bluff. Enraged, he begins to strangle her, throws her down on the couch, jumps on top of her, fuming about the fact that she questions his authenticity. A three-minute scene.

The film had been shot three years before. In the meantime, Katja had gotten married to a man she loves deeply, and she has obviously matured significantly since the filming. The two actors will present a theatrical performance of a scene, chosen by Pierre, that consists of a lot of text by Pierre and a great deal of reaction shots of Katja. The time lapse and the shift in medium will make it difficult for the audience to judge whether any differences between the film and the performance on Saturday night are due to the dreamwork or to uncontrolled variables. A highly flawed experiment! That, and having three minutes to explain it all to an audience of Freudians, while I am ostensibly of the Jungian persuasion .... Foolishly, I rush in.

Intentional dreaming attempts to set up a communication between waking and dreaming. We know from neuroscience that dreams are not primarily cognitive events. Embodied emotion appears to be the shaper of dreams. The two iconic adversaries in current laboratory dream research, Mark Solms and Allan Hobson, agree about the fact that brain imaging REM data show "a preferential activation of limbic and paralimbic regions in the forebrain ... [implying] ... that *dream emotion may be a primary shaper of dream* plots rather than playing a secondary role."[1]

Based on this well-established scientific theory, it is clear that one cannot just ask the dreaming imagination a cognitive question. It would be like speaking Chinese to a Spaniard. Intentional dreaming is like placing a call, inviting the creative imagination to pick up and respond. We have to translate our outgoing call into a set of embodied emotional states, into the language of dreaming. Ever since antiquity, placing the call has been named "dream incubation." In her book *Dreamwork for Actors*, Janet Sonenberg calls it "seeding the dream."

Before we start with Katja's incubation, I need to explain briefly the method of embodied imagination as I practice it. Based on the definition of image from the standpoint of dreaming as a quasi-physical environment in which we find ourselves, it is necessary to access a state of consciousness close to dreaming in order to gain entry to this image realm. The closest we can approach dreaming without being asleep is in the hypnagogic state, the state of consciousness we pass through in the process of falling asleep. The hypnagogic state is well documented in dream laboratory research and consists of two phases: the waking hypnagogic state and the sleeping hypnagogic state, with the transition between them being usually imperceptible. The sleeping hypnagogic state is called "sleep-onset." After REM sleep, this is the most creative state of the dreaming imagination. Dreams are reported in 95% of sleep laboratory awakenings that occur during REM sleep, while the corresponding figure for sleep-onset awakenings is 70%. REM sleep is difficult to access and finds the brain in a delirious state (as Allan Hobson notes in his 1999 book *Dreaming as Delirium: How the Brain Goes out of Its Mind*[2]). During sleep-onset, the dreaming corresponds to a brain-set relatively similar to the waking brain and as such is partially accessible to waking consciousness. The waking hypnagogic state is of a twilight nature and the dreamer is able to experience images as environments. This state of consciousness also appears naturally during flashbacks after severe traumatic moments, such as war or rape, when the experiencer suddenly finds himself or herself back in a quasi-physical simulation of the environment in which the trauma happened. A flashback, like an image, is not just visual: it is an environment that elicits responses from all the senses. The twilight hypnagogic state, therefore, does not give rise to narrative memories, but to flashbacks. A narrative memory in neuroscience is called an explicit memory, a memory *about* an event and is related strongly to the hippocampus region of the brain. A flashback is an implicit memory, a fully embodied emotional re-living of an event, involving primarily the limbic regions such as the amygdala. As a method, embodied imagination helps the experiencer to enter into a waking hypnagogic state that leads him or her into a flashback of a previously experienced environment. This flashback gives rise to a complex embodied state. The state is then etched into the body as a sense memory, a technique derived from acting.

A beautiful description of the sense memory technique is given by Andy Serkis, the brilliant actor who plays Gollum in the movie trilogy *The Lord of the Rings*. Gollum's famous voice, one of the most memorable elements in both Tolkien's *The Hobbit* and his *The Lord of the Rings* trilogy, became Andy's touchstone and key to the character. "I had an emotional root to that sound," he says. "For me, it is where his pain is trapped. That emotional memory is trapped in that part of his body, his throat. In just doing the voice, I immediately got into the physicality of Gollum, and embodied the part as I would if I were playing it for real."[3]

A complex image gives rise to a multiplicity of such embodied states as Serkis mentions, which are each imprinted as sense memories in different parts of the body. This creates a "memory body." During the apotheosis of embodied imagination, called the composite, all embodiments are triggered simultaneously, giving rise to an intricate network of states. The following work is a demonstration of this.

Katja's character has just snorted coke before the scene begins. As the character, she can feel how the effect of the coke enters in through the back, moves up her chest, bends her backwards and comes over her like a wave, her jaws tighten, her eyes open wide as she holds on to the sink. At the same time the character feels pleasantly distant from the world. We locate this embodied state as a sense memory in the point of entry in her back, between the shoulders, from where the coke impulse spreads throughout her body. We focus on this point of entry until it is solidly engraved as a sense memory. When this sense memory location is tripped at some later moment, Katja will be instantly aware of each element in the coke scene with all the accompanying feelings and sensations. In the same way, we focus upon other emotions: her desire to win and to exercise control over Pierre, a desire located in her neck; the moment of fright, located in the back of the throat; and her dread, located in her hands. Then I help her identify with Pierre—feeling what he experiences—by having her become fully aware of his grip on her throat: she feels the sensations of strangulation, senses the pressure of the hands, and feels the intention in them. She can sense in his hand how Pierre is straining to contain himself until he bursts all over her. She traces his strain and explosion to his belly, where it settles as another location in her sense memory body.

This last embodiment, accessed through an identification with Pierre's character, is based on the central idea of embodied imagination, derived from the work of Corbin, namely, that each image element is an embodiment of its own intelligence. An image environment, which always consists of a variety of elements, is a network of intelligences.

An intelligence alien to the protagonist (usually called "I") may be accessed by way of identification. When fully identified with an alien character, the experiencer enters the subjectivity of "other," without "other" losing his fundamental otherness. This I call *paradoxical introception.* Katja feels Pierre's subjective experience of strain and explosion, all the while being aware it is not her own experience as Katja.

At this point in the technique we are dealing with three fundamentally different "bodies": two image bodies and one memory body. The image bodies stem from the identification with image intelligences in the image-environment, either protagonist or other, Katja Stuurman and Pierre Peters; the memory body is the result of sense memory imprints upon the body in the physical environment, Katja Schuurman's. While in the waking hypnagogic state, the experiencer is in a dual consciousness: one awareness is fully in the quasi-physical image environment, while the other is fully aware of the fact that she is surrounded by imagination and is simultaneously in a physical environment outside the image in a body-in-the-room. The latter awareness is employed for the memory body: while Katja is in a paradoxical introception of Pierre, the resulting sense memory, the strain in his belly, is implanted in Katja's body-in-the-room.

Ivon Voss, an accomplished Dutch dreamworker, is my assistant in this project. She makes notes and feeds them back to me when I lose track of the elements in the complexity of body states we end up with. In the end, I help Katja to hold all the states together; she is able to do this after a few minutes of concentrated practice. She remarks how frequently her mind is all over the place, and that it feels helpful to be able to contain all these impulses in a single *physical* awareness. Her body-in-the-room is now "tattooed" with a network of sense memories that embody the essential composition of the scene. This body Katja will call up for half a minute before going to bed at night in order to attract dreaming by way of a complex "magnetic" field. By including an element of Pierre's experience we not only incubate Katja's character, but the relationship between them as well.

During the week, we get anxious phone calls that she is not dreaming. She's trying too hard. I tell her to drink two large glasses of water before going to bed and to put a pad and pencil in the bathroom.

Usually, the whole process of trying to catch a dream after starting out the night in the character's body shapes the subsequent dreams increasingly. Like an anxious magnet, it attracts unfamiliar imagination from elsewhere.

In Pierre's dream after his incubation, this process of giving over the reins to the *involuntary* imagination may be portrayed in the image of his being obliged to travel due north by boat, and placing a call to a woman who has to help him get to the other side but has never done this before. At first, she is very reluctant to get him the transportation, but finally he convinces her to do so. It reminds me of the instruction given to the actor to call upon the dreaming to follow the compass due north to the other side, that is, to the *involuntary* creative imagination (portrayed as a hesitating female helper who has never done this before and is *unwilling* at first), to find fresh inspiration—a process the actor has never before attempted. In Pierre's dream, the woman-from-the-other-side is both an evil cackling witch and a beautiful transcendent image of a woman. This double-ness heralds an experience that is simultaneously out of control and intensely frightening to the habitual self on the one hand, while giving access to the beauty of the inspiring image on the other. As RSC actor Naomi Frederick told us in the quote above, giving over the reins to the involuntary imagination, while bringing precious rewards, is far from comfortable, provoking eerie echoes of the unknown. This is not gratuitous improv; it carries the germs of witchcraft and possession.

That Friday, at the end of her dreaming week, we return with Katja to the same foyer in the Schouwburg. The camera woman is ready—I do not get lost in the bowels of the building. Katja has caught two images. She is very apologetic. No narratives, just images. I am pleased. This work is more indebted to images than to narrative. Narrative makes us try to figure things out and search for clues and plot, the unavoidable Sherlock Holmes task of classical dream interpretation, which may quicken the mind, but often dissociates from body. To do her work correctly, the actor needs to embody text in a spontaneous act of physical intelligence. Image environments possess the actor and infuse her with fresh physical information, giving access to a source of continuous unselfconscious character formation.

Katja dreams of her parents' home; she is sitting around a rectangular table with three characters—two of them familiar: her husband and her sister; the third arising from the collective imagination: a fat soap actor. In a second image she finds herself in a store. Behind a white counter, abusing customers, is an angry young woman who does not want to be there.

Let us keep in mind that we are taking the perspective that *these are vicarious images dreamed by proxy for the character*. We are not interested in Katja's personal associations, which would lead us into the world of the actor, not that of the character. We assume that the character's world has created this environment, knowing that this meta-perspective arises from the phenomena just as little, or as much, as the conviction that Katja's dreams are about Katja; that Katja dreams about her familiars does not mean that these figures are identical to the physical people whose likeness they bear. Her physical husband sleeps next to her, possibly involved in a dreaming of his own, and her factual sister is doing god-knows-what. Upon awakening, we know that dreamed presences are simulacra, quasi-physical imitations, not physical beings. The assumption that an imitation corresponds to its physical counterpart is an implicit meta-position, always a conjecture, and can never be demonstrated.

Michael Taussig, in his groundbreaking book *Mimesis and Alterity*, describes a fetish among the Cuna people, a curing figurine, which is a copy of an actual figure of a white colonizer.

> With this we are plunged, so I believe, into a paradox—namely that the copy, magically effective as it is, with the point-for-point correspondences of body part to body part, ... is *not a copy*—not a copy, that is, in the sense of being what we might generally mean when we say a "faithful" copy. Yet for it to be (magically) effective on the real world of things, persons, and events, it would very much seem that it has to be just that—a "faithful" copy ....[4]

In the meta-position corresponding to the act of dreaming by proxy, we may understand all the elements of Katja's dream as fetishes containing the efficacy of the character for whom she dreamed them. A meta-position is taken up for the sake of expedience: in therapeutic dreamwork it is frequently profitable to assume that an imitation symbolizes the original; in theater dreamwork it is not.

I begin with two quick silent assessments: the first dream environment feels familiar and safe, while the second is pervaded by an air of threat; and the fat soap actor, introduced with a giggle as "my sister's boyfriend, which in real life he is not," is the most ahistorical presence. I assume that if I start out with this character we will not instantly get into a confusion between simulacrum and physical counterpart. Katja knows for a giggle-provoking fact that the soap actor is not her sister's boyfriend. So there we enter.

I help her observe the environment, the wooden quality of the table, the light coming in through the window. Fat-Man's body is large, very different from Katja's physical self, which is lithe and petite. I help her sense into the voluminous body of the big man. After identifying with his presence, she can feel an unusual spaciousness, especially in the chest. Her own body is much more compact. She breathes in deeply.

Next we look at the sister. The presence looks different from her actual sister. This character is considerably calmer looking. We focus upon the difference between the actual sister and the dream-sister, since deviations from the factual point to strong imaginative activity. Dream-Sister's calm is felt as a quiet in the stomach. Finally, I help her concentrate her attention upon her husband. As she senses deeply into their merged state, she feels his presence fused with her left shoulder, as if they were Siamese twins.

The camera woman shoots our closed-eyed conversation from the hip.

Now we shift our attention to the young woman behind the counter. She is mean to the customers. As Katja is able to identify with this woman, who is a little younger than herself, she instantly feels the woman's intense frustration in the throat. She says nasty things to try to rid herself of the frustrating feelings, a strategy that results in little shocks and brief eruptions of relief. But the frustration is too great to be gotten rid of entirely. This frustrates the store clerk even more. She moves lightly for an instant, but then heavily with frustration once again. It is felt in the throat and the jaws.

Katja Schuurman ends up with a body composed of stability in the belly, ample breath in the chest, intense frustration in the throat and jaws, which can only be partially defused by nastiness—all of which is suffused with a symbiotic desire to merge. The character Katja Stuurman in the scene to be performed is intensely frustrated with Pierre Peters. Despite the wounding exchange of nastiness, she is unflappable, having enough breath and stamina to trick Peters into a confession, while at the same time struggling with a desire to merge and get through to him. The embodied composite seems relevant.

Saturday night, after the extensive three-minute in-depth explanation of my work, the Schouwburg audience is shown a five-minute clip of the incubation work with Katja and Pierre, plus a few minutes of Katja's dreamwork, from which the nastiness and angry frustrations have erroneously been edited out, leaving the audience a false pretty picture without inherent tensions. Then I work with Pierre's dream. This is the first time ever that this method has been applied outside of the rehearsal room, in front of an audience. The safety level is well below zero. I have been allotted 20 minutes, which is very brief for a piece of dreamwork.

Pierre and I are sitting on two large comfortable chairs center stage, with Ivon Voss behind us on an ottoman taking notes as my prompter, stage left is the sofa on which the actors will re-enact the scene, stage right is another comfortable chair with its back to the audience, from which Katja observes my work with her scene partner.

In the dream, Pierre sits, phone in hand, calling a woman who is supposed to help him to get to the other side on his journey due north. The intense necessity to get to the other side is present in his shoulders. I feel in my body the urgency to travel with Pierre to the land of dreams, the other side, in order to get our information. The woman of his dreams is initially not helpful. She has a cackling voice, unpleasant, like that of a witch. When he lets her presence pervade him, it feels like a dark skeleton all through his body. I flash upon Pierre Peters' skeleton in the closet, his murdered wife, and sense the magnetic north pole drawing us in. Some teenagers high up in the gallery begin to giggle in vicarious shame. It distracts me momentarily. Then the dream woman becomes calm, like a Madonna, just observing him. She will be helpful, looks beautiful and eerie, making him feel estranged from himself with a fear of the unknown in his belly. I think of the presence of a murdered woman making the murderer feel forever alien to himself, dissociated by necessity.

Then we get to a dream taking place in a wartime bunker. (How appropriate for the war-torn fight between Katja and Pierre!) It feels oppressive, experienced as a strong pressure on the chest, combined with a desperate hope that he will get out of this mercifully. The pressure increases as we are both aware of sitting here on stage, caught, not able to leave, observed by over 700 people. The pressure becomes unbearable, but Pierre is able to contain it, wondering how he will ever extricate himself from this oppressive field. Only my knowledge that Pierre Peters is being trapped by Katja, ensnared by his inevitable past, and will end his life in prison, which is foreshadowed in the scene about to be played (starting with Katja's taunting opening gambit, "You have never been to Yugoslavia!"), gives me the conviction not to end the experiment here and now. Pierre Bokma looks like an animal in a trap. At the same time, we are *enacting* the entrapment. I vaguely sense that I have trapped Bokma in this situation on the stage for my experiment, with everyone watching. It is as though I am holding him down, like Peters does Katja. I feel helpless and under unbearable pressure, unable to change it. Sweat pearls upon my upper lip. I cannot do anything but wait until the vise holding both of us in its implacable grip relaxes.

In the last image, there is a man who gets into quarrels with everyone. He kicks people, an action that gets focused in Pierre's left leg. A good omen for the epitome of a quarrel scene between Pierre and Katja. Now I help Pierre focus on the composite of embodied states distributed all over his body. The oppression in the chest becomes unbearable because of the exposed setting in which the work is being conducted. All other states recede. I am unable to prevent this single overwhelming state from taking over, and we lose much of the differentiation we had been able to achieve. I am caught in the same oppression, both as oppressor and oppressed. By now the trap is a dissociated state oppressing both of us. There is no consciousness available to make our getaway, as the prison doors echo with the metallic slam of lockdown. I am relieved to leave the stage and let them play the scene.

The dramatic intensity is of such obvious electricity that it makes their performance in the movie three years earlier pale before it. Pierre's language is deadly menacing, his behavior unbearably oppressive, pushing her down in their mutual anguish and rage. At the same time, a single tear rolls off Katja's cheek, taking the full three minutes of the performance to complete its course. In all her eruptive frustration, she never feels crushed by his pressure, she tells us after the show, but is most starkly aware of the impossibility of her wish, based on her desire for fusion, to get through to this man.

The audience seems spellbound, holding still for a moment after the end of the performance, before erupting into a heartfelt applause.

Later, I hear that some in the audience have concluded that the Schouwburg performance had little to do with the dreamwork, since the dreams had been *obviously* personal and unrelated to the characters.

## *NOTES*

[1] J. A. Hobson, "The New Neuropsychology of Sleep: Implications for Psychoanalysis," *Neuro-psychoanalysis: An Interdisciplinary Journal for Psychoanalysis and the Neurosciences* 1, no. 2 (1999): 166.

[2] J. A. Hobson, *Dreaming as Delirium: How the Brain goes out of its Mind* (Cambridge, MA: The MIT Press, 1999).

[3] Andy Serkis, "The Lord of the Rings," 2000-2007, <http://www.serkis.com/cinlotr.htm> (July 28, 2007).

[4] Michael Taussig, *Mimesis and Alterity: A Particular History of the Senses* (New York: Routledge, 1993), p. 52.

# Returning Soul to the World: Culture and Community

Simply said, you make soul by living life, not by retreating from the world into "inner work" or beyond the world in spiritual disciplines and meditation removes .... [but rather by leaving behind] the Cartesian split between inner and outer—good soul inside and the world, the flesh, and the devil outside ...."

—James Hillman, *We've Had a Hundred Years of Psychotherapy—and the World's Getting Worse,* pp. 50-51

"So, I want to clear this up here, because Keats's phrase which has sustained my therapy for so long, contains a major mistake! It actually neglects the world, even while finding a soul use for it. You go through the world for your own sake, making your own soul. But what about the world's soul, Michael? What about the *anima mundi* and making that?"

—James Hillman, *We've Had a Hundred Years of Psychotherapy—and the World's Getting Worse,* p. 54

Mary Watkins is a core faculty member and Coordinator of Community and Ecological Fieldwork and Research in the M.A./Ph.D. Depth Psychology Program at Pacifica Graduate Institute. In 1974, she completed *Waking Dreams* while studying with James Hillman at the Jung Institute in Zürich. As a member of the early archetypal psychology group, she was inspired by Hillman's commitment to the imaginal and to seeing through. This led to the publication of *Invisible Guests: The Development of Imaginal Dialogues* in 1986. Since the 1980s, her work has focused on creating bridges between Euro-American depth and archetypal psychologies and psychologies of liberation from Latin America, Africa, and Asia. The latter is explored in her new book, *Toward Psychologies of Liberation* (Palgrave Macmillan), co-authored with Helene Shulman Lorenz.

25

# "Breaking the Vessels": Archetypal Psychology and the Restoration of Culture, Community, and Ecology

MARY WATKINS

> Breaking the vessels is the return, the turn again to the world, giving back what we have taken from it by storing inside ourselves its soul. By this return we regard the world anew, having regard for it as it shows its regard for us and to us in its face.
>
> —James Hillman, "*Anima Mundi*: The Return of the Soul to the World"[1]

In mystical Judaism, the original creation of the world went awry when the vessels intended to contain God's divine radiance burst, releasing shards of the divine into every being and thing. Each of these shards is said to be encased by a hard seed-covering, a husk (*klipoth)* that obscures the sacred. In this creation myth, human beings are enjoined to restore the world through both mystical prayer (*tikkun nefresh*) and the repair of the world (*tikkun olam*). In *tikkun olam*, we are to liberate and then gather together the sparks of divinity by recognizing the sacred in every being and thing through dialogical relations.[2] Since creation was disrupted before it was finished, "restoration" is not imagined as a return to a previous idyllic state. Instead, restoration refers to living into possibilities for creation that manifest messianic goals of peace, justice, and sacred relations.

In his 1982 essay "*Anima Mundi*: The Return of the Soul to the World," Hillman breaks the primary vessel of Jungian analysis, the dyadic relationship anchored in a focus on the intrapsychic. He rejects the equation of the soul with subjectivity, noting the way it colludes with a sense of the material, public, and external world as dead and soulless, and of the self as cordoned off from culture, nature, and the built environment: "As the soul is without world, so the world is without soul."[3]

For Hillman, a "soul-spark" is not only within each of us, but in animals, plants, and "man-made things of the street."[4] He likens these sparks to the "seminal images" that offer themselves in the sensuous presentation of each particular, in its "availability to imagination" and its presence as a "*psychic* reality."[5]

The breaking of the analytic container releases the idea of psychopathology to be applied more widely. Hillman announces:

> My practice tells me that I can no longer distinguish clearly between neurosis of self and neurosis of world, psychopathology of self and psychopathology of world. Moreover, it tells me that to place neurosis and psychopathology solely in personal reality is a delusional repression of what is actually, realistically, being experienced. This further implies that my theories of neurosis and categories of psychopathology must be radically extended if they are not to foster the very pathologies which my job is to ameliorate.[6]

Breakdown, he argues, must now be seen in nuclear plants, the "traffic system, the school systems, the courts and criminal justice system, giant industries, municipal governments, finance and banking."[7] Hillman argues that by overfocusing on an individual's projections onto others, analysis ignores the projections on to us "by the unconsciousness of the world": "the world is inundating me with its unalleviated suffering."[8] Once awakened from an "anaesthetized slumber of subjectivism," Hillman hopes, we can then "analyze social forces [and] environmental conditions" with the same acuity formerly "reserved only for [ourselves]."[9]

Re-recognizing psyche beyond the intrapsychic opens the way for a psychopathology of the world, and a call for a *psychotherapeia*, a care of the soul of the world. Hillman's own break with the confinement of soul work within analytic practice encourages archetypal psychology to approach community, cultural, and ecological concerns. His soulful work on a wide variety of social and ecological issues, including transportation, city, environment, war, money, and welfare, announces a radical widening of the scope of archetypal psychology. This widening of focus places Hillman in alignment with many early psychoanalysts in Vienna and Berlin, and with subsequent branches of psychoanalysis that have concerned themselves with the cultural dimensions of psyche, collapsing the strict dichotomizing of internal and external, and of the private and the public.[10] Hillman's archetypal approach, however, offers a distinctive orientation to cultural, community, and ecological work, an orientation that I will take this opportunity to outline.

For the last decade, Hillman's work has been a founding and central pillar in the inspiration, design, and curriculum of the M.A./Ph.D. Depth Psychology Program at Pacifica Graduate Institute. My examples of Hillman's orientation are drawn from the work of doctoral students in this program, where I have coordinated depth psychological community and ecological fieldwork and research since 1997. These adult learners come to a study of depth psychology from a wide variety of disciplines, such as architecture, urban planning, the arts, law, prison reform, filmmaking, medicine, hospice work, media studies, organizational development, and psychotherapy. In our program, we have begun not with a clinical focus, but with the aim of creating and nourishing the practice of depth psychological mindedness in a wide variety of settings. Each year, in their fieldwork and research, students practice the application of depth psychological theories and approaches to community and ecological issues, paying attention to the interfaces between individual psychological suffering and cultural pathology in their efforts to restore liveliness and depth of insight. Their fieldwork experience allows them new vantage points on depth theory and practice, helping them to engage in critique, affirmations, and extensions of depth theories and methods.

Through immersion in community and ecological contexts, over five hundred improvisational works have been created that bridge depth psychological theory with "restoration" in the areas of community, culture, and ecology.[11] Looking back over this burgeoning body of work, I want to describe some of the key themes in Hillman's archetypal psychology that have inspired and influenced the cultural, community, and ecological work of a new generation of depth and archetypal psychologists. How have and how might central ideas of archetypal psychology—*notitia*, aesthetic response, beauty and ugliness, multiplicity, dialogue, pathologizing, seeing through, archetypal dominants, holding reflection and action together, the call of the world soul, the imaginal—orient us as we work with psyche in the world? I offer this mapping of ideas and the kinds of work they have inspired not only to pay homage to Hillman's vision, but to hold open our imagination about the wide range of depth psychological engagement that is needed and possible.

## *Notitia*

How are the archetypal and depth psychologically minded to enter into the fray of community and ecological work? Over lunch in 1981, I posed this question to Hillman around the nuclear dilemma. I was called by nuclear holocaust dreams and active imaginations to witness and address the nuclear, but felt unprepared by depth theory and my largely intrapsychically oriented psychotherapeutic training and daily work. Hillman used the analogy of a therapist beginning an hour with a new patient and said something like the following:

> When you start, you are completely helpless. You don't know a thing. The person may tell you a dream, and at first that only makes it worse, as it seems strange and incomprehensible. But things make you curious. You keep listening, *noticing*, not knowing what to do, and acknowledging your felt inferiority. Slowly you begin to see things, dimly as though in the dark. You keep listening, *noticing*, and following, and gradually a way is made.

*This* I did know how to do, and I began to see how it was possible to translate this way of proceeding clinically into encounters with cultural and environmental issues.

Hillman, like Sufi mystical poets before him, describes the heart's characteristic action not as feeling, but as sight. He says, "individuating begins with noticing, paying attention to the specifics of what is actually there so that it can become fully what it is."[12] All cultural and ecological work needs to be continually grounded in what Hillman calls "*notitia.*"

Noticing involves a gift of careful attention that is sustained, patient, subtly attuned to images and metaphors, tracking both hidden meanings and surface presentations. The practice of noticing addresses our "deprivation of intimacy with the immediate environment," which Hillman diagnosed in 1982.[13] Depth engagement begins with careful noticing: a "being-with" that is a form of doing that allows intimacy with a situation to develop.

The dwelling and participating with that careful noticing requires opens pathways to the depths of a phenomenon. Like a lover's careful noticing of the beloved, such attention finds ways of caring that are not superimposed, but arise from the ground of relationship spawned by careful attention. For Hillman, the activity of noticing is a countercultural one, resisting the mania of hyperactivity and overarousal that the dominant culture encourages. Paradoxically, the first step in archetypal activism is to stop. Only then do we discover ourselves already within a world that we can notice more deeply. This noticing is akin to Freud's basic method of free association, in which the analyst resists an overfocus and a premature directedness that issues from the ego. Instead, the analyst is encouraged to enjoy a widening of awareness and an evenly hovering attention so that new perceptions can emerge.[14] In American culture, slowing down is necessary not only to noticing, but also to the essential work of mourning, to which we will soon turn.

Because we have associated a turn to the world with a turn toward the public and toward action, it is difficult initially to discover a way of being with an area of concern in the world that is slow, observant, and participatory, and that invites reverie, image, and insight. We are used to going into a situation with something we are going to share or impose, some aim clearly in mind. This ego orientation makes it difficult to see and understand the place at which we have arrived. We have dragged our agenda and presuppositions with us. Depth psychological engagement with the soul of the world begins differently, more as an apprenticeship, an openness to being tutored. It requires the vulnerability of coming without a plan or of knowing that the plan we arrive with will soon dissolve as we find the ideas we have come with inadequate to the situation we find ourselves in.

Many of us are starved for this mode of engagement in the world. We are exhausted by wrestling with situations in the world through our work and other commitments and we take solace in a remove from the world. We have not learned how to be present to the interiority of each situation we enter, resting in a whole-hearted attentiveness. This takes time. When we learn how to make this shift, work in the world is no longer pitted against individual soul work. The two flow together, each a source of both challenge and restoration.

In her fieldwork Rosmarie Bogner[15] extended her architecturally oriented practice of listening to landscapes to listening carefully to the town of Ketchum, Idaho. Such listening for Bogner formed the basis of an attempt to harmonize human dwelling with the surrounding ecosystem. As she tried to "notice" her Idaho town, she meditated on buildings, spending time with them, and taking careful pictures of them. Through this noticing, she found herself in reverie with these structures, listening to their sense of being crazily juxtaposed to surrounding buildings, inquiring into their desire and distress, their sense of history. This kind of listening, where noticing joins forces with reverie, was necessary before there could be meaningful consultation with the architectural planning process in her town.

In love with the valley she lives in, a landscape and bioregion endangered by development, Laura Mitchell[16] apprenticed herself to the creek bed, to the dwindling fauna and flora, to earth and rock formations. In her careful noticing over time, her knowledge of the valley's peril became particularized and her advocacy on behalf of the area deepened. This noticing formed the basis of her participation with local groups in discerning the fate of the land. Advocacy flowed from the erotic connection engendered by noticing. Learning from others also attentive to this place, Mitchell proposed the idea of ecoimaginal identity, shifting her focus not only to how we become attuned to the places that home us, but also to how we are constituted by them and the imaginal activity they spark within us.

Mike Denney,[17] a physician, noticed that a young male coma patient seemed to be spiritually affecting his caregivers. Having been trained to assume that coma patients are non-expressive, he was surprised to realize that those around the patient were acting as though communication was happening. Apprenticing himself to the young man's mother, the physical therapist, and several other caregivers, Denney began to develop the capacity to sense the subtle field of communication between himself and his patient. He too began to partake in the sacred experience of being-with. How, he then wondered, is this dimension related to medicine? How can we heal the rift that our allegiance to science and its secularized ways of being have established in Western practices of healing? These questions opened dialogue among nurses and doctors in his hospital setting, leading to a widening of their field of attention while tending the ill.

Gay Bradshaw's[18] work in interspecies communication and the traumatic effects of habitat destruction on animals began with years of devoted living with and careful noticing of animals. Through this noticing, she was able to slip out of the anthropocentric grasp that Hillman sees as plaguing psychology.[19] By refusing the usual privileging of human language, she invited the animals' lived realities and communicative efforts to come forward to her attention. These shifts were necessary to understanding the applicability of human trauma theory to animals and their communities. This opened to work that led to advocacy to stop the forces that undermine animal well-being as well as to an engagement in restorative work in animal healing.

Noticing requires a de-centering from the heroic ego, an activation of what Hillman has called the imaginal ego. We need to step aside, but not to the distance of an objective observer. The stepping aside is an interior move away from premature intentions forged in isolation. Contrary to the dictates of natural science, it clears the way for greater intimacy and opens up the possibilities of collaboration.

## Aesthetic Response: Beauty and Ugliness

> But the deepest evil in the totalitarian system is precisely that which makes it work: its programmed, single-minded monotonous efficiency; bureaucratic formalism, the dulling daily service, standard, boring, letter-perfect, generalities, uniform. No thought and no responsiveness. Eichmann .... So, the question of evil, like the question of ugliness, refers primarily to the anaesthetized heart, the heart that has no reaction to what it faces, thereby turning the variegated sensuous face of the world into monotony, sameness, oneness. The desert of modernity.
>
> —James Hillman, *The Thought of the Heart and the Soul of the World*[20]

Hillman describes "noticing" as the basis of classical depth psychology; the noticing of dream images, of bodily feelings, memories, omissions, and slips of tongue. This noticing contributes to an awakening. This same noticing must, he says, be extended to the world from which we have withdrawn our attention. We need, he says, a "depth psychology of extraversion," through which depth can be found "in the objects, in the images presented by the world."[21] When we begin to notice the world, we are struck by both ugliness and beauty. Hillman, unlike Jung, links this aesthetic response with the ethical. It "does not replace the ethical," but it gives "sensate images that direct our longings toward ideals," visions that we can "become seduced by."[22] Hillman argues that we have repressed our aesthetic involvement with the world, numbing our perception of both beauty and ugliness. Once awakened, aesthetic response—be it "naïve recoil or desirous advance"—pulls us into relationship with the polis and with politics. We awake from conformity, says Hillman, and can no longer think that our miseries are wholly occasioned by our personal relationships. "Beauty evokes love," says Hillman.[23] Aesthetic response fuels protest.

In Deborah Mac Williams'[24] work the devotion to the beauty of place led to her intense grief about its desecration in the anonymity and ugliness of strip malls and through careless development in her city of Bend, Oregon. She realized that addressing this desecration depended on her confronting numbed responses. Mac Williams and her co-researchers got out of their cars and walked the unfriendly and ugly strips they usually tried to ignore. Using clay, image, and words, these participants struggled to give form to their reactions to the lifeless asphalt tracts their town was giving way to. Here a love for and advocacy of the beauty of place feeds the intent to note carefully what is ugly and create a psychic space to bear the feelings of mourning, disgust, impotence, and sorrow that arise. From this starting point, reveries of the deeply desired could unfold, offering a path to active participation and creation in the design of the city.

Nancy Welliver[25] is a scientist who works in nuclear waste management at the Hanford Nuclear Site in Washington. She has allowed herself to be open to the environmental catastrophe that has unfolded over sixty years of nuclear contamination there, studying the environmental changes that have occurred both at Hanford and in Nagasaki. Nagasaki was destroyed in 1945 with plutonium processed at Hanford. Knowing the insufficiency of words to convey this tragic situation, she has explored combining images from Hanford and Nagasaki with early music devoted to Mary.

> My belief is that post-Enlightenment images cannot adequately express the profound psychological and somatic fallout of the

> Bomb. It is time to return to something more ancient. This presentation of a series of images and music illustrates what I believe to be an overwhelming grief for the way in which humanity has chosen to deploy the intellectual mastery of nature's secrets to create the Enlightenment's most frightening and misused contribution to Western culture. In an effort to reach back past this heritage, I take the viewer through time, to the ancient Nichiren Buddhist practice of chant and to the Western medieval and Renaissance periods when chants to the Virgin Mary and other goddesses were sung. This ancient music is layered with images of Hanford, Nagasaki, and the Virgin of the Urakami Cathedral. The Cathedral was destroyed and the Virgin burned black in the 1945 atomic fire. Onlookers are invited to view Hanford, Nagasaki, and the destruction of both environments through a mythological lens.

Welliver's visual juxtaposition of two cities intertwined in their destinies, Nagasaki and Hanford, conveys a deep truth: the land of the "victor" is currently more deeply disturbed than even the object of the bomb's original destructive energy, Nagasaki. Hanford is a literal and metaphorical wasteland. Vast portions of its 600 square miles are no longer habitable. Its former verdant orchards are destroyed. Much of its land is soaked with radioactive and poisonous chemicals from abandoned reactors and plutonium processing buildings. Ironically, the land is teeming with animals and plants because of the lack of human inhabitants. These living creatures are often laden with radioactivity and are routinely put to death to prevent radiation from spreading over the range of their habitat. The towns within Hanford's borders are ghost towns and will likely remain so in perpetuity. Working with image and music, Welliver finds a way to memorialize and mourn what is difficult to grasp in its extremity. Without this grasp, transformation of the mentality that continues to produce Hanford-like scapes is impossible.

## Depression

Hillman has consistently advocated for the necessity of entering and bearing depression, that soul movement that slows or stops us, pulling us downwards, away from habitual activities. In *Suicide and the Soul*,[26] Hillman describes the surprising energy that arises from yielding to the difficult images of suicidal ideation. He advises analysts not to ignore and starve, through inattention, the nightmares and "daymares" of depression, but to trust that attention to them will release an autonomous vitality from within the difficult images themselves. Hillman's return of the soul to the world has also broken our containing understanding of the causes of depression. Hillman argues that depression must not be seen only as a result of personal history and problems, but that it is a response to a world shared with others. As we widen our attention, we discover that the hoarding of soul within interiority has served a defensive function, protecting us from the tragedies and travesties in our midst.

Our emergence into a felt sense of interdependence is paradoxically marked by both depression and joy. Welliver reports that finding a visual and musical language to present what she witnessed at Hanford has released a new sense of vibrancy and health. The same was true for Mac Williams, who, while beginning her fieldwork from a sense of overwhelming grief for the environment, found that her mourning gave way to a joy born of engagement.

Robert J. Lifton describes the current age as one of psychic numbing.[27] There is no way to restore our sensitivity without bearing the grief we so actively defend against. Regardless of the area of our engagement in the world, the capacity to turn toward depressive feelings, to accept a sense of being overwhelmed and inadequate to the situation is necessary. If we are to break our attention free from its circumscription by purely personal pursuits, we will find ourselves feeling small, amidst many bits and pieces that do not seem to cohere into any understandable patterns.

## Multiplicity

Psyche as described by Hillman is polytheistic, sounding forth a complex layering of often contradictory and paradoxical voices of multiple figures and perspectives. The "heroic ego" is that part of us that attempts to deny and silence this multiplicity, asserting unilateral power and control. It denies diversity and eschews dialogue, proceeding with a monologue that does not understand its own viewpoint as a perspective. The multiplicity of the psyche arises spontaneously, however, and when repressed or negated, it voices itself through symptom and pathology. The methodology for understanding and healing in Jung and Hillman calls for an attempt to bracket the dominating and oppressive aspects of the ego, making space for the unlistened-to and the silenced to speak directly. One turns to the margins of awareness, to greet and coax other points of view into dialogue, and to listen to what has been voiced but unheeded.

Archetypal psychology's radical critique of a colonizing form of ego consciousness that feigns singleness or unity has its analog in cultural and ecological life. This should not be surprising, since we each tend to internalize the pattern of relations prevalent in the dominant culture in which we are located. The heroic ego might well be named the colonizing ego, to mark its connection to the colonial era, a time stained by the exploitation and oppression of the many by the few.[28]

The multiplicity of psychic voices includes the multiplicity of cultural voices that go unheeded by dominant cultural forces. As with the individual, the neglected, unheard, repressed, and denied viewpoints assert themselves through symptom and pathology. Thus, an archetypal psychologist attuned to psyche in the world listens for the multiplicity of viewpoints that comprise situations and events. She is attentive to the dynamics that prevent certain voices from speaking or being heard, and she works to create situations in which these can come to voice and be heard and in which those who are accustomed to speaking over the voices of others can learn the value of listening.

Sandra Paul[29] found herself struggling with both a distance from the earth in her North Carolina community and alienation between the cultural groups that compose its citizenry. While the beauty of the earth is often referred to in her community, it is often treated as only a commodity. To gain a better understanding of the gaping wound between self and earth, self and other, that she carried—and that she felt much of her community to carry—she decided to interview elder women about their relation to the earth and to neighboring cultural groups. She was careful to include individuals from each of the main cultural groups that comprised her community: Cherokees, African-Americans, Euro-American longtime southerners, and recent Euro-American émigrés from the North. The lack of dialogue between these women in their everyday lives extended back generations, both to the forced march of the Cherokee from their lands, and to the forced exile of Africans from Africa and their further domination through the institution of slavery. As the historical narratives of their families crisscrossed, the defensive silence between them in the present became understandable. For instance, a Euro-American woman's great-great-grandfather was an army escort for Cherokee families during their forced displacement. One African-American woman had ancestors who were owned by the ancestors of current Euro-American families residing in the town.

The way in which Christianity had led some to treat the land as lifeless was contrasted starkly with the earth-centered Cherokee cosmology. Paul sees healing in her community as entailing a hosting of dialogue among its multiple cultural groups. Such a dialogue holds several seeds of possibility for a deepened sense of community in the present, for historical healing, and for the sharing of indigenous ecological sensibilities with settlers who may not yet have experienced an ecstatic and grief-laden relationship to the earth and its other-than-human inhabitants and presences.

## Dialogue

In both Jungian and archetypal work, the bridging of the conscious and the unconscious occurs through dialogue, as in the practice of active imagination. Such bridging activates what Jung called the transcendent function. Hillman uses the language of "soul" for the space that opens up through dialogue.

Cheryl Hashman Sheinman[30] worked with the idea of dialogue in a large conservative Jewish synagogue in South Florida that was dominated by a few loud voices. As members of the community began to engage in dialogue, some voices began to be listened to for the first time. In addition, as the group heard more about previously unknown perspectives, they developed the capacity to begin to listen for the voice of the soul of the temple. It became clear that such active efforts to connect across diverse perspectives through dialogue can give rise to a soulful experience that transcends any individual voice. Opening a sacred space for mindful dialogue also melted away illusions of consensus on charged and crucial matters, such as Israeli-Palestinian relations.

Paul Jones,[31] an urban planner in Flagstaff, Arizona, explored how to listen to a city from a depth-psychological perspective. He began to see that few were actually involved in the city planning process. What dreams did they have for it? As he stretched to see Flagstaff from other ethnic, class, and cultural points of view, he found himself in unfamiliar places and conversations. As he witnessed art-making within the marginalized communities of Flagstaff, it became clear how vibrant a city it could be if more of its residents were invited to the table.

Jim Gossett's[32] fieldwork involved the threat and shadow of violence in the wake of the naming of a national monument near Escalante, Utah. Here the environmental disputes and the rapid onslaught of ecotourism affected Native American communities, centuries-old ranching families, and a Latter-Day Saints community. Community dialogue directed at metabolizing the changes was absent. Gossett, grounding himself in careful noticing and listening to members of the different groups and his own psychic resonance to them and their land, imagined ways to use dialogue to bridge the divide that violence otherwise threatened to widen.

## Pathologizing

> You know, the soul is always being rediscovered through pathology. … The world has become full of symptoms.
>
> —James Hillman, *We've Had a Hundred Years of Psychotherapy*[33]

Hillman turns our attention to the pathological and the symptomatic. He directs us to bend towards the wounded, the twisted and deformed, to listen into what they have to say to us. We are not to move quickly to an eradication of symptom, but to listen carefully to its messages. To do so requires us to participate alongside that which suffers, to apprentice ourselves to that which we might otherwise try to dominate, to hear its critique and discern its implicit vision. Hillman turns directly to pathology, particularly attentive to it as a critique of "normal" or dominant consciousness.

Matthew Green, in his archetypally inspired cultural work with adolescent Chicano boys in Oceano, California, had to listen past as well as into the job he was assigned: teenage pregnancy prevention. While the goal seemed well-intentioned, it was imposed from outside the boys' community. Other "symptoms" for these boys included poverty, drug use, a high dropout rate at school, and gang affiliation. Green reflects,

> I have come to realize that this model, which is based on the strategy of finding the "cause" and then developing the best "solution" to eradicate it, never asks an essential question: "What might the unwanted teen pregnancy epidemic be telling us

> about our society, ourselves, the community in which the teens live, about the teens themselves?" Without asking this question I sense that we can never really come to terms with the dilemma of unwanted teen pregnancy. Until we hear what it is trying to say, it will keep saying it in this or other ways, despite all our prevention efforts. Unknowingly the model serves to hide, and even deny, the essence of the dilemma. Most tragically, the structures and actions of these programs proposed by this model inhibit us from becoming aware of and fully experiencing the reality of who and what we are as a society. What we do not realize is that our strategy of attempting to "eradicate" the problem without listening into what it is telling us cuts us off from experiencing soul.[34]

Here Green attempts to enact Hillman's methodology of "seeing through" the way the "problem" is initially posed. Following Hillman in giving attention to the pathologized, Green works carefully to listen into the boys' experiences, desires, and hopes, rather than imposing the agenda of the state agency on them.

Working alongside them to help them fulfill their goal of creating a teen center and striving to promote a milieu in which they can enjoy handball tournaments, dance, rap, Djing, and Graffiti art, Green listened in to the stories they told as well as the stories that seemed present, yet untold. He worked with his resistances so that he might be able to listen without moralizing to the lyrics of the boys' favorite rap songs as well as to the emerging narratives of gang conflict. "I tried to suspend my vision for them and see instead what their vision might be saying to me." Just how had these families come to live in Oceano? What were their stories of immigration and struggle? He wondered what the feeling of shame that he sensed in the boys was about. The adolescents and adult men began meeting in *circulos*, or councils, and this made it possible for the community to listen deeply to the concerns and histories of each of its members. Their choice of this form reclaimed an indigenous tradition that their forebears had used in pre-colonial times. From these circles, an oral history project for the community was launched. As the boys engaged in these activities, they were openly shunned by many in the larger community, making the dynamics of oppression that their stories spoke about even more palpable. One boy said, "Matthew, you don't know how it feels to live this every day!" Hillman's words were a mantra: "The study of lives and the care of souls means above all a prolonged encounter with what destroys and is destroyed, with what is broken and hurts—that is, with psychopathology."[35]

## "Seeing Through"

> First there is the psychological moment, a moment of reflection, wonder, puzzlement, initiated by the soul which intervenes and countervails what we are in the midst of doing, hearing, reading, watching. With slow suspicion or sudden insight we move through the apparent to the less apparent. We use metaphors of light—a little flicker, a slow dawning, and a lightning flash—as things become clarified. When the clarity has itself become obvious and transparent, there seems to grow within it a new darkness, a new question or doubt, requiring a new act of insight penetrating again toward the less apparent.
>
> —James Hillman, *Re-Visioning Psychology*[36]

Hillman asserts that "[w]e are always in the embrace of an idea," that "our wrestling with ideas is a sacred struggle," "that soul-making takes place as much through ideation as in personal relationships or meditation."[37] Indeed, his opus is a staggering gift teaching us at *every* turn how to live in relationship to ideas: loving them, critiquing them, turning them, seeing through them, being devoted to them, being animated by them, sacrificing to them, caring for and tending them. Without such careful attention to ideas, he says, psyche turns to ideologies. Indeed, breaking the norms of knowing by "seeing through" is fundamentally related to breaking the oppressive aspects of human existence.[38] When ideas are not seen through, the sense of reality they spawn is experienced as natural and inevitable. It is the process of seeing through that liberates us to create with ideas rather than merely be a victim of them. This seeing through is never done once and for all, but is a continual process. Hillman calls us to situate our ideas and practices within the historical and cultural context from which they arise, to see each idea as one perspective among many—each with its own history and consequences.

In the context of her creative writing classes at a state penitentiary, Suzan Still[39] committed herself to an ongoing process of seeing through the ideas by which this system of incarceration functions. Throughout her time at the prison, she encountered rules against "overfamiliarity."

Forbidden to respond to her students' letters, not even allowed to call them by their first name, she began to see a system of progressive dehumanization that is focused on treating the men, whose poems moved her to tears, as raw commodities to be profited from. Following the implications of the commodification of prison labor and the corporatization of the American penal system, Still exposes the profit incentive that is fed by the *failure* to rehabilitate inmates. To withhold normal human relations from prisoners, to treat them as numbers and as a disposable resource is consistent with the idea of profiting from them as though they were abject objects. Longer prison stays and increased recidivism mean larger corporate profits, while at the same time it re-inscribes the institution of slavery and the related practice of "apartheid" under the rubric of punishment.

The kind of seeing through of ideas that Still's work embodies moved her to an ethic of soulful participation and intimate familiarity with her students, and stimulated both her and them to envision actively together a restorative justice system that does not flay the very skin of the soul. She confessed that she felt most at home and alive with these men, whose lives necessitated their own seeing through of gross senses of failure and inadequacy, of violence that was received and perpetuated, and of a system that preys upon their mistakes. In such work, the depth of "down" and "in" is joined with the depth "between" self and other.

## Archetypal Dominants

As Still saw through to the archetypal ideas structuring our prisons, she found the shadow fantasies of the *senex*: "imaginings around how to control, suppress, repress, disempowered, punish, humiliate, depotentiate, depersonalize and dehumanize."[40] Hillman's own cultural work is wedded to his early and abiding interest in exposing and learning from the archetypal dominants in our experiences. Here "seeing through" allows insight into persistent patterns that unconsciously repeat outside of awareness.

In his fieldwork, Craig Chalquist made a pilgrimage to the sites of the original California missions established by the Spanish Catholic Church in its colonizing move up the coast of California.[41] Open to his and others' dreams and fantasies, he researched each place's history, looking for persistent archetypal chords that affect its inhabitants over generations. Ruth Meyer,[42] a psychohistorian, followed Clio, the muse of history, in her study of historians' imaginal lives around the historical period that fascinates and compels their scholarship. Phillip Gibson[43] turned to African Verdun cosmology in his attempt to understand the embrace of the cadence call in the U.S. military at the moment of its racial desegregation. Tracing the cadence call's root in Verdun worship, Gibson reflects on the integration of African-based ecstatic practices into the U.S. induction of young men into the warrior archetype.

## Reflection And Action

> Ideas allow us to envision, and by means of vision we can know. ... But when an insight or idea has sunk in, practice visibly changes. The idea has opened the eye of the soul. By seeing differently, we do differently. Then "how" is implicitly taken care of.
>
> —James Hillman, *Re-Visioning Psychology*[44]

As Still listens to the burning, lava-like poems of her prison students, her seeing through is ignited into a liberatory potential, and she imagines with her prison poets how our culture might reverse its draconian soul-killing proclivities and create a system of justice worthy of the name. Meyer re-imagines and practices the teaching of history in such a way as to invite her students into an empathic engagement with the historical moment being studied. Gibson educates fallen warriors within the justice system who are struggling to understand the deformation of their psychic landscape as it was inflicted on them by their training as army recruits and soldiers. Seeing through begins a momentum that often delivers us into grief and outrage, making necessary the tasks of address, protest, creation, and restoration.

For Hillman, "action and idea are not inherent enemies, and they should not be paired as a contrast."[45] He sees reflection as an activity, and action as always enacting an idea. Hillman speaks of our need to bring soul into action, and action into soul.

From the perspective of archetypal psychology, social activism can be grounded in noticing, reflecting, seeing through, in reverie and dialogue, in aesthetic sensitivity. Pathology is not overridden by premature eradication, but needs to be listened to with patience for its insights. While the will and the discipline of the ego are often necessary, they are in service to the erotic field of interconnection engendered by these practices. "Love, too," says Hillman, "can be a method of psychologizing, of seeing into and seeing through, of going ever deeper."[46]

Hillman's archetypal psychology and Paulo Freire's radical liberatory pedagogical praxis[47] share the space created by the dual conjunctions of reflection and action and of love and seeing though. Freire's work approaches love through justice, while Hillman arrives at love through beauty. Each understands how radically necessary de-ideologization is for moving towards the effort of re-visioning and both appreciate the creative actions needed to embody the process. In Freirean work, seeing through is understood as "conscientization," or the development of a critical consciousness of the ideas and ideologies that structure everyday reality. Such insight opens the way for annunciation, the imagining of alternative groundings of "reality" and ways of being. Students studying at the boundaries of depth and liberation psychologies are taking Hillman's sensibilities into the areas of justice and human rights, feminist and cultural studies, community education and the arts, and the addressing of collective trauma, including racism, poverty, forced migration, and the destruction of neighborhoods and wild corners. Here, archetypal and liberation psychologies are being stewed together to create new variants of community, cultural, and ecological work that are infused with the sensibilities outlined above.[48]

## The Call Of The World Soul

When we begin to notice the world attentively, we find ourselves particularly attuned to certain issues, problems, and situations. Particular aspects of the world soul call out to us, as though we have been singled out by our unique combination of temperament, history, wounds, and passions. The path of individuation is in part a fine-tuning to the ways in which we are called and obligated. Both individuation's meandering path *and* its insistent directives reflect the ways in which the world has entered, formed, and spoken to us. The kind of activism Hillman describes arises less from egoic intention than from the slow dilation of the self that Walt Whitman lyricizes, that rhythm of sympathetic inhalation of the world into the self, and the creative and erotic exhalation of the self toward the world that signals our belonging.[49]

The desire and energy for witness emerges in strange ways: dreams, visions, recurring images, unbidden feelings, and preoccupying thoughts. Sometimes they emerge from the center of our concern and intention. At other times something from the margin of our awareness whispers insistently, asking for our attention. Each path provides the possibility of healing a stance of bystanding. Paradoxically, living into the interdependent web of which we are a part does not deplete us, but provides membership in a gift economy where it is possible to draw sustenance from beyond narrowly defined selves. As Lewis Hyde puts it, "Our generosity may leave us empty, but our emptiness then pulls gently at the whole until the thing in motion returns to replenish us."[50]

## The Imaginal

It was through my interest in the imaginal that I came to Hillman's work, and it is to the primacy of the imaginal that my students and I continually return. Released from the confines of subjectivism, we continually re-discover how the imaginal registers, conveys, and amplifies the calls of the world. It awakens us through image and animated perceptions to what suffers and to what is beautiful. With exacting specificity, free-rising images convey the way the soul perceives the daily realities we live amidst. Through its stark and direct renderings, the imaginal cuts through our denial, dissolving our distance from grief and outrage.

When perceived through the heart, the imaged presentation of "what is" leads to longings and imaginings of what might be. The imaginal surpasses the given, announcing the transgressive. For this reason, cultural work on every continent encourages the arts, knowing that they will give birth to images of the deeply desired, utopic images toward which a community orients itself in common striving.

Brent Blair, a liberation arts educator working with teenage boys incarcerated at Central Juvenile Hall, East Los Angeles, offered his students the opportunity to learn about and then deconstruct and reconfigure the myth of Orpheus. Their theater work enabled this tale to evoke the struggles and tragedies of their journeys into that darkness they lived within our inner cities and the prisons too often connected with them. "In the end," says Blair, their dramatic work was "a testimony to the ineffability of the human spirit to awaken possibility in an atmosphere of such defeat."[51] In such work with image, not only does one find archetypal threads that can be followed to diverse collective mythic traditions, but one encounters the not-yet-thought, unexpected conjunctions and barely tolerated desires that point towards new possibles. For these reasons, openness to the imaginal and to the arts in all their forms is never merely an adjunct to cultural, community, and ecological work, but essential and indivisible from it.

## Coda

Alive in all of Hillman's work is a penetrating questioning, a bursting open of the terms in which we might otherwise seek a false sense of security. Here we find a steady refusal to turn the gaze from what is difficult, from what suffers. A devotion to beauty awakens us, and challenges us to act on behalf of what we love.

One night in 1999, when Hillman was visiting with my students, they succeeded in coaxing him into commenting on the question of praxis around their community and ecological fieldwork and research. He replied:

> Think of when you are sailing. You are never on course. You are always correcting. Only through these constant corrections do you find your course. You need to ask yourself, "Am I too personal here, thinking only of my own 'growth'? Am I too much like a 'missionary' there, bringing 'light' to these people?" The movement, movement through it, is part of the essence. ... At any moment as you travel on a circle you can think, "I got it." You fix on the point and can easily go off on a tangent. *The plan is the sensitivity ....*

Regardless of the topic he touches, Hillman's work teaches us sensitivity. While goals are not to be utterly abandoned, they are not to be taken literally but as "guiding fictions."[52] We reflect on them, looking for the ideas and myths that animate them, and the shadow they are capable of casting. The vessels we have so carefully crafted must also be broken, not as a pure act of destruction, but as part of an ongoing process of seeing through and re-creation that demands our thinking, imagining, acting, and our looking again with what Hillman calls "the eye of the heart."

## NOTES

[1] In James Hillman, *The Thought of the Heart and the Soul of the World* (Woodstock, CT: Spring Publications, 1992), p. 129.

[2] Martin Buber, *The Way of Man* (London: Routledge, 2002).

[3] Hillman, *Thought of the Heart,* p. 95.

[4] *Ibid.*, p. 101.

[5] *Ibid.*

[6] *Ibid.*, p. 93.

[7] *Ibid.*, p. 96.

[8] *Ibid.*, p. 99.

[9] *Ibid.*, p. 100.

[10] Mary Watkins, "Sketches for the Recovery of Night Vision: Re-Orienting Depth Psychology to Engage the Inconvenient Truths of the 21st Century," see <www.online.pacifica.edu/watkins> (May 8, 2008).

[11] For a list of representative projects, sites, and guidelines, see <www.online.pacifica.edu/depthfieldwork> (July 15, 2006).

[12] Hillman, *Thought of the Heart,* p. 52.

[13] *Ibid.*

[14] Mary Watkins, "Depth Psychology and the Liberation of Being," in *Pathways into the Jungian World: Phenomenology and Analytical Psychology,* ed. R. Brooke (London: Routledge, 2000).

[15] Rosmarie Bogner, "Toward Ketchum's Architectural Design Guidelines," Community/Ecological Fieldwork paper, Depth Psychology Doctoral Program, Pacifica Graduate Institute, 1999.

[16] Laura H. Mitchell, "The Eco-Imaginal Underpinnings of Community Identity in Harmony Grove Valley: Unbinding the Ecological Imagination," Ph.D. dissertation, Pacifica Graduate Institute, 2005.

[17] Mike Denney, "Interview with a Coma Patient," Community/Ecological fieldwork, Depth Psychology Doctoral Program, Pacifica Graduate Institute, 1999.

[18] G. A. Bradshaw, Mary Watkins, "Trans-Species Psychology: Theory and Praxis," *Spring 75, Part I—Psyche and Nature* (Fall 2006): 69-94.

[19] James Hillman, "Justice, Beauty, and Destiny as Foundations for an Ecological Psychology," in *City and Soul*, ed. Robert J. Leaver (Putnam, CT: Spring Publications, 2006), p. 211.

[20] Hillman, *Thought of the Heart,* pp. 62, 64.

[21] James Hillman, "Aesthetic Response as Political Action," in *City and Soul,* ed. Robert J. Leaver (Putnam, CT: Spring Publications, 2006), p. 143.

[22] *Ibid.,* p. 152.

[23] *Ibid.,* p. 154.

[24] Deborah Mac Williams, "To Know a Place," Community/Ecological fieldwork, Depth Psychology Doctoral Program, Pacifica Graduate Institute, 1999.

[25] Nancy Welliver, "Nagasaki and Hanford: A Tale of Two Cities," Community/Ecological fieldwork, Depth Psychology Doctoral Program, Pacifica Graduate Institute, 2007, p. 1.

[26] James Hillman, *Suicide and the Soul* (Dallas, TX: Spring Publications, 1976).

[27] Robert J. Lifton, February 2007, from the author's notes of Lifton's lecture delivered to the International Trauma Studies Program, Columbia University, New York.

[28] Helene Schulman Lorenz and Mary Watkins, "Depth Psychology and Colonialism: Individuation, Seeing Through, and Liberation," in *Psychology at the Threshold,* ed. Dennis Slattery and Lionel Corbett (Einsiedeln, Switzerland: Daimon Verlag, 2002), pp. 281-298.

[29] Sandra Paul, "Sacred Connections through Women's Stories," Community/Ecological fieldwork, Depth Psychology Doctoral Program, Pacifica Graduate Institute, 1999.

[30] Cheryl Hashman Sheinman, "Introduction of a Dialogue Group in a Contemporary, Conservative Jewish Synagogue," Community/Ecological fieldwork, Depth Psychology Doctoral Program, Pacifica Graduate Institute, 2000.

[31] Paul Jones, "The City Revealed: Uncovering Soul in a City through Voices from Its Edges," Community/Ecological fieldwork, Depth Psychology Doctoral Program, Pacifica Graduate Institute, 2000.

[32] Jim Gossett, "Monumental Rupture," Community/Ecological fieldwork, Depth Psychology Doctoral Program, Pacifica Graduate Institute, 2000.

[33] James Hillman and Michael Ventura, *We've Had a Hundred Years of Psychotherapy—and the World's Getting Worse* (New York: HarperCollins Publishers), p. 4.

[34] Matthew Green, "Re-Thinking Our Work with At-Risk Youth," Community/Ecological fieldwork, Depth Psychology Doctoral Program, Pacifica Graduate Institute, 2000, p. 9.

[35] James Hillman, *Re-Visioning Psychology* (New York: Harper & Row, 1975), p. 56.

[36] *Ibid.*, 140.

[37] *Ibid.*, pp. 121, 115.

[38] Mary Belenky, Blythe Clinchy, Nancy Goldberger, and Jill Tarule, *Women's Ways of Knowing: The Development of Self, Voice, and Mind* (New York: Basic Books, 1986).

[39] Suzan Still, "The Hero's Journey: Breaking Depth Psychology *into* Prison" and "We Wish We Could Write This in Fire: Writings of Marginalized Men," Community/Ecological fieldwork, Depth Psychology Doctoral Program, Pacifica Graduate Institute, 1998 and 1999 respectively.

[40] *Ibid.*, p. 15.

[41] Craig Chalquist, *Terrapsychology: Re-Engaging the Soul of Place* (New Orleans, LA: Spring Journal Books, 2007).

[42] Ruth Meyer, *Clio's Circle: Entering the Imaginal World of Historians* (New Orleans, LA: Spring Journal Books, 2006).

[43] Phillip Gibson, "The Singing and Dancing God of War," Pacifica Graduate Institute, unpublished paper.

[44] Hillman, *Re-Visioning Psychology*, pp. 121-122.

[45] *Ibid.*, p. 116.

[46] *Ibid.*, p. 136.

[47] Paulo Freire, *Pedagogy of the Oppressed* (New York: Continuum, 1989).

[48] Mary Watkins, "Seeding Liberation: A Dialogue between Depth Psychology and Liberation Psychology," in *Depth Psychology: Meditations in the Field*, ed. Dennis Slattery and Lionel Corbett (Einsiedeln, Switzerland: Daimon Verlag, 2000); Mary Watkins and Helene Lorenz, *Toward Psychologies of Liberation* (London/New York: Palgrave Macmillan, 2008).

[49] Lewis Hyde, *The Gift: Imagination and the Erotic Life of Property* (New York: Vintage Books, 1979).

[50] *Ibid.*, p. 23.

[51] Brent Blair, "Looking in Darkness," Depth Psychology Doctoral Program, Pacifica Graduate Institute, 2000, unpublished paper, p. 1.

[52] James Hillman, "Goals for Dallas," in *City and Soul*, ed. Robert J. Leaver (Putnam, CT: Spring Publications, 2006), p. 275.

Robert Leaver is a community psychologist, facilitator, and teacher. He is the convener of New Commons—a think, link, and do tank. His current focus is Crafting Communities, Making Places with Character in villages, cities, networks, and organizations. Leaver holds a B.A. in Psychology from Roger Williams College and an M.S. in Child Development and Family Relations from the University of Rhode Island. He has taught psychology, organizational theory, and entrepreneurship at various Rhode Island colleges and currently serves on the faculty of Boston College's Leadership for Change. His publications include a chapter entitled "The Commonwealth Organization," in *Rediscovering the Soul of Business: A Renaissance of Values* (1995) and several monographs on 21st-century organization and community building. His most recent work with James Hillman involved compiling and editing *City and Soul*, Volume 2 of the *Uniform Edition of the Writings of James Hillman* (2006).

# 26

# The Work of James Hillman: City and Soul, and Providence, RI

ROBERT LEAVER

Without images, we tend to lose the way. ... The soul wants its images, and when it doesn't find them, it makes substitutes: billboards and graffiti, for instance. ... How we see into each other, look at each others' faces, read each other—that is how soul contact takes place. ... We also need body places. Places where bodies see each other, meet each other, are in touch with each other, like the people who leave their offices in Paris and swim in the Seine River. ...This emphasizes the relationship of body to the daily life of the city, bringing one's physical body into the town. In other words, I am emphasizing the place of intimacy within a city, for intimacy is crucial to the soul. ... A city that neglects the soul's welfare makes the soul search for its welfare in a degrading and concrete way, in the shadow of those same gleaming towers. ... The soul that is uncared for turns into an angry child.[1]

## I. Hillman's Doggedness

As an archetypal psychologist, what does James Hillman have to say to us about cities? Why such a long-standing interest in cities since his co-founding of the Dallas Institute for Humanities and Culture in 1973 and the resulting early writings on city and soul?

One answer can be found in the Greek word for city, *polis*—the throng and energy of people. Other psychologists define psyche in terms of what is inside us or in relation to another person. For Hillman, psyche has to relate deeply to what is *out there* and animate the archetypes. This move takes in not just what lies inside, but also outside and around us as well.[2] For Hillman, cities consciously or unconsciously evolve us, and our culture, and do so more than we care to acknowledge.

Building on the *polis* ... in ancient Greece the city was about spectacle and spectators—people seeing and being with others. Without a vital *polis*, the self remains recessed and not engaged. We exist only in the presence of other spectators and spectacles.

Hillman nudges us to attend to the city: to open our eyes and look, and let our hearts feel the buildings, the public sculptures, the public squares as alive. He wants us to know that city *is nature, that nature is* not just what we encounter when we go into the woods. Hillman wants us to know that streets are for slow walking, to take in the city's soul. The mind alone will not move the culture. For a culture to move, it must be felt through the valve of aesthetics—a breathing in—that is ever so present in cities.

Hillman sees city-making as an act of soul-making. The city is where soul can enter and be noticed because cities, more than most places, represent more complex archetypal patterns. For example, our traditional city council chamber is patterned after the Greek public stage, where democracy was in action. This Greek theatre was the stage—the *pynx*—perfectly designed so that all present could hear and see each other. Further, in cities, pathologies smolder. Messes are ever-present. Cities are intense Petri dishes in which we may observe people living and working. Eyes connect. People meet. Together, they walk and talk, coming back from lunch. Old men play chess with life-sized pieces in an old park in Zürich. A city is never finished. This hum of the *polis*—the energy of the throng—makes cities rich repositories of soul and culture, and in turn, cities shape the people living in them, deepening soul and culture.

Archetypal psychology is known as an inclusive movement or "invisible college." It welcomes in psychology, mythology, story and poetry, art, culture and public life, and much more. As an invisible college, "the movement" has no campus. Instead, the invisible college evolves through common themes and inquiries that bind thinkers and practitioners together throughout the world. What better place than cities to connect thinkers and practitioners doing the work of archetypal psychology?

Hillman loves to push the edges, to make the invisible more visible, and to honor what should remain invisible. He is not interested in what we know; instead he heads out to uncover and name the unspoken, the unsaid, or the yet-to-be-said. Hillman invites us to read the signs in the culture based on what the archetypes and myths reveal. He left clinical practice about twenty years ago to become a therapist of our culture. He now engages in a therapy of ideas with the aim of both dislodging unhealthy ideas and healing the culture. And cities are one rich place to engage in a therapy of ideas.

## II. Core Ideas of City and Soul

### Cities Entertain Ideas, Hold Images

At the end of a century, the myths, the stories, and the forms that shaped it crumble. The next century cannot be a repetition of the previous one. Rather, the next century begs for new stories and new forms to evolve to shape the next myth.[3] The future is not a fresh start; rather, the new story and form blends what fits from the past with what has to be freshly developed. Cities most often lead the conversations that evolve our culture. And the next stage in the evolution of cities will need ideas dancing everywhere. Hillman works in the world of ideas—both by *manufacturing* and challenging them, He writes:

> ... [W]here do you go to play with ideas? ... Where can we go to imagine an idea and move it further? ... [Nowhere in our society are we encouraged to] let the idea swim way out and reel it back in again. ... One of the great difficulties in our American life is that we don't have places for entertaining ideas. And that is precisely what we're supposed to do with an idea: entertain it. This means having respect for ideas themselves: letting them come and go without demanding too much from them at first,

> like their origins ..., their popularity ..., their logic .... Why can't they be a little crazy? We admit our feelings are crazy. ... [M]aybe our ideas have arms and legs, too, and are crazy and want to get out and meet other ideas, air themselves, spend time with each other in public. The ideas themselves, not the people in whom they occur. Just the ideas wanting to appear and be received, welcomed, entertained for a while.[4]

Through his European sensibilities, Hillman slows us down to a more measured pace, in contrast to the hastiness and impatient speed of America. He is less interested in explaining or validating what is or what we do based on current convention. He wants us to stop responding automatically and realize that what we think and what we do is shaped by images and archetypes. For example, "the ideas we have that we do not know we have ... have a hold on us."[5] His written harangues aim at dislodging imprisoning ideas and opening our psyches up to entertaining more liberating ideas. This is his therapy of ideas at work.

Hillman finds that Americans are too preoccupied with action. We do not entertain ideas merely for the sake of their beauty. We rush to judgment, closing out other possibilities. Standing on the shoulders of Carl Jung, Hillman invites us to stop analyzing the meaning of an image in a dream; instead, he advises us to "stick with the image,"[6] and allow the image to do its work. An image or idea comes with an imperative; it wants something of us. It will not get satisfaction until you move *with* it. Go where the image takes you; it knows what to do. For Hillman, there is action in letting the image pull you because your psyche is in motion, thinking, feeling what the image reveals.

The American mind thinks of "change" as going west for a fresh start, discarding the past, leaving stuff behind. Hillman views change differently, whether it concerns individuals, organizations, or cities. We cannot disregard the past and just "go west." Instead, we must name what remains changeless, immutable, and even messy, and what is open to change.[7] The soul comes alive from experiencing the changeless anchors and is thus granted permission to explore change.

## Polytheism for Cities

Archetypal psychology steers clear of anything mono. This psychology is polytheistic: it considers the many. Conversations in cities about planning, budgeting, or zoning often get stuck because each voice holds his or her way of thinking to be the one and only right way. For example, in most U.S. cities, it is the practical people who run municipal affairs, and the artistic people are largely marginalized, despite the occasional endowment or token grant. Consequently, artists view themselves as disconnected from "Joe Citizen" and all too often steer clear of engaging in civic affairs.

A way out of this standoff is for cities to engage in community conversations. Hillman puts forth three realms of experience to frame such conversations: the concrete, the psychological, and the mythical.[8] It is a trilogy of need, want, and desire, or fact, conversation, and story. Each layer of experience feels distinct to the observing psyche. Each layer reveals elements of soul. The concrete is our world of facts; everything is singular and matter of fact: mono. Our needs are located here. The psychological is our world of two: a conversation back and forth with another. Tensions arise. Here we experience the presence, and often difference, of the other person. Our wants come into play; there is often tension and dissension. The third realm is the mythic, with its multiples and its many possibilities. The mythic realm holds images, stories, and endless connectivity, which is often beyond the comprehension of the human mind. This is the realm of the unexplainable—the poetic basis of mind. Desire and longing reside here. This is where a city's destiny is lodged.

Cities with soul revel in engaging the three realms, with their citizens as members of the *polis*. In concrete terms, we have crumbling infrastructure and potholes. So we complain or try to fix the problem. In psychological terms, we go about doing the business of the city, having meetings, engaging in debate, holding conversations, or feeling the pulse of the crowds in the streets. And in mythical terms, we feel the origins of the place, its layers of memory laid down by previous creators, its longing to shape the city's destiny. A city of soul, a city of character of place, traverses all three of these realms.

## *Anima Mundi*—Soul of the World

Hillman invites us into the soul of the world—*anima mundi*—the large animated sphere swirling around us. It is an old soul, deep with layers of tradition and innovation. Wake up: the soul of the world is alive and longs for you to attend to it. Everyday things in the world pulse with life: rocks, fish, trees, and city streets—all are animated. Look around. Feel the particulars. It is the soul of the world as our patient—not us—that needs attention. If people respected all things as animated with soul, there would be less trashing of the natural world.

In archetypal psychology, soul and spirit are different. Spirit swiftly transcends, soars, and wants to leave the messes behind. It has a quick, ascending tone. Spirit is above, where it is pure and clear. What lie below are soul and a murky descent. Soul is the layering of experience, the mess, the incompleteness, culturally crafted over time in a mythic sense. Since soul is below, you drop into it. Soul is a slower mode of being than spirit. Soul has rough edges and quirks. The soul of a city includes the often unwanted—the strip club, the homeless, the hidden "sad bar" behind the black glass we hurriedly walk by.

Soul is vast and empty until we enter "it" with ideas, images, actions, and above all, longing. The soul of the world says, "I am nothing unless you move in me."[9] The romantics say, "Tell me what you long for and I will tell you who you are."[10] Cities long for people to move inside them and thus to be making soul.

And when you read vision statements put out by cities, you realize that they tend to be full of spirit and not much soul. So we have much work to do to get soul talked about more.

## Beauty and Aesthetics

Beauty animates the world soul, and thus our cities. Beauty is not just what is considered pretty. Beauty is not limited to the art on the walls of urban galleries. In fact, to animate the soul of the world, beauty must be released from the "temporary prisons" of office lobbies and museums—the most often assumed only right place for art. Instead, beauty is *the* city. Beauty is revealed in the city street life of people and the public places. It is present in the old buildings that tell stories of memory … "once upon a time that building was the counting house for the ships arriving in the port of Providence." It is the experience of the strange nooks and streets that twist and then stop and go nowhere. It is the look of the battered street sign on which the words are barely readable. It is felt in the cries of kids outside in the street or the look of the weathered faces of the elders of the city. In cities, such beauty lies in wait, ready to ambush us and surprise us with its wonder, as it did Gabriel Garcia Márquez, who found magic in the ordinary chores of being.

Aesthetics and beauty are joined at the hip, or, put another way, beauty touches our senses through aesthetics. Aesthetics enables us to gasp in awe, "to breathe in" through our senses, our heart and bodies tingling. Aesthetics slows us down ... we are temporarily in a moment of stillness in which we feel and imagine our self to be a bit fuller, more powerful, or sad, but most of all emotionally connected to the soul of the world. Aesthetics is the vibe in each particular "pull"—like the face of someone walking towards us or an unexpected turn in a city street. Something is asked of us. We stop to take in an unusual window; we stop to talk. This response is aesthetic and so beauty is present. Such expressions of beauty allow the soul of the world to feel a bit blessed.

## Natural Beauty without Nature

For James Hillman, one does not have to go to the woods to find nature or beauty: it is everywhere in our cities. Hillman wants to free the definition of nature from the limits of natural things only, such as the woods, and disentangle the need for beauty from the need for nature. Beauty is everywhere in everything we see and touch—in the office, in the funky coffee shop, in the old faces of the street. When we make this move, "we no longer have to split the natural from the urban. Surely it is as natural for humans to build burial grounds, market places, and form political and social communities ... as it is for them to gather nuts and berries. ... Cities belong to human nature; nature does not begin outside the city walls."[11]

## The Walking Cure

"A city that offers no walking offers no dwelling for the mind nor soul. We may be *driving* ourselves crazy by not attending to the fundamental need for walking. When walking we release anxiety."[12] The city is for walking with all our senses engaged: our eyes, our ears, our feet. Old cities have grown from the patterns of our feet or the patterns of cows. When we walk we feel the mazes and amazements of what has gone before us. So cities serve as dwelling places where we can get in touch with memories and our own better health. Further, by getting out of cars, we reduce our carbon footprint and help slow global warming.

## Character Forms in Community

Archetypal psychology moves our frame of mind beyond the individual, beyond *my* problems, beyond *my* lost lover. Hillman has a revolutionary view of self (or character, a term he uses often).

> The idea of self has to be redefined. … [S]elf is [often viewed as] the interiorization of the invisible God beyond. … I would rather define self as *the interiorization of community*. [Thus, a self is what people, ideas, and things you bring in from "out there" from the soul of the world.] … If self were defined as the interiorization of community, then the boundaries between me and another would be much less sure. I would be with myself when I'm with others. I would not be with myself when I'm walking alone or meditating or in my room imagining or working on my dreams. In fact, I would be estranged from myself.
> And "others" would not include just other people, because community … is something more ecological … [a] psychic field. And if I'm not in a psychic field with others—with people, buildings, animals, trees—I *am* not. … "I am because I party." *Convivo ergo sum.*[13]

Cities are one form of psychic field, shaping who we are and what we do. Hillman's rant against psychotherapy: therapy has not kept up. It isolates people from the stuff of the world. It separates people from the culture and the *polis* (the literal throng and energy of the people), where self—character—has the opening to step into its destiny. Counter to this soul opening is therapy, stepping in, shutting out vital experience: instead of engaging the culture or the polis by taking political action, we internalize "the stuff" as *my* problem. Therapy deadens rather than activates us, whereas in community, especially in cities, there is the chance that something "out there"—such as a toxic building—will enrage us into taking action and thus bring us closer to our character.

This psychic field of the city is inclusive of differences. In the city, our character and ideas have the opportunity to develop more fully and dynamically than, say, in the suburbs, which are mostly about sameness, with little experience of difference. Character is formed from encountering differentness, other faces—the faces of characters both present and past. In the city, one can sense the layers of memory that are present, layers by which one remembers the faces and words of the ghosts and ancestors who have gone before and built what one is now walking through. This memory is triggered by the place's culture as well as by the buildings. Cities provide the differentiation and complexity that the soul longs for. Its rough edges, its quirks, even its incompleteness—all these are essential ingredients to hew character and enliven the polis.

In his poem, "The Second Coming," Yeats says: "... The falcon cannot hear the falconer; / Things fall apart; the center cannot hold; / Mere anarchy is loosed upon the world ...."[14] The center of democracy will hold only when we see and feel the faces of others. Cities are the best natural container for faces to see faces. As Levinas says: "[T]he bare face of another is where ethics lies."[15] If we truly see the face of others, we cannot turn away from our service to the common good. If we all head for the woods and isolation and assume that cities are dead, Yeats's center will not hold, the culture will crumble ....

The *polis* longs for us to "mix it up" with others. Despite our feisty, distinctly American need for independence and privacy, there is something equally hardwired about our need to be with others. The human dilemma is how to handle the creative tension between self (or "I want to be alone") and others. And it is with others that our character is formed.

## III. Providence: A City of Justice, Beauty and Destiny[16]

The job of the citizen is to tune the vibe of the city. You are not here primarily to build the buildings or fix the infrastructure, but to make the city human again. The Greeks named the city vibe the *polis*—the throng of the people, or the oil that greased the wheels of Athenian democracy. As soul-makers of Providence, its citizens "oil this place" to create the conditions that will make the practice of democracy run more smoothly. The rebirth of Providence is about its people rising up after a long sleep of introversion. A city is nothing without its people being engaged as citizens.

As a city, Providence means two things: (1) it is a physical place, and (2) it is the sense of destiny implicit in the definition of providence, the noun, as "the timely preparation for future eventualities."[17] Soul-making in this city requires its citizens to pursue three timeless Hillman longings, three ideas (not literalisms to quantify): justice, beauty, and destiny:[18]

- Justice: our ongoing struggle to make our co-existence and co-participation with other people and with the planet possible;
- Beauty: our receptivity—heart open, senses alive and on fire—to the city's unfolding as a large work of public art, a receptivity that comes from walking the city, breathing in the life of the city with heart aroused, taking in the sensory particulars of the experience we know as Providence;
- Destiny: our realization that we are meant for something, something is wanted of us—moments of feeling necessary—beyond our immediate personal concerns, the pull of the distinct call to live our Providence.

By combining these three timeless values in distinctive ways, Providence can get in touch with providence and better understand its character of place. Here is a sampling of how Providence lives these three longings. We display our *beauty* on a walk along cobblestoned Pine Street or having coffee after a concert at the all-night 1940s Haven Brothers Diner, wheeled in each evening to its reserved spot next to City Hall. We foster *justice* through the existence of over fifteen innovative and engaged citizen associations such as the Downtown Neighborhood Association. We live the *destiny* of our place by being quirky, creative, open, and entrepreneurial, by believing that small is beautiful, and by practicing diversity in diversity with little ethnic isolation. Our destiny is *in* our founding story, as told by Roger Williams, the founder of RI who, when faced with the "my way or the highway" attitude of the Massachusetts Puritans and a warrant for his arrest, got out of town and put a stake in the ground for religious freedom, which eventually developed into a cornerstone of democracy in the U.S. Williams embedded in our state constitution the words: "to go forth as a bold and lively experiment for the religious freedom for all."[19] Williams adamantly wrote of soul freedom for all citizens as a guiding principle in creating Rhode Island as an active, lively experiment.

As a city, we will experience our Providence when we own *our* sense of place—what we stand for and want to see manifested. To be true to ourselves, to our character, we must own soul freedom and not succumb to the preservationist view of Providence (keep things as they are) or the usual general projection of what a city is about (compare ourselves to Boston or New York, say, and come up short). Remember, Providence wants something unique from us, and we must keep unfolding what our city demands of us.

## All Citizens Are Artists

Each city needs to work out its own understanding of beauty, justice, and destiny, and in order to get it right we need to consider the thoughts of James Hillman on the power of citizens to animate aesthetics and beauty in making a city:

> If artists are like the City's watchdogs, the barking guardians of immediate un-anesthetized noticing, then a first priority of any city is to increase the participation of its artists and to make life for them more possible—not "easy" or recognized or successful, merely *possible*.
>
> By "artists" please don't hear me to mean … those with professional artistic skills. No. The artist that the city needs to favor is anyone whose perception and action embodies subversive, discomforting, aesthetic noticing—preacher, journalist, photographer, humorist, thinker, investor. Any citizen at all is an artist when he or she cuts through cant, demands quality, and refuses to be anesthetized.
>
> Artists are not those who have taste, but those who *do* taste, and see the world. They do not have special senses, sensibilities, sensitivities; they simply sense as men and women of senses, sensing what goes on, and responding 100% to the city, to its discomforts and outrages by being equally discomforting and outrageous.
>
> The artist furthermore—and you are beginning to see that what I am calling artists others might call citizens—is always altogether engaged … in work time and free time, functional and aesthetic, practical and ideal. What happens in the street, what he or she smells and touches has no less importance than Major Policies and Great Ideas. The citizen as artist leaves nothing to George, and nothing to Sam. He [or she] is the eternal busybody.[20]

My questions to the citizen artists of Providence are: What annoys you about your city? What needs more aesthetic, public attention in Providence so we can breathe in our *polis*? Where will we create the next public places that will serve as common ground for neighborhoods and ethnic groups to gather? Where are we ready to be outrageous?

## Our Daily Practice as Citizens of Providence

In 1987, a rug dealer from India was part of my life for the summer. He spent the night at a party I hosted in Newport, RI walking about the room introducing himself like this: "And so Robert, how *do you* serve the world?" I still tingle when I hear his question, and I am still pursuing the answer. I invite the citizens of Providence to live the rug dealer's question, but with a tweak: How do you serve Providence?

Here are some suggestions for how individuals as citizen artists can activate the hum of the *polis*, the throng of fellow citizens, and move their city to touch the hearts of more of its people:

- Engage in public actions that move the city from discomfort to more comfort and from comfort to more discomfort, knowing that city-making is never finished, knowing that comfort and discomfort are an essential creative tension that we have to handle.
- Remember that our eyes gazing into another's eyes on the city streets is the core of our humanity. The eyes of others bond us all in civil community. Community is possible only when we are vulnerable in the face of others from all stations in life and all walks of life. As Levinas tells us, ethics lies in the face.[21]
- Hold public conversations with friends and strangers in the streets. Linger with others. Slow it all down so that there is time to converse on a street corner as an act of living our democracy. Make public conversations on the streets a daily ritual, like a prayer.
- Say hello to strangers; let your eyes meet the eyes of others.
- Publicly notice Providence's quirky nooks and crannies as sacred gifts to talk about with others. Animate our quirks, such as the Haven Brothers Diner, or the cobblestones on Pine Street. Reveal to others the city's gifts—streets such as Westminster Street, with its intact 19th-century look and feel as a streetscape. Andrés Duany, the new urbanist planner and a frequent visitor to Providence to help us plan the city, sees Westminster Street as the last jewel of an 18th-century street in America, with its old European design and feel.
- Walk slowly—eyes wide open to take in the gaze of others and the surprises of Providence.
- Walk, with your head up, looking, sensing and tasting the city's people and buildings instead of looking down at your feet or above to the skies.

These acts of soul-making are our work as citizens to mold this city for the greater good. Publicly engaging people and animating our place are our obligations as citizens. These acts of caring for people and place are democracy in action.

## IV. Providence Fragments

The following fragments and isolated bits reveal that some of Hillman's questions and ideas still dance in the Providence culture. They are drawn from a formal talk and two community conversations in which Hillman engaged community leaders of Providence in 2005 and 2006. The focus of these gatherings was "Providence and Beyond: Sustainable Cities? Sustainable Suburbs?"[22] Participants were consciously invited for their diversity of views and backgrounds: developers, city planners, academics, public artists, elected officials, business owners, community activists, and environmentalists. The framework for the conversation: the next questions, images, ideas, and creative tensions to shape Providence. Five questions raised by Hillman in the conversation were:

- How do we green a city? What is the green fantasy?
- Does aesthetics cost more?
- What kind of bridges can be built between sections and classes of the city? Who comes to meetings about the city?
- How do we know when the city is working? Promoting "good" news on the media: What is real local news?
- What is typically Providence? How to characterize the essence of this city? Who are Providence's ancestors and ghosts whose presence is still shaping Providence?

These Hillman questions are still nudging us along in Providence. Below are two of Hillman's questions with notes of his responses teased out from a back-and-forth community conversation between him and the other participants.

### What Kinds of Bridges Can Be Built between Parts of the City?

***Hillman:*** The great industrial cities of the past century had three elements that brought diverse people together in the cities: public transportation, department stores, and baseball parks. What will the next public meeting places for our cities be? What do we come to cities for today? Consider making known what people come to cities for these days: protection and security, hospitality, courts and justice, pageants and displays. And in Providence you have Water Fire, an ancient ritual of water, fire, people, and music, attended by 100,000 people each night. And, my boat ride last year to ceremonially ignite the fires was tribal and soulful. Our old cities were built on the tomb of a figure whom the citizens owed something to. How do we put in place the next kinds of urban worship spots? Today, in cities we are on our own. We are moving towards a Greek-city-state-like structure because the Feds are backing off. So we have to be more loyal to our places and the fantasies of our place.

### How Do We Know the City Is Working? Promoting Good News on the Media: What Is Real Local News?

*Hillman:* Begin by transforming the idea of what is local news. News was created as a public service and we must get back to that founding principle. News is what the people talk about in the city, all people and not just the TV guys. Telling local stories takes more time than watching TV and that's a good thing. It is time to share each other's struggles as news: the developments in the city … gossip … where is the money going? As citizens think about what you need to know to help you, help each other foster the *polis*.

## V. The Next Stage in the Evolution of Cities

In what fresh ways will James Hillman and archetypal psychologies handle the next evolution of cities?

### A New Profession: Community Psychologist

Many of the current ways of approaching city-making isolate disciplines and often make them compete for attention and resources. It is time for a new profession, or rather, a team of professionals, that places front and center their new work of tuning the psychology of the community. And archetypal psychology is one discipline able to weave together the diverse elements of architecture, planning, public art, and much more.

## Cities as Inter-Cultural Places

Community is defined as the shared experience of the ties that bind us to others in ways that matter, beyond our sense of self. As there are distinct senses of place, there are different kinds of community. Some communities, such as those of the Shakers, have close ties with little room for variation. Other communities have loose ties, such as those found in Los Angeles.

In the evolution of community in the U.S., we began as a mono culture. Then came the great "melting pot," as we opened our arms to the first immigrants. Of late, the focus has been on multi-culturalism, which welcomes diversity and does not dissolve diverse customs and languages into one homogeneous broth. Now something else is required.

Immigrants flock to our cities for work as well as to remain connected to their culture of origin through proximity to other immigrants from their ethnic group. With their arrival, cities are seeding a inter-cultural milieu. Immigration today is less European/Mediterranean-dominated than it was in the past, and represents a greater diversity of cultures—African, Middle-Eastern, Asian—with a variety of customs and symbols. This requires us to think and act more inter-culturally, that is, we work together directly for the benefit of the whole.[23]

## Democracy in Action Again

Creating more places to practice (that is, get ready for and then exercise) democracy requires the blending of the discipline of aesthetics, the built environment, and social justice. Richard Sennett[24] describes the two building blocks of Athenian democracy as the *agora* (the marketplace), for the practice of democracy, and the *pynx* (equivalent to today's city council chambers), the formal place for the exercise of democracy. To animate democracy, citizens need more places distributed throughout our cities to practice and then to act more democratically than we have until now.

## 21st-Century Buildings

It is estimated that a one-degree rise in mean global temperature will obliterate parts of coastal Maine, parts of Manhattan, and the entire Jersey coast within 20 years. Climate change will lead to fewer cars and trucks on the roads and more localism and regionalism. Some of the changes in our lifestyle will come in the form of self-contained eco-green buildings, localized energy production, and a closed-loop city ecosystem in which "one person's waste is another's food."[25]

The nature of buildings will change too. The next generation of sustainable, green, high-performance buildings will not necessarily look like our preserved old buildings or our more recent modern ones. Green building materials and ecological design considerations will challenge architects and planners to move beyond repeating history or perpetuating modernism and instead create an elegant, aesthetic that defies category. Not only the architecture but also the mechanics of buildings will be designed for the long-term and for disassembly. Parts will be designed to be reused, and whole sections, such as a bedroom, will be have the possibility of being moved to another house when the kids grow up and leave. In this way, less goes to the city dump—or floats on a barge in the ocean, to be dumped eventually in someone else's backyard. Most recently constructed buildings have a financial shelf-life of 15 years. After the investment has been paid off, the building is often torn down to make room for another 15-year building. In all cases, the rubble is sent to the landfill. This practice will change too. We need buildings that are built like cathedrals—to last forever—yet are ready to be disassembled and reassembled elsewhere at any moment.

## Our "Fall" into Place and Community—Ground Zero and Katrina

Two seldom-integrated foundations have shaped American culture, have influenced how we engage in commerce and how we create our culture. 9/11 and Katrina—two colossal disasters—ruptured our two-part foundation. At Ground Zero, American commerce was hit. The towers were built by technology, and destroyed in an instant by technology. The destruction was accomplished in mere minutes. Arising from the ruble was a man of spirit—a hero—Rudolph Giuliani, who so quickly rallied the *polis*, righting the ship. His call was to save New York.

His eagerness and haste to right the ship cut short a beautiful experience. In the wake of the Twin Towers' collapse, there were reports in New York, for a week or so, of acts of kindness and a sense of community. In the wake of the event, the feminine longing for connection and soul entered and stayed for a while.[26] As the business of the city again took over, the feminine and the soul withdrew its temporary visible presence. To enter a place and be felt, soul requires sustained slowness.

In New Orleans, one of the prime centers of American culture was smashed by Hurricane Katrina. New Orleans is about music, story, old buildings, and a vibe that is a defining characteristic of the culture of most old industrial American cities. New Orleans was built by hand, over centuries. Nature destroyed it, slowly, over many days, with water and mud—two marks of the presence of soul. As is characteristic of soul, no one single Giuliani-like spirit rose up—though such an out-front leader kept being asked for on the coast of Louisiana. Without a "Giuliani," leadership in Katrina-ravaged New Orleans was assumed to be lacking. Yet, we heard stories of small acts of bravery and compassion by unknown local "heroes." These small acts of kindness express the more invisible soul or call for "leaderful-ness,"[27] as opposed to the visible spirit and the swift-acting heroics of a single charismatic leader. The "slower" feminine was more pervasive, and still lingers, in New Orleans.

The destroyed towers and flooding are "tough" urban problems to tackle: decaying infrastructure vs. modern technology; the marked difference between a slick new building built by technology in New York (amortized to last 15 years!) and the old buildings of New Orleans, built by hand to last more than a lifetime. A premium was placed on charisma as *the* true measure of leadership. On one hand, the public call in New York was for the rebuilding of the "Center of World Commerce" as quickly as possible. On the other hand, the call for New Orleans—a vital piece of Americana, with its street musicians and storytellers—was to dismantle the city (or at least large sections of it). But in fact, America longs for both. In the call to eliminate New Orleans as a city we hear, not the struggle between economics and culture, but rather the push for the supremacy of American culture as defined in terms of the high "European" arts of New York City. The supposed supremacy of commerce and high culture over street culture is still an ongoing urban problem.

We need both the masculine and the feminine to be engaged in order for our culture to be whole. The masculine drives for independence and distinction. The feminine has a longing for connection and community. This call for a sense of place and community is a not sexist parting of the ways, with men doing one thing and women doing another! No, it is a call to revive the psychological power of making places and making community by hand, by and for the community. The two callings remain the same, but the actions—like running a local farm or holding a coffee hour—will be different today.

## Six Slow Movements for Cities

Life is short, we must move slowly.[28]

Six movements demonstrate localism and slowness on the rise.

**Slow Cities**: This movement began in Italy in 1999, when the mayors of four cities got together to define guiding principles for their cities: less pollution, the conservation of local aesthetic traditions, the fostering of local crafts, produce, and cuisine, and the effort to make citizens aware of the pleasures and rewards of the leisurely rhythms of life.

**Slow Community Conversation**: The new commons is not a single physical place, like the old New England commons, where cattle grazed and the first town meetings were held and public notices were posted. The new commons is many places. It is many things. It cuts across and blends neighborhoods, disciplines, and classes. It is part town hall, part grange hall, and part third place, like Ray Oldenburg's coffee and barbershops of old.[29] Further, it is the call to build the next generation of fourth places: the public realm that goes beyond parks and squares. The new commons is the 21st-century version of the bazaars of ancient Istanbul or Lisbon, where goods were bought and sold in dense spaces of trading. The hum of the *polis* was felt in such places. In ancient Greece, the *agora*—the bazaar—was the training ground for democracy, which was executed in the more formal Greek *pynx*, or theater. The *agora* is what the new commons strives to re-create.

**Slow Learning:** This is, in part, "stealing time from the culture"[30] for reflection in a hurried world. If we do not stop and reflect publicly, we will keep doing what we have always done, even though it was conceived for a time that is now gone forever. Additionally, slow learning understands the local knowledge, or the place's "metis."[31] That is, it knows about how local practices and wisdom move in a community, since each place behaves differently based on its individual "metis." Most people fail to understand the particulars of a place because they are blinded by, and thus impose on the locality, a global, generalized, abstract standard. Abstract standards reveal generalities and not the particulars of a place's nuances and detailed local understandings.

**Slow Food:** This is not only about the local production of food, but also about the slow experience of tasting it. When we eat slowly, we are *in* conversation with others and their faces at our table. The slow-food movement was born in Italy as a counter-reaction to the announcement that a McDonald's would be built on a cherished piazza. In a post-peak-fossil-fuel world, cities and their surrounding regions will have to produce much of their food locally. The Intervale in Burlington, Vermont produces about 8% of the city's fresh food and does so from an old dump farmed by 13 entrepreneurial farmers.

**Slow Money:** This is the work of Woody Tasch and the Investors' Circle. It uses patient capital (slow returns) to invest in American companies committed to sustainability. The Circle has over 400 investors throughout the U.S. While most second-tier cities keep complaining that they are not keeping up with the fast, large money movements of Boston, Silicon Valley, or New York, the time has come for smaller cities to promote a slow money, or bootstrapping, economy.

**Slow Building:** The next buildings and public places that will be created in our cities will require an unfolding.[32] As an architect, Christopher Alexander sits on the land, walks the land, and feels the land, until the building or public space that the land and the people want comes into his heart and then into view. For Alexander, it is a partnership involving the land, the people, and the professionals. Alexander's timeless method of planning first defines the public realm and how people want to walk in it, then designs and locates buildings and pedestrian paths to service these needs.

Each of these urban challenges "holds a place" for the insights of archetypal psychologies, because when it is engaged in cities, archetypal psychology brings questions and ideas to move the story along. Hillman tells the story of Oedipus on the road out of Thebes—his beginnings—moving to Colonus, his preparation for ends. On the walk he is blind and inflated: "Set my consciousness straight and the city will be straight."[33] Hillman calls this hubris. Oedipus is no longer the inquisitor who saves the city by action. In Colonus, he learns to bless the city by his death and moves from piety to libations. In Colonus, he touches the city, listens to it, and takes in where the city is now. Anima and images are the method in Colonus. On the road from Thebes to Colonus we dream the myth of cities along. And that is what our cities today long to do next. And archetypal psychology serves as an essential frame for the next generation of practitioners who are striving to make city with soul.

## *NOTES*

[1] James Hillman, "City and Soul," in *City and Soul*, Uniform Edition of the Writings of James Hillman, Vol. 2, ed. Robert Leaver (New York: Spring Publications, 2006), pp. 20-26. This quote is an extract from the article by the same name in the Uniform Edition that the author has had for years, passed on to him as a typewritten handout.

[2] James Hillman, *Re-Visioning Psychology* (New York: Harper and Row, 1975).

[3] Michael Meade, from lecture notes taken by the author during men's work conferences with Robert Bly, James Hillman, and Michael Meade, 1989.

[4] James Hillman, "Entertaining Ideas" in *Stirrings of Culture,* ed. Robert J. Sardello and Gail Thomas (Dallas, TX: The Dallas Institute of Humanities and Culture, 1986), p. 3.

[5] James Hillman, from lecture notes taken by the author during the men's work conferences with Robert Bly, James Hillman, and Michael Meade, 1989.

[6] *Ibid.*

[7] *Ibid.*

[8] Ibid.

[9] Hillman, *Re-Visioning Psychology.*

[10] Robert Bly, from lecture notes taken by the author during the men's work conferences with Robert Bly, James Hillman, and Michael Meade, 1989.

[11] James Hillman. "Natural Beauty without Nature: Re-founding the City," 1995, audiotape of a lecture given at Leslie College, Boston, Massachusetts. Sound Horizons, New York, NY, 1995.

[12] James Hillman, "Walking," in *City and Soul*, Uniform Edition of the Writings of James Hillman, Vol. 2, ed. Robert Leaver (New York: Spring Publications, 2006), p. 253.

[13] James Hillman and Michael Ventura, *We've Had a Hundred Years of Therap—and the World's Getting Worse* (New York: Harper Collins, 1992), p. 40.

[14] William Butler Yeats, *The Collected Poems of W. B. Yeats* (New York: The Macmillan Company, 1956), pp. 184-185.

[15] Emanuel Levinas, quoted in James Hillman, *The Force of Character and the Lasting Life* (New York: Random House, 1999), pp. 141-142.

[16] Excerpted from a talk given by the author to the members of the new down-city residents association of Providence, RI, in June 2005.

[17] Oxford Compact English Dictionary (Oxford: Oxford University Press, 2003).

[18] James Hillman, "Justice, Beauty and Destiny as Foundations for an Ecological Psychology," in *City and Soul*, Uniform Edition of the Writings of James Hillman, Vol. 2, ed. Robert Leaver (New York: Spring Publications, 2006), pp. 207-216.

[19] This is the origin myth of Rhode Island based on actual language in the state constitution of Rhode Island.

[20] James Hillman, "Imagining Buffalo," in *City and Soul*, Uniform Edition of the Writings of James Hillman, Vol. 2, ed. Robert Leaver (New York: Spring Publications, 2006), pp. 295-296.

[21] See note 15 above.

[22] You can read excerpts of the Hillman Conversations by going to <http://www.newcommons.com/page/87041/> (November 10, 2007). The origins of "Providence and Beyond" was the June 2005 symposium, "Transforming Urban Communities," sponsored by the Royal Society of Art in Providence, RI.

[23] Charles Landry, keynote address at the Transforming Urban Communities symposium, June 2005, Providence, RI.

[24] Richard Sennett, "The Spaces of Democracy," *Harvard Design Magazine* 8 (Summer 1999).

[25] William McDonough and Michael Braungart, *Cradle to Cradle* (New York: North Point Press, 2002). The aim of the book is to have us think of designing everything so that whatever is created is another product's food.

[26] James Hillman, "Ground Zero: A Reading," in *City and Soul*, Uniform Edition of the Writings of James Hillman, Vol. 2, ed. Robert Leaver (New York: Spring Publications, 2006), p. 406.

[27] Joseph Raelin, *Creating Leaderful Organizations* (San Francisco, CA: Berrett-Koehler Publishers, 2003). Leaderfulness is Joe Raelin's idea of moving beyond charismatic leadership as the only model of leadership to bringing out leadership qualities in everyone.

[28] A saying from Thailand, quoted by the poet Naomi Shiob Nye, from notes taken by the author at the "Great Mother Conference," Maine, 1997.

[29] Ray Oldenburg, *The Great Good Place* (St. Paul, MN: Paragon House, 1989).

[30] The mantra of mythologist, Michael Meade, from lecture notes taken by the author during the men's work conferences with Robert Bly, James Hillman, and Michael Meade, 1989.

[31]James C. Scott, *Seeing like a State: How Certain Schemes to Improve the Human Condition Have Failed* (New Haven, CT: Yale University Press, 1998), p. 311.

[32] Christopher Alexander, *The Nature of Order: An Essay on the Art of Building and the Nature of the Universe* (Berkeley, CA: The Center for Environmental Structure, 2002). Throughout this volume and the other three in the Alexander series, "unfolding" is what Alexander sees as the next way to build a building, contrary to the formula building of most of today's architecture.

[33]Karl Kerényi and James Hillman, "Oedipus Revised," in *Oedipus Variations* (New York: Spring Publications, 1991), p. 150.

Ronald Schenk received his Master's degree in Social Work from Washington University, St. Louis, Missouri, and his initial training in psychoanalytic psychotherapy in New Haven, Connecticut. He lived and worked with the Navajo Native Americans before receiving a Ph.D. in Psychology at the University of Dallas, specializing in Phenomenological Psychology. He trained in Jungian Analysis with The Inter-Regional Society of Jungian Analysts, where he has been a Senior Training Analyst for many years and has served in several administrative capacities, most recently as President. He is currently in private practice and teaches in Dallas and Houston. His interests are in clinical training, cultural psychology, and postmodernism. He has written three books, *The Soul of Beauty: A Psychological Investigation of Appearance* (1992), which gives an aesthetic perspective on depth psychology; *Dark Light: The Appearance of Death in Everyday Life* (2001), a collection of essays on culture and imagination; and *The Sunken Quest, The Wasted Fisher, The Pregnant Fish: Post-modern Reflections on Depth Psychology* (2001). The present essay is part of a larger work in progress, *9/11, Enron, "Katrina": Terror, Destruction and American Soul.*

# 27

# 9/11, The Twin Towers, and American Soul

RONALD SCHENK

## 9/11 AND THE APPEARANCE OF THE OTHER

... Beauty's nothing
but the beginning of Terror we're still just able to bear
...

—Ranier Maria Rilke, *Duino Elegies*

Death is the mother of beauty; ...

—Wallace Stevens, "Sunday Morning"

... [A] letter always arrives at its destination.

—Jacques Lacan, Seminar on *The Purloined Letter*

After the dust settled and the magnitude of the effect of the terrorist strikes on the World Trade Center emerged—thousands of people killed, billions of dollars worth of property destroyed, an ensuing retaliatory military campaign of unknown cost and duration, political crisis throughout the Middle East, a severe deepening of an economic recession, the psyche of America revealed as fundamentally fearful and insecure—after all this, what remains most indelibly in the mind are the images, the sheer immensity and power of them, staggering, almost intolerable, each exuding its own terror, its own sexuality, its own beauty:

- a sudden boom, a lush orange billowing fire in the sky, showers of burning birds;
- a rain of bodies—images America did not want to see in photographs—some in flames, diving corporate angels, Blake's terrified, tumbling souls down descending into the hyle, or the contorted figures of Bosch's souls plopping on sidewalks and people like the frogs of Exodus;
- "To Carthage then I came /Burning burning burning burning"[1];
- steady long lines descending, individuals stopping, risking life and limb to help and to hold while obstructing burdened rescuers climbing in counterpoint;
- intimate communications between loved ones before death, while communication breakdown brings death;
- everywhere the search for authority, while the voice of authority instructs workers to return to their offices, which turn into tombs;
- firefighters and police officers arguing over who is in charge while top-level officials locate their headquarters in the very locations that are the most endangered;
- spontaneous choices as to whether to go up or down, ascent ending in death and descent in life;
- and suddenly what was unimaginable to all except a few firefighters and a demolition engineer, the sky falling in a booming tidal wave of collapse amidst a mushrooming cloud, burying and decapitating individuals while crowds run through the streets in horror, straight out of Godzilla movies;
- "London Bridge is falling down falling down falling down"[2];
- and then nothing … but the weighing heavy presence of absence;
- "Have a Nice Day" had turned to havoc universal, gall had burst its bladder, another beast had emerged in slouch, and the moment bowed down.

Although the rescue operation itself was imbued with brave action, which included actually reaching one of the damaged floors in the South Tower (the first to fall), and the successful evacuation of thousands, it was also fraught with scenes of confusion and chaos as in the fog of a battle zone. Many of the rescue workers were not under anyone's command and the police and fire departments were not in communication with each other. Some rescuers were suspected of looting. Fire fighters climbing the stairs were using outmoded communications equipment that did not work, trying to get to a fire their superiors had determined could not be fought, while actually hindering evacuation of workers. Many fire fighters stayed in the buildings either too exhausted to move or uninformed of the order to evacuate. As one firefighter later said, it is too simplistic to make the event one of heroism or blame. "It was a series of random events that killed thousands and saved hundreds. Not many people did anything right that day, but not many people did anything wrong that day either."[3] Another firefighter declared, "I saved one person that day and that was me, and it was by running for my life."[4]

After the crashes, silence descended as an underworld emerged, Dis-appearing—sirens sounding perpetual alarm; individuals and crowds like gaggles of ghosts wandering the streets covered in ash; shadowy workers quietly sifting through the ruins in eerie gray light; search dogs going crazy at the smell of dead humanity but finding no flesh; gnarled, twisted, jagged forms of broken steel looming; the smells—putrid, acrid, overly sweet—permeating everything; below, fires that would not go out, above, emptiness; finally, small altars and memorials of flowers appearing here and there on sidewalks while tiny bone fragments in plastic bags were delivered to the doors of families:

> "My name is Ozymandias, king of kings;
> Look on my works, ye Mighty, and despair!"
> Nothing beside remains. Round the decay
> Of that colossal wreck, boundless and bare
> The lone and level sands stretch far away.[5]

The images carried the complexities and paradoxes of an epic. It was a piece of art, the plot and effects of which put Hollywood to shame,[6] the mind boggled by the imagination, organization, and discipline that was unfolding—terrorist authors and actors, an unwitting cast of thousands and a crew of hundreds, all a part of the whole production, the scope of which no one had any clue.

Nineteen individuals, each armed with only a small cutting tool, bring the most powerful nation in history, a nation that spends billions of dollars each year on defense and security, to its knees. The very symbols of the nation's technological and economic superiority, the jet and the skyscraper, become instruments of its own destruction, revealing the terror of its technology and the violence of its architecture, jets as phallic bombs, skyscrapers as tombstones, and oil, the life flow to which the nation is addicted, fueling the flames which bring about the fall.

It was at once

- a deconstructive event, the huge appearance of the Other as "the direct experience of the Real,"[7] or the world of the "all" signifier shattering the world of the totally signified, authenticity as violent transgression penetrating the insular numbness of programmed Western consciousness enveloped in a life of corporate advertisement;
- an archetypal event, its imagery through the ages and across cultures signaling the "call from without" of cosmic change;
- a mythic event, a story of the tragic hero whose fault, hubris, or inability to see, gives rise to a violent fall enacting sacrifice, manifested not only in the massive loss of life and fortune, but in the flow of blood donations;
- a Biblical event, evoking Old Testament images—Babel, Sodom and Gomorrah, Samson and the fall of the Philistines, David and Goliath ("... but who is David and who is Goliath?" asked a schoolboy in the Bronx), the downfall of Nebuchadnezzar, the Lord as a refiner's fire, as well as Mammon (the New Testament god of money), and Jesus overturning the tables of the money changers in the Temple—all giving a sense of divine punishment, divinity presenting its earthly form in a cosmic hierarchy.

## "God Bless America," "Let's Roll," "Keep Buying"

The American imagination could not deepen to meet the depth of the images by which it was confronted and flattened, and instead turned to a fundamental American myth of entitled innocence. There was the appeal to transcendent spirit—not just the calls for God's blessing, but the overt blending of God and country—followed by a tidal wave of blind patriotism, people literally wrapping themselves in the flag, the sales of flags skyrocketing, flag designs on Christmas cards and decorations, interminable patriotic anthems, the nation blitzed by advertising campaigns evoking patriotic songs, slogans, and themes, each pointing to a fundamental American assumption that is no different from those of the terrorists—we are God's children. Like the terrorists, Americans instantly assigned the mantel of "hero," its singular category of virtue, to a designated few warriors—firefighters and police officers—and separated itself from the "other," signified as "evil." Immediately came the inevitable calls for action—Do something. Retaliate. "Let's roll." Finally, just as the terrorists no sooner express their connection with God than they think of *jihad*, Americans no sooner linked themselves to God than they thought of the economy. Keep buying, spending. Don't let terrorism keep us from consuming. In short, America could not stretch its imagination beyond "good" and "evil" to a sense of tragedy through suffering appearing as a means of achieving awareness and change.

What unfolded after the fall of the towers was the image of a holy trinity—God, country, and economy—inextricably linked in the American consciousness as its governing story. Americans are a people "under God." The world is America's to dominate. God blesses America technologically by keeping the economy ascending in America's limitless "pursuit of happiness."

It is tempting to think of 9/11 in dualistic terms of worlds at war—a jet-propelled, unstoppable spirit force meeting a mammoth, towering, consuming world of immovable matter, each with its own respective goal of intangible well-being and tangible self-interest. A closer look reveals that each "world" holds the other.[8] The "spiritual" world of fundamentalist Islam turns to violent material enactment and the "material" world of global capitalism embraces the transcendent spirit of a people "under God."

Spirit and matter, each starts from a different place, but collision and collapse evoke a third world of irony—a hazy, smelly, shadowy, mercurial, flickering underworld of depths, emptiness, smallness, shadows, and twilight. Following classical distinctions, this third orientation encircling spirit and matter is that of *psyche*. Soul connects and envelops the spiritual and the material and sees each in the other, the two worlds interacting through imagination.

Carl Jung, hearkening to a universal tradition, indicated that the world itself had a soul, *anima mundi*, a life in which humans participate and which calls for human reflection. The idea of *anima mundi* resonates with the idea held by contemporary physicists that maintains that the cosmos itself has a consciousness. Jung depicted *anima mundi*, like all manifestations of soul, as presenting itself in images that carry meaning in and of themselves.[9] For the French psychoanalyst, Jacques Lacan, the idea of *anima mundi* would indicate the Other, an encompassing symbolic matrix or structure with its own subjectivity out of which another subjectivity evolves in reciprocal gaze and which already reflects the latter's behavioral patterns.

We are who we are through the eye of an other. Modern consciousness and the world are mutually other to each other. "I" and "other" always interpenetrate. Soul permeates the world—each culture, country, and city, each place, thing, and event having its own subjectivity, its own essence—and humans are the other reflecting that life. The world has its own desire and depth, its own underworld, its own dis-ease through which it makes its appearance and becomes a part of psychology. Psychology becomes political via *anima mundi.*

The other is the "not me" standing in counter position while watching "me" in my habitual way of seeing and experiencing. When the other as world calls through traumatic violence, depth psychology asks, "What does this say about us and our condition?" Does traumatic experience indicate a national essence or identity? How did we, through our character, help to create this event? What does the other want of us? From this position of uncertainty, we would respond to the fall of the twin towers by seeing it in terms of *anima mundi* and more particularly in terms of the nation and its soul, and by focusing on the mythical meaning inherent in the particularity of the images themselves.

## The Twin Towers

> The trade-center towers could be the start of a new skyscraper age or the biggest tombstones in the world.
>
> —Ada Louise Huxtable, *The New York Times* architecture critic, 1966[10]

> … the fire … writhes inside
> It is hard.
> But that I had done a bit more …
> Had the towers stood up for just one minute longer …
> It is hard.
>
> —Leslie Robertson, WTC Chief Engineer[11]

The twin towers of the World Trade Center, soaring above the world like classic hero twins, were built in the 1960s and 70s by two brothers who were among the world's wealthiest men, David and Nelson Rockefeller, and the Port Authority of New York and New Jersey. The Port Authority was an agency with a reputation for having an arrogant, ultramasculine, militaristic culture of competitiveness driven by the quest for self promotion, dominating power, and profit. It was headed by Austin Tobin, of whom it was said that he was "wired into power and power seemed to radiate out from his presence."[12] The World Trade Center project was managed by Guy Tozolli, the ambitious former planner of the New York World's Fair, and an authoritarian in style, who demanded absolute loyalty to what he called "The Program." A construction manager described the attitude with which the WTC was built: "We were the elite. There was nothing we couldn't do. There was no challenge that we couldn't tackle. There were no rules we couldn't find a way around—without being illegal—to get the thing done."[13]

The Port Authority itself was established in 1921 to assess the New York area's transportation needs in such a way that systems could be built that would transcend interstate conflict. In particular, it was to address the problem of transporting goods between docks in Brooklyn and Manhattan and the New Jersey mainland, a problem that remains to this day. The World Trade Center, as a real estate project, was a diversion from the Port Authority's chartered purpose of facilitating transportation and improving commerce and trade. Originally meant to be located on the east side of Manhattan as a modest building housing only agencies central to transportation, it ended up as the world's tallest building structure, and was ultimately used to lease private office space. Rockefeller and Tozolli eventually chose a building design that emphasized largess and symbolized a dominance that would attract both notoriety and money. The project quickly took on a tone of spiritualized inflation. The idea for it to be the tallest building in the world came from the Port Authority's female public relations director, Lee Jaffe, and as one engineer said, "We all thought it was like building the Pyramids. It was the eighth wonder of the world."[14]

From its conception to its destruction, the bigness of the WTC made it a target. With 10% of the office space in Manhattan, the WTC eventually came to be a mixed blessing for lower Manhattan. It served as a home to a diversified mini-city of mostly private businesses and agencies, while for the world it came to be the symbolic center of global capitalism and a two-time target for terrorists. Even in its origins, the building of the World Trade Center was opposed by many sectors of the New York business and real estate worlds. Theodore Kheel, a labor mediator, declared that the Port Authority was a "dangerously short-sighted and rigid conservative money machine harnessed to serve, not the public interest, but the private vision of an opportunistic management." For Kheel, the World Trade Center was the "clearest sign of the Port Authority's intellectual bankruptcy and arrogant indifference to the real needs of community."[15] Lawrence Wien, baron of Manhattan real estate, headed the Committee for a Reasonable World Trade Center and prophetically suggested that an airplane might hit the twin towers.

Representatives from the field of architecture were similarly appalled by the Twin Towers. Michael Lewis referred to them as "swagger buildings—arrogant, proud and strutting objects that are physical manifestations of America's competitive culture."[16] Wolf von Eckardt wrote for the *Washington Post*, "There is the fascination of the tower's ugliness. Man's tallest buildings to date defy their surroundings, man's most wondrous, skyscraping community. The 110-story Brobdingnagian shafts stand with blunt, graceless arrogance at the western edge of Manhattan island, seeming to tilt that wonder with overbearing size and hubris."[17]

Although the WTC was conceived and built in the service of an ultra aggressive towering ambition, its architect, Minoru Yamasaki, was an emotionally and physically sensitive man with a fear of heights, who thought of it as a symbol of peace. Yamasaki was also the architect for one of the world's most despised and failed public housing projects, Pruitt Igoe in St. Louis, Missouri, which was explosively demolished shortly after work on the Twin Towers was completed, paradoxically anticipating the similar demise of its sibling structures. Tozolli chose Yamasaki in part because he would follow Tozolli's program, and in part because Tozolli was impressed by the way Yamasaki's building for the Consolidated Gas Company in Detroit pulled the eye upward, evoking the sense of a medieval cathedral. Tozolli told Yamasaki, "President Kennedy is going to put a man on the moon. You're going to figure out a way to build me the tallest buildings in the world."[18]

Historically, skyscrapers are the descendants of medieval cathedrals and the church steeples of the Enlightenment, giving a spiritual background to an economic function. Skyscrapers have had three distinct architectural periods. Those of the first generation, built at the end of the 19th and the beginning of the 20th century, were constructed around an exterior iron frame that supported the building from the outside, providing a great deal of interior space but having the disadvantage that their floors were vulnerable to pancaking on top of one another during fires. In the second stage, the buildings were fortified with steel frames encased in concrete that ran throughout the structure; this reduced the danger of collapse considerably but introduced the disadvantage of heavy columns in the interior, which took up valuable space. Extant examples of this type are the Woolworth Building (1913), once called the "cathedral of commerce," the Empire State Building (1931), which itself survived an airplane crash in 1945, and 90 West Street (1907), which survived the fires that brought the downfall of the more modern 7 World Trade. Chief Engineer Leslie Robertson constructed the Twin Towers in an innovative third style, combining aspects of the previous two by putting the load-bearing steel pillars on the perimeter and buttressing them with trusses of flooring, forming a tube-shaped structure of steel frame and concrete surrounding a core of steel reinforcing. Lightweight steel plates between the upright pillars kept the building from swaying too much in high winds. The towers, despite their height, would be relatively light in weight, and in their monolithic form they evoked a transcendent feeling. Yamasaki liked the aesthetics of the bamboo pole style and the strength it would provide, while Tozolli liked the large amount of rental space the design made available.

In short, the Twin Towers were created in the service of a larger-than-life spirit as a symbol of world domination, with an emphasis on lightweight technology and with profit as the foundational priority—all three being fundamental features of an American soul founded upon spiritual entitlement, aggressive domination, and economic self-interest as revealed by 9/11.

## The Twin Towers as Symbol

Osama bin Laden, the leader of al Qaeda, the militant group that carried out the attacks on the towers, referred to them as "those awesome symbolic towers."[19] For the builders they represented dominance, while to the popular American mind their height gave a sense of spiritual ascendance, much as a spaceship liftoff does. To the outside world they signified arrogance and exceptionalism. American dominance in world trade is manifested in the phenomenon of globalization, that is, in the worldwide expansion of the reach of the American economy through corporate enterprise, an expansion that has disadvantaged poor countries, co-opted their resources, and exploited their cheap labor.

Towers that reach for the heavens universally symbolize spiritual pride and hubris, qualities that inevitably result in their fall at the hands of the gods. In the Old Testament, the Tower of Babel was built by men to "make a name" and to put their power in the place of Yahweh's. In the ancient Tarot deck of cards, the image representing "The Tower" shows a tall stone structure struck and broken by lightning and flames, its crown toppled. A king and queen tumble out of its windows, falling headlong to the ground. Meanings include "destruction," "coming of a new age," "the fall of Adam," "the materialization of spirit," "the fall of the House of Life infested with evil," "the demise of Falsehood," "trial by fire," "the jaws of Dis," "the eye of God," "the king must die," "freedom from old structures," "catastrophe," and "complete and sudden change."

The symbolism of the Twin Towers and America's response to the terrorist attacks both show how the well-being of the economy is like a spirit force or god in the American psyche. This sense of the economy as god is mirrored in the pantheon of the ancient Greeks, where the god Hermes was the divinity of commerce. For the Greeks, Hermes was god of the marketplace and all liminal places of transition or trade. He ruled over windfall profits and catastrophic losses. He was the divinity in charge of the spread of wealth and the taking of wealth in the form of robbery. He was god of the favorable moment as well as the calculated risk.

Hermes' altars were called herms. In their primitive form they were stone heaps set up along the roadside where sacrifices could be offered and also pilfered. In their sculpted form, herms were stone columns, four-sided pillars with a head at the top placed at the entrances to cities and homes. The phallic form of the herms bespoke their significance as indicators of vitality. In this light, the Twin Towers can be seen as America's phallic herms honoring America's allegiance to the economy as a psychological divinity.

In sum, the symbolic meaning of the towers spans many levels—from dominance and arrogance to a deeper indicator of the American character as fundamentally linked to the economy as god.

## The Fall of the Towers

In constructing the towers, Leslie Robertson took into account the force of a jet plane slamming into the building. In fact, both towers withstood the impact of a 767, and the structure of the buildings allowed for the escape of most of the 25,000 people working below the level of impact. The collapse of the buildings came about when the intense heat of the burning buildings (over 2000° C), generated by flaming jet fuel from the fully loaded planes (10,000 gallons), caused the steel structures to fold. The north tower caved in when the damaged internal core pillars eventually gave way. The south tower collapsed because the connectors—which attached the floor trusses to the upright steel pillars on the exterior walls with two bolts each—could hold no longer under the intense heat of the fire. It is thought that the major factor in the collapse of both buildings was not so much the architectural design, but the disintegration of the inexpensive foam fire protection, which either had worn away over time or was blown away by the impact of the plane.[20] In addition, the stairwells of both buildings (except for one in the south tower) were either blocked or unprotected from the fire because they were lined with inexpensive drywall rather than with the old-fashioned concrete casings; the people on the floors above the level of impact were thus trapped at the top of the building. In short, it was not the design of the structure so much as the vulnerability of the building material to heat that caused the towers to fall.

If the towers reflect an American myth of spiritual ascendance, political dominance, and economic self-interest, then the failure to give priority to the details of the internal structure are indicative of a shadow in this myth. Further, the mythical meanings of "tower" as well as the etymology of the word "disaster" (literally, "separated from the stars") suggest that there is a larger intention to the collapse of the Twin Towers. If their fiery fall is a wake-up call from the world-as-other that sees us, how can we understand the metaphor more concretely? Staying with the precise images of the towers' fall, is there something too excessive in the American character that needs to be limited or grounded or is there something in the American attitude toward the world that is trapped in the elevated air, not well connected, weak at the core, closed off, burned out, or that cannot stand the heat or needs empty space?

## Gathering Up the Pieces

American consciousness is busted into, and an opening is created. America sees the other seeing it. If the towers were glass mirrors in which America saw itself only as sheer dominating power, then their absence creates a void that not only calls us to an appreciation of the beauty of emptiness, but allows the other in the world to inform us as American. The writer Jack Miles has said that piety, "that set of graceful accepting, and otherwise positive attitudes that one may choose to cultivate toward relationships that are not a matter of choice," is achieved ultimately within the context of danger.[21] The terrorist strikes and the fall of the Twin Towers have made all Americans pious in the sense of accepting the fact that they are American. Confrontation with Islamic fundamentalism forces America to look at its own "fundament," its ground, its myth. We cannot change our mythology of self-interest, but we can open it up and deepen it.

James Hillman has described America as a place of animal life, characterized by the animal's attunement to its surroundings, its acceptance of its place in the world order, and its mode of being through display.[22] Hillman sees this life as encroached upon by Europeans with the same fantasies that dominate our lives today, transcending oppression through development, progress, problem solving, technology, all for a "freedom" that is practiced as an unlimited potential for accumulation and consumption. I would suggest that these fantasies *are* America's myth, a myth of utopian innocence as prefigured in America's Judeo-Christian heritage as the descendents of the Children of God and anticipated by Alexis de Tocqueville, who saw American democracy as leading to a form of collective mindlessness that gives itself over to an invisible authority.

If, as Anthony Lane suggests, the fall of the Twin Towers presented the reverse image of a spaceship launch,[23] and if, as Robert Romanyshyn asserts, space flight represents a leaving of earth in search of a spiritual home,[24] then the fall of the towers might represent a return to the animal world and its consciousness of community. The fall would indicate to America that descent and reflection are valid modes alongside soaring and building and growing and developing. The earth-shaking effect of a handful of men with simple box cutters, as well as the image of workers sifting through tons of rubble for small fragments, would indicate that there is a value to the small world, taking us back to de Tocqueville's observation that the soul clings to small things. We might realize the need for a deeper understanding of our sense of money and the economy (and their spiritual roots), as well as the need for a more imaginative way of incorporating them into our daily lives. The background maze of paradoxical political and economic connections in the world community—the bin Laden and Saud families' corporate connections with the West and the Bush family, Bush presenting the Taliban with congratulations and a check for its efforts in the war on drugs, Americans helping the al Qaeda and the Taliban to build infrastructure in Afghanistan's struggle against the Soviet Union, America providing Saddam Hussein with materials to build weapons of mass destruction in its war against Iran, the infusion of consumer values into Middle-Eastern life and the use of corporate wealth by terrorists—all these would indicate the irony at play in the *anima mundi* and the need for an interrelational attitude toward the world.

Through terrorism, fear and trembling have been established in our daily lives as important parts of our psychological life. It is not that every human being has the right to live without fear, but rather that through fear, every human being lives a totality. The terrorists' use of the religious imagination in their actions opens us to imagination itself as a means by which to moderate the rationalism that dominates our lives. Finally, the small altars and memorials on the sidewalks of Manhattan as well as the call for a permanent memorial on the site of Ground Zero would reflect the need for a continuous presence of memory—not just for the victims, but for our indulgences and our fear, for the universal images that tell us we are not the sole makers of our world, and for the life of the world informing us. Like Philemon and Baucis of old, we would make space for the gods themselves who make themselves known through disasters—Mnemosyne as memory, Poseidon, old earth shaker, Sophia, the wisdom of the Earth, Hermes of the marketplace—all as foundations of our daily lives.

For the last word, let us turn back to the Middle East, to Afghanistan, and to its most renowned citizen, the poet Rumi, who lived at the time of another terror, the Crusades of European Christians against Muslims in the Holy Land. Rumi's wise man rode around on a stick horse in the company of village children. After reining his horse in, he might say to us that America has been dozing long enough in Egypt, that the towers' twin fall was a forced climb to the execution place, and that now America has a chance because a window has opened—to the slow struggling wisdom of a one-year-old, walking.

## *NOTES*

[1] T. S. Eliot, "The Waste Land," III, lines 307-308.

[2] *Ibid.*, V, line 426.

[3] Jim Dwyer, Kevin Flynn, and Ford Fessenden, "9/11 Exposed ...," *New York Times*, July 7, 2002.

[4] Angus Gillespie, *Twin Towers: The Life of New York City's World Trade Center* (New York: New American Library, 2002), p. 246.

[5] Percy Shelley, "Ozymandias."

[6] Lawrence Wright reports in his book *The Looming Tower: Al-Qaeda and the Road to 9/11* (New York: Knopf, 2006, pp. 303, 309), that the jihadist architects of 9/11 watched Hollywood movies on videotape in refining their plot.

[7] Slavoj Zizek, *Welcome to the Desert of the Real: Five Essays on September 11 and Related Dates* (New York: Verso, 2002), p. 5.

[8] Ironically, one of the victims of 9/11 was John O'Neil, who at the time was Security Director of the World Trade Center. For years he had worked in the FBI as Chief of Counterterrorism and, realizing the danger presented by bin Laden, had worked diligently to track him down. In fact, O'Neil and bin Laden had much in common in their private lives, personalities, and core values, while representing seemingly different worlds. See Wright, especially pp. 208, 345-52.

[9] One of the images that Jung designates as a symbol of the *anima mundi*, the fiery wheel, was made manifest by the terrorists. Jung writes, "Setting fire to the wheel is ... a figurative expression for a catastrophic revolt of all the original components of the psyche, a conflagration resembling panic or some other uncontrollable, and hence fatal outburst of emotion." (C. G. Jung, *Aion, The Collected Works of C. G. Jung*, trans. R. F. C. Hull, vol. 9ii (Princeton, NJ: Princeton University Press, 1969), p. 137.

[10] James Glanz and Eric Lipton, "The Height of Ambition," *The New York Times Magazine,* September 8, 2002, p. 34.

[11] John Seabrook, "The Tower Builder," *The New Yorker*, November 19, 2001.

[12] Gillespie, p. 24.

[13] *Ibid.*, p. 63.

[14] Glanz and Lipton, p. 42.

[15] Gillespie, pp. 135-136.

[16] *Ibid.*, p. 265.

[17] *Ibid.*, p. 140.

[18] Glanz and Lipton, p. 38.

[19] Daniel Benjamin, "The 1,776-Foot-Tall Target," *The New York Times*, March 23, 2004.

[20] Louis DiBono, the head of the company contracted by Tozolli to apply the fire protection, was apparently involved with the Mafia and was murdered by John Gotti for "the sin of disrespect"—the underworld as the shadow of the towers as icons of the ascending spirit.

[21] Jack Miles, "In Impious America," *Spring* 52 (1992): 22-26.

[22] James Hillman, "Culture and the American Soul," *Spring* 62 (1997): 26-31.

[23] Anthony Lane, "This Is Not a Movie," *The New Yorker*, September 24, 2001.

[24] Robert Romanyshyn, *Technology as Symptom and Dream* (New York: Routledge, 1989).

# The Personal

Moved by a new idea or spiritual impetus, anima is right there, wanting to make it personal, asking, "How does it relate?" and "what about me?" These torturing incursions of soul into spirit and spirit into soul are the syzgy in action. This is the *coniunctio*.

—James Hillman, *Anima: An Anatomy of a Personified Notion*, p. 183

Lyn Cowan has been a practicing Jungian analyst since 1980. She is a former president of the Inter-Regional Society of Jungian Analysts and served as its Director of Training for six years. She also held a professorship for ten years in the doctoral program in Clinical Psychology at Argosy University (Minneapolis). After two years of teaching and lecturing at the C. G. Jung Center of Houston, Texas, she returned home to St. Paul, Minnesota. She is the author of three books: *Portrait of the Blue Lady: The Character of Melancholy* (2004), *Tracking the White Rabbit: A Subversive View of Modern Culture* (2002), and *Masochism: A Jungian View* (1982). She lives close to three very inviting rabbit holes.

28

# The Archetype of the Personal: A Memoir Scrap

LYN COWAN

For a long time in my younger days I secretly (well, maybe not so secretly) identified with Alice, the one who visits Wonderland and quests after the wisdom of the March Hare, the self-satisfaction of the Cheshire Cat, the perfect logic of the Red Queen, and the fearless compulsion of the White Rabbit. I wandered through the Wonderland of archetypal psychology, a place inhabited by eloquent theorists that eventually came to be my intellectual home, even though I am not interested in having an intellectual home. While I have changed my mind several times about a lot of things, the imaginal place where I have lived for three decades has not been painted over with dramatically different colors for years. It does have many overstuffed closets where I store memory clippings from my life, both before I moved in and more recently. Many of the permutations one undergoes in Wonderland have to do with dis-identifying with Alice, who, as a rather literal-minded lover of convention, does not know how to interact with the residents very well. While I fell into this "place," much as Alice did when she fell down the rabbit hole, at some point in the passage of thirty years I came to recognize Wonderland as my home, and my neighbors here are far more likeable and interesting than Alice.

I see myself in this wonderland as a sort of intellectual Bag Lady, in the style of Trudy, Lily Tomlin's marvelous creation. I am happy to have little theoretical baggage—nothing that needs proving, defending, or polishing: just enough to orient me through the practice of analysis and to serve as a lens through which I can unmyopically observe my personal life and see if theory matches experience. I park transiently on other people's doorstep, ripping off an idea here, a partial thought there, and then I cobble them together into something resembling "found art," which becomes a book or essay or other piece of work that other people can use. Some assembly is required. In the vocabulary of archetypal psychology, you could say I am a child of mercurial Hermes, part thief, part con-artist, and part messenger.

My brand of archetypal psychology, admittedly stolen, is a way of understanding the psyche that can accommodate the great richness and depth of psychic life while preserving nuance and subtlety—both great movements from one paradigm to another and small shifts as individual attitudes change. It is a vivifying perspective, reflecting the already-animated life of the psyche.

As the Cheshire Cat seemed able to do, you can operate in almost any style of consciousness that is in the ascendant at the moment, either by the moment's necessity or by congruency with your own temperament. Jung said, "Reality is what works in the human soul," and I for one am thankful that we do not have to be content with only one reality. In years of teaching clinical psychology doctoral students, I have been constantly shocked and depressed at how insistent most of them are that there be only *one* reality, which they innocently define as the collectively defined "reality" that gets you a high-paying job after graduation without requiring much mental effort. Here again, I remember the tested wisdom of Trudy, the Bag Lady: "Reality is the leading cause of stress amongst those in touch with it. I can take it in small doses, but as a lifestyle I found it too confining."

When I first went to Zürich for analytical training in 1973, after nearly three years of analysis, one divorce, and two college degrees, my formal psychological education consisted of having read two volumes of Jung's *Collected Works* (numbers 10, *Civilization in Transition* [1964] and 11, *Psychology and Religion* [1958]) and one book by James Hillman, *Insearch: Psychology and Religion.* Other than the speeches of Queen Elizabeth I, these three books were the only things that really made sense or "spoke to me." They opened up worlds of ideas, and I discovered I liked having ideas, even if they were not my own. I remember distinctly a particular moment on an afternoon in June, sitting in my backyard reading Hillman's book, feeling my sluggish academically-deadened mind beginning to expand as if frantically growing billions of new cells. Now and then my heart lurched as I read words that held some deep mystery as well as satisfying logic, and I thought then that someday, maybe I too might have an original idea. For that moment, though, and as it turned out for years thereafter, it was enough to dine at other theorists' tables, where I have been well fed, and have even been able to pass on some prime cuts to newcomers.

But arriving in Zürich meant only arriving in Zürich literally. I was not able to go anywhere psychologically with my pulsing new hope of insearching, did not think of author James Hillman as an actual, living, human being, and had no idea how I was going to pay for training. And most distressing of all, I had no idea what "psychological" meant. That I was an hysterical personality seemed clear, but the possibilities of that escaped me. I had yet to discover that I was even more a devotee of Dionysus than of Hermes. In fact, I knew nothing about either of them, or the rest of their weird mythical families. In further fact, I had no real understanding of what mythology had to do with psychology.

Like most poverty-stricken and introverted candidates at the Zürich Institute, I stayed by myself most of the time, except for a small group of us that met weekly to study and prepare for the Propaedeuticum exams. And like many new arrivals in Zürich, I began by going to every lecture that was offered, realizing I had a huge knowledge deficit to fill. By the end of the first semester I was overloaded, had taken in more of Marie-Louise von Franz's genius than I could digest, was depressed (because I knew I would never recognize a patient's mother complex or transference even if it hit me in the face), was rapidly going under financially, and at the age of thirty was limping around on a cane because of a formerly bad knee gone bad again. My analyst was hospitalized for two months with pneumonia and I still did not have a transference onto him, which added to my worry that my individuation was not processing. Feeling somewhat put-upon by an unconcerned universe, I was gradually taken over by terminal homesickness, but I did not have any way of understanding that psychologically either.

Then the gods, who were still hidden from my view, intervened in the form of a friend who told me that James Hillman—the mythical author of my backyard epiphany—was looking to hire someone to do some typing for him. I had considerable experience as a typist, which in the late 1960s was my means of support, could do 100 words per minute on a manual machine, but assumed there were dozens like me who were equally qualified and that the job was already filled. Two weeks later, the friend called again to say Hillman was still looking. So, desperate for money and not conscious enough to be intimidated, I called James Hillman and said I was interested in the job.

"Aha!" he cried happily into the phone. "And what is your background?"

"Medieval history," I said. "B.A. and M.A."

"Aha!" he said again, "Then you know Latin?"

This gave me pause, as I failed to see the connection between knowing Latin and knowing how to type.

"Well, some. I took a course in it."

"Excellent! Excellent!" he said, and I could see the smile right through the telephone line. "Then you know how to hyphenate!"

"Yes," I replied, once more confident, "I am a very good hyphenator." There had to be a connection between Latin and hyphenating, since mythical author James Hillman was making one, but I decided not to ask what it might be.

"Great! You've got the job. It isn't really typing. It's operating the composer for Spring Publications. Go over to Spring House and tell Valerie we talked and you're now on staff. Good-bye." Suddenly I was an employee, albeit with a clandestine job, which paid meagerly in cash under the table. Only later did I learn that a composer, in those pre-computer, pre-word-processing days was a large, glorified IBM Selectric typewriter that justified margins, had changeable font heads, limited memory, and was the machine on which books were published. In my way of personifying, before I knew what personifying was, I developed a love-hate relationship with that machine, which I named Mephistopheles because it was a devil to keep running properly. At Spring House, formerly a glove manufacturing site, the composer sat on a just-big-enough wooden table with a rudimentary chair in a small room that was always freezing, with a tiny space heater that was helpless against the chronic Zürich chill. Think Dickens and you have the scene.

And that was the beginning of my rookie year as an archetypal psychologist.

But being at Spring House was in every other way close to salvation for me, because it was the beginning of my real psychological education. It was an extraordinarily gifted group of people who worked and/or congregated there, and without realizing it, I had already entered an archetypal realm where the imagination created new realities every day, all of them intellectually stimulating and vaguely dangerous, as new ideas are. Hillman also put me in charge of answering the hate mail Spring received from irate subscribers who inexplicably resented waiting six months or more for their copy of *Spring Journal.*

There was another, huge bonus to this involvement at Spring. Hillman (who had become Jim) asked me to type his final draft of *Re-Visioning Psychology*, and that was the project that completely changed the course of my thinking. It was like climbing inside another person's remarkable mind and watching it work, hearing it use language that kept opening up wondrous new realms of ideas, of learning, of ways to think mythically, to live psychologically.

At the same time that I was completely absorbed in typing the *Re-Visioning* manuscript and later doing the index for it, I went to hear Jim's ten-lecture series at the Institute on Alchemy. The subject of alchemy, so esoteric and incomprehensible to me as Jung wrote about it, turned out to be a whole new language of metaphor I could grasp quite naturally, and gave me the first solid sense—a material, almost tactile sense—of how the psyche worked and *felt.* That gave me the golden key to open the enormous treasure house of Jung's work, and Freud's work, and now Hillman's.

It was through the opening of alchemy and the fortuitously acquired job, which consisted only of typing and making sure those hyphens were in the right place, that I discovered the psychological life, and that it was something one actually *lived*, not merely theorized about or conceptualized into abstractions. I felt a flicker of hope that I might yet be able eventually to recognize someone's mother complex or transference when it walked into my future consulting room.

I began typing Jim's manuscript as a novice to this kind of archetypal thinking. My mind was continuing the expansion it had begun earlier in my backyard. As I went more deeply into the book, page by typewritten page, I began to feel like Dante being led out of a dark wood by the poet Virgil. I began to see countless mysteries of the world and all its hidden places, the endless varieties of psychic life. All this was too grand and rich for my mortal mind to encompass, but it was enough at the beginning to know they were there. Happily, my Virgil was just a telephone call away, so when I mentally stalled at some new perspective, some odd angle upon which Jim was expounding, I just called and asked him to explain it, so I could know what I was typing. This was not only delightful and exciting, it was the most formative experience of my psychological education. And it was not lost on me that the brand name of the typewriter I was using was "Hermes."

One episode stands out because it had to do with a key element in archetypal thinking: there is a passage in *Re-Visioning Psychology* where Hillman talks about "psychological faith" (in the chapter on "Personifing or Imagining Things").

> Psychological faith begins in the *love of images*, and it flows mainly through the shapes of persons in reveries, fantasies, reflections, and imaginations. Their increasing vivification gives one an increasing conviction of having, and then of being, an interior reality of deep significance transcending one's personal life.[1]

I very much wanted to transcend my personal life. But the word "faith" was too encrusted with old conventional religious ideas for me to grasp it in this different context. So I called Jim and told him I was confused about what he meant by "psychological faith" and could he please explain that. And in a typical response he said, "Oh yes. A very important idea. I have some additions, let me bring them over and I'll explain about faith." So while I sat in one of my two chairs in my room in Zürich, Jim paced around and in his usual animated way explained the meaning and context of psychological faith. It was about having faith in, trusting, giving credence to, the reality of imaginal fantasies, to the figures and movements in an imaginal world that is hidden from the eye that sees only literally. It meant believing that the soul's faith, as he wrote, "makes me possible as a personification of psyche."[2]

I was elated. The more I went on typing, the more I could feel the number of my brain cells multiplying exponentially by the billions and beyond. My personal neurotic hang-ups and inferiorities paled in significance beside this breathtaking vista of psychic realms. But while the elation carried me for a long time, my personal neurotic hang-ups and inferiorities did not stay pale or insignificant, but seemed to become darker and heavier. I was starting to live what I was learning but had not yet found the emotional bridge to connect living with learning.

I was only vaguely aware that this emotional element was missing and so I did not know what to call it. While the ideas of the newly emerging archetypal psychology were thrilling and convincing and illuminating, I could not quite get a visceral connection that would help me understand my personal tangled psyche, could not shine the new light of understanding into the dark corners of my own inarticulate soul. My own conscious *experience* of the archetypal dimension, the numinosity, the living sense of mythic figures, was missing.

Then one afternoon it hit me. I had become friends with Spring's production manager (and so much more), Valerie Donleavy (later Valerie Lopez), and was visiting her flat. I left at about five o'clock. It was sometime in early April, the sky was the color of a battleship and the Zürich air damp and chill and hostile as always. I was crossing the narrow street—odd and frustrating that I cannot now remember the name of that street—when suddenly I was struck forcefully with a visceral, heart-seizing realization: *Valerie was an archetype!* Or, putting it more accurately, she *embodied* a style of archetypal consciousness that I found compelling, fascinating, a bit intimidating, and deeply emotionally stirring. And it was not just her British accent. There was a psychic figure in the backdrop. Valerie was a Big Sister with a maternal quality, something foreign to my actual experience, but the longing for which I recognized in myself at that moment. Suddenly I realized I had separated Valerie the person from Valerie-as-archetypal-image, a move which is, really, the whole of it and the rabbit-hole of it, because if you can make this move, you are inside Wonderland. It was like watching a play and simultaneously glimpsing what was going on behind the curtain. ("Seeing through," as Jim put it.) The moment of crossing that anonymous street was fraught (to use one of Valerie's favorite words) with implication, significance, resonating depth, great possibilities. So caught up in the magic of the experience, I do not remember getting to the other side of the street.

I wish I could say I was launched on my way to becoming a brilliant theorist in the field of archetypal psychology as a result of this fraught street-crossing episode, but it did not happen. My mind does not bend in that direction, I do not have the right inclination for theory—not my archetypal pattern, you might say. But the path I took instead led me to a way of practicing analysis that in turn sharpened my psychological acuity, and set me on a course that I think fate intended from the beginning: to write psychologically about life rather than to write about psychology. Hermes once again has primacy of place.

The dominant archetype at this point in my life seems to be the archetype of the personal. This is the fantasy I am living at present, an imaginal idea that my personal life and my memories of its past have a context. I have become fascinated with the historical and cultural context in which this life has been and is being lived. This is not a private thing—I am hardly the only 65-year-old person who is interested in the context of one's life. Given an archetypal vantage point, I can both live and observe this "personal life" at the same time, with more or less success depending on how much sleep I have had. And there is a psychological bonus, since according to Jung, I am on the right track towards another fantasy, that of "individuation": my dreams have become increasingly, impenetrably obscure as I get older, and his definition of reality as whatever works in the human soul has become more liberating and satisfying.

John Fowles, the British writer, once said that questions are a form of life, answers are a form of death. The warp of my mind has always leaned toward questions and still does—I figure the answers, like death, will come in their own time so I don't have to pursue them. This is the same kind of liberation one gains from an understanding and experience of the archetypal dimension, that wonderland place where I have become not merely an occupant, but a resident. The Mad Hatter is a good neighbor, we share similar neurotic styles. The regular tea party with close friends and stimulating colleagues has grown less and less comprehensible, more and more interesting and provocative. I look for guests to join us who are able to see the invisible.

> "Have some wine," the March Hare said in an encouraging tone. Alice looked all around the table, but there was nothing on it but tea. "I don't see any wine," she remarked. "There isn't any," said the March Hare.

Poor Alice, as Lewis Carroll often referred to her. She never got to read *Re-Visioning Psychology*, never grasped the psychological faith of the March Hare and so never discovered that just because something is not there, it does not mean you cannot have it. Even the erratic movements of the Red Queen did not encourage Alice to reflect more deeply on her own apparent displacement in a world of images. It is worth a lot to discover that the examined life—including the parts you cannot see—is, as Plato pointed out, the only kind worth living. I will continue to live mine in Wonderland, for as long as my archetypal neighbors keep imagining a life for me.

## *NOTES*

[1] James Hillman, *Re-Visioning Psychology* (New York: Harper Colophon Books, 1975), p. 50.

[2] *Ibid.,* p. 51.

KAZUHIKO HIGUCHI was born in Yokohama and currently resides and works in Kyoto, Japan. In 1958, he joined the Andover Newton Theological School in Boston, where met John Billinsky, and where he subsequently completed his S.T.M. (Master of Sacred Theology) in 1960 and his D.Min. in 1975. He attended the C. G. Jung Institute in Zürich, beginning in 1964, and had analytical dream work with James Hillman when Hillman was the Institute's Director of Studies. He became a member of IAAP in 1983. He is now President of the Association of Jungian Analysts, Japan (AJAJ) and Vice President of the International Society for Sandplay Therapy (ISST), as well as President of the Japanese Association of Sandplay Therapists (JAST). Among the Japanese people, he is widely known as one of the pioneers who introduced Jungian psychology and archetypal psychology into Japan. He has translated two of Hillman's books into Japanese: *Insearch: Psychology and Religion* and *Suicide and the Soul.*

# 29

# Being and Non-Being: Fullness and Emptiness

KAZUHIKO HIGUCHI

[*Note: When Kazuhiko Higuchi celebrated his 77$^{th}$ birthday, James Hillman sent him a short story, "A Tale of Two Tigers," as a birthday gift. This short essay is a return salute to Hillman.*]

One of the most basic aspects of the foundational Western Psychic Tree, as I understand it, is the verse from Exodus that reveals the Divine Name. "God said to Moses, 'I am he who is.'" (Exodus 3:14). The god of Moses is. He has being. My own Eastern Evolutionary Tree is very different. In Japan, the beginning of all that exists is not an Ultimate Being, but Great Emptiness. This emptiness is not the opposite of being, not nothingness or a sterile void. Rather, it is a ground of emptiness that is pregnant with possibility and full of potential. In the East, everything begins with this empty non-being that, nonetheless, can take on form and become visible.

One gets a taste of this interplay of form and emptiness in the interaction of characters in Japanese Noh. Every Noh play begins with the appearance of an initial character, who, through his spiritual and psychic sensibility, calls forth from the invisible realm the main character in the drama. The initial character, the *waki*, never wears a mask. In many plays, the *waki* is a traveling monk. He pauses on his pilgrimage at a place where he senses spiritual energy and begins to pray. He continues to pray for the well-being of all that he senses there, revealing his deep compassion. Moved by this kind attention, the main character, or *shite*, slowly appears from the invisible realm. The *shite* can be of either gender but is always masked. He or she may change masks several times during the recitation of the story, which often begins with a regret or grudge that he or she is carrying from a previous existence. Wearing different masks, the main character tells his or her tale, taking on the faces of the psychic characters from his or her past that have influenced and inspired his or her core personality. When the story has been heard and witnessed, the main character fades back into the foundational emptiness from which he or she came. On the surface, things appear to be as they were before. This Eastern drama has a very different feel from the stories of the West, which tend to have characters or beings that interact with one another as they engage in relationship, conflict, and resolution.

This drawing out of the story that is enacted in Noh theater is comparable to the drawing out from the unconscious that is the work of analysis. In the coaxing out that occurs, the multiple faces, and eventually the true face, of the characters appear. The *waki*'s receptivity, sensibility, and compassion make the apparition possible. The *shite*'s story can be fully, truthfully told.

In a similar vein, an important aspect of my own work in Japan has been the conception and formation of a technique based on the psychology of C. G. Jung that I have called Fantasy Group. Here too, the invisible can sometimes be made visible. In one exercise, a large sheet of white paper is provided to each group of five to ten participants. Each person is invited to use finger paint to create a picture, maintaining complete silence, of whatever he or she wishes. Naturally, since the paper is shared, many issues related to aesthetics, territory, and time/space are manifested. There is no predetermined time limit for the exercise and sometimes these themes are explored at length, in a silent war of wills, and end only when the participants have no paint or energy left to continue. Similar exercises are engaged in with clay, paper collage, and other expressive modalities. After each exercise, the participants are invited to speak, with the guidance of a moderator, about their symbols, images, process, and experience. The Japanese are often less talkative than their Western counterparts, especially in connection with their interior experience. However, if something touches their deeper unconscious feelings, they may talk on and on, unable to bring their discussion regarding their insights and new awareness to a close. This embodying of symbol in paint and clay, and the embodied experience of using such mediums, has great relevance for the participants.

At the end our time together, we have a group ceremony and ritually burn or destroy all that was created with paint, paper, and clay. In this way, the images themselves disappear, fading back into the invisible realm. Yet, they also remain impressed on our hearts. As in the Noh play, it is as it was before, but not essentially as it was before. In Buddhism it is sometimes said that insight is the mother of the Buddhas.

Much of my work with the Fantasy Groups here in Japan is the legacy of my meetings with Jim Hillman. I first met Jim in Zürich in 1964. Much later, in 1982, he came to Kyoto and attended one of our Fantasy Groups. He told me then of a dream he had had as his airplane made its way across the Pacific Ocean. He had dreamed of a solar eclipse. His soul sensed that he was traveling from the land of the sun to the moon realm. He was moving from a culture of great Being to one of great Emptiness, from focused sunlight to reflective moonlight. The sun was in eclipse.

Over the ensuing years, we have met in many places. When I first went to Zürich, I was like the traveling monk in the Noh play. In my wanderings here and there, I came upon Jim in the great mountain land of Switzerland. I stopped because I felt that this was a place where something vital could happen. Perhaps there are not so many places on earth where we perceive such a strong sense of spiritual essence. I felt it there in Zürich, and in all the other loci—Ascona, Paris, San Francisco, Thompson, Florence, Nara, and Kyoto—where Jim and I crossed paths. I am always grateful to meet him. We never know for certain which of us is playing the role of *waki* and which the role of *shite*. We are ever moving back and forth between Sun and Moon, West and East, Being and Emptiness. I treasure his roles as both in my life's play. I am grateful for our many years of friendship.

On my 77$^{th}$ birthday, he sent me a beautiful story, "The Tale of Two Tigers." With deep thanks for that tale, I return to him a message from the Tiger of the East to the Tiger of the West. In the *I Ching*, the tenth hexagram is Lu/Treading (Conduct). "Treading: treading upon the tail of the tiger. It does not bite the man. Success." I pray for the continuing success and longevity of the Western Tiger who inhabits, so skillfully, the one world of being and non-being.

Kyoto, January 2007

NOEL COBB was born and brought up in the United States, but currently lives and works in London, England. He has a degree in philosophy from the University of Michigan and one in psychology from the University of Oslo. He had his Jungian training analysis in London and has practiced as a psychotherapist since 1980. In 1987, he co-founded, with Eva Loewe, The London Convivium for Archetypal Studies, and the following year they started publishing *SPHINX: A Journal for Archetypal Psychology and the Arts*. His publications include several journal articles, books, and volumes of poetry. His *Archetypal Imagination: Glimpses of the Gods in Life and Art* was published in 1992.

# 30

# An Open Letter to James Hillman

NOEL COBB

London, 2008

Dear James,

Do you remember, we talked over lunch one day in London of our "Imaginal Family Trees"? It turned out that there were many people in the branches of our Trees who existed for us in common.

This reminded me of Goethe's expression: "elective affinity." The Jungian analyst, Buntie Wills, who first suggested I read your book on Jung's Psychological Types in 1977, knew I would feel a psychological kinship with you. Later, another Jungian analyst confirmed this, suggesting I consider convening a forum in England for the dissemination of your work and the new field of "Archetypal Psychology." That group came to be known as "The London Convivium for Archetypal Studies," and for over ten years we hosted you and other kindred souls, such as Christopher Bamford, Ean Begg, Peter Bishop, Ed Casey, Murray Cox, Francesco Donfrancesco, Francis Huxley, Eva Loewe, Thomas Moore, Enrique Pardo, Ginette Paris, Linda Proud, Kathleen Raine, Anthony Rooley, Gail Thomas, Alfred Ziegler.

In 1988, the Convivium gave birth to the annual, *SPHINX—A Journal for Archetypal Psychology and the Arts,* co-designed and co-edited with Eva Loewe. There, fine poetry can be found by Charles Baudelaire, Robert Bly, Coleman Barks, Jules Cashford, the Poet of the Homeric Hymns, Federico Garcia Lorca, Pablo Neruda, Francis Ponge, Jalaluddin Rumi, Jeremy Reed, Rainer Maria Rilke, Thomas R. Smith, Gary Snyder, William Stafford, Arsenyi Tarkofsky, and Georg Trakl; and philosophy by A. H. Armstrong, Gaston Bachelard, Henry Corbin, Ed Casey, Paul Kugler, David Miller, Kathleen Raine, and, of course, James Hillman. There were paintings by Carlo Mattioli, Mario Fallani, and Emma Ronay as well as goldsmith work by Kevin Coates.

Mentioning all these names gives some indication of the larger family of kindred souls that were drawn into the orbit of the Convivium. James, you were the central inspiration behind all this. The beauty and imagination that happened all through these years, whether in performances, talks, readings, discussions, dances, exhibitions, or recitals, and all the written work of SPHINX was directly and (often) indirectly the result of your own passionate enthusiasm for beauty and imagination—and for Soul-Making.

My own debt to you and archetypal psychology is immense. Through you, I was first made aware not only of the term "soul-making" and its relevance to psychotherapy, but also of the immense resonance it has (as described in John Keats' great letter to his brother George) for the work of Psychological Alchemy initiated by Carl Jung. The subsequent deepening of this idea throughout the years in your own books and papers has led me to infinitely precious sources of rare wisdom. Through your re-vivification, not only of the works of Heraclitus, Homer, Plotinus, and Ficino, but also of Bachelard, Freud, and Jung, you have helped to stem the destructive impact of Television, Mobile Telephones, E-mails, and the Internet on the warmth and vitality of the Thought of the Heart.

And most of all, I thank you for your deep commitment to *Anima Mundi.* You have given me words and thoughts to express my perceptions and feelings of "a World Ensouled"—beyond individual soul-making. By calling attention to the Soul of the World as the main priority to be reckoned with in our lives, you have shown in so many differentiated ways how our psychologically impoverished lives can find true meaning at last.

Please accept these few poems, gathered around the reality of "soul-making," as an offering at the Imaginal Banquet to be given in your honour in 2008.

With much affection,

Noel

---

## Falling out of the Skin into the Soul

Staring into archangelic incandescence,
Andrei Rublev saw burning gold exfoliate:
The shocking flicker of breathing forms.

How many times in free fall through the Bardo did you fear
The speed of impact would destroy you? Yet, the sweet
Pandemonium of life was always there to greet you.

When you were sewn into your skin, where was the soul?
Nina Simone, singing "Mr. Bojangles" reminds us
Of the Pietà. The soul bears untold years of loss.

Singing all the way from Malaga to the Alhambra
El Tenazas, "The Tenacious One," arrives, walking.
One lung dead from a knife-fight. A stopped clock of pain.

Does Deep Song come from inscrutable moonlight?
Or is it God who screams? Voice, zigzagging
Like a wounded moth in air perfumed by blood and roses.

It takes a shipwreck to call us back to beauty.
Yes, Pablo, we die in darkness, darkness. Only then
Finally here: falling out of the skin into the soul.

## God's Face

I do not want to hear again how captured macaques writhe,
Test-fed drugs through tubes down their throats; how they
Helplessly wring their tiny hands and stare at the sky.

Say you are born as an animal, chances are
You will be used for your meat, your milk, your glands,
Your horns, teeth, tusks, feathers, skin, and fur.

The animal-headed Gods of the Upper Nile
Tried to teach us Beauty, Justice, Virtue, Wisdom.
All day the butcher downstairs chops up animals.

How I love the animal-bright look in your eyes!
And when you weep for the animals' pain, I ask myself:
How many lifetimes does it take for the heart to open?

Because Melampous saved the murdered snake's orphans,
They later licked his ears clean, so he could understand
The ancient words of birds and be a healer.

Under the trees a distraught dervish prays: "O God,
Show me your Face!" A drunk leans out the Tavern window,
Shouting, "Have you never noticed the grace of a tiger?"

## WEIGHING THE SOUL

"Surely if the soul exists it can be weighed!"
Cried Arthur Koestler, planning to weigh a man at death.
A steel bed was designed to measure change in milligrams.

The man's last breath went out. No weight was lost.
Old Koestler and his wife committed double suicide.
Did no soul suffer then when darkness fell at noon?

But suppose the soul is the savour, the flavour, the taste
Of things: the juice, the rasa of the raga, pressed out
By the winepress of our love for what's beyond us.

Don't you think the grape cries out, "Spare me! The pressure
Of the winepress feels like death!" Though the vintner answers
"Our art frees Marsyas's soul forever from his skin."

Each Renaissance has its scheming Joe McCarthy
Stealing the ladder from between the captive soul
In the tower and her selfless lover on the ground.

What weight then made Sandro Botticelli run and throw
His pagan paintings on the flames? If we do not save
The soul, who will? Weightless, it can still be burnt alive.

## Curious Reassurance

The blackbird sings and in its song the world soul sings.
A song without words. A song at dawn for the sun,
Returning. A song at night for the sun's grave going.

Steeped in remotest reverie, the poet marinates
In metaphorical mystery, like the hanks and loops
Of Moroccan yarn boiled in vats of indigo dye.

The schoolboy lies on his back in the grass, in love
With the changing shapes of feminine clouds. Nervous,
Gary Cooper waits for night and breathless Ingrid Bergman.

If there is solitude, if we protect and cherish it,
If there is only time enough, if the crush of life
Does not blot out the blackbird's song, if there is solitude—

Knowing that the gibbons of Sumatra still hoo-hoo
And glide through the tops of vertiginous trees, gives
Curious reassurance to the poet on London Bridge.

The poet listens to the silence in the blackbird's song.
The poet listens even as death everywhere advances.
The blackbird sings and in its song the world soul sings.

## The Melancholy Humour

These are the signs: dryness, heaviness, sluggishness,
Lack-lustre eyes, a neglect of one's appearance, a mournful
Look. Inwardly, an excess of Saturn and black bile.

There always are two choices: appease the gloomy God
By being more like him, or curb his sway
By calling on the help of Jupiter, the Sun, and Venus.

If it suits you, then wear black, visit graveyards,
Stay alone, read Gilgamesh, grow sad with mathematics.
Listen to the sombre drone of Dowland's *Lachrimae.*

Or go outside, away from ugly buildings, on paths
Through leafy oak, near the sound of water. Wear gold,
Hear Mozart, burn aromatic myrrh, smell jasmine.

For softening the melancholy humour, Ficino
Recommends a melt-in-the-mouth made of almonds, sugar,
Saffron, cinnamon, pine-nuts, and rose-petal syrup.

It's May and cherry blossom time again! And, Oh!
The grateful soul wants to dance among the clouds
Of pink blossom, but for the bodies bleeding in the streets.

## Why Rumi Stayed Awake

Before the rain the night is full of listening.
Each rosebush is a giant ear, listening
To the sighs of a hundred thousand sleepers.

The breathing of the world asleep is such music
To the rose. The noises of the day destroy
The rose's pleasure hearing raindrops forming far away.

To be awake when all else is sleeping
Was Rumi's great desire. With the ears of the rosebush
He heard the dreams of the wooddove and the robin.

A ball of bones and bright feathers holds a whole world.
The robin hops on legs thin as straws.
Without love, who would wish to exist?

What does the robin dream? What do men and women
Dream? Who cares what robins dream, except the poet?
When Rumi stayed awake all night, it was because of love.

There are those who say that after death there is nothing.
Tell that to the rosebush and hear her gentle laughter:
"Some people sleep so deep they lose all sense of dreaming."

## The Clover's Breath

Someone in us is suspicious of our desire to be
Generous. We have signed up with the Merchants of Greed.
Colourful ads warn us not to give to the Poor.

Because his paintings hang so quietly
On the plush gallery walls, we search for any trace
Of negligence in Vermeer's household books.

The sun sheds its light on even the darkest moon
And rain falls without ever asking for pay. Unabashed,
The Zebra nakedly displays its exuberant art.

Unpleasant things appear when we think we have won.
So many shadows creep into the poem before we reach
The end. Right now large numbers are ramming the door.

Hooked and tangled in the nylon lines of arctic trawlers
One hundred thousand albatross are killed each year.
The Ancient Mariner killed one and disaster struck.

Still, we trust the Worker Bees of the World to return
Laden with praise from the sweet mouths of clover.
The clover's sweet breath is its gift to us all.

---

David H. Rosen, M.D., a Jungian analyst, holds the McMillan Professorship in Analytical Psychology, and is Professor of Humanities in Medicine and Professor of Psychiatry & Behavioral Science at Texas A&M University. He is the author of over ninety scholarly articles and eight books including *The Healing Spirit of Haiku*, co-authored with Joel Weishaus (2004); *Transforming Depression: Healing the Soul Through Creativity* (2002); *Evolution of the Psyche*, co-authored with Michael Luebbert (1999); *The Tao of Jung: The Way of Integrity* (1997). For more information, visit his website: http://psychology.tamu.edu/Faculty/Rosen/index.html, or e-mail him at: drosen@psych.tamu.edu.

31

# Better with Time: Honoring James Hillman

DAVID H. ROSEN

Full of fiery rage and brilliance, James Hillman faced and overcame suicide (*Suicide and the Soul,* 1964), something I call "egocide and transformation."[1] Carl Jung, too, went through the same experience when he broke from Sigmund Freud.[2] In *Suicide and the Soul,* a seed was sown for the soul to emerge and flower in *Re-Visioning Psychology* (1976). Hillman discloses in the "Preface: A Memoir" for the 1992 edition of *Re-Visioning Psychology,* that his books are him. In other words, if you want to know Hillman read his books. This parallels the adage: "All writing is autobiographical." Natalie Goldberg's words ring true, "Writing is deeper than therapy. You write *through* your pain, and even your suffering must be written out and let go of."[3] Likewise, this is the essence of *The Wounded Researcher,*[4] and I would add, The Wounded Healer as well as The Wounded Writer—all three are embodied by Hillman. Also in the "Preface: A Memoir" mentioned above, Hillman reveals that the original version of his Terry Lectures (1972), which form the basis of *Re-Visioning Psychology,* was rejected by Yale University Press. Characteristic of Hillman, and a model to us all, he persisted and rewrote his *magnum opus.* Not only was it subsequently published by Harper & Row in 1976, but it was nominated for a Pulitzer Prize.

Like a fine red wine, Hillman gets better with time. *Healing Fiction* (1983) was first published three years before his sixtieth birthday. *We've Had a Hundred Years of Psychotherapy—and the World's Getting Worse* (with Michael Ventura, 1992) was published when he was sixty-six. *The Soul's Code: In Search of Character and Calling* (1997), published one year after Hillman turned seventy, is about *telos, à la* Plato and Aristotle, and about realizing one's full potential. *The Force of Character and the Lasting Life* (2000), published six years before he turned eighty, depicts how one's character develops and ripens naturally over time.

Hillman, like Jung, incarnates what the Zen Master Gempo Yamamoto used to say, "At the age of sixty, one is more efficient than at fifty; seventy is more useful than sixty; eighty is more effective than seventy. But our real life begins after we depart from the corporeal body."[5] Hillman has been true to himself and as Soen Nakagawa Roshi says, "If you cannot return home, yourself is not your true self."[6]

Out of Darkness
Raging Fire—
Re-birth of soul

## *NOTES*

[1] David H. Rosen, *Transforming Depression: Healing the Soul Through Creativity*, 3rd ed. (York Beach, ME: Nicolas-Hays, 2002).

[2] David H. Rosen, *The Tao of Jung: The Way of Integrity* (New York: Penguin Books, 1997), pp. 65-66.

[3] Natalie Goldberg, *Writing Down the Bones: Freeing the Writer Within* (Boston, MA: Shambhala Publications, 1986), p. 114.

[4] Robert D. Romanyshyn, *The Wounded Researcher: Research with Soul in Mind* (New Orleans, LA: Spring Journal Books, 2007).

[5] E. T. Shimano, K. Tanahashi, and R. S. Chayat, eds., *Endless Vow: The Zen Path of Soen Nakagawa* (Boston, MA: Shambhala Publications, 1996), p. 8.

[6] *Ibid.*, p. 130.

Spring Journal Books

## Studies in Archetypal Psychology Series

*Series Editor*
Greg Mogenson

### Other Titles in the Series

The Collected English Papers of Wolfgang Giegerich
Vol. 1: The Neurosis of Psychology: Primary Papers towards a Critical Psychology
Vol. 2: Technology and the Soul: From the Nuclear Bomb to the World Wide Web
*Wolfgang Giegerich*

Dialectics & Analytical Psychology: The El Capitan Canyon Seminar
*Wolfgang Giegerich, David L. Miller, Greg Mogenson*

Raids on the Unthinkable: Freudian *and* Jungian Psychoanalyses
*Paul Kugler*

Northern Gnosis: Thor, Baldr, and the Volsungs in the Thought of Freud and Jung
*Greg Mogenson*

The Essentials of Style: A Handbook for Seeing and Being Seen
*Benjamin Sells*

The Wounded Researcher: A Depth Psychological Approach to Research
*Robert Romanyshyn*

The Sunken Quest, the Wasted Fisher, the Pregnant Fish: Postmodern Reflections on Depth Psychology
*Ronald Schenk*

Fire in the Stone: The Alchemy of Desire
*Stanton Marlan, ed.*

After Prophecy: Imagination, Incarnation, and the Unity of the Prophetic Tradition
*Tom Cheetham*